The Self-Taught Cloud Computing Engineer

A comprehensive professional study guide to AWS, Azure, and GCP

Dr. Logan Song

BIRMINGHAM—MUMBAI

The Self-Taught Cloud Computing Engineer

Group Product Manager: Preet Ahuja

Publishing Product Manager: Suwarna Rajput

Senior Editor: Isha Singh

Technical Editor: Nithik Cheruvakodan

Copy Editor: Safis Editing

Project Coordinator: Shagun Saini

Proofreader: Safis Editing

Indexer: Rekha Nair

Production Designer: Joshua Misquitta

Marketing Coordinator: Rohan Dhobal

First published: August 2023

Production reference: 1240823

Packt Publishing Ltd

Grosvenor House

11 St Paul's Square

Birmingham

B3 1RB, UK.

ISBN 978-1-80512-370-5

www.packtpub.com

To God, for your amazing grace.

To my mother, Shuiming Tang, and to the memory of my father, Ada Song, for your sacrifices and love.

To my wife, Tracey, for your unconditional love and support.

To my daughter, Nancy, for showing me what talent and hard work can achieve. Congrats on your success at Princeton University and Stanford University.

To my son, Neil, for your strong passion, deep critical thinking, and self-learning. May God bless your life at Yale University.

To my daughter, Nicole, for your compassion and endurance. May God guide you in your future.

Foreword

In today's fast-paced digital landscape, where technology shapes the way we live and work, cloud computing has emerged as a transformative force. Its power to revolutionize businesses, accelerate innovation, and enable modern technology is immeasurable. As the demand for cloud expertise continues to soar, there is a pressing need for comprehensive resources to equip more individuals with the knowledge and skills in this dynamic realm.

The Self-Taught Cloud Engineer by Logan Song fills this void admirably. As one of the world's leading **Subject Matter Experts (SMEs)** in cloud computing, Logan brings forth a wealth of wisdom, insights, and practical guidance in this remarkable book. Within its pages lies an extraordinary learning journey that will empower readers to grasp the intricacies of the three most prominent clouds on Earth: Amazon web services, Google Cloud, and Microsoft Azure.

This book transcends mere technical jargon and dives deep into the essence of cloud computing. Logan begins by laying a solid foundation of cloud computing concepts and services, ensuring readers comprehend the fundamentals before embarking on their transformative journey. The exploration commences with an immersive experience within the AWS cloud. By meticulously unraveling the intricacies of AWS services, ranging from compute and storage to network, database, big data, machine learning, and security, Logan offers invaluable insights into best practices for service design and deployment.

The journey continues to Google Cloud, where Logan expertly highlights its similarities and differences from AWS. Here, readers will explore the bedrock of Google Cloud's infrastructure services, delve into the realm of data analytics and machine learning, and uncover the robust security services that safeguard organizations' digital assets. This comparative study equips learners with the necessary mindset to evaluate and leverage the unique strengths of each cloud platform.

No comprehensive cloud education would be complete without an examination of Microsoft Azure, and Logan seamlessly integrates Azure into the learning journey. By collating the knowledge acquired about the previous two clouds, readers gain a holistic understanding of cloud computing. Stepping into the next level, the Azure segment delves into foundational services, data analytics, machine learning, and security features, enabling learners to expand their repertoire of cloud skills and become well-rounded cloud professionals.

But this book goes beyond technical instruction. In its final part, Logan shares his personal cloud journey, where he underwent a profound transformation from a traditional advisory IT infrastructure architect to a chief cloud architect and professor. Through his captivating narrative, he imparts the secret ingredients of his success: a perpetually grateful disposition and an unwavering commitment to lifelong learning. These invaluable lessons, intertwined with his own experiences, will inspire readers to adopt a positive mindset and embrace the challenges and opportunities that lie ahead.

As I reflect on the significance of *The Self-Taught Cloud Engineer*, I am reminded of the huge potential that lies within each of us. The power to shape our destinies, build successful careers, and contribute meaningfully to the digital era is within our grasp. This book serves as an indispensable guide, empowering individuals to unlock the full potential of cloud computing and become the cloud superheroes our world desperately needs.

Yu Meng, Ph.D.

IEEE Senior Member

MIT App Inventor Certified Expert Trainer

ISEF Grand Prize Judge

Contributors

About the author

Dr. Logan Song is the cloud director and chief cloud architect at Dito LLC, a Google Partner company. With over 25 years of professional experience, Dr. Song is highly skilled in enterprise information technology architecture, specializing in cloud computing and machine learning. Dr. Song has led numerous data center virtualization and cloud projects in Fortune 500 companies and government agencies. He holds numerous cloud certifications in AWS, Azure, and Google Cloud.

Dr. Song holds a Ph.D. in industrial engineering, an MS in computer science, and a BS in electrical engineering. Currently, he is an adjunct professor at the University of Texas in Dallas, teaching graduate courses in cloud computing and machine learning.

I want to thank the Packt team: Isha Singh, Shagun Saini, Suwarna Patil, and the reviewers and editors, who have worked so hard to make this book possible.

I am full of gratitude to all my friends, teachers, classmates, colleagues, and coworkers for the help they have provided to me in my life.

lifelong learning. These invaluable lessons, intertwined with his own experiences, will inspire readers to adopt a positive mindset and embrace the challenges and opportunities that lie ahead.

As I reflect on the significance of *The Self-Taught Cloud Engineer*, I am reminded of the huge potential that lies within each of us. The power to shape our destinies, build successful careers, and contribute meaningfully to the digital era is within our grasp. This book serves as an indispensable guide, empowering individuals to unlock the full potential of cloud computing and become the cloud superheroes our world desperately needs.

Yu Meng, Ph.D.

IEEE Senior Member

MIT App Inventor Certified Expert Trainer

ISEF Grand Prize Judge

Contributors

About the author

Dr. Logan Song is the cloud director and chief cloud architect at Dito LLC, a Google Partner company. With over 25 years of professional experience, Dr. Song is highly skilled in enterprise information technology architecture, specializing in cloud computing and machine learning. Dr. Song has led numerous data center virtualization and cloud projects in Fortune 500 companies and government agencies. He holds numerous cloud certifications in AWS, Azure, and Google Cloud.

Dr. Song holds a Ph.D. in industrial engineering, an MS in computer science, and a BS in electrical engineering. Currently, he is an adjunct professor at the University of Texas in Dallas, teaching graduate courses in cloud computing and machine learning.

I want to thank the Packt team: Isha Singh, Shagun Saini, Suwarna Patil, and the reviewers and editors, who have worked so hard to make this book possible.

I am full of gratitude to all my friends, teachers, classmates, colleagues, and coworkers for the help they have provided to me in my life.

About the reviewers

Dharmesh R. Vaya is a cloud technologist known for his ability to develop enterprise applications on cloud platforms and foster a spirit of innovation among teams, with a rich experience in banking, e-commerce, and media/entertainment, to name a few. In his professional journey, he has close to 17 years of IT experience and works as a solutions architect at Palo Alto Networks, where he specializes in Prisma Cloud, for securing cloud workloads, and is a thought leader around DevSecOps and related technologies.

He is a recognized Google Developer Expert for the Google Cloud Platform & Payments category. He actively speaks at various international conferences, sharing his experience/learnings with the broader tech community.

I would like to thank my colleagues, mentors, and community members for all the guidance and support that have defined me as a professional. Grateful for you folks! I'm forever indebted to my parents for all their support and blessings. I'm super thankful to my family for giving me support and strength through this journey. I owe this to you all.

With over 20 years of experience in software, DevOps, and cloud engineering, **Raymond J. Hill** has become a trusted authority in the industry. Offering a broad spectrum of expertise, from IT support to leading high-performing engineering teams across various clients, Raymond's experience is as diverse as it is extensive. This vast technical and leadership experience lends them a unique and insightful perspective on the interplay of technology, management, and client delivery.

I'd like to thank my family and friends, who understand the time and commitment it takes to review books, write code, lead teams effectively, and everything else required to be a tech nerd. None of this would be possible without their support.

Chirag Nayyar has studied the cloud since 2013 and is a solutions consultant for a cloud consulting company. He assists customers in developing their public cloud adoption framework, strategy, and implementation plans.

In addition to his job, he participates in cloud communities as a speaker and co-organizer, and runs a YouTube channel where he provides guidance on various cloud platforms, including how to prepare for certifications.

I want to express my gratitude to my wife for always being there for me.

Table of Contents

Table of Contents

3

Amazon Networking Services 45

4

Amazon Database Services 79

5

Amazon Data Analytics Services 105

6

Amazon Machine Learning Services   145

7

Amazon Cloud Security Services   177

Part 2: Comprehending GCP Cloud Services

8

9

10

Part 3: Mastering Azure Cloud Services

12

Microsoft Azure Cloud Foundation Services   309

13

Azure Cloud Database and Big Data Services   335

14

Azure Cloud AI Services   357

15

Azure Cloud Security Services   381

11

Google Cloud Security Services   285

Part 3: Mastering Azure Cloud Services

12

Microsoft Azure Cloud Foundation Services   309

13

Azure Cloud Database and Big Data Services 335

14

Azure Cloud AI Services 357

15

Azure Cloud Security Services 381

Preface

Cloud computing came into our world in 2006, about 60 years after the first computer emerged. Cloud computing provides a brand-new concept of computing power services such as elastic, self-provisioning, and on-demand. In a traditional computing data center model, computing infrastructure is conceived as physical hardware with space, compute and network equipment, admin staff, physical security, and capital expenditure – entailing a long procurement cycle, big maintenance costs, and a lumbering structure. The new cloud computing model builds the computing infrastructure as software that matches your business needs: provisioning and terminating computing resources on-demand, scaling the computing resources up and down elastically and automatically, deploying the cloud resources as immutable code with version control, and paying for what you use.

Amazon Web Services (**AWS**) was the first cloud service, followed by Microsoft Azure and **Google Cloud Platform** (**GCP**). These are the three main clouds that are dominating the world, and this book helps you to learn about and master all of them and build a successful career in cloud computing.

Who this book is for

The book is for individuals in the information technology domain, whether you are a beginner looking to start your cloud computing journey or an experienced professional seeking to expand your skills. Our interactive study book is designed to empower you with the knowledge and practical experience necessary to excel in the world of cloud computing. With the detailed roadmap in the book, you will be able to complete a comprehensive cloud learning journey and develop a successful cloud computing career thereafter.

What this book covers

Chapter 1, Amazon EC2 and Compute Services, introduces AWS cloud compute services including EC2, among others.

Chapter 2, Amazon Cloud Storage Services, delves into AWS cloud storage services including EBS, EFS, S3, and so on.

Chapter 3, Amazon Cloud Networking Services, discusses AWS cloud networking services, including VPC, Amazon Direct Connect, Amazon **Domain Name Service** (**DNS**), and **Content Delivery Network** (**CDN**).

Chapter 4, Amazon Cloud Database Services, covers relational databases, NoSQL databases, and data warehouses in the AWS cloud.

Chapter 5, Amazon Cloud Big Data Services, explores AWS big data services for data ingestion, storing, processing, and visualization in the Amazon cloud.

Chapter 6, Amazon Cloud Machine Learning Services, examines AWS cloud **machine learning (ML)** services, including SageMaker and AWS ML API services.

Chapter 7, Amazon Cloud Security Services, addresses AWS cloud security services for hardening the Amazon cloud environment.

Chapter 8, Google Cloud Foundation Services, covers **Google Compute Engine (GCE)**, **Persistent Disks (PDs)**, network storage (Filestore), **Google Cloud Storage (GCS)**, Google VPC, and VPC peering.

Chapter 9, Google Cloud Data Services, covers GCP data services such as Cloud SQL, Firestore, Datastore, and Bigtable; and GCP big data services, including BigQuery, Pub/Sub, Dataproc, Dataflow, and so on.

Chapter 10, Google Cloud AI Services, examines GCP ML services, focusing on GCP Vertex AI and AI APIs.

Chapter 11, Google Cloud Security Services, discusses GCP security services including endpoint security, network security, data security, and **Security Command Center (SCC)**, which is the focal point of this chapter.

Chapter 12, Azure Cloud Foundation Services, explores the concepts of Azure cloud virtual machines and disk storage, file storage, **Binary Large Object (BLOB)** storage, queue storage, table storage, Azure vNets, and peering.

Chapter 13, Azure Cloud Data Services, covers Azure cloud-managed database services such as relational databases (Azure SQL Database), NoSQL databases (Azure Cosmos DB), and cache databases (Azure Cache for Redis), and discusses Azure big data services including Azure Data Factory, Azure Databricks, and Azure HDInsight.

Chapter 14, Azure Cloud AI Services, discusses Azure Machine Learning workspaces and Azure Cognitive Services, including the Azure OpenAI service.

Chapter 15, Azure Cloud Security Services, covers Microsoft Azure cloud security, including Azure security best practices, the Azure cloud security reference architecture, and an Azure security case study of a real-life project.

Chapter 16, Achieving Cloud Certification, reviews cloud certification roadmaps for AWS, Azure, and GCP, develops cloud exam strategies, and analyzes practice questions for seven cloud certification exams.

Chapter 17, Building a Successful Cloud Computing Career, discusses the cloud job market and the soft skills in a cloud career, and I share my own cloud story.

To get the most out of this book

To get the most out of this book, study the chapters to master the basic concepts, learn by doing all the lab examples in the chapters, study the certification exam contents, and go on to achieve cloud certifications.

If you are using the digital version of this book, we advise you to type the code yourself or access the code from the book's GitHub repository (a link is available in the next section). Doing so will help you avoid any potential errors related to the copying and pasting of code.

Download the example code files

You can download the example code files for this book from GitHub at `https://github.com/PacktPublishing/Self-Taught-Cloud-computing-Engineer`.

If there's an update to the code, it will be updated in the GitHub repository.

We also have other code bundles from our rich catalog of books and videos available at `https://github.com/PacktPublishing/`. Check them out!

Conventions used

There are a number of text conventions used throughout this book.

`Code in text`: Indicates code words in text, database table names, folder names, filenames, file extensions, pathnames, dummy URLs, user input, and Twitter handles. Here is an example: "Using `putty` to connect to a Linux instance, install `mysql client pkg` and connect to the RDS endpoint."

A block of code is set as follows:

```
Create database school;
Create table school.students (
    StudentID int primary key,
    LastName varchar(100),
    FirstName varchar(100),
    City varchar(100)  );
```

When we wish to draw your attention to a particular part of a code block, the relevant lines or items are set in bold:

```
Create database school;
Create table school.students (
    StudentID int primary key,
    LastName varchar(100),
```

```
    FirstName varchar(100),
    City varchar(100)  );
```

Any command-line input or output is written as follows:

```
gcloud functions deploy image_checking  --trigger-resource  z04092023-
upload --trigger-event google.storage.object.finalize --runtime
python37
```

Bold: Indicates a new term, an important word, or words that you see on screen. For instance, words in menus or dialog boxes appear in **bold**. Here is an example: "Click **Explore table items**."

> **Tips or important notes**
> Appear like this.

Get in touch

Feedback from our readers is always welcome.

General feedback: If you have questions about any aspect of this book, email us at customercare@ packtpub.com and mention the book title in the subject of your message.

Errata: Although we have taken every care to ensure the accuracy of our content, mistakes do happen. If you have found a mistake in this book, we would be grateful if you would report this to us. Please visit www.packtpub.com/support/errata and fill in the form.

Piracy: If you come across any illegal copies of our works in any form on the internet, we would be grateful if you would provide us with the location address or website name. Please contact us at copyright@packt.com with a link to the material.

If you are interested in becoming an author: If there is a topic that you have expertise in and you are interested in either writing or contributing to a book, please visit authors.packtpub.com.

Share your thoughts

Once you've read *The Self-Taught Cloud Engineer,* we'd love to hear your thoughts! Scan the QR code below to go straight to the Amazon review page for this book and share your feedback.

https://packt.link/r/180512370X

Your review is important to us and the tech community and will help us make sure we're delivering excellent quality content.

Download a free PDF copy of this book

Thanks for purchasing this book!

Do you like to read on the go but are unable to carry your print books everywhere?

Is your eBook purchase not compatible with the device of your choice?

Don't worry, now with every Packt book you get a DRM-free PDF version of that book at no cost.

Read anywhere, any place, on any device. Search, copy, and paste code from your favorite technical books directly into your application.

The perks don't stop there, you can get exclusive access to discounts, newsletters, and great free content in your inbox daily

Follow these simple steps to get the benefits:

1. Scan the QR code or visit the link below

https://packt.link/free-ebook/978-1-80512-370-5

2. Submit your proof of purchase
3. That's it! We'll send your free PDF and other benefits to your email directly

Part 1:
Learning about
the Amazon Cloud

This first part kicks off the cloud journey by introducing the Amazon cloud. In this part, we will digest the concept of cloud computing and examine the AWS cloud services, including compute, storage, networking, database, big data, machine learning, and security, aiming for a comprehensive understanding of the Amazon cloud and obtaining hands-on skills in the AWS cloud.

This part comprises the following chapters:

- *Chapter 1, Amazon EC2 and Compute Services*
- *Chapter 2, Amazon Cloud Storage Services*
- *Chapter 3, Amazon Cloud Networking Services*
- *Chapter 4, Amazon Cloud Database Services*
- *Chapter 5, Amazon Cloud Big Data Services*
- *Chapter 6, Amazon Cloud Machine Learning Services*
- *Chapter 7, Amazon Cloud Security Services*

1

Amazon EC2 and Compute Services

Amazon Web Services (**AWS**) is a cloud computing platform offered by Amazon. It provides a wide range of cloud-based services, including compute, storage, networks, databases, data analytics, **machine learning** (**ML**), and other functionality that can be used to build scalable and flexible applications. We will start our Amazon cloud learning journey from the AWS compute services—specifically, **Elastic Compute Cloud** (**EC2**), which was one of the most basic and earliest cloud services in the world.

In this chapter, we will cover the following topics:

- **The history of computing**: How the first computer evolved from physical to virtual and led to cloud compute

- **Amazon Global Cloud Infrastructure**: Where all the AWS global cloud services are based

- **Building our first EC2 instances in the Amazon cloud**: Provision EC2 instances in the AWS cloud, step by step

- **Elastic Load Balancers** (**ELBs**) and **Auto Scaling Groups** (**ASGs**): The framework providing EC2 services elastically

- **AWS compute – from EC2 to containers to serverless**: Extend from EC2 to other AWS compute services, including **Elastic Container Service** (**ECS**), **Elastic Kubernetes Service** (**EKS**), and Lambda

By following the discussions in this chapter, you will be able to grasp the basic concepts of cloud computing, AWS EC2, and compute services, and gain hands-on skills in provisioning EC2 and compute services. Practice questions are provided to assess your knowledge level, and further reading links are included at the end of the chapter.

The history of computing

In this section, we will briefly review the computing history of human beings, from the first computer to Amazon EC2, and understand what has happened in the past 70+ years and what led us to the cloud computing era.

The computer

The invention of the computer is one of the biggest milestones in human history. On December 10, 1945, **Electronic Numerical Integrator and Computer (ENIAC)** was first put to work for practical purposes at the University of Pennsylvania. It weighed about 30 tons, occupied about 1,800 sq ft, and consumed about 150 kW of electricity.

From 1945 to now, in over 75 years, we human beings have made huge progress in upgrading the computer. From ENIAC to desktop and data center servers, laptops, and iPhones, *Figure 1.1* shows the computer evolution landmarks:

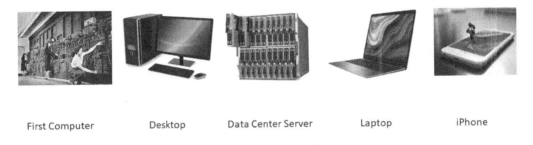

First Computer　　　Desktop　　　Data Center Server　　　Laptop　　　iPhone

Figure 1.1 – Computer evolution landmarks

Let's take some time to examine a computer—say, a desktop PC. If we remove the cover, we will find that it has the following main *hardware* parts—as shown in *Figure 1.2*:

- **Central processing unit (CPU)**
- **Random access memory (RAM)**
- **Hard disk (HD)**
- **Network interface card (NIC)**

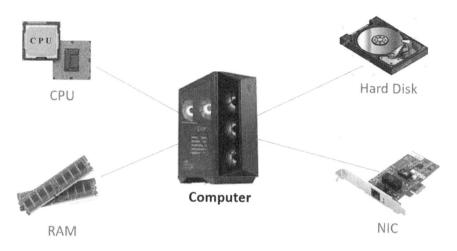

Figure 1.2 – Computer hardware components

These hardware parts work together to make the computer function, along with the *software* including the **operating system** (such as Windows, Linux, macOS, and so on), which manages the hardware, and the **application programs** (such as Microsoft Office, web servers, games, and so on) that run on top of the operating system. In a nutshell, hardware and software specifications decide how much power a computer can serve for different business use cases.

The data center

Apparently, one computer does not serve us well. Computers need to be able to communicate with each other to fulfill network communications, resource sharing, and so on. The work at Stanford University in the 1980s led to the birth of Cisco Systems, Inc., an internet company that played a great part in connecting computers together and forming the intranet and the internet. Connecting many computers together, *data centers* emerged as a central location for computing resources—CPU, RAM, storage, and networking.

Data centers provide resources for businesses' information technology needs: computing, storing, networking, and other services. However, the concept of data center ownership lacks flexibility and agility and entails huge investment and maintenance costs. Often, building a new data center takes a long time and a big amount of money, and maintaining existing data centers—such as tech refresh projects—is very costly. In certain circumstances, it is not even possible to possess the computing resources to complete certain projects. For example, the Human Genome Project was estimated to consume up to 10,000 trillion CPU hours and 40 exabytes (1 exabyte = 10^{18} bytes) of disk storage, and it is impossible to acquire resources at this scale without leveraging cloud computing.

The virtual machine

The peace of physical computers was broken in 1998 when VMware was founded and the concept of a **virtual machine** (**VM**) was brought to Earth. A VM is a software-based computer composed of virtualized components of a physical computer—CPU, RAM, HD, network, operating system, and application programs.

VMware's hypervisor virtualizes hardware to run multiple VMs on bare-metal hardware, and these VMs can run various operating systems of Windows, Linux, or others. With virtualization, a VM is represented by a bunch of files. It can be exported to a binary image that can be deployed on any physical hardware at different locations. A running VM can be *moved* from one host to another, *LIVE*—so-called" v-Motion". The virtualization technologies virtualized physical hardware and caused a revolution in computer history, and also made cloud computing feasible.

The idea of cloud computing

The limitation of data centers and virtualization technology made people explore more flexible and inexpensive ways of using computing resources. The idea of cloud computing started from the concept of *"rental"*—use as needed and pay as you go. It is the on-demand, self-provisioning of computing resources (hardware, software, and so on) that allows you to pay only for what you use. The key concept of cloud computing is *disposable computing resources*. In the traditional information technology and data center concept, a computer (or any other compute resource) is treated as a *pet*. When a pet dies, people are very sad, and they need to get a new replacement right away. If an investment bank's trading server goes down at night, it is the end of the world—everyone is woken up to recover the server. However, in the new cloud computing concept, a computer is treated as cattle in a herd. For example, the website of an investment bank, zhebank.com, is supported by a *herd* of 88 servers—www001 to www88. When one server goes down, it's taken out of the serving line, shot, and replaced with another new one with the same configuration and functionalities, automatically!

With cloud computing, enterprises are leveraging the **cloud service provider** (**CSP**)'s *unlimited* computing resources that are featured as global, elastic and scalable, highly reliable and available, cost-effective, and secure. The main CSPs, such as Amazon, Microsoft, and Google, have global data centers that are connected by backbone networks. Because of cloud computing's pay-as-you-go characteristics, it makes sense for cost savings. Because of its strong monitoring and logging features, cloud computing offers the most secure hosting environment. Instead of building physical hardware data centers with big investments over a long time, virtual software-based data centers can be built within several hours, immutable and repeatedly, in the global cloud environment. Infrastructure is represented as code that can be managed with version control, which we can call **Infrastructure as Code (IaC)**. More details can be found at https://docs.aws.amazon.com/whitepapers/latest/introduction-devops-aws/infrastructure-as-code.html.

EC2 was first introduced in 2006 as a web service that allowed customers to rent virtual computers for computing tasks. Since then, it has become one of the most popular cloud computing platforms available, offering a wide range of services and features that make it an attractive option for enterprise customers. Amazon categorizes the VMs with different EC2 instance types based on hardware (CPU, RAM, HD, and network) and software (operating system and applications) configurations. For different business use cases, cloud consumers can choose EC2 instances with a variety of instance types, operating system choices, network options, storage options, and more. In 2013, Amazon introduced the **Reserved Instance** feature, which gave customers the opportunity to purchase instances at discounted rates in exchange for committing to longer usage terms. In 2017, Amazon released EC2 Fleet, which allows customers to manage multiple instance types and instance sizes across multiple **Availability Zones** (**AZs**) with a single request.

The computer evolution path

From ENIAC to EC2, a computer has evolved from a huge, physical unit to a disposable resource that is flexible and on-demand, portable, and replaceable, and a data center has evolved from being expensive and protracted to a piece of code that can be executed globally at any time on demand, within hours.

In the next sections of this chapter, we will look at the Amazon Global Cloud Infrastructure and then provision our EC2 instances in the cloud.

Amazon Global Cloud infrastructure

The **Amazon Global Cloud Infrastructure** is a suite of cloud computing services offered by AWS, including compute, storage, databases, analytics, networking, mobile, developer tools, management tools, security, identity compliance, and so on. These services are hosted globally, allowing customers to store data and access resources in locations that best meet their business needs. It delivers highly secure, low-cost, and reliable services that can be used by almost any application in any industry around the world.

Amazon has built physical data centers around the world, in graphical areas called AWS Regions, which are connected by Amazon's backbone network infrastructure. Each Region provides full redundancy and connectivity among its data centers. An AWS Region typically consists of two or more AZs, which is a fully isolated partition of the AWS infrastructure. An AZ has one or more data centers connected with each other and is identified by a name that combines a letter identifier with the region's name. For example, `us-east-1d` is the d AZ in the `us-east-1` region. Each AZ is designed for fault isolation and is connected to other AZs using high-speed private networking. When provisioning cloud resources such as EC2, you choose the region and AZs where the EC2 instance will be sitting. In the next section, we will demonstrate the EC2 instance provisioning process.

Building our first EC2 instances in the Amazon cloud

In this section, we will use the AWS cloud console and CloudShell command line to provision EC2 instances running in the Amazon cloud—Linux and Windows VMs, step by step. Note that the user interface may change, but the procedures are similar.

Before we can launch an EC2 instance, we need to create an AWS account first. Amazon offers a *free tier* account for new cloud learners to provision some basic cloud resources, but you will need a credit card to sign up for an AWS account. Since your credit card is involved, there are three things to keep in mind with your AWS 12-digit account, as follows:

- Enable **multi-factor authentication** (**MFA**) to protect your account

- You can log in to the console with your email address, but be aware that this is the root user, which has the superpower to provision any resources globally

- Clean up all/any cloud resources you have provisioned after completing the labs

Having signed up for an AWS account, you are ready to move to the next phase—launching EC2 instances using the cloud console or CloudShell.

Launching EC2 instances in the AWS cloud console

Logging in to the AWS console at `console.aws.amazon.com`, you can search for EC2 services and launch an EC2 instance by taking the following nine steps:

1. **Select the software of the EC2 instance**: Think of it just like selecting software (OS and other applications) when purchasing a physical desktop or laptop PC.

   In AWS, the software image for an EC2 instance is called an **Amazon Machine Image** (**AMI**), which is a template that is used to launch an EC2 instance. Amazon provides AMIs in Windows, Linux, and other operating systems, customized with some other software pre-installed:

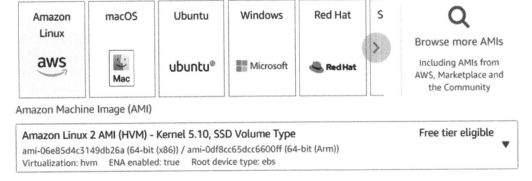

Figure 1.3 – Selecting an AMI

As shown in *Figure 1.3*, we have chosen the Amazon Linux 2 AMI, which is a customized Linux OS tuned for optimal performance on AWS and easy integration with AWS services, and it is free-tier eligible.

In many enterprises, AMI images are standardized to be used as **seeds** to deploy EC2 instances—we call them **golden images**. A production AMI includes all the packages, patches, and applications that are needed to deploy EC2 instances in production and will be managed with secure version-control management systems.

2. **Select the hardware configuration of the EC2 instance**: This is just like selecting hardware—the number of CPUs, RAM, and HD sizes when purchasing a physical desktop or laptop PC. In AWS, the hardware selection is to choose the right EC2 instance type—Amazon has categorized the EC2 hardware configurations into various instance types, such as **General Purpose**, **Compute Optimized**, **Memory Optimized**, and so on, based on business use cases. Some AWS EC2 instance types are shown in *Figure 1.4*:

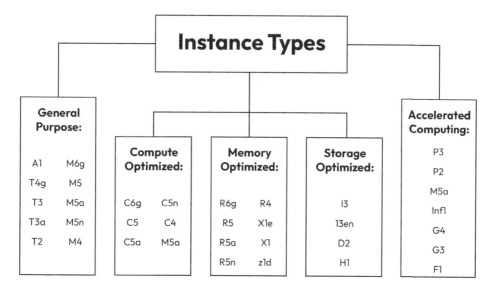

Figure 1.4 – EC2 instance types

Each instance type is specified by a category, family series, generation number, and configuration size. For example, the p2.8xlarge instance type can be used for an Accelerated Computing use case, where p is the instance family series, 2 is the instance generation, and 8xlarge indicates its size is 8 times the p2.large instance type.

We will choose t2.micro, which is inexpensive and free-tier eligible, for our EC2 instances.

3. **Specify the EC2 instance's network settings**: This is like subscribing to an **Internet Service Provider** (**ISP**) for our home PC to connect to a network and the internet. In the AWS cloud, the basic network unit is called a **Virtual Private Cloud** (**VPC**), and Amazon has provided a default VPC and subnets in each region. At this time, we will take the default setting—our first EC2 instance will be placed into the default VPC/subnet and be assigned a public IP address to make it internet-accessible.

4. **Optionally attach an AWS Identity and Access Management (IAM) role to the EC2 instance**: This is something very different from traditional concepts but is very useful for software/ applications running on the EC2 instance to interact with other AWS services.

    With IAM, you can specify who can access which resources with what permissions. An IAM role can be created and assigned with permissions to access other AWS resources, such as reading an **Amazon Simple Storage Service** (**Amazon S3**) bucket. By attaching the IAM role to an EC2 instance, all applications running on the EC2 instance will have the same permissions as that role. For example, we can create an IAM role, assign it read/write access to an S3 bucket, and attach the role to an EC2 instance, then all the applications running on the EC2 instance will have read/write access to the S3 bucket. *Figure 1.5* shows the concept of attaching an IAM role to an EC2 instance:

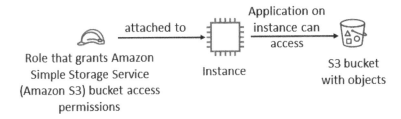

Figure 1.5 – Attaching an IAM role to an EC2 instance

5. **Optionally specify a user data script to the EC2 instance**: User data scripts can be used to customize the runtime environment of the EC2 instance—it executes the first time the instance starts. I have had experience using the EC2 user data script—at a time when the Linux system admin left my company and no one in the company was able to access a Linux instance sitting in the AWS cloud. While there exist many ways to rescue this situation, one interesting solution we used was to generate a new key pair (public key and private key), stop the instance, and leverage the instance's user data script to append the new public key to the EC2-user user's **Secure Shell** (**SSH**) profile, during the instance starting process. With the new public key added to the EC2 instance, the ec2-user user can SSH into the instance with the new private key.

6. **Optionally attach additional storage volumes to the EC2 instance**: This can be thought of as buying and adding additional disk drives to our PC at home. For each volume, we need to specify the size of the disk (in GB) and the volume type (hardware types), and whether encryption should be used for the volume.

7. **Optionally assign a tag to the EC2 instance**: A tag is a label that we can assign to an AWS resource, and it consists of a key and an optional value. With tags, we attach metadata to cloud resources such as an EC2 instance. There are many potential benefits of tagging in managing cloud resources, such as filtering, automation, cost allocation and chargeback, and access control.

8. **Setting a Security Group (SG) for the EC2 instance**: Just like configuring firewalls on our home routers to manage access to our home PCs, an SG is a set of firewall rules that control traffic to and from our EC2 instance. With an SG, we can create rules that specify the source (for example, an IP address or another SG), the port number, and the protocol, such as HTTP/HTTPS, SSH (port 22), or **Internet Control Message Protocol (ICMP)**. For example, if we use the EC2 instance to host a web server, then the SG will need an SG rule to open ports for `http (80)` and `https (443)`. Note that SGs exist outside of the instance's guest OS—traffic to the instance can be controlled by both SGs and guest OS firewall settings.

9. **Specify an existing key pair or create a new key pair for the EC2 instance**: A key pair consists of a public key that AWS stores on the instance and a private key file that you download and store on your local computer for remote access. When you try to connect to the instance, the keys from both ends are matched to authenticate the remote user/connections. For Windows instances, we need to decrypt the key pair to obtain the administrator password for logging in to the EC2 instance remotely. For Linux instances, we utilize the private key and use SSH to securely connect to the cloud instance. Note that the only chance to download an EC2 key pair is during the instance creation time. If you've lost the key pair, you cannot recover it. The only workaround is to create an AMI of the existing instance, and then launch a new instance with the AMI and a new key pair. Also, note that there are two formats for an EC2 key pair when you save it to the local computer: the `.pem` format is used on Linux-based terminals including Mac, and the `.ppk` format is used for Windows.

Following the preceding nine steps, we have provisioned our first EC2 instance—a Linux VM in the AWS cloud. Following the same procedure, let us launch a Windows VM. The only difference is that in *step 1*, we choose the Microsoft Windows operating system— specifically, **Microsoft Windows Server 2022 Base**—as shown in *Figure 1.6*, which is also free-tier eligible:

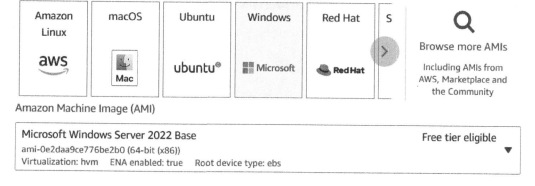

Figure 1.6 – Selecting Microsoft Windows as the operating system

So far, we have created two EC2 instances in our AWS cloud—one Linux VM and one Windows VM—via the AWS Management console.

Launching EC2 instances using CloudShell

We can also launch EC2 instances using the command line in CloudShell, which is a browser-based, pre-authenticated shell that you can launch directly from the AWS Management Console. Next are detailed steps to create an EC2 Windows instance in the `us-west-2` Region:

1. **From the AWS console, launch CloudShell** by clicking the CloudShell sign, as shown in *Figure 1.7*:

aws
Services
Search
[Alt+S]
Oregon
Logan
EFS
IAM

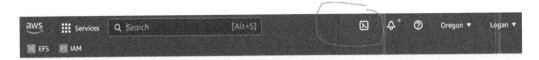

Figure 1.7 – Launching CloudShell from the AWS console

2. **Find the AWS AMI image ID** in the `us-west-2` region, with the following CloudShell command – the results are shown in *Figure 1.8*:

```
[cloudshell-user]$ aws ec2 describe-images --region us-west-2
```

[cloudshell-user@ip-10-6-69-82 ~]$ aws ec2 describe-images --region us-west-2
{
"Images": [
{
"Architecture": "x86_64",
"CreationDate": "2021-11-13T17:14:15.000Z",
"ImageId": "ami-0ef0b498cd3fe129c",
"ImageLocation": "068169053218/dremio-daasExecutor-test-76bd55f5-32ee-491c-86ab-2fcb6eecdec7",
"ImageType": "machine",
"Public": true,
"OwnerId": "068169053218",
"PlatformDetails": "Linux/UNIX",
"UsageOperation": "RunInstances",
"State": "available",

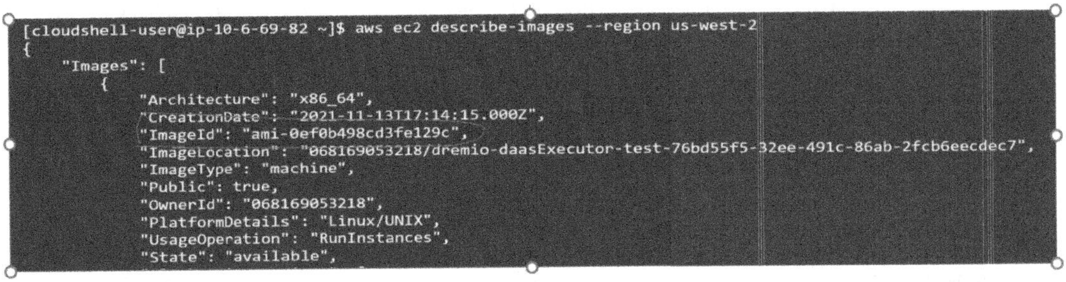

Figure 1.8 – Finding the Linux AMI image ID

3. **Find the SG name** we created in the previous section, as shown in *Figure 1.9*:

```
[cloudshell-user@ip-10-6-69-82 ~]$ aws ec2 describe-security-groups
{
    "SecurityGroups": [
        {
            "Description": "launch-wizard-1 created 2023-01-26T22:34:24.105Z",
            "GroupName": "launch-wizard-1",
            "IpPermissions": [
                {
                    "FromPort": 3389,
                    "IpProtocol": "tcp",
                    "IpRanges": [
                        {
                            "CidrIp": "129.110.242.32/32"
                        }
```

Figure 1.9 – Finding the SG name

4. **Find the key pair** we created in the previous section, as shown in *Figure 1.10*:

```
[cloudshell-user@ip-10-6-69-82 ~]$ aws ec2 describe-key-pairs
{
    "KeyPairs": [
        {
            "KeyPairId": "key-092be0798f7c7883b",
            "KeyFingerprint": "c7:4d:81:09:8c:3d:cb:db:b0:47:ee:4e:21:dd:53:cd:54:5a:65:72",
            "KeyName": "mywestkp",
            "KeyType": "rsa",
            "Tags": [],
            "CreateTime": "2023-01-26T22:35:40+00:00"
        }
    ]
}
```

Figure 1.10 – Finding the key pair name

5. **Create an EC2 instance** in the us-west-2 region, using the aws ec2 run-instances command, with the following configurations we obtained from the previous steps. A screenshot is shown in *Figure 1.11*. The instance ID is called out from the output

AMI:

ami-0ef0b498cd3fe129c

SG:

launch-wizard-1

Key pair:

mywestkp

Instance type:

t2.micro

```
aws ec2 run-instances --image-id ami-0ef0b498cd3fe129c --count 1
--instance-type t2.micro --key-name mywestkp --security-groups
launch-wizard-1 --region us-west-2
```

```
[cloudshell-user@ip-10-6-69-82 ~]$ aws ec2 run-instances  --image-id ami-0ef0b498cd3fe129c  --count 1  --instance-type t2.micro --
key-name mywestkp --security-groups launch-wizard-1 --region us-west-2
{
    "Groups": [],
    "Instances": [
        {
            "AmiLaunchIndex": 0,
            "ImageId": "ami-0ef0b498cd3fe129c",
            "InstanceId": "i-00398bfb35733237a",
            "InstanceType": "t2.micro",
            "PublicDnsName": "",
```

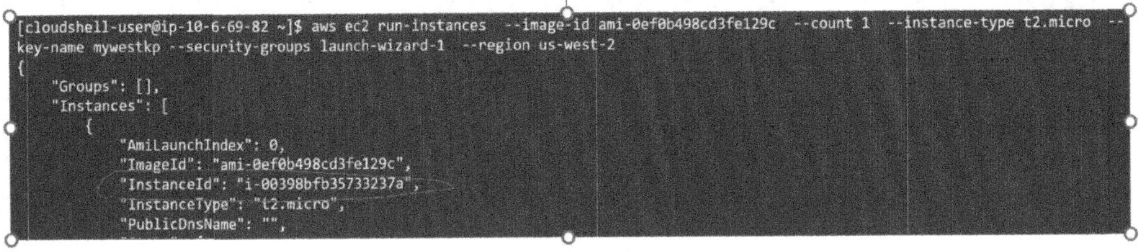

Figure 1.11 – Launching an EC2 instance

6. **Examine the details of the instance** from its InstanceId value. As shown in *Figure 1.12*, the instance has a public IP address of 35.93.143.38:

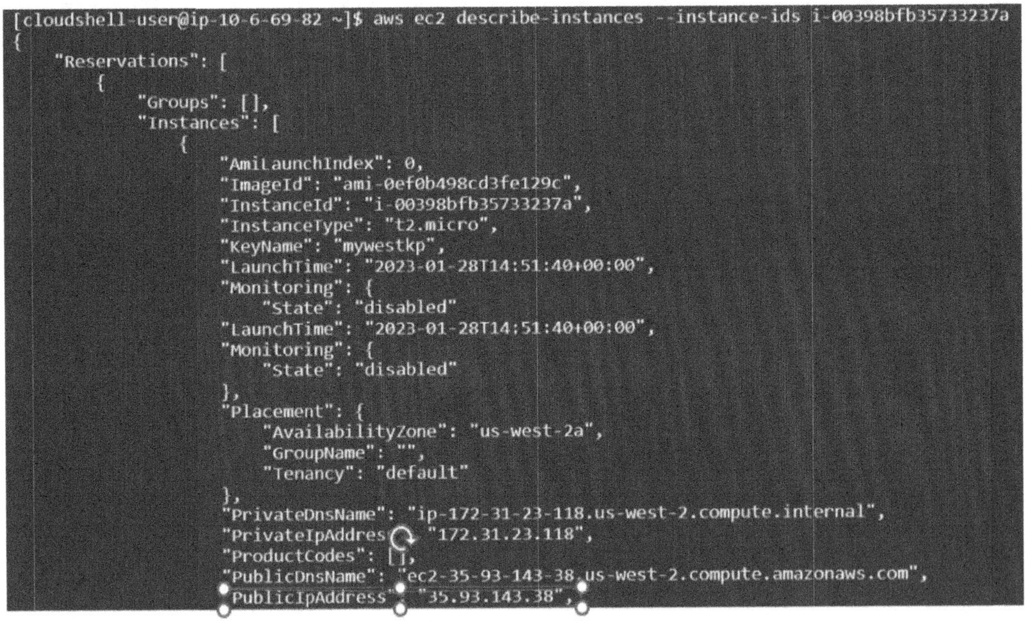

```
[cloudshell-user@ip-10-6-69-82 ~]$ aws ec2 describe-instances --instance-ids i-00398bfb35733237a
{
    "Reservations": [
        {
            "Groups": [],
            "Instances": [
                {
                    "AmiLaunchIndex": 0,
                    "ImageId": "ami-0ef0b498cd3fe129c",
                    "InstanceId": "i-00398bfb35733237a",
                    "InstanceType": "t2.micro",
                    "KeyName": "mywestkp",
                    "LaunchTime": "2023-01-28T14:51:40+00:00",
                    "Monitoring": {
                        "State": "disabled"
                    "LaunchTime": "2023-01-28T14:51:40+00:00",
                    "Monitoring": {
                        "State": "disabled"
                    },
                    "Placement": {
                        "AvailabilityZone": "us-west-2a",
                        "GroupName": "",
                        "Tenancy": "default"
                    },
                    "PrivateDnsName": "ip-172-31-23-118.us-west-2.compute.internal",
                    "PrivateIpAddress": "172.31.23.118",
                    "ProductCodes": [],
                    "PublicDnsName": "ec2-35-93-143-38.us-west-2.compute.amazonaws.com",
                    "PublicIpAddress": "35.93.143.38",
```

Figure 1.12 – Finding the EC2 instance's public IP address

So far, we have created another EC2 instance using CloudShell with command lines. Note that CloudShell allows us to provision any cloud resources using lines of code, and we will provide more examples in the rest of the book.

Logging in to the EC2 instances

After the instances are created, how do we access them?

SSH is a cryptographic network protocol for operating network services securely over an unsecured network. We can use SSH to access the Linux EC2 instance. **PuTTY** is a free and open source terminal emulator, serial console, and network file transfer application. We will download PuTTY and use it to connect to the Linux VM in the AWS cloud, as shown in *Figure 1.13*:

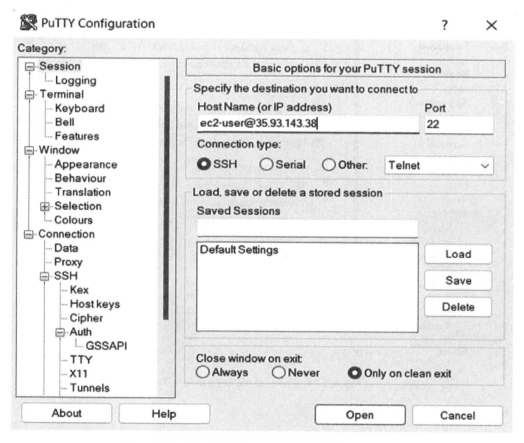

Figure 1.13 – Using PuTTY to connect to the Linux instance

As shown in *Figure 1.13*, we entered `ec2-user@35.93.143.38` in the **Host Name (or IP address)** field. `ec2-user` is a default user created in the guest Linux OS, and `35.93.143.38` is the public IP of the EC2 instance. Note we need to open the SSH port (`22`) in the EC2 instance's SG to allow traffic from our remote machine, as discussed in *step 8* of the *Launching EC2 instances in the AWS cloud console* section earlier in the chapter.

We also need to provide the key pair in the **PuTTY Configuration** window by going to **Connection | SSH | Auth**, as shown in *Figure 1.14*:

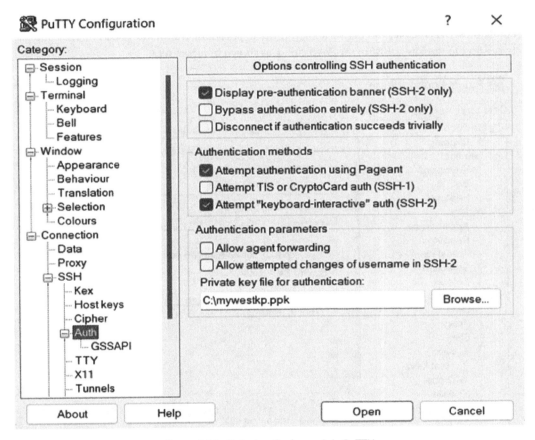

Figure 1.14 – Entering the key pair in PuTTY

Click **Open**, and you will be able to SSH into the Linux instance now. As shown in *Figure 1.15*, we have SSH-ed into the cloud EC2 instance:

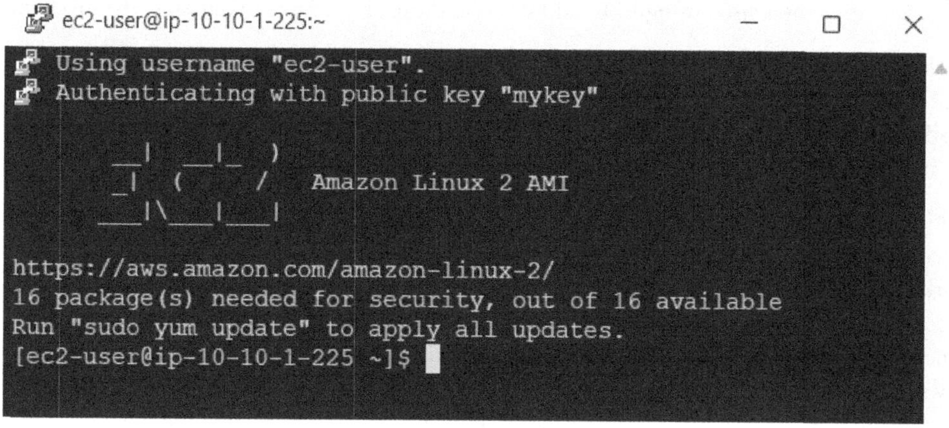

Figure 1.15 – SSH-ing into ec2-1 from the internet

Since we are using a Windows terminal to connect to the remote Linux instance, the key pair format is `.ppk`. If you are using a Mac or another Linux-based terminal, you will need to use the `.pem` format. These two formats can be converted using the open source software PuTTYgen, which is part of the PuTTY family.

With a Linux-based terminal including Mac, use the following command to connect to the cloud Linux EC2 instance:

```
ssh -i keypair.pem ec2-user@35.93.143.38
```

`keypair.pem` is the key pair file in `.pem` format. Make sure it's set to the right permission using the `chomd 400 keypair.pem` Linux command. `ec2-user@35.93.143.38` is `user@` EC2's public IP address. The default user may change to `ubuntu` if the EC2 instance is an Ubuntu Linux distribution.

For the Windows EC2 instance, just as we access another PC at our home using **Remote Desktop Protocol (RDP)**, a proprietary protocol developed by Microsoft that provides a user with a graphical interface to connect to another computer over a network connection, we use RDP to log in to the Windows EC2 instance in the AWS cloud. By default, RDP client software is installed on our desktop or laptop, and the Windows EC2 instance has RDP server software running, so it becomes very handy to connect our desktop/laptop to the Windows VM in the cloud. One extra step is that we need to decrypt the administrator's password from the key pair we downloaded during the instance launching process, by going to the AWS console's **EC2 dashboard** and clicking **Instance | Connect | RDP Client**.

ELB and ASG

We previously briefed the "cattle in a herd" analogy in cloud computing. In this section, we will explain the actual implementation using ELBs and ASGs and use an example to illustrate the mechanism.

An ELB automatically distributes the incoming traffic (workload) across multiple targets, such as EC2 instances, in one or more AZs, so as to balance the workload for high performance and **high availability** (**HA**). An ELB monitors the health of its registered targets and distributes traffic only to the healthy targets.

Behind an ELB, there is usually an ASG that manages the fleet of ELB targets—EC2 instances, in our case. ASG monitors the workload of the instances and uses auto-scaling policies to scale—when the workload reaches a certain up-threshold, such as CPU utilization of 80%, ASG will launch new EC2s and add them into the fleet to offload the traffic until the utilization drops below the up-threshold. When the workload reaches a certain down-threshold, such as CPU utilization of 30%, ASG will shut down EC2s from the fleet until the utilization rises above the threshold. ASG also utilizes a health-check to monitor the instances and replace unhealthy ones as needed. During the auto-scaling process, ASG makes sure that the running EC2 instances are loaded within the thresholds and are laid out across as many AZs in a region.

Let us illustrate ELB and ASG with an example. `www.zbestbuy.com` is an international online e-commerce retailer. During normal business hours, it needs a certain number of web servers to work together to meet online shopping traffic. To meet the global traffic requirements, three web servers are built in different AWS regions—North Virginia (`us-east-1`), London (`eu-west-2`), and Singapore (`ap-southeast-1`). Depending on the customer browser location, Amazon Route 53 (an AWS DNS service) will route the traffic to the nearest web server: when customers in Europe browse the retailer website, the traffic will be routed to the `eu-west-2` web server, which is really an ELB (or **Application Load Balancer** (**ALB**)), and distributed to the EC2 instances behind the ELB, as shown in *Figure 1.16*.

When Black Friday comes, the traffic increases and hits the ELB, which passes the traffic to the EC2 instance fleet. The heavy traffic will raise the EC2 instances' CPU utilization to reach the up-threshold of 80%. Based on the auto-scaling policy, an alarm will be kicked off and the ASG will automatically scale, launching more EC2 instances to join the EC2 fleet. With more EC2s joining in, the CPU utilization will be dropped. Depending on the Black Friday traffic fluctuation, the ASG will always keep up to make sure enough EC2s are working on the workload with normal CPU utilization. When Black Friday sales end, the traffic decreases and thus causes the instances' CPU utilization to drop. When it reaches the down-threshold of 30%, the ASG will start shutting down EC2s based on the auto-scaling policy:

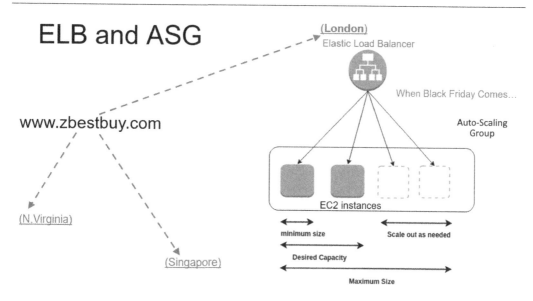

Figure 1.16 – ELB and ASG

As we can see from the preceding example, ELB and ASG work together to scale elastically. Please refer to https://docs.aws.amazon.com/autoscaling/ec2/userguide/autoscaling-load-balancer.html for more details.

AWS compute – from EC2 to containers to serverless

So far in this chapter, we have dived into the AWS EC2 service and discussed AWS ELB and ASG. Now, let's spend some time expanding to the other AWS compute services: ECS, EKS, and Lambda (serverless service).

We have discussed the virtualization technology led by VMware at the beginning of the 21st century. While transforming from physical machines to VMs is a great milestone, there still exist constraints from the application point of view: every time we need to deploy an application, we need to run a VM first. The application is also tied up with the OS platform and lacks flexibility and portability. To solve such problems, the concept of **Docker** and **containers** came into the world. A Docker engine virtualizes an OS to multiple apps/containers. A Docker image is a lightweight, standalone, executable package of software that includes everything needed to run an application: code, runtime, system tools, system libraries, and settings. A container is a runtime of the Docker image, and the application runs quickly and reliably from one computing environment to another. Multiple containers can run on the same VM and share the OS kernel with other containers, each running as isolated processes in user space. To further achieve fast and robust deployments and low lead times, the concept of **serverless** computing emerged. With serverless computing, workloads run on servers behind the scenes. From a developer or user's point of view, what they need to do is just submit the code and get the running results back—there is no hassle of building and managing any infrastructure platforms at all, while resources can continuously scale and be dynamically allocated as needed, yet you never pay for idle time as it is pay per usage.

From VM to container to serverless, Amazon provides EC2, ECS/EKS, and Lambda services correspondingly.

Amazon ECS is a fully managed container orchestration service that helps you easily deploy, manage, and scale containerized applications using Docker or Kubernetes. Amazon ECS provides a highly available and scalable platform for running container-based applications. Enterprises use ECS to grow and manage enterprise application portfolios, scale web applications, perform batch processing, and run services to deliver better services to users.

Amazon EKS, on the other hand, is a fully managed service that makes it easy to deploy, manage, and scale Kubernetes in the AWS cloud. Amazon EKS leverages the global cloud's performance, scale, reliability, and availability, and integrates it with other AWS services such as networking, storage, and security services.

Amazon Lambda was introduced in November 2014. It is an event-driven, serverless computing service that runs code in response to events and automatically manages the computing resources required by that code. Amazon Lambda provides HA with automatic scaling, cost optimization, and security. It supports multiple programming languages, environment variables, and tight integration with other AWS services.

For more details about the aforementioned AWS services and their implementations, please refer to the *Further reading* section at the end of the chapter.

Summary

Congratulations! We have completed the first chapter of our AWS self-learning journey: cloud compute services. In this chapter, we have thoroughly discussed Amazon EC2 instances and provisioned EC2 instances step by step, using the AWS cloud console and CloudShell command lines. We then extended from EC2 (VM) to the container and serverless concepts and briefly discussed Amazon's ECS, EKS, and Lambda services.

In the next chapter, we will discuss Amazon *storage* services, including block storage and network storage that can be added and shared by EC2 instances, and the Simple Storage Service.

At the end of each chapter, we provide practice questions and answers. These questions are designed to help you understand the cloud concepts discussed in the chapter. Please spend time on each question before checking the answer.

Practice questions

1. Which of the following is not a valid source option when configuring SG rules for an EC2 instance?

> A. Tag name for another EC2 instance
>
> B. IP address for another EC2 instance
>
> C. IP address ranges for a network
>
> D. SG name used by another EC2 instance

2. An AWS cloud engineer signed up for a new AWS account, then logged in to the account and created a Linux EC2 instance in the default VPC/subnet. They were able to SSH to the EC2 instance. From the EC2 instance, They:

> A. can access www.google.com
>
> B. cannot access www.google.com
>
> C. can access www.google.com only after they configure SG rules
>
> D. can access www.google.com only after they configure **Network Access Control List** (**NACL**) rules

3. Alice launched an EC2 Linux instance in the AWS cloud, and then successfully SSH-ed to the instance from her laptop at home with the default ec2-user username. Which keys are used during this process?

> A. ec2-user's public key, which is stored on the EC2 instance, and the private key on the laptop
>
> B. The root user's public key on the EC2 instance
>
> C. ec2-user's public key, which is stored on the laptop
>
> D. ec2-user's private key, which is stored on the cloud EC2 instance
>
> E. ec2-user's symmetric key, which is stored on both the laptop and EC2 instance

4. www.zbestbuy.com is configured with ELB and ASG. At peak time, it needs 10 AWS EC2 instances. How do you make sure the website will never be down and can scale as needed?

> A. Set ASG's minimum instances = 2, maximum instances = 10
>
> B. Set ASG's minimum instances = 1, maximum instances = 10
>
> C. Set ASG's minimum instances = 0, maximum instances = 10
>
> D. Set ASG's minimum instances = 2, maximum instances = 2

5. A middle school has an education application system using ASG to automatically scale resources as needed. The students report that every morning at 8:30 A.M., the system becomes very slow for about 15 minutes. Initial checking shows that a large percentage of the classes start at 8:30 A.M., and it does not have enough time to scale out to meet the demand. How can we resolve this problem?

A. Schedule the ASGs accordingly to scale out the necessary resources at 8:15 A.M. every morning

B. Use Reserved Instances to ensure the system has reserved the capacity for scale-up events

C. Change the ASG to scale based on network utilization

D. Permanently keep the running instances that are needed at 8:30 A.M. to guarantee available resources

6. AWS engineer Alice is launching an EC2 instance to host a web server. How should Alice configure the EC2 instance's SG?

A. Open ports 80 and 443 inbound to 0.0.0.0/0

B. Open ports 80 and 443 outbound to 0.0.0.0/0

C. Open ports 80 and 443 inbound to 10.10.10.0/24

D. Open ports 80 and 443 outbound to my IP

7. An AWS cloud engineer signed up for a new AWS account, then logged in to the account and created an EC2-1 Windows instance and an EC2-2 Linux instance in one subnet (172.31.48.0/20) in the default VPC, using an SG that has SSH and RDP open to 172.31.0.0/16 only. They were able to RDP to the EC2-1 instance. From the EC2-1 instance, they:

A. can SSH to EC2-2

B. can ping EC2-2

C. cannot ping EC2-1

D. cannot SSH to EC2-2

8. www.zbestbuy.com has a need for 10,000 EC2 instances in the next 3 years. What should they use to get these computing resources?

A. Reserved Instances

B. Spot Instances

C. On-demand instances

D. Dedicated-host instances

9. AWS engineer Alice needs to log in to an EC2-100 Linux instance that no one can access since the AWS engineer who was managing it left the company. What does Alice need to do?

    A. Generate a key pair, and add the public key to EC2-100 using `user-data`

    B. Generate a key pair, and add the public key to EC2-100 using `meta-data`

    C. Generate a key pair, and copy the public key to EC2-100 using **Secure Copy Protocol** (**SCP**)

    D. Remove the old private key from EC2-100

10. An AWS architect launched an EC2 instance using the `t2.large` type, installed databases and web applications on the instance, then found that the instance was too small, so they want to move to an `M4.xlarge` instance type. What do they need to do?

Answers to the practice questions

    1. A

    2. A

    3. A

    4. A

    5. A

    6. A

    7. A

    8. A

    9. A

10. One way is to stop the instance in the AWS console and start it with the `M4.xlarge` instance type.

Further reading

For further insights into what you've learned in this chapter, refer to the following links:

- `https://aws.amazon.com/ec2/`
- `https://aws.amazon.com/ecs/`
- `https://aws.amazon.com/eks/`
- `https://aws.amazon.com/lambda/`

- `https://docs.aws.amazon.com/autoscaling/ec2/userguide/autoscaling-load-balancer.html`
- `https://docs.aws.amazon.com/ec2/`
- `https://aws.amazon.com/blogs/compute/`

2
Amazon Cloud Storage Services

We explored Amazon EC2 and compute services in the previous chapter and provisioned EC2 instances in the Amazon cloud, including Windows and Linux instances. In this chapter, we will discuss Amazon cloud storage, including the block cloud storage that can be attached to an EC2 instance, the network filesystem cloud storage that can be shared by many EC2 instances, and the object cloud storage storing objects in the cloud. We will cover the following topics in this chapter:

- **Amazon Elastic Block Store (EBS)**: Provides block-level storage volumes to EC2 instances. We will show how to create and attach storage volumes to EC2 instances and use them as primary storage.

- **Amazon Elastic File System (EFS)**: Provides scalable and fully managed filesystem storage to be shared by EC2 instances and on-premises resources.

- **Amazon Simple Storage Service (S3)**: Provides object storage that can store and retrieve any amount of data from anywhere on the web.

- **Amazon Snowball** and **Snowmobile**: Physical data transfer services for transferring large amounts of data into or out of the AWS cloud.

- **Accessing S3 from EC2 instances**: By leveraging an EC2 IAM role, EC2 instances can easily access S3 and take advantage of S3's scalable, durable, and highly available storage services for your applications running on EC2.

Following the discussions in this chapter and integrating the EC2 knowledge and skills learned from the last chapter, you will be able to dive deep and understand why we need to and how to create block storage, network filesystem storage, and simple storage in the cloud, how you can transfer storage from your on-premises data centers to the cloud, and how to access the cloud storage from an EC2 instance.

Understanding EBS

When we run out of storage on our home PC, we usually buy a new disk drive, shut down the computer, install the disk drive, reboot the computer to recognize the new disk drive, and then log into the computer guest OS to format the new disk drive and start using it.

This type of disk storage is called *block storage*, which is a technology that controls storage on the computer, using a block as the storing unit. It takes the data to be stored, divides it into blocks of equal sizes, and stores the data blocks on the underlying physical storage. With block storage, a block is the unit for data storing and retrieving, and only changes to the blocks are written to the disk. For example, when you change a sentence in a Microsoft Word doc and save the doc, only the blocks that store the sentence were updated to the physical disk drive, in contrast to *object storage*, which uses an object (such as a fingerprint file) as a storing unit - any *partial* changes to the object will update the *whole* object. Object storage stores the whole object as a unit, which has metadata for object retrieval.

Block storage is usually formatted by the computer's guest OS to form a filesystem. If the disk drive is locally attached to the computer and formatted, it will be a local filesystem. A local filesystem can be shared with another computer through a network, and it is called a *network filesystem* from the remote computer's point of view. When you write to a file on a network filesystem, the changed portion is updated to the source disk drive via the network. The filesystem has a directory/folder hierarchy and stores files with blocks. Block storage uses disk drive blocks directly for reading and writing. The concepts of object storage, filesystem, and block storage are illustrated in *Figure 2.1*:

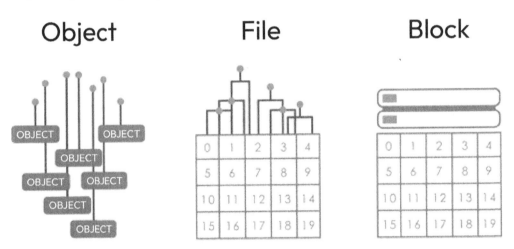

Figure 2.1 – Object storage, filesystem, and block storage

How do we add disk storage to an EC2 instance in Amazon cloud? Instead of buying a new disk drive for our home computer, we create a virtual disk drive in the AWS cloud, called an **EBS** volume. Instead of shutting down a computer and physically installing a disk drive to it, we attach the EBS volume to an EC2 instance on the fly (without shutting down the instance), and then format the disk from the guest OS. Much simpler than our earlier example of adding a physical disk to a PC, we create a virtual disk drive in the AWS cloud, called an **EBS** volume, and attach it to an EC2 instance on the fly.

With only a couple of clicks, we add disk storage to the instance and format it to use. Here are the detailed steps:

1. **Log into the Linux instance and check its existing disk storage:**

   Log into the Linux instance we launched earlier, and run the following OS commands:

   ```
   sudo su     (become the superuser in the Linux system)
   fdisk -l    (list the disks visible in the Linux system)
   ```

   As shown in *Figure 2.2*, the preceding command lists all the disks and one 8 GB disk drive, which is the root disk for the guest OS:

   ```
   [ec2-user@ip-172-31-22-204 ~]$ sudo su -
   [root@ip-172-31-22-204 ~]# fdisk -l
   Disk /dev/xvda: 8 GiB, 8589934592 bytes, 16777216 sectors
   Units: sectors of 1 * 512 = 512 bytes
   Sector size (logical/physical): 512 bytes / 512 bytes
   I/O size (minimum/optimal): 512 bytes / 512 bytes
   Disklabel type: gpt
   Disk identifier: 61856571-99DD-4505-96FC-1DD8820522F6

   Device       Start      End  Sectors Size Type
   /dev/xvda1    4096 16777182 16773087   8G Linux filesystem
   /dev/xvda128  2048     4095     2048   1M BIOS boot
   ```

   Figure 2.2 – Check the Linux instance disk storage

2. **Create an Amazon EBS volume:**

   Go to **AWS console | EC2 instance dashboard | Elastic Block Store | Volumes**, and we can see the root EBS volume of the instance, as shown in *Figure 2.3*. Click on **Create Volume**:

   Figure 2.3 – The EBS volume for the EC2 instance

   In the new window shown in *Figure 2.4*, fill in the details such as volume size, type, and AZ, then click **Create volume**. Based on performance and price, Amazon EBS provides three different volume types: **Solid State Drive (SSD)** volumes, **Hard Disk Drive (HDD)** volumes, and previous-generation volumes. More details are available from https://docs.aws.amazon.com/AWSEC2/latest/UserGuide/ebs-volume-types.html.

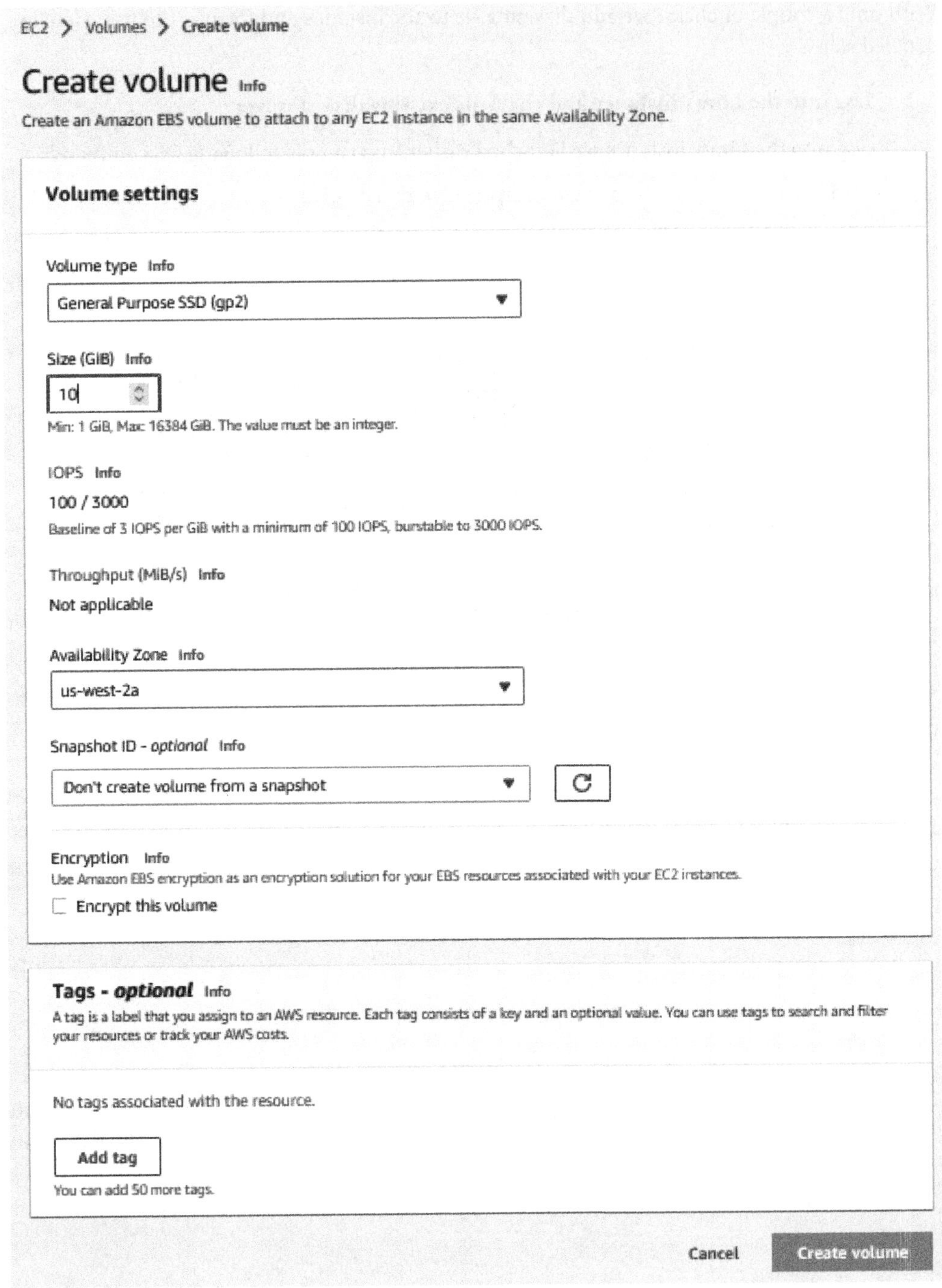

EC2 > Volumes > **Create volume**

Create volume Info

Create an Amazon EBS volume to attach to any EC2 instance in the same Availability Zone.

Volume settings

Volume type Info

General Purpose SSD (gp2)	▼

Size (GiB) Info

10	⬍

Min: 1 GiB, Max: 16384 GiB. The value must be an integer.

IOPS Info

100 / 3000

Baseline of 3 IOPS per GiB with a minimum of 100 IOPS, burstable to 3000 IOPS.

Throughput (MiB/s) Info

Not applicable

Availability Zone Info

us-west-2a	▼

Snapshot ID - *optional* Info

Don't create volume from a snapshot	▼	C

Encryption Info

Use Amazon EBS encryption as an encryption solution for your EBS resources associated with your EC2 instances.

☐ Encrypt this volume

Tags - *optional* Info

A tag is a label that you assign to an AWS resource. Each tag consists of a key and an optional value. You can use tags to search and filter your resources or track your AWS costs.

No tags associated with the resource.

Add tag

You can add 50 more tags.

Cancel   **Create volume**

Figure 2.4 – Create an EBS volume

3. **Attach the new EBS volume to the Linux EC2 instance:**

    Now, we will see two EBS volumes. Choose the newly created volume and select **Attach volume** from the drop-down **Actions** menu, as shown in *Figure 2.5*:

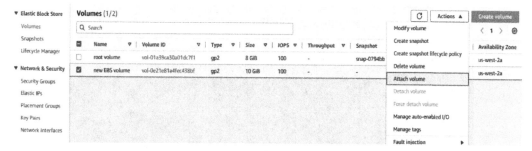

Figure 2.5 – Attach the EBS volume

    Select the EC2 instance we created earlier in the pop-up window. Click **Attach Volume**, as shown in *Figure 2.6*:

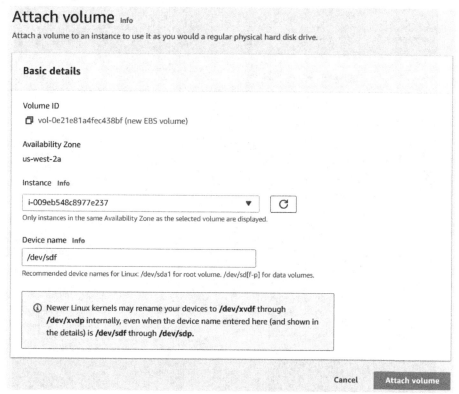

Figure 2.6 – Attach the EBS volume to the EC2 instance

4. **Go back to the Linux Guest OS, format the new disk, and use the storage:**

    Afterward, the EBS volume is attached to the instance. On the Linux Guest OS, run `fdisk -l` again. We now see two disk drives, including the new 10 GB disk drive. Run the Linux command `mkfs` to create a new filesystem from the newly added disk, make a new directory/ ebs and `use mount` to mount the filesystem to `/ebs1`, as shown in *Figure 2.7*. We are now using the new disk storage:

```
[root@ip-172-31-22-204 ~]# fdisk -l
Disk /dev/xvda: 8 GiB, 8589934592 bytes, 16777216 sectors
Units: sectors of 1 * 512 = 512 bytes
Sector size (logical/physical): 512 bytes / 512 bytes
I/O size (minimum/optimal): 512 bytes / 512 bytes
Disklabel type: gpt
Disk identifier: 61856571-99DD-4505-96FC-1DD8820522F6

Device        Start       End  Sectors Size Type
/dev/xvda1     4096 16777182 16773087   8G Linux filesystem
/dev/xvda128   2048     4095     2048   1M BIOS boot

Partition table entries are not in disk order.


Disk /dev/xvdf: 10 GiB, 10737418240 bytes, 20971520 sectors
Units: sectors of 1 * 512 = 512 bytes
Sector size (logical/physical): 512 bytes / 512 bytes
I/O size (minimum/optimal): 512 bytes / 512 bytes
[root@ip-172-31-22-204 ~]# mkfs /dev/xvdf
mke2fs 1.42.9 (28-Dec-2013)
Filesystem label=
OS type: Linux
Block size=4096 (log=2)
Fragment size=4096 (log=2)
Stride=0 blocks, Stripe width=0 blocks
655360 inodes, 2621440 blocks
131072 blocks (5.00%) reserved for the super user
First data block=0
Maximum filesystem blocks=2684354560
80 block groups
32768 blocks per group, 32768 fragments per group
8192 inodes per group
Superblock backups stored on blocks:
        32768, 98304, 163840, 229376, 294912, 819200, 884736, 1605632

Allocating group tables: done
Writing inode tables: done
Writing superblocks and filesystem accounting information: done

[root@ip-172-31-22-204 ~]# mkdir /ebs1
[root@ip-172-31-22-204 ~]# mount /dev/xvdf /ebs1
[root@ip-172-31-22-204 ~]# cd /ebs1; touch x
[root@ip-172-31-22-204 ebs1]# ls
lost+found  x
```

Figure 2.7 – List disks and format the new disk

5. **Increase the EBS storage as needed**

   After an EBS volume is attached to the Linux instance and made a useable filesystem by the guest OS, we can increase the EBS volume size and extend the filesystem at any time, with two steps:

   - Increase the size of the EBS volume in the AWS console

   - Extend the filesystem on the Linux Guest OS

More details are available at `https://docs.aws.amazon.com/AWSEC2/latest/UserGuide/modify-ebs-volume-on-instance.html`.

In the preceding example, we created an Amazon EBS volume and attached it to the Linux instance, then formatted the disk to a filesystem, and used it from the instance guest OS. The filesystem is expandable at any time as needed. For EC2 instances with Windows guest OS, you will use the `format` command to format the new disk and label it with a drive letter such as D, E, and so on. More details are available from `https://www.bu.edu/comtech/students/technical-guides/hardware/how-to-format-hard-drives/`.

In the next section, we will discuss Amazon EFS and demonstrate how to create and use it for multiple EC2 instances as a network filesystem.

Understanding EFS

An Amazon EBS volume can be created and attached to an EC2 instance, but usually, it is not meant for many instances to share. Amazon EFS provides simple, scalable, elastic file system storage that can be shared among many EC2 instances on the AWS Cloud and servers on-premises. With only a couple of clicks, we can create and share Amazon EFS to EC2 instances easily. Here are the detailed steps:

1. **Create an Amazon EFS filesystem**

   Log into the AWS console, go to the EFS service, and create a filesystem, as shown in *Figure 2.8*:

Figure 2.8 – Create the Amazon EFS filesystem (1)

I. Click "Create file system":

In the pop-up window, provide a name for the EFS filesystem and choose a storage class: a One Zone EFS filesystem stores data at the AZ level, and a `standard` filesystem stores data redundantly across multiple AZs in the same region. Note that there is no need to specify the size of the EFS filesystem since it scales elastically depending on the EC2 instances' demands on the shared filesystem. Click **Create**, as shown in *Figure 2.9*. The EFS filesystem is now created:

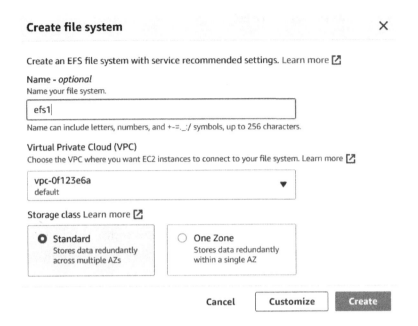

Figure 2.9 – Create the Amazon EFS filesystem (2)

2. **Attach the created EFS filesystem to a Linux instance:**

Review the EFS filesystem and click the **Attach** tab, as shown in *Figure 2.10*:

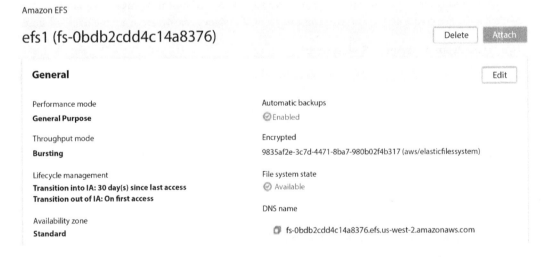

Figure 2.10 – Review the Amazon EFS filesystem

Then click the **Using the NFS client tab**, then copy the Linux `sudo mount` command, as shown in *Figure 2.11*:

Attach

Mount your Amazon EFS file system on a Linux instance. Learn more ☑

⦿ Mount via DNS	○ Mount via IP

Using the EFS mount helper:

```
sudo mount -t efs -o tls fs-0bdb2cdd4c14a8376:/ efs
```

Using the NFS client:

```
sudo mount -t nfs4 -o nfsvers=4.1,rsize=1048576,wsize=1048576,hard,timeo=600,retrans=2,noresvport fs-0bdb2cdd4c14a8376.efs.us-west-2.amazonaws.com:/ efs
```

Figure 2.11 – Copy the mount command

Go to the Linux guest OS, use mkdir to create a new directory, and mount the EFS filesystem to the directory using the `sudo mount` command copied earlier. As you can see from *Figure 2.12a*, the new filesystem is now ready for reading and writing:

```
[root@ip-172-31-26-122 /]# mkdir /efs1
[root@ip-172-31-26-122 /]# sudo mount -t nfs4 -o nfsvers=4.1,rsize=1048576,wsize=1048576,hard,timeo=600,
retrans=2,noresvport fs-0bdb2cdd4c14a8376.efs.us-west-2.amazonaws.com:/ /efs1
[root@ip-172-31-26-122 /]# cd /efs1; cp /etc/hosts .
[root@ip-172-31-26-122 efs1]# ls
hosts
[root@ip-172-31-26-122 efs1]# touch x
[root@ip-172-31-26-122 efs1]# ls
hosts  x
```

Figure 2.12a – Mount the EFS file system to a Linux Instance

3. **Verify the EFS filesystem is shared from another Linux instance:**

    Log into another Linux instance in the same region, use mkdir to create a directory, and **mount** *the same EFS filesystem* to the local directory. You will find that the filesystem is shared among the two EC2 instances with read and write, as shown in *Figure 2.12*:

```
[root@ip-172-31-31-184 ~]# sudo mount -t nfs4 -o nfsvers=4.1,rsize=1048576,wsize
=1048576,hard,timeo=600,retrans=2,noresvport fs-0bdb2cdd4c14a8376.efs.us-west-2.
amazonaws.com:/ /efs2
[root@ip-172-31-31-184 ~]# ls /efs2
hosts  x
[root@ip-172-31-31-184 ~]#
```

Figure 2.12b – Verify the shared EFS filesystem on another Linux instance

With a few clicks, we have created an EFS filesystem and shared it among two EC2 Linux instances in the same region. In the next section, we will investigate the AWS object storage: S3.

Understanding S3

As we have discussed, Amazon EBS is block storage that can be attached to an EC2 instance. Amazon EFS is an elastic filesystem storage that can be shared among EC2 instances. Now, we will examine Amazon's object storage: S3.

S3 is object-based storage and is a public end point accessible globally via the web and other means. In S3, objects or files are stored in a bucket (*folder*). S3 is a universal namespace storage, which means the names must be unique globally. While there is unlimited storage for S3 customers, each object or file is limited to 0 TB to 5 TB in size.

Amazon S3 offers a range of object-level storage classes that are designed for different use cases:

- `S3 Standard`, with 4x9 (99.99%) availability and durability.

- `S3 Standard-Infrequent` (Standard-IA), with 3x9 (99.9%) availability and 11x9 durability.

- `S3 Reduced` Redundancy Storage with 3x9 availability and 4x9 durability.

- `S3 Intelligent-Tiering`, which places the objects to the right tier based on access activities.

- `Glacier` is for archive only, with 11 x 9 data durability. You can choose from different archive storage classes optimized for different access patterns and storage durations.

Amazon S3 offers versioning to manage different versions of an object in the same bucket, so we can easily recover an object from both unintended user actions and application failures.

Amazon S3 offers life cycle management that manages the automatic movement of objects between different S3 storage classes. With life cycle management, you can configure a set of rules that automatically transition objects from one storage class to another storage class at a specified condition, to minimize storage costs or optimize performance as needed. S3 life cycle management offers an easy way to manage object storage rate and cost for long-term storage and to configure actions and configurations for expiration, including the permanent deletion of objects.

Figure 2.13 shows an example of life cycle management: the current version of S3 objects will sit in Standard S3 class for 30 days, then transition to Standard-IA for 100 days, then move to AWS Glacier, and will be permanently deleted after 455 days:

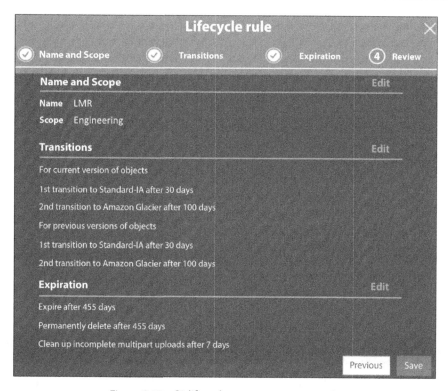

Figure 2.13 – S3 lifecycle management example

AWS S3 storage provides a simple and easy-to-use storage service that integrates well with the other AWS services. But how to transfer a big amount of data from on-prem to the AWS cloud? We will answer this question in the next section.

Understanding Snowball and Snowmobile

To help customers transfer a huge amount of data (close to petabytes) to the cloud, Amazon offers data transportation services including AWS Snowcone, AWS Snowball, and AWS Snowmobile.

AWS Snowcone is a small, rugged, but secure and versatile device that can help organizations to extend their AWS infrastructure to the edge and enable them to do fast data transfers. With Snowcone, you can collect, process, and transfer data to AWS, either offline by shipping the device or online with AWS DataSync.

AWS Snowball is an appliance-based data transfer service that uses secure, portable storage devices that are delivered to your doorstep, for you to load your data and then send it back to AWS after the data transfer is complete. The data is encrypted during the transferring process, leveraging Amazon S3 for secure storage and Amazon **Key Management Service (KMS)** for encrypting the data on the device. An AWS Snowball appliance provides up to 80 TB of usable HDD storage.

AWS Snowmobile is a truck-based data transfer service that uses a secure truck with 100 **Petabytes (PB)** storage capacity, to be dispatched to your site, and connected to your network to perform high-speed data transfer. The truck will be driven back to AWS to transfer the data to your cloud accounts. During the whole process, data is encrypted at rest and in transit. AWS Snowmobile also provides users with analytics and reporting capabilities during the data transfer process.

Accessing S3 from EC2 instances

Now that we have launched an EC2 instance in *Chapter 1* and created S3 buckets in *Chapter 2*, naturally, we will ask the question: do my EC2 instances have access to my S3 buckets?

To answer this question, we need to look at it from two perspectives:

- S3 is a public endpoint, so the EC2 instance needs to have a public IP address.

  However, that's not enough – when you log into the EC2 instance, and run the command (as shown in the following figure):

  ```
  aws s3 ls
  ```

  You will find that there are no S3 buckets listed:

```
[ec2-user@ip-172-31-28-114 ~]$ aws s3 ls
Unable to locate credentials. You can configure credentials by running "aws configure".
```

Figure 2.14 – No S3 bucket is found from EC2

- To have an EC2 instance access S3 buckets, we need to assign an IAM role to the EC2 instance. Recall that we briefly covered this in the EC2 section in *Chapter 1*:

  An IAM role can be assigned with permissions to access other AWS resources, such as reading an Amazon Simple Storage Service (S3) bucket. By attaching the IAM role to an EC2 instance, all the applications running on the EC2 instance will have the permissions of that role.

Here, *the applications running on the EC2 instance* include a terminal/shell running on the EC2 instance. Let us implement this step by step, starting from an EC2 role creation:

1. Log into the AWS console, go to the IAM services, and click **Create role** as shown in *Figure 2.15*:

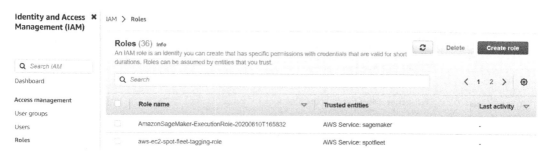

Figure 2.15 – Create an IAM role

2. In the pop-up window, choose **AWS service** under **Trusted entity type**, and **EC2** as the use case, then click **Next**, as shown in the following figure:

Figure 2.16 – Selecting a trusted entity type

3. In the **Add permissions** tab, type **AmazonS3** as the filter and then choose **AmazonS3FullAccess**, and click **Next**, as shown in *Figure 2.17*:

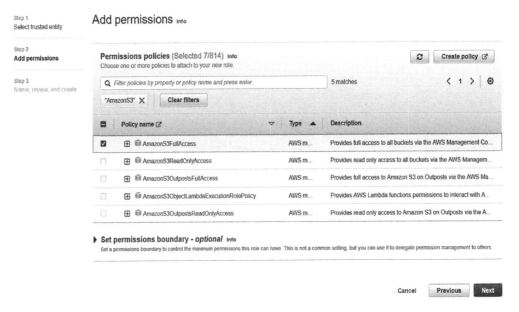

Figure 2.17 – Add permission to the role

4. Review the role name and click **Create role**, as shown in *Figure 2.18*:

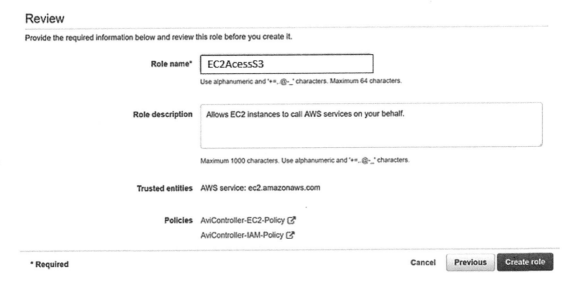

Figure 2.18 – Review and create role

5. After the IAM EC2 role is created, we need to attach it to the EC2 instance named **test**. Navigate to the EC2 dashboard and select our instance, then go to **Actions** -> **Security** -> **Modify IAM role**, as shown in *Figure 2.19*:

Figure 2.19 – Modify the IAM role to the instance

6. In the new window, choose the role we created earlier, and then click **Update IAM role**, as shown in *Figure 2.20*:

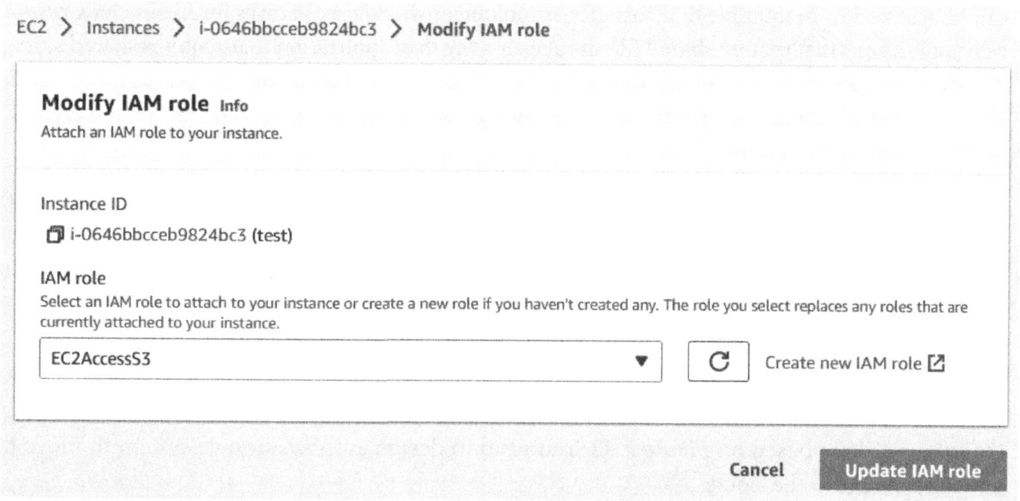

EC2 > Instances > i-0646bbcceb9824bc3 > **Modify IAM role**

Modify IAM role Info

Attach an IAM role to your instance.

Instance ID

  i-0646bbcceb9824bc3 (test)

IAM role

Select an IAM role to attach to your instance or create a new role if you haven't created any. The role you select replaces any roles that are currently attached to your instance.

EC2AccessS3   ▼ | C | Create new IAM role ☑

Cancel   **Update IAM role**

Figure 2.20 – Update the IAM role to the instance

7. Now, go back to the EC2 instance and run the following command:

```
aws s3 ls
```

Now, the S3 buckets for the AWS account will be listed, as shown in *Figure 2.21*:

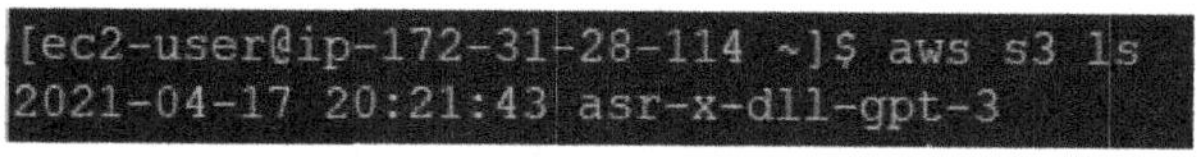

```
[ec2-user@ip-172-31-28-114 ~]$ aws s3 ls
2021-04-17 20:21:43 asr-x-dll-gpt-3
```

Figure 2.21 – List the S3 bucket on the EC2 instance

By attaching the EC2 role to the EC2 instance, all the applications running on the instance will be able to assume the EC2 role's permissions. However, there is one question remaining: what if the EC2 instance does not have a public IP address? Can it still access the S3 buckets? The answer is yes, and we will explore and implement it in *Chapter 3, AWS Networking Services*.

Summary

Congratulations! We have completed *Chapter 2* of our AWS self-learn journey: *Amazon Cloud Storage Services*. In this chapter, we introduced the Amazon EBS and EFS concepts, provisioned block storage and network filesystems for EC2 instances step by step, and then discussed the Amazon S3 services and Amazon data transfer services: Snowcone, Snowball, and Snowmobile.

As you can see, AWS provides these storage solutions to meet different business needs. Amazon EBS provides block storage volumes for EC2 instances, and some use cases include running a database that needs high-performance block storage, hosting a website that requires persistent storage, or an application that requires low-latency access to data. Amazon EFS provides a shared filesystem that can be accessed from multiple EC2 instances simultaneously. Some use cases for EFS include running web applications that require shared file storage, or a big data application that requires shared storage. Amazon S3 provides object storage that is highly scalable and durable. Some use cases for S3 include storing and sharing files, images and videos, hosting a static website with static assets, and archiving data for long-term retention.

So far, we have covered the compute services and storage services from the Amazon cloud. In the next chapter, we will discuss the AWS network services. As we stated earlier, a single computer without networking is useless. It is the networks that make all the computers and services communicate and integrate to achieve business goals.

Practice questions

Questions 1-4 are based on *Figure 2.22*. You need to design an AWS storage system to move the on-prem storage to the cloud:

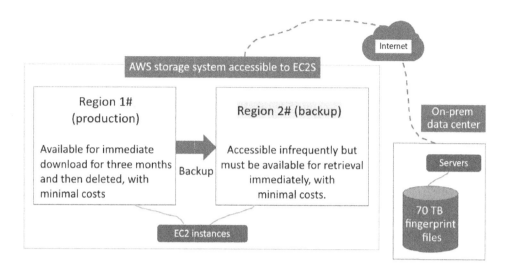

Figure 2.22 – An AWS system storage

1. How will you choose production storage in Region 1#?

   A. EBS

   B. S3

   C. Glacier

   D. EFS

2. How will you design cloud storage in Region 2#?

   A. Amazon Glacier with expedited retrievals

   B. Amazon S3 Standard-Infrequent Access

   C. Amazon EFS

   D. Amazon S3 Standard

3. What's the best way to transfer files from on-prem to Region 1#?

   A. Amazon transfer with multi-part uploading

   B. AWS Snowball

   C. AWS Snowmobile

   D. AWS Transfer using direct-connect networks

4. What's the best way to back up from Region 1# to Region 2#?

    A. Amazon S3 Cross-Region Replication

    B. AWS Snowball or Snowmobile

    C. Copy the video records from the cloud to a third-party data center

    D. Migration using direct-connect networks between regions

5. For Amazon S3, what is the largest object that can be uploaded in a single PUT?

    A. 5 gigabytes

    B. 5 terabytes

    C. 500 megabytes

    D. 5 telebytes

6. Which of the following statements is true?

    A. EBS volumes are ephemeral.

    B. EBS volumes can be attached to an EC2 instance in another AZ.

    C. EBS volumes can be attached to an EC2 instance in another Region.

    D. EBS volumes can be attached to certain EC2 instances simultaneously.

7. Company XYZ requires you to preserve, restore, and retrieve immediately every version of every file that you have stored in the AWS cloud. Which service should you use?

    A. S3 One Zone-IA

    B. S3 Standard with versioning enabled

    C. S3 Glacier

    D. S3 Reduced Storage with versioning enabled

8. An AWS engineer created an EC2 instance with a public IP address and an S3 bucket in the same Region. What do they need to do to have the instance read from and write into the S3 bucket?

9. An AWS engineer created an EC2 instance with no public IP address and an S3 bucket in the same Region. What do they need to do to enable the instance to read from and write into the S3 bucket?

10. After mounting an Amazon EFS to the EC2 instance, do you need to format mkfs to it?

Answers to the practice questions

1. B.
2. A.
3. B.
4. A.
5. A.
6. D.
7. B.
8. Create an EC2 role that has read and write access to the S3 bucket, and assign the role to the EC2 instance.
9. Create a VPC endpoint for S3. Create an EC2 role that has read and write access to the S3 bucket, and assign the role to the EC2 instance.
10. No.

Further reading

For further insights into what you've learned in this chapter, refer to the following links:

- https://aws.amazon.com/ebs/
- https://aws.amazon.com/efs/
- https://aws.amazon.com/s3/
- https://docs.aws.amazon.com/ebs/index.html
- https://docs.aws.amazon.com/efs/index.html
- https://docs.aws.amazon.com/s3/index.html

3
Amazon Networking Services

In the previous chapters, we learned about Amazon compute and storage services, focusing on EC2, EBS, EFS, and S3. We provisioned EC2 instances and the cloud storage that can be used by EC2 and other services. In this chapter, we will discuss Amazon cloud networking, where all the cloud resources are connected and communicate with each other.

We will cover the following topics in this chapter:

- Computer network basics – the fundamental network concepts, such as IP address, network address, and CIDR notation.

- Amazon **Virtual Private Cloud** (**VPC**) – the Amazon cloud network where EC2 and other services communicate with each other. We will provision VPCs, subnets, and EC2 instances in the VPC/subnets and explore EC2 instance communications within the VPC and to the internet.

- AWS network security – this becomes a priority once our VPC and EC2 instances are exposed to the internet. We will show how to build and configure network firewalls for cloud resource protection.

- AWS Direct Connect – the information highway connecting your private on-premises data centers to the AWS public cloud to form a hybrid cloud.

- The Amazon cloud **Domain Name System** (**DNS**) – Route 53 is a reliable and scalable DNS service that provides essential functionality for hosting and managing your domains and resources in the AWS cloud.

- The Amazon **Content Delivery Network** (**CDN**) – CloudFront is an AWS CDN service that delivers content, such as web pages, videos, and images, to users with low latency and high speeds.

Cloud networking is one of the most important AWS services. By learning about the basic cloud networking concepts and practicing the fundamental skills in this chapter, you will build a solid and strong foundation for constructing your AWS cloud framework. We will start the chapter by reviewing computer network basics.

Reviewing computer network basics

In *Chapter 1*, we learned that a computer network is a collection of interconnected devices, such as computers, servers, printers, and other devices, that are linked together to share resources and communicate with each other. A subnet, or subnetwork, is a smaller network that is created by partitioning a larger network into smaller segments, typically used to improve network performance, security, and management. Each subnet is identified by a unique network address, and devices within the same subnet share the same network address prefix. Each device has a unique address in the network/subnet. For a computer to talk to another one in a computer network, it must have an address for communication, which we call an **IP address**.

IP address

An **IP address**, or an **Internet Protocol** address, is a numerical address assigned to a device in a computer network for communication with the other devices that are also assigned IP addresses. An IP address serves as an identifier for the device on the network and allows it to send and receive data. There are two versions of IP addresses in use today: IPv4 and IPv6. IPv4 addresses consist of four decimal numbers separated by dots, while IPv6 addresses use a hexadecimal format with eight sets of four characters separated by colons. We will mainly use IPv4 in our book. *Figure 3.1* shows a fictitious website, www.zeebestbuy.com, and its IP address

zeebestbuy.com

172.217.9.36

10101100. **11011001**. 00001001.**00100100**

Figure 3.1 – An IP address

As we can see, an IPv4 address can be represented by four decimal numbers, 172.217.9.36, or by 4 bytes (32 bits) of binary numbers, 10101100.11011001.00001001.00100100. Since an IP address has 4 bytes or 32 bits, the total number of addresses in this IP space is 2^{32}. We cannot put this number of computers in one network, so we need to develop a way to separate the network into subnets, which requires something called **Classless Inter-Domain Routing (CIDR)**.

CIDR

CIDR is a method used to allocate IP addresses in networks and specify network addresses. In the CIDR notation, a network address is represented by an IP address followed by a slash (/) and a number indicating the number of bits in the network address. For example, the CIDR notation 172.217.9.0/24 represents a network address – the first 24 bits (10101100.11011001. 00001001) represent the network portion and are *fixed*, and the remaining 8 bits represent the host portion and are *varied* (from 00000000 to 11111111). For the subnet 172.217.9.0/24, since 24 bits out of 32 are fixed and 8 bits are variable, there are $2^8=256$ IP addresses in the subnet:

172.217.9.0 to 172.217.9.255. *Figure 3.2* shows CIDR notations for some subnets, from /32 to /24, and the available IP addresses for the subnets:

Subnet Mask Hierarchy

Subnet Mask	CIDR	Binary Notation	Available Addresses Per Subnet
255.255.255.255	/32	11111111.11111111.11111111.11111111	1
255.255.255.254	/31	11111111.11111111.11111111.11111110	2
255.255.255.252	/30	11111111.11111111.11111111.11111100	4
255.255.255.248	/29	11111111.11111111.11111111.11111000	8
255.255.255.240	/28	11111111.11111111.11111111.11110000	16
255.255.255.224	/27	11111111.11111111.11111111.11100000	32
255.255.255.192	/26	11111111.11111111.11111111.11000000	64
255.255.255.128	/25	11111111.11111111.11111111.10000000	128
255.255.255.0	/24	11111111.11111111.11111111.00000000	256
255.255.254.0	/23	11111111.11111111.11111110.00000000	512
255.255.252.0	/22	11111111.11111111.11111100.00000000	1024
255.255.248.0	/21	11111111.11111111.11111000.00000000	2048
255.255.240.0	/20	11111111.11111111.11110000.00000000	4096
255.255.224.0	/19	11111111.11111111.11100000.00000000	8192
255.255.192.0	/18	11111111.11111111.11000000.00000000	16384
255.255.128.0	/17	11111111.11111111.10000000.00000000	32768
255.255.0.0	/16	11111111.11111111.00000000.00000000	65536
255.254.0.0	/15	11111111.11111110.00000000.00000000	131072
255.252.0.0	/14	11111111.11111100.00000000.00000000	262144
255.248.0.0	/13	11111111.11111000.00000000.00000000	524288
255.240.0.0	/12	11111111.11110000.00000000.00000000	1048576
255.224.0.0	/11	11111111.11100000.00000000.00000000	2097152
255.192.0.0	/10	11111111.11000000.00000000.00000000	4194304
255.128.0.0	/9	11111111.10000000.00000000.00000000	8388608
255.0.0.0	/8	11111111.00000000.00000000.00000000	16777216

Figure 3.2 – CIDR notation

With IP address and network address notations, we can construct any networks and connect them with routing devices. And that's how we build the internet, which will be discussed next.

The internet

The internet is a global network of interconnected computer networks that allows the exchange of information and communication among users around the world. It is composed of millions of devices, including computers and networking hardware devices, and software applications, protocols, and standards that enable these devices to communicate and share data with each other.

At a high level, the internet is made up of physical infrastructure, such as computers, routers, and switches. A router is a network device that connects multiple networks and routes data packets between them. Routers use a route table to determine the best path for data packets to take between networks, and they can be used to filter and direct traffic based on various criteria, such as port numbers, IP addresses, and protocols. Each subnet must be associated with one and only one route table. A switch is a network device that connects multiple devices within a network. Switches use MAC addresses to direct traffic to the correct device and can be used to segment networks and improve performance by limiting the amount of traffic that flows through each segment.

On the internet, routers, switches, and computers work together, under network routing protocols such as **Transmission Control Protocol** (**TCP**) and IP. Just like computers have evolved from physical machines to virtual machines, networks have evolved from hardware-based physical networks to software-based virtual networks. In the next section, we will discuss Amazon VPC, which is a virtual network in the cloud.

Understanding Amazon Virtual Private Cloud

A VPC is a network in the Amazon cloud. With Amazon VPC, you can assign custom IP address ranges, create subnets, and configure route tables, network gateways, and security settings. You can launch instances in a specified subnet of a VPC. By default, you can create five VPCs per AWS account per region, and you can increase this default quota by contacting Amazon cloud support. AWS VPC provides several benefits over traditional data center-based network designs, including the following:

- **High availability**: Amazon VPC is software based. Within a VPC, the routers are virtual and provide high availability. VPCs are regional in AWS and thus a VPC can span multiple AZs, with each subnet mapping to an AZ.

- **Flexibility**: Amazon VPC provides the flexibility to design and build your network topology to meet your specific business and technical requirements. With Amazon VPC, you select the IP address range for VPCs and subnets, configure route tables, and associate them with subnets.

- **Isolation**: Amazon VPC provides isolation of cloud resources, allowing you to create separate virtual networks for different applications or workloads, for example, separate a production VPC from a development VPC. A VPC is logically isolated from other VPCs in the same AWS account.

- **Time and cost effectiveness**: Amazon VPCs are created and used at no cost. Since they are virtual, you can provision VPCs and subnets on the fly and reduce the cost of your network infrastructure.

- **Security**: In the Amazon cloud, you can define **Network Access Control Lists** (**NACLs**) to control traffic in and out of subnets.

- **Connectivity to on-premises**: You can configure Amazon VPC to connect the virtual network to an on-premises data center using a VPN or AWS Direct Connect. This allows enterprises to extend their existing IT infrastructure to the cloud and access AWS services securely.

Next, we will provision our VPC networks in the Amazon cloud. We will use the AWS cloud console to show how to create a VPC and subnet. We will use CloudShell to create an AWS cloud, including a VPC, subnets, and instances, and then configure the VPC/subnet/EC2 instances for internet access. Let's start with the first part of building our AWS cloud framework.

Part one – creating a VPC with subnets

In the first part, we will use the AWS console to create a VPC and a subnet under the VPC, to demonstrate how to use the AWS console in creating networks in the cloud.

Creating a VPC and a subnet using the AWS cloud console

Log in to the AWS console, search for VPC services, and select **Create VPC**, then fill in the VPC settings. Enter my vpc1 for the name. For simplicity, we will select **No IPV6 CIDR block** and choose a CIDR of 10.10.0.0/16 for our VPC. Click **Create VPC**, as shown in *Figure 3.3*:

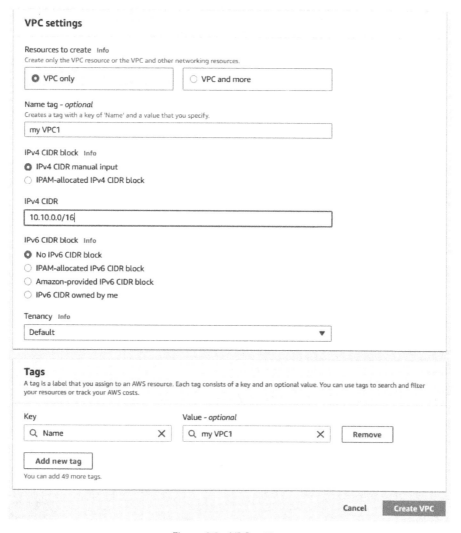

Figure 3.3 – VPC settings

After the VPC is created, go back to the VPC dashboard and then to **Subnets**, then click **Create subnet**. Fill in the subnet settings; choose **my VPC1** as the VPC, enter `public-subnet` as the name, set its CIDR to `10.10.1.0/24`, and click **Create subnet**, as shown in *Figure 3.4*:

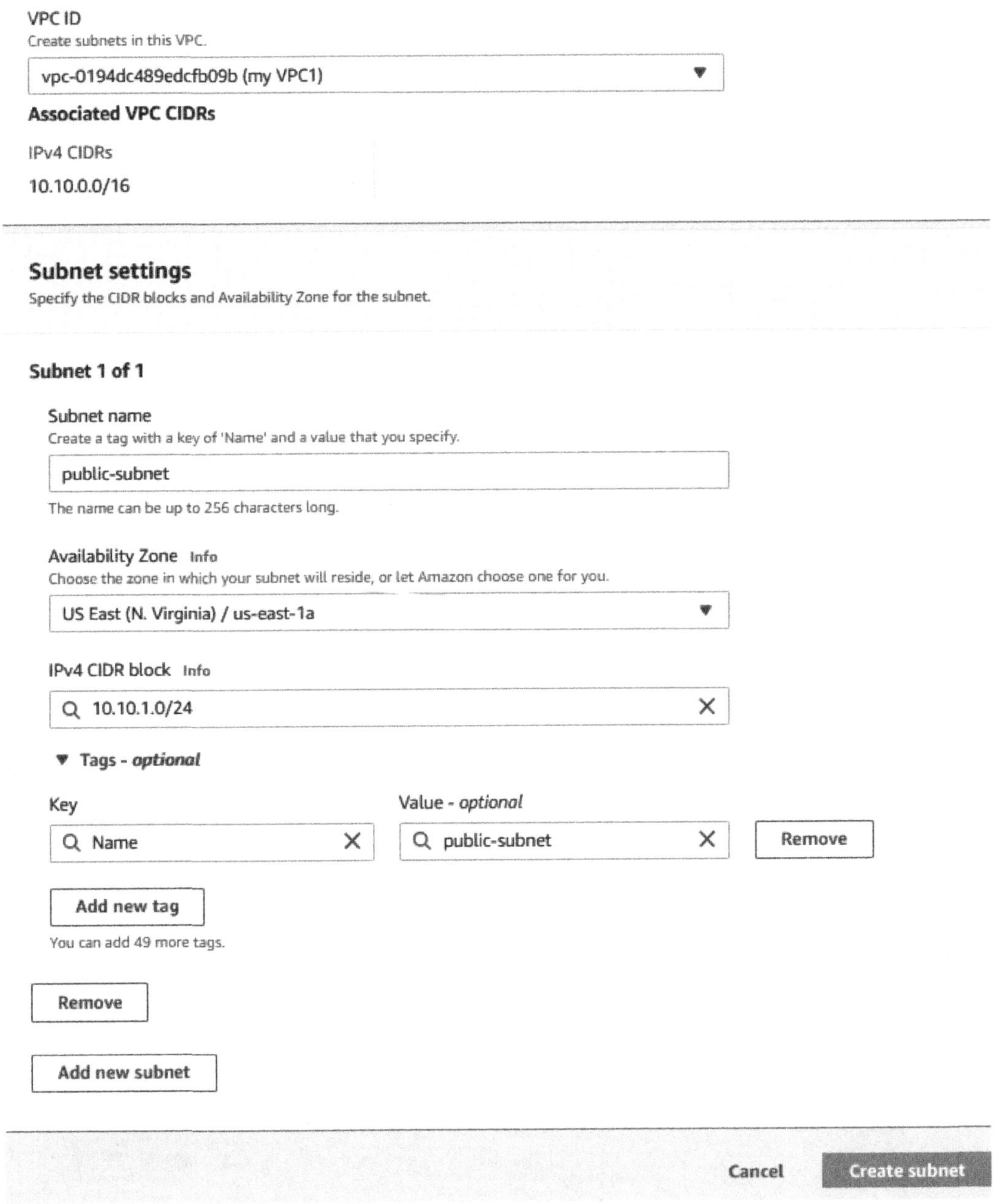

VPC ID
Create subnets in this VPC.

vpc-0194dc489edcfb09b (my VPC1)   ▼

Associated VPC CIDRs

IPv4 CIDRs

10.10.0.0/16

Subnet settings
Specify the CIDR blocks and Availability Zone for the subnet.

Subnet 1 of 1

Subnet name
Create a tag with a key of 'Name' and a value that you specify.

public-subnet

The name can be up to 256 characters long.

Availability Zone Info
Choose the zone in which your subnet will reside, or let Amazon choose one for you.

US East (N. Virginia) / us-east-1a   ▼

IPv4 CIDR block Info

Q 10.10.1.0/24   ✕

▼ Tags - *optional*

| Key | Value - *optional* | |
| Q Name   ✕ | Q public-subnet   ✕ | Remove |

Add new tag
You can add 49 more tags.

Remove

Add new subnet

Cancel   **Create subnet**

Figure 3.4 – Subnet settings

> **Note**
>
> As we discussed earlier, a VPC with an IPv4 CIDR block of `10.10.0.0/16` has 65,536 total IP addresses and can be divided into subnets. For each subnet, there are some addresses reserved for Amazon. For example, the subnet `10.10.1.0/24` has a total of 256 total IP addresses, but the following 5 IP addresses are reserved, thus leaving 251 IP addresses available to create EC2 instances in the subnet:
>
> `10.0.1.0`
>
> Network address
>
> `10.0.1.1`
>
> Internal communication
>
> `10.0.1.2`
>
> DNS resolution
>
> `10.0.1.3`
>
> Future use
>
> `10.0.1.255`
>
> Network broadcast address

Creating an AWS cloud network using CloudShell

As we discussed earlier, we can also use AWS CloudShell to create and manage any cloud resources with the **Command Line Interface (CLI)**. In this section, we will use CloudShell to recreate a VPC named **VPC1** and two subnets named **public-subnet** and **private-subnet** under VPC1, in the US-west-2 region, and launch two instances – one Linux instance in **public-subnet** with a public IP address and another Linux instance in **private-subnet** without a public IP address:

1. **Create VPC1**:

```
aws ec2 create-vpc --cidr-block
10.10.0.0/16 --tag-specifications
ResourceType=vpc,Tags='[{Key=Name,Value="VPC1"}]'
```

```
[cloudshell-user@ip-10-2-126-119 ~]$ aws ec2 create-vpc \
>    --cidr-block 10.10.0.0/16 \
>    --tag-specifications ResourceType=vpc,Tags='[{Key=Name,Value="VPC1"}]'
{
    "Vpc": {
        "CidrBlock": "10.10.0.0/16",
        "DhcpOptionsId": "dopt-f8579e9d",
        "State": "pending",
        "VpcId": "vpc-0e6043d6091faa7cd",
        "OwnerId": "317332158300",
        "InstanceTenancy": "default",
        "Ipv6CidrBlockAssociationSet": [],
        "CidrBlockAssociationSet": [
            {
                "AssociationId": "vpc-cidr-assoc-04116e8e5e98b256f",
                "CidrBlock": "10.10.0.0/16",
                "CidrBlockState": {
                    "State": "associated"
                }
            }
        ],
        "IsDefault": false,
        "Tags": [
            {
                "Key": "Name",
                "Value": "VPC1"
            }
        ]
    }
}
```

Figure 3.5 – Create VPC1

2. **Create public-subnet and private-subnet in VPC1**, as shown in *Figure 3.6*:

```
aws ec2 create-subnet --vpc-id vpc-0e6043d6091faa7cd \
--cidr-block 10.10.1.0/24 --tag-specifications ResourceType=subn
et,Tags='[{Key=Name,Value="public-subnet"}]'
aws ec2 create-subnet --vpc-id vpc-0e6043d6091faa7cd --cidr-
block 10.10.2.0/24 --tag-specifications ResourceType=subnet,Tags
='[{Key=Name,Value="private-subnet"}]'
```

```
[cloudshell-user@ip-10-2-126-119 ~]$ aws ec2 create-subnet \
>     --vpc-id vpc-0e6043d6091faa7cd \
>     --cidr-block 10.10.2.0/24 \
>     --tag-specifications ResourceType=subnet,Tags='[{Key=Name,Value="private-subnet"}]'
{
    "Subnet": {
        "AvailabilityZone": "us-west-2a",
        "AvailabilityZoneId": "usw2-az1",
        "AvailableIpAddressCount": 251,
        "CidrBlock": "10.10.2.0/24",
        "DefaultForAz": false,
        "MapPublicIpOnLaunch": false,
        "State": "available",
        "SubnetId": "subnet-0328a7940791d9fc0",
        "VpcId": "vpc-0e6043d6091faa7cd",
        "OwnerId": "317332158300",
        "AssignIpv6AddressOnCreation": false,
        "Ipv6CidrBlockAssociationSet": [],
        "Tags": [
            {
                "Key": "Name",
                "Value": "private-subnet"
            }
        ],
        "SubnetArn": "arn:aws:ec2:us-west-2:317332158300:subnet/subnet-0328a7940791d9fc0",
        "EnableDns64": false,
        "Ipv6Native": false,
        "PrivateDnsNameOptionsOnLaunch": {
            "HostnameType": "ip-name",
            "EnableResourceNameDnsARecord": false,
            "EnableResourceNameDnsAAAARecord": false
        }
    }
}
```

Figure 3.6 – Create subnets

3. **Create two EC2 instances**, one in each subnet. EC2-1 is in the public subnet and is assigned a public IP address, while EC2-2 is in the private subnet and does not have a public IP address. The commands are as follows and a screenshot is provided in *Figure 3.7*:

```
aws ec2 run-instances --image-id ami-0ef0b498cd3fe129c --count
1 --instance-type t2.micro --subnet-id subnet-0871b6aaa7092c075
--key-name mywestkp --region us-west-2  --associate-public-ip-
address
aws ec2 run-instances --image-id ami-0ef0b498cd3fe129c –count 1
--instance-type t2.micro --subnet-id subnet 0328a7940791d9fc0
--key-name mywestkp --region us-west-2 --no-associate-public-ip-
address
```

```
[cloudshell-user@ip-10-6-43-95 ~]$ aws ec2 run-instances --image-id ami-0ef0b498cd3fe129c --count 1 \
> --instance-type t2.micro --subnet-id subnet-0328a7940791d9fc0 \
> --key-name mywestkp --region us-west-2  --no-associate-public-ip-address
{
    "Groups": [],
    "Instances": [
        {
            "AmiLaunchIndex": 0,
            "ImageId": "ami-0ef0b498cd3fe129c",
            "InstanceId": "i-0288c5d94570afe62",
            "InstanceType": "t2.micro",
            "KeyName": "mywestkp",
            "LaunchTime": "2023-02-14T01:56:33+00:00",
            "Monitoring": {
                "State": "disabled"
            },
            "Placement": {
                "AvailabilityZone": "us-west-2a",
                "GroupName": "",
                "Tenancy": "default"
            },
            "PrivateDnsName": "ip-10-10-2-11.us-west-2.compute.internal",
            "PrivateIpAddress": "10.10.2.11",
```

Figure 3.7 – Create instances

Figure 3.8 shows a network diagram of the VPC we have built so far, including VPC1, its two subnets, and the two instances – EC2-1 in the public subnet and EC2-2 in the private subnet:

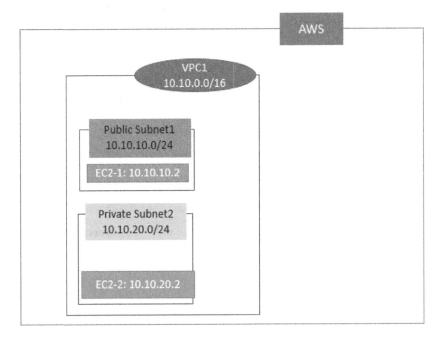

Figure 3.8 – VPC network

Now that we have provisioned VPCs/subnets/EC2 instances, it's time to discuss how to access them from the internet.

Accessing the EC2 instances from the internet

While VPCs are isolated networks in the cloud, there are needs to access an EC2 from the internet and for the EC2 instances to access the internet, such as to patch the guest OS. For the EC2-1 instance in public subnet1 in VPC1 to communicate with the internet, we need to open a route from the public subnet to the internet, with three steps:

1. **Create IGW1 and attach it to VPC1**

    To open a route from our VPC to the internet, we need to create an **Internet Gateway** (**IGW**) and attach it to VPC1.

    From the AWS console, go to the VPC dashboard and find the **Internet Gateway** section. Click **Create internet gateway**, and in the new window, provide a name tag for the IGW. We will call it IGW1, as shown in *Figure 3.9*:

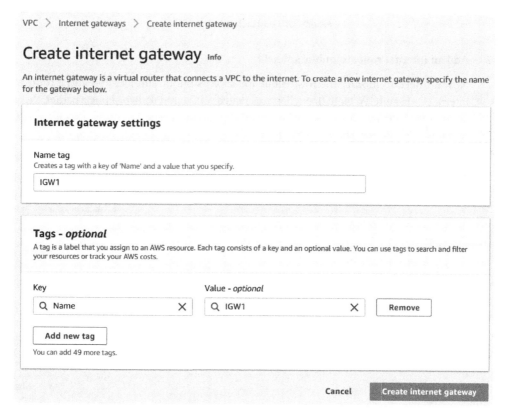

Figure 3.9 – Create IGW1

Attach IGW1 to VPC1, as shown in *Figure 3.10*.

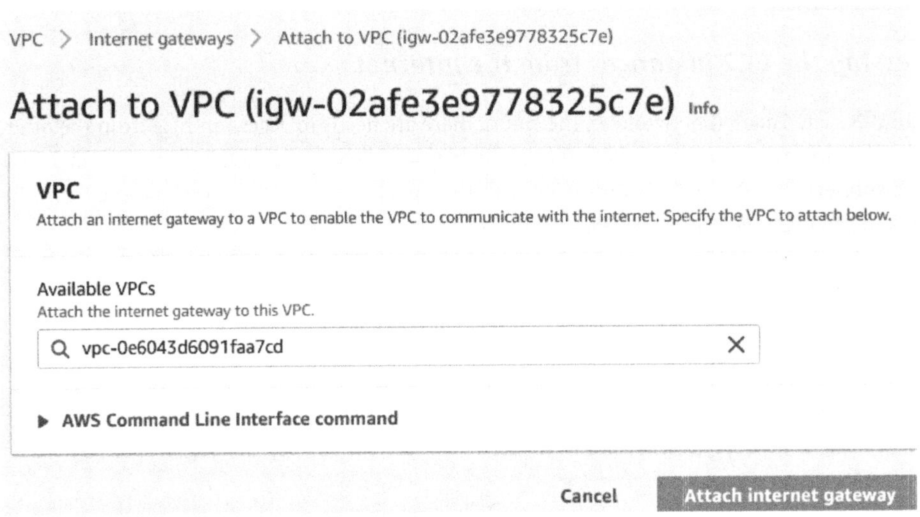

Figure 3.10 – Attach IGW1 to VPC1

2. **Add an internet route to public subnet1**

    Now we need to modify the route table for VPC1's public subnet1 and add a route to the internet – via an IGW. Note that when we created VPC1 and its two subnets earlier, there was an *invisible* VPC router created to route the traffic within VPC1; all subnets with a VPC are routable. We will now check out the route table for VPC1, as shown in *Figure 3.11*:

Figure 3.11 – Route table for VPC1

Click **Edit routes** and add a new route with a destination of 0.0.0.0/0 (meaning anywhere) and a target of IGW1, which is the IGW we created and attached to VPC1 earlier. Click **Save changes**, as shown in *Figure 3.12*:

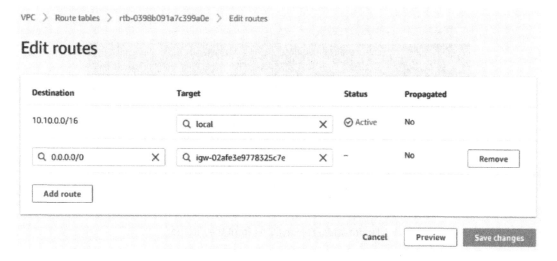

Figure 3.12 – Add internet route to route table

Go back to the route table and then to **Subnet association** | **Edit subnet associations** and associate the route table with the public subset we created earlier, as shown in *Figure 3.13*:

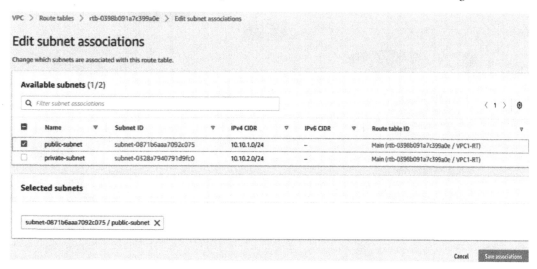

Figure 3.13 – Associate route table to subnet

Click **Save associations**. Now, we have built a route from VPC1 to the internet, so all internet traffic will go to IGW1 as the next hop.

3. **SSH to the EC2 instance in the public subnet**

In *Chapter 1*, we have introduced PuTTY to SSH into the Linux EC2 instances in the cloud. Now, we SSH through the internet into the EC2-1 instance, as shown in *Figure 3.14*:

```
ec2-user@ip-10-10-1-225:~                                    —   □   ✕

Using username "ec2-user".
Authenticating with public key "mykey"

    _|  _|_  )
   _|  (   _|  /      Amazon Linux 2 AMI
  _| \__|_|_|

https://aws.amazon.com/amazon-linux-2/
16 package(s) needed for security, out of 16 available
Run "sudo yum update" to apply all updates.
[ec2-user@ip-10-10-1-225 ~]$
```

Figure 3.14 – SSH to EC2-1 from the internet

We have set up the route between the EC2-1 instance and the internet. *Figure 3.15* shows the AWS network we have built so far:

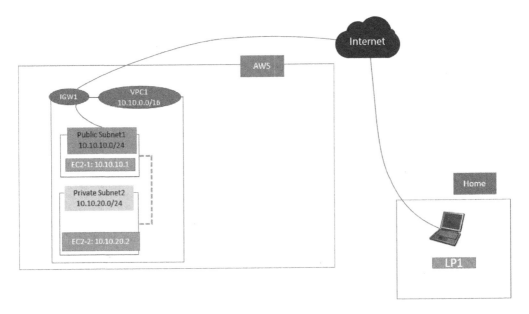

Figure 3.15 – AWS cloud with internet access

Now, let's add more VPC/subnet/EC2 instances to the cloud.

Part two – Provisioning more cloud resources and connecting them together

In this part, we will add more VPCs, subnets, and EC2 instances into the cloud and connect them together by peering the VPCs.

Provisioning more cloud resources

With the same procedure, let us create VPC2, subnet8 in VPC2, and an EC2 instance in subnet8. The network architecture is shown in *Figure 3.16*. Note EC2-2 and EC2-8 do not have public IPs assigned:

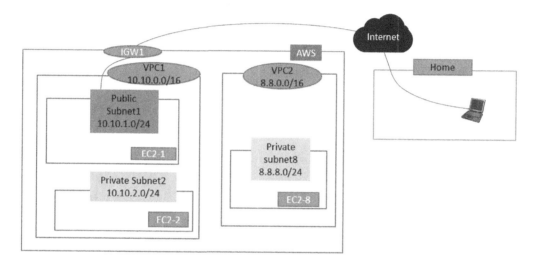

Figure 3.16 – VPC network architecture

As we addressed earlier, all EC2 instances in the same VPC can communicate with each other. From EC2-1, we can ping EC2-2 after we have configured EC2-2's SG to allow ICMP (ping) from EC2-1. However, we cannot ping EC2-8 from EC2-1, since there are no routes between them. Let's resolve this issue by *peering* VPC1 and VPC2 together.

Peering the VPCs

In the Amazon cloud, we can peer two VPCs in the same AWS account, no matter which region they sit in, and we can also peer two VPCs in different AWS accounts, provided they agree on peering with each other. The following figure provides an example of peering two VPCs in the same account. From the AWS console, go to the VPC dashboard and then click **Peering connections** | **Create peering connection**. Fill in the peering name, a local VPC to peer with (VPC1), and another VPC to peer with (in my account and this region, it is VPC2). Then, click **Create peering connection**, as shown in *Figure 3.17*:

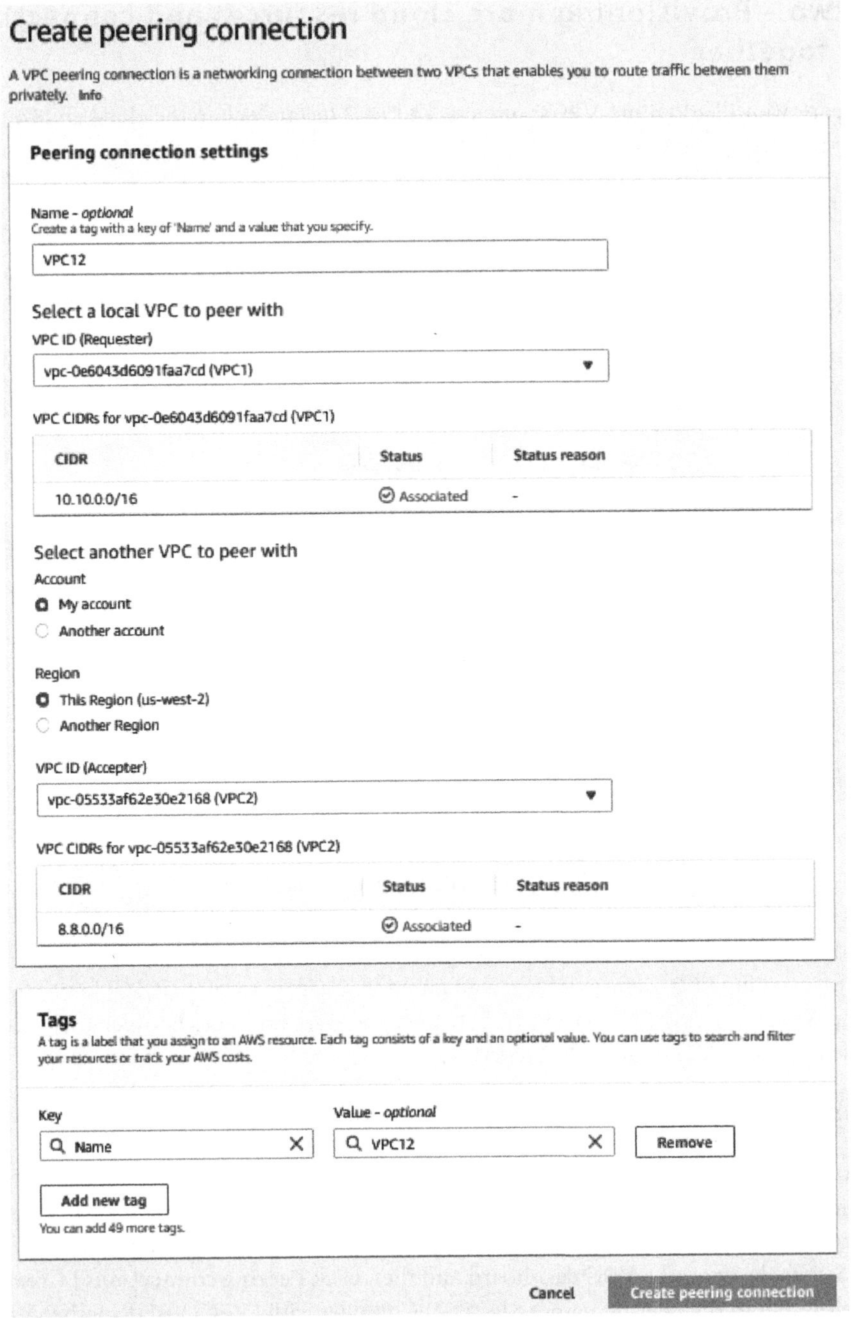

Create peering connection

A VPC peering connection is a networking connection between two VPCs that enables you to route traffic between them privately. Info

Peering connection settings

Name - *optional*
Create a tag with a key of 'Name' and a value that you specify.

VPC12

Select a local VPC to peer with

VPC ID (Requester)

vpc-0e6043d6091faa7cd (VPC1) ▼

VPC CIDRs for vpc-0e6043d6091faa7cd (VPC1)

CIDR	Status	Status reason
10.10.0.0/16	⊘ Associated	-

Select another VPC to peer with

Account
● My account
○ Another account

Region
● This Region (us-west-2)
○ Another Region

VPC ID (Accepter)

vpc-05533af62e30e2168 (VPC2) ▼

VPC CIDRs for vpc-05533af62e30e2168 (VPC2)

CIDR	Status	Status reason
8.8.0.0/16	⊘ Associated	-

Tags

A tag is a label that you assign to an AWS resource. Each tag consists of a key and an optional value. You can use tags to search and filter your resources or track your AWS costs.

Key	Value - *optional*	
🔍 Name ✕	🔍 VPC12 ✕	Remove

Add new tag
You can add 49 more tags.

Cancel   Create peering connection

Figure 3.17 – VPC peering

The connection is now in the *pending status*. Click it and accept the peering request, then it will be in the active state. The bridge is now built, but we still need to configure the routes between VPC1 and VPC2 – that is, configure route tables on both VPCs.

Go to the VPC dashboard and then to **Route tables,** select the VPC1 route able, **Edit routes**, then add a route from VPC1 to VPC2 (8.8.0.0/16) with the target of the peering connection (VPC12). Click **Save changes**. This is shown in *Figure 3.18*:

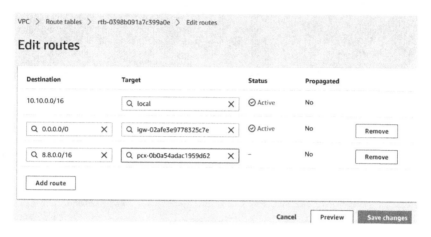

Figure 3.18 – Edit routes for the VPC1 route table

Repeat the preceding steps for the VPC2 route table – add a route from VPC2 to VPC1 (10.10.0.0/16) with the **peering connection** (VPC12) as the target. Then, associate it to the subnet (8.8.8.0/24).

There is one more thing to do. Go to the EC2 dashboard and then to **EC2-8 | Security | Security Group | Edit inbound rules**, and add a rule to EC-8's security group to allow ping from VPC1. Then, click **Save rules**, as shown in *Figure 3.19*:

Figure 3.19 – Edit SG inbound rules for EC2-8

Now, let's verify that EC2-1 and EC2-8 can communicate with each other. Go back to EC2-1's guest OS terminal and try to ping EC2-8 (the IP address is 8.8.8.43). We can see it is working, as in *Figure 3.20*:

```
[ec2-user@ip-10-10-1-225 ~]$ ping  8.8.8.43
PING 8.8.8.43 (8.8.8.43) 56(84) bytes of data.
64 bytes from 8.8.8.43: icmp_seq=1 ttl=255 time=0.955 ms
64 bytes from 8.8.8.43: icmp_seq=2 ttl=255 time=0.553 ms
64 bytes from 8.8.8.43: icmp_seq=3 ttl=255 time=0.495 ms
^C
--- 8.8.8.43 ping statistics ---
3 packets transmitted, 3 received, 0% packet loss, time 2023ms
rtt min/avg/max/mdev = 0.495/0.667/0.955/0.206 ms
```

Figure 3.20 – Ping EC2-8 from EC2-1

Figure 3.21 shows the AWS VPC network we have built so far:

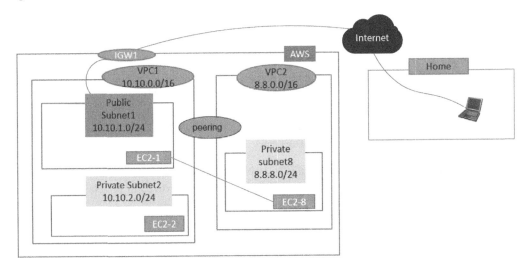

Figure 3.21 – VPC network with peering

Now, we have opened communication channels between EC2-1 in the public subnet and the internet via IGW1. But what about the EC2-2 and EC2-8 instances that are in the private subnets of VPC1 and VPC2? In the next section, we will discuss a way for EC2-2 and EC2-8, the two instances that do not have public IP addresses, to access the internet.

Creating a Network Address Translation (NAT) gateway

A NAT gateway allows EC2 instances in a VPC to go outbound to resources on the internet, but does not allow inbound traffic to the EC2 instance from the internet. Different from the IGW way in which we assign public IP addresses to EC2, here we use NAT to map EC2's private IP addresses to the NAT's public address for outbound requests and map the public IP address back to the EC2 private IP addresses for inbound responses. Take the following steps:

1. **Create a public NAT gateway**. Go to the VPC dashboard and then to **NAT gateways | Create NAT gateway**. Fill in the name (NAT1) and subnet (public subnet) and click **Allocate Elastic IP** to get an **Elastic IP** (**EIP**) for NAT1, then click **Create NAT gateway**, as shown in *Figure 3.22*.

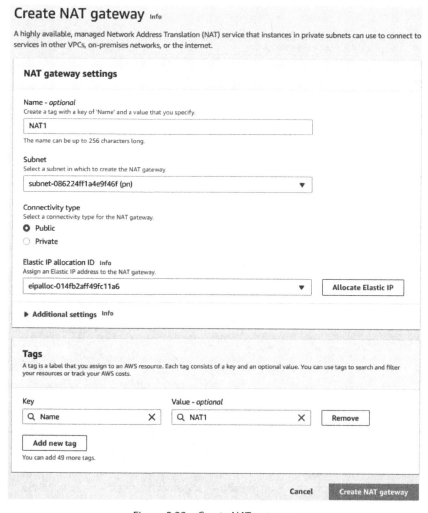

Figure 3.22 – Create NAT gateway

2. **Set up the private subnet route table:**

    After the NAT gateway is created, navigate to the VPC dashboard and then **route tables** and create a new route table called `VPC1PriRT` under VPC1. Add a route under **Destination** (`0.0.0.0/0`) using `NAT1` we created earlier as the target, then click **Save changes**, as shown in *Figure 3.23*. Then, associate the route table to the private subnet.

Figure 3.23 – Edit routes for the private subnet route table

3. **Validate internet access from EC2-2**

Now, SSH to EC2-1 (via the IGW), then SSH from EC2-1 to EC2-2 (make sure the SG for EC2-2 allows SSH traffic from EC2-1, and the private key is copied to EC2-1) and execute the `curl www.google.com` command. As shown in *Figure 3.24*, it works (the curl messages are partially shown)!

```
[ec2-user@ip-10-10-1-229 ~]$ ls -l
total 4
-r-------- 1 ec2-user ec2-user 1675 Feb 15 16:10 mykey.pem
[ec2-user@ip-10-10-1-229 ~]$ ssh 10.10.2.249 -i mykey.pem
The authenticity of host '10.10.2.249 (10.10.2.249)' can't be established.
ECDSA key fingerprint is SHA256:AYodQL9fBbvln6XRQLbHSjkNtbsFGevS7CqHSmr2vrk.
ECDSA key fingerprint is MD5:77:e0:ec:a4:40:61:95:68:c3:94:ba:62:98:23:35:7f.
Are you sure you want to continue connecting (yes/no)? yes
Warning: Permanently added '10.10.2.249' (ECDSA) to the list of known hosts.

       __|  __|_  )
       _|  (     /   Amazon Linux 2 AMI
      ___|\___|___|

https://aws.amazon.com/amazon-linux-2/
[ec2-user@ip-10-10-2-249 ~]$ curl www.google.com
<!doctype html><html itemscope="" itemtype="http://schema.org/WebPage" lang="en"
><head><meta content="Search the world's information, including webpages, images
, videos and more. Google has many special features to help you find exactly wha
```

Figure 3.24 – Access www.google.com from EC2-2

Now, we have implemented the AWS cloud architecture shown in *Figure 3.25*, and successfully connected EC2-1 to the internet via IGW1 and EC2-2 via NAT1-IGW1:

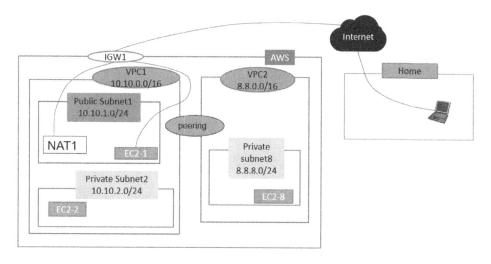

Figure 3.25 – AWS VPC architecture

As a practice lab, configure subnet8 to allow EC2-8 outbound access to the internet (but not inbound from the internet).

Part three – hardening AWS network security

Since we opened VPC1 to the internet, security has become a very important factor. Here, we will discuss the configurations in VPC to harden the security of the VPC and the cloud resources sitting in it. We will discuss two topics: VPC firewalls and VPC endpoints.

VPC firewalls

From *Chapter 1*, we know that a key pair and security groups are used to protect EC2 instances. Here, we will review **SGs**, which are virtual firewalls for EC2 instances and have the following features:

- Act as a virtual firewall that controls the inbound and outbound traffic for one or more EC2 instances

- Can be used to allow or deny traffic based on IP address, port number, and protocol (such as TCP or UDP)

- Can be associated with one or more EC2 instances or with a specific network interface of an instance

- Support the principle of least privilege, which means that only necessary traffic is allowed to reduce the attack surface and improve security

- Are stateful, which means that any traffic that is allowed to come into the EC2 instances will be allowed to go out; any traffic that is allowed to go out will be allowed to come in

Let me use an example to explain the term *stateful*. As shown in *Figure 3.26*, you have a PC at home with the IP address 54.24.12.19 that needs to SSH to an EC2 instance in the Amazon cloud with the address 10.10.1.1. Since the SG has an inbound rule open for SSH at port 22 from 54.24.12.19, the packet (source IP: 54.24.12.19, source port: 2000, destination IP: 10.10.1.1, and destination port: 22) is allowed to go into the EC2 server. When the packet is received by the EC2 instance, it will compile a return packet (source IP: 10.10.1.1, source port: 22, destination IP: 54.24.12.19, and destination port: 2000). The SG is stateful, meaning that the return packet will be allowed to go out, and there is no need to add any outbound rules for the packet:

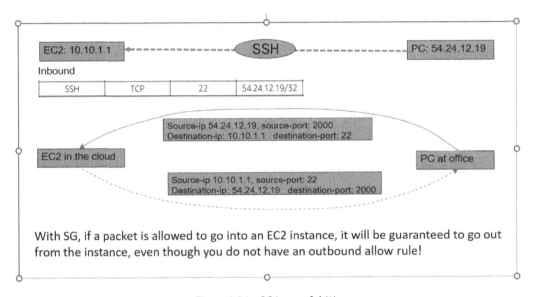

Figure 3.26 – SG is stateful (1)

Figure 3.27 shows another SG example for outbound traffic. You have an EC2 instance in the Amazon cloud with the IP address 10.10.1.1 and need to access a web server running on an office PC with the address 54.24.12.19. Since the SG has an outbound rule open for port 80 from 10.10.1.1, the packet (source IP: 10.10.1.1, source port: 1234, destination IP: 54.24.12.19, and destination port: 80) will be allowed to go out to the PC server. When the packet is received by the web server, it will compile a return packet (source IP: 54.24.12.19, source port: 80, destination IP: 10.10.1.1, and destination port: 1234). The SG is stateful, meaning that the return packet will be allowed to come in, and there is no need to add any inbound rules for the packet:

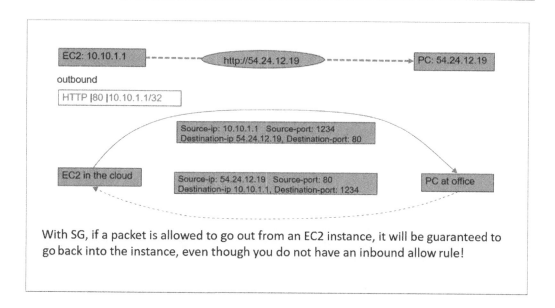

Figure 3.27 – SG is stateful (2)

An NACL is another type of firewall at the subnet level, and it has the following features:

- It is used to allow or deny traffic based on the IP address, port number, and protocol

- It is evaluated before SGs and applies to all instances in a subnet, whereas security groups are associated with individual instances

- It supports numbered rules that are evaluated in order, with the lowest number taking precedence

- It is stateless, which means that any traffic that is allowed to go into the EC2 instances is not guaranteed to be allowed to go out, and we need an NACL rule to explicitly specify the outbound permission

Let us use an example to explain the term *stateless*. As shown in *Figure 3.28*, you have a PC at home with the IP address 54.24.12.19 and need to SSH to an EC2 instance in the Amazon cloud with the address 10.10.1.1. Since the NACL has an inbound rule to allow for SSH traffic at port 22 from 54.24.12.19, the packet (source IP: 54.24.12.19, source port: 2000, destination IP: 10.10.1.1, and destination port: 22) is allowed to go into VPC1. When the packet is received by the EC2 instance, it will compile a return packet (source IP: 10.10.1.1, source port: 22, destination IP: 54.24.12.19, and destination port: 2000). Because NACLs are stateless, the return packet may not be allowed to go out, and you will need to add an outbound rule for the packet:

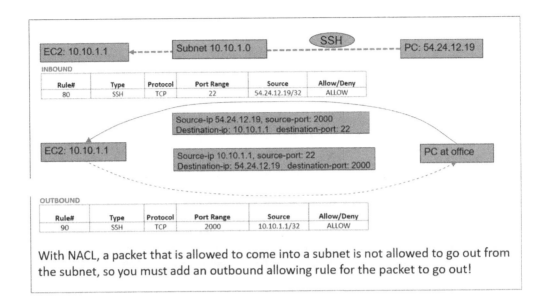

Figure 3.28 – NACL is stateless (1)

Figure 3.29 shows another example of outbound traffic. You have an EC2 instance in the Amazon cloud with the IP address 10.10.1.1 and need to access a web server running on a PC with the address 54.24.12.19. Since the NACL has an outbound rule to allow traffic to go out from port 80 from 10.10.1.1, the packet (source IP: 10.10.1.1, source port: 1234, destination IP: 54.24.12.19, and destination port: 80) will be allowed to go out to the PC server. When the packet is received by the web server running on the PC, it will compile a return packet (source IP: 54.24.12.19, source port: 80, destination IP: 10.10.1.1, and destination port: 1234). The NACL is stateless, meaning that the return packet may not be allowed to come in, unless there is an explicit inbound rule added to allow the packet to come back in:

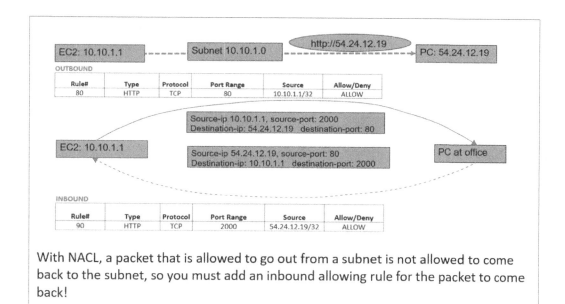

With NACL, a packet that is allowed to go out from a subnet is not allowed to come back to the subnet, so you must add an inbound allowing rule for the packet to come back!

Figure 3.29 – NACL is stateless (2)

As we have learned from the preceding discussions, SGs and NACLs provide protection to the cloud resources inside a VPC, such as EC2 instances. But what about EC2 instances in a VPC to access an S3 bucket? We will introduce VPC endpoints for S3 next.

VPC endpoints

In the previous sections, we learned that an IGW provides inbound and outbound communication with internet resources, and NAT only provides outbound internet access for private cloud resources. Any EC2 instances that have internet access can access public endpoints such as S3 buckets after being assigned an EC2 role that has permission to access the buckets. However, due to security reasons, some companies do not allow internet trespassing to access AWS public endpoints from VPC resources. To that end, VPC endpoints were introduced.

A VPC endpoint for S3 is a way to access S3 resources privately within an Amazon VPC without using a public IGW, a VPN connection, or NAT devices. Using the network diagram shown in *Figure 3.30*, we will create a VPC endpoint for S3 and provide S3 bucket access for an EC2-2 instance that has no public IP addresses:

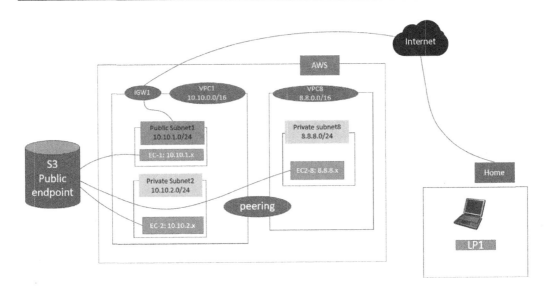

Figure 3.30 – VPC network diagram

Here are the detailed steps:

First, we need to create an EC2 role that has access to the S3 bucket and assign the role to our EC2 instance. We discussed and did this in the previous chapter, and now we create the endpoint:

1. Create a VPC endpoint for S3 in the us-east1 region:

    I.   Log in to the AWS Management Console and navigate to the Amazon VPC console. Click on **Endpoints** in the left-hand menu. Click the **Create Endpoint** button.

    II. Fill in the endpoint settings in the new pop-up window, as shown in *Figure 3.31*:

        `vpc-s3-endpoint` is the name

        Select **AWS services** as the service category

        Select **com.amazonaws.us-east-1.s3** as the service name

        Select **VPC1** to create the endpoint

        Select the **VPC1-Pri** route table to associate with the endpoint

        Enable policies for resource-based policies to control access to the bucket

    III. Click **Create endpoint** to create the VPC endpoint.

2. Now you can verify S3 access from EC2-2, which does not have internet access.

Create endpoint Info

There are three types of VPC endpoints – Interface endpoints, Gateway Load Balancer endpoints, and Gateway endpoints.
Interface endpoints and Gateway Load Balancer endpoints are powered by AWS PrivateLink, and use an Elastic Network
Interface (ENI) as an entry point for traffic destined to the service. Interface endpoints are typically accessed using the public
or private DNS name associated with the service, while Gateway endpoints and Gateway Load Balancer endpoints serve as a
target for a route in your route table for traffic destined for the service.

Endpoint settings

Name tag - *optional*
Creates a tag with a key of 'Name' and a value that you specify.

```
vpc-s3-endpoint
```

Service category
Select the service category

- ● **AWS services**
  Services provided by Amazon

- ○ **PrivateLink Ready partner services**
  Services with an AWS Service Ready designation

- ○ **AWS Marketplace services**
  Services that you've purchased through AWS Marketplace

- ○ **Other endpoint services**
  Find services shared with you by service name

Services (1/3)   ⟳

`Q Filter services`   ⟨ 1 ⟩   ⚙

Service Name: com.amazonaws.us-east-1.s3 ✕   **Clear filters**

	Service Name ▽	Owner	▽	Type
◉	com.amazonaws.us-east-1.s3	amazon		Gateway
○	com.amazonaws.us-east-1.s3	amazon		Interface
○	com.amazonaws.us-east-1.s3-outposts	amazon		Interface

VPC
Select the VPC in which to create the endpoint

VPC
The VPC in which to create your endpoint.

```
vpc-0d90c4e16d2e815a2 (VPC1)          ▼    ⟳
```

Route tables (1/2) Info   ⟳

`Q Filter route tables`   ⟨ 1 ⟩   ⚙

	Name ▽	Route Table ID	▽	Main
☐	VPC1RT	rtb-0595676d643322bb5 (VPC1RT)		Yes
☑	VPC1-Pri	rtb-0fa2616ffbf955b3c (VPC1-Pri)		No

Figure 3.31 – VPC endpoint settings

So far, we have provisioned VPCs, subnets, and EC2 instances in the AWS cloud, and discussed their security hardening. What about the network connections between the public cloud and the on-premises data centers? Let's look at that in the next section.

Understanding Amazon Direct Connect

Amazon Direct Connect is a network service that provides a dedicated and private connection between your on-premises data center environment and the virtual data centers in the cloud. This connection is a private, high-speed, low-latency connection that is not accessible over the public internet. With Amazon Direct Connect, the connection between your on-premises environment and the AWS cloud will have guaranteed bandwidth and performance.

To set up AWS Direct Connect, you'll need to follow these steps:

1. **Review the prerequisites**: Before you begin, make sure you have an AWS account and access to the AWS Management Console, a Direct Connect location, and a device that can connect to the Direct Connect location.

2. **Request a connection**: Log in to the AWS Management Console and go to the Direct Connect console. Choose a Direct Connect location and request a new connection. Provide details such as your connection name, port speed, and virtual private gateway.

3. **Choose a Partner**: Choose a Direct Connect Partner who can provide a network connection between your on premises environment and the Direct Connect location.

4. **Configure the connection**: Once the connection has been approved by the Direct Connect Partner, you'll receive a **Letter of Authorization and Connecting Facility Assignment (LOA-CFA)** document. You'll need to provide this document to the colocation facility where your equipment will be located. You'll also need to configure your routers to connect to the Direct Connect location.

5. **Test the connection**: After the connection is set up, test it to make sure it's working properly. You can do this by creating a test VPC and connecting to it from your on-premises environment.

6. **Start using Direct Connect**: Once you're confident that the connection is working as expected, you can start using Direct Connect to connect to your AWS resources.

More details are available at `https://docs.aws.amazon.com/directconnect/latest/UserGuide/getting_started.html`.

To secure the traffic over Amazon Direct Connect, you can set up a VPN over an Amazon direct connection, extend your private network into AWS, and securely access resources running in the cloud. To set up a VPN over Amazon Direct Connect, you will need to configure a virtual private gateway in your AWS VPC and a customer gateway in your on-premises environment and configure a VPN connection between the two gateways. More details are available at `https://aws.amazon.com/premiumsupport/knowledge-center/create-vpn-direct-connect/`.

As a basic network service, DNS plays a critical role in networking and the internet. When we extend our network from on-premises to the cloud, how does DNS work in the cloud? We will examine this in the next section.

Understanding Amazon DNS – Route 53

Amazon Route 53 is a scalable and highly available DNS web service provided by AWS. Some details about AWS Route 53 are as follows:

- It provides translation from human-readable names (such as `example.com`) into IP addresses that computers use to connect to network resources

- It can also be used to route traffic to AWS resources, such as EC2 instances, S3 buckets, and load balancers

- It offers features such as latency-based routing, geo DNS, health checks, and DNS failover, which help improve the performance, availability, and reliability of applications

- It integrates with other AWS services, such as CloudWatch and CloudTrail, to provide additional monitoring and logging capabilities

Amazon Route 53 supports the following routing policies:

- **Simple routing**: Uses one Route 53 server

- **Weighted round-robin routing**: Assign weights to Route 53 server rotations

- **Latency routing**: Route traffic based on latencies

- **Geolocation routing**: Route traffic based on the location of users

- **Geoproximity routing**: Route traffic based on the location of resources

- **Failover routing**: Route traffic to the failover site when the primary site is not reachable

- **Multivalue answer routing**: Distributes DNS responses across multiple IP addresses – up to eight healthy records can be selected at random

More details on Amazon Route 53 can be found at `https://aws.amazon.com/route53/`.

In the next section, we will cover the AWS CDN, which provides efficient delivery of cloud content, such as photos and PDF files.

Understanding the Amazon CDN

The Amazon CDN is called Amazon **CloudFront** (**CF**). It is a global delivery service that leverages edge locations to securely deliver content with low latency and high speed. CF is integrated with AWS cloud services, and has the following features:

- It is a global network of edge locations that cache and deliver content (such as web pages, videos, and software downloads) to end users with low latency and high data transfer speeds.

- It can be used to distribute both static and dynamic content from AWS and non-AWS origin servers, such as EC2 instances, S3 buckets, and on-premises servers.

- It offers features such as content compression, SSL/TLS encryption, and custom domain names, which help improve the security, reliability, and performance of applications.

- It has a pay-as-you-go pricing model, with no upfront costs or minimum fees. The cost is based on the amount of data transferred, the number of requests made, and the edge locations used.

More details about Amazon CF can be found at `https://aws.amazon.com/cloudfront/`.

Summary

In this chapter, we discussed the Amazon cloud network – VPC, Direct Connect, Route 53, and the CDN, CF. We focused on building a small AWS cloud, by provisioning VPCs, subnets, EC2 instances, and peering VPCs, and setting up internet access for the EC2 instances. We discussed AWS VPC network security and compared the differences between SGs and NACLs. At the end of the chapter, we briefly looked at AWS Direct Connect, providing a connection between on-premises and the Amazon cloud, Amazon Route 53, and Amazon CF concepts and features. In the next chapter, we will discuss database concepts and introduce Amazon cloud database services.

Practice questions

1. What is the main function of an **Internet Gateway** (**IGW**) in AWS VPC?

   A. To provide **Network Address Translation** (**NAT**) for instances in the VPC

   B. To allow instances in the VPC to communicate with other resources outside the VPC

   C. To restrict access to the VPC to only authorized users or resources

   D. To provide load-balancing capabilities for instances in the VPC

2. Which of the following is not a valid use case for a NAT gateway in Amazon VPC?

   A. Allowing instances in a private subnet to access the internet

   B. Enabling communication between two VPCs in different regions

   C. Enabling communication between a VPC and an on-premises network

D. Enabling communication between a VPC and a third-party service that requires a whitelisted IP address

3. Which of the following statements is true about AWS security groups?

A. Security groups are stateless, meaning that inbound and outbound rules must be specified separately

B. Security groups are attached to individual instances, not to a VPC

C. Security groups can be used to restrict inbound and outbound traffic based on IP addresses or port numbers

D. Security groups can be used to allow traffic from a specific IP address range requiring a VPN connection

4. Which of the following is a key difference between an AWS SG and NACL?

A. Security groups can only be applied at the subnet level, while NACLs can be applied at the instance level

B. Security groups are stateful, meaning that they automatically allow return traffic for allowed inbound traffic, while NACLs are stateless

C. Security groups can only allow traffic based on IP addresses, while NACLs can allow or deny traffic based on IP addresses, port numbers, or protocols

D. Security groups can be used to create complex security policies that can filter traffic at multiple layers, while NACLs are simpler and more restrictive in nature

5. Which statement about AWS Direct Connect is true?

A. It is a service that allows you to securely connect your on-premises network to AWS over the public internet

B. It is a service that allows you to create a private, dedicated network connection between your on-premises infrastructure and AWS

C. It is a service that enables you to register domain names and route traffic to AWS resources

D. It is a service that provides managed DNS hosting and traffic management capabilities for your domain names

6. Which of the following is not a valid reason to use AWS Direct Connect?

A. To reduce bandwidth costs for accessing AWS services

B. To improve the reliability and performance of your network connections to AWS

C. To improve the security of your network connections to AWS

D. To access AWS services from a location where internet access is not available

7. What is AWS Route 53?

A. A service that enables you to register domain names and route traffic to AWS resources

B. A service that provides managed DNS hosting and traffic management capabilities for your domain names

C. A service that enables you to establish a private, dedicated network connection between your on-premises infrastructure and AWS

D. A service that allows you to securely connect your on-premises network to AWS over the public internet

8. Which of the following is a valid use case for Route 53 traffic routing policies?

A. Distributing traffic evenly across multiple EC2 instances in a single Availability Zone

B. Directing traffic to the nearest AWS region based on the location of the user

C. Balancing traffic across multiple AWS accounts using weighted routing

D. Limiting the amount of traffic that can be sent to a specific AWS resource

9. What is AWS CloudFront?

A. A service that allows you to run containers on AWS using Docker

B. A service that enables you to manage and store large amounts of data in the cloud

C. A **Content Delivery Network** (**CDN**) that speeds up the delivery of your static and dynamic web content

D. A service that provides serverless computing capabilities for running code in response to events

10. Which of the following is a valid use case for AWS CloudFront?

A. Storing and managing large volumes of data for analysis using AWS analytics services

B. Running containers on AWS using Kubernetes

C. Hosting a website that requires complex server-side processing and database access

D. Accelerating the delivery of content to users worldwide, especially those in remote or high-latency locations

Answers to the practice questions

1. B
2. B
3. C
4. B
5. B

6. D

7. B

8. B

9. C

10. D

Further reading

For further insights into what you've learned in this chapter, refer to the following links:

- `https://aws.amazon.com/vpc`

- `https://docs.aws.amazon.com/vpc/index.html`

- `https://aws.amazon.com/vpc/faqs/`

- `https://aws.amazon.com/getting-started/hands-on/getting-started-create-vpc/`

- `https://docs.aws.amazon.com/directconnect/index.html`

- `https://aws.amazon.com/directconnect/faqs/`

- `https://aws.amazon.com/getting-started/hands-on/getting-started-dc/`

- `https://docs.aws.amazon.com/cloudfront/index.html`

- `https://aws.amazon.com/cloudfront/faqs/`

- `https://aws.amazon.com/getting-started/hands-on/get-started-with-cloudfront/`

- `https://docs.aws.amazon.com/Route53/index.html`

- `https://aws.amazon.com/route53/faqs/`

- `https://aws.amazon.com/getting-started/hands-on/get-started-route-53/`

4

Amazon Database Services

Amazon database services provide a scalable, flexible, and high-performance solution for a wide range of applications and workloads. These services are fully managed, meaning that AWS handles the underlying infrastructure and administration tasks such as managing high availability and scalability. This allows users to focus on their data and applications. They also integrate with other AWS services, allowing for seamless integration with other parts of an AWS application stack.

In this chapter, we will cover the following Amazon database services:

Amazon cloud relational databases: Fully managed AWS relational databases that can be used for transactional applications, reporting and analytics, and content management, including **Amazon Relational Database Service (RDS)** for traditional databases such as MySQL, MariaDB, PostgreSQL, Oracle, SQL Server, and **Amazon Aurora** for a high-performing, MySQL and PostgreSQL-compatible database.

Amazon cloud NoSQL databases: Fully managed AWS NoSQL databases that can handle large volumes of unstructured data with high scalability and availability, including **Amazon DynamoDB**, a key-value and document database, and **Amazon DocumentDB**, a MongoDB-compatible document database.

Amazon cloud in-memory caching: Fully managed AWS in-memory data caching services that can be used to improve application performance by caching frequently accessed data, including **Amazon ElastiCache** for **Redis** and **Memcached**.

Amazon Cloud Data Warehousing: Fully managed data warehousing services that can be used to store and analyze large volumes of structured and unstructured data, including **Redshift** for large-scale data warehousing, and **Amazon EMR (Elastic MapReduce)** for processing large datasets using Apache Hadoop, Spark, and other big data tools. We will focus on Redshift in this chapter and discuss the others in the next chapter.

By following these topics in this chapter, you will understand the basic concepts and gain hands-on skills with Amazon cloud database services. If you are familiar with database basics and **structured query language (SQL)**, a programming language for storing and processing information in a relational database, you can skip the first section. The examples shown in this chapter are also available in the GitHub repository for this book: `https://github.com/PacktPublishing/Self-Taught-Cloud-computing-Engineer`.

Database basics

A **database** is an organized collection of data that is stored and managed on a computer. It allows for efficient storage, retrieval, and management of data, which can be used for a wide range of applications, such as websites, mobile apps, financial systems, and more. A database consists of one or more tables that contain related data. Each table contains rows and columns, where the columns represent the attributes or fields of the data, and the rows represent the individual instances or records of the data. There are many different types of databases:

- **Relational databases**: These are the most common type of database, where structured data is organized in a tabular format with rows and columns. Data is organized into tables, and relationships between tables are established through keys.

- **NoSQL databases**: These databases are designed to handle unstructured or semi-structured data that cannot be easily organized into tables. Instead, they use document-based, key-value, or graph-based approaches to store and organize data.

- **Object-oriented databases**: These databases store data as objects rather than in a tabular format. They are designed to work with object-oriented programming languages, such as Java, C++, and so on.

- **Data warehouses**: These databases are used to store large amounts of data from different sources, such as transactional systems, social media, and other data sources. They are designed to support complex data analysis and reporting

Overall, databases are an essential tool for managing and organizing data and are used in many different industries and applications. They provide a scalable, efficient, and secure way to store and manage data, which can be accessed by multiple users and applications at the same time. We will discuss each of them in the upcoming sections.

Relational databases

A relational database stores and organizes data in tables or relations, with each table representing a specific entity or concept. The tables are made up of columns and rows, where each column represents a particular attribute or characteristic of the entity, and each row represents a specific instance or record of the entity. We use a schema to define the structure of a database, including the tables and relationships between them.

A schema is a map of how data is stored and organized in the database. It has tables and keys including a **primary key** and a **foreign key**. A primary key is a column or group of columns in a table that uniquely identifies each row in that table: no two rows have the same value in the primary key column(s). Primary keys are important for maintaining the integrity and consistency of the data in the database, as they ensure that each record can be uniquely identified and retrieved. A foreign key is a column in one table that refers to the primary key of another table. It establishes a link or relationship between the two tables, enabling data to be retrieved from multiple tables at the same time. Foreign keys are essential for maintaining referential integrity in a database, which means that data in one table must always correspond to data in another table.

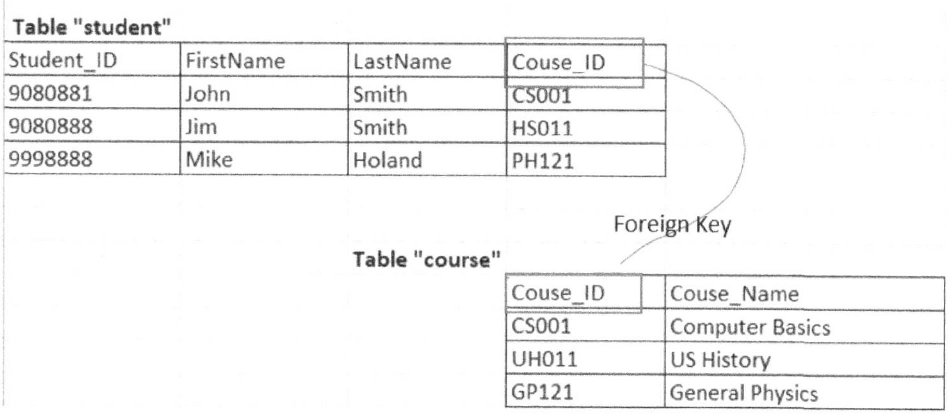

Table "student"

Student_ID	FirstName	LastName	Couse_ID
9080881	John	Smith	CS001
9080888	Jim	Smith	HS011
9998888	Mike	Holand	PH121

Foreign Key

Table "course"

Couse_ID	Couse_Name
CS001	Computer Basics
UH011	US History
GP121	General Physics

Figure 4.1 – Database schema

Figure 4.1 shows a small database consisting of two tables: a `student` table and a `course` table. The primary key for the `course` table is `Course_ID`, which is also a foreign key in the `student` table. This relationship defines the database schema and allows you to retrieve information about both students and the courses they take using a single query.

Relational databases use **Structured Query Language** (**SQL**) to create, manipulate, and retrieve data. SQL allows users to write complex queries that can extract specific data from one or more tables, based on various conditions or criteria. The ability to query data in this way makes relational databases a powerful tool for data management and analysis. The following examples create a database called `school`, and create a table called `students` in the database, with `StudentID` as the primary key:

```
Create database school;
Create table school.students (
    StudentID int primary key,
    LastName varchar(100),
    FirstName varchar(100),
    City varchar(100)  );
```

Relational databases have **Atomicity, Consistency, Isolation, and Durability** (**ACID**) to ensure data reliability and transactional integrity in database transactions. More details are available at https://aws.amazon.com/relational-database/.

NoSQL databases

NoSQL databases were designed to handle unstructured or semi-structured data and to support highly scalable and distributed systems. Different from relational databases , which rely on structural data models, NoSQL databases use a more flexible, non-relational data model such as key-value pairs, documents, graphs, and other formats. There are several different types of NoSQL databases, including document-oriented databases, key-value stores, graph databases, and column-family stores. Each type has its unique strengths and weaknesses and is best suited for different types of applications and data models.

NoSQL databases are more flexible since there is no schema among the tables. The following example shows a `Student` table that has entries with the key-value format:

```
Student =
{ "Student class number" : 101,
"Student details": [


{"Student name" : "John Smith", "Born City" : "Houston", "Course_
taking" : "CS201"},


{"Student name" : "Jim Smith", "Born City" : "Plano", "Age" : 20},


{"Student name" : "Neil Armstrong", "Age" : 18, "Course_taking" :
"CS202"}


{"Student name" : "Neil Smith", "Age" : 21, "Born City" : "Chicago"}

],}
```

NoSQL databases are not a replacement for traditional relational databases. Rather, they are complementary technology that can be used in conjunction with them to address specific data management needs.

In-memory cache databases

An **in-memory cache database**, also known as an **in-memory data grid**, is a type of database that stores data entirely in RAM for very fast data access and retrieval. In-memory cache databases are often used to accelerate the performance of high-traffic, latency-sensitive applications.

Here are some examples of in-memory cache databases:

- **Redis:** In addition to being a popular NoSQL database, Redis can also be used as an in-memory cache database. It supports a wide range of data structures and can be used for caching, messaging, and more.

- **Memcached**: A high-performance, distributed in-memory cache database that is widely used for caching web applications. It can be used to store key-value pairs and can be accessed from multiple servers in a cluster.

In-memory cache databases are often used in conjunction with other databases, such as a traditional disk-based relational database, to provide a fast and efficient caching layer for frequently accessed data.

Data warehouses

The goal of a **data warehouse** is to provide a comprehensive, unified view of an organization's data so that it can be used for decision-making, reporting, and other analytical purposes. They are also optimized for fast querying and reporting and often use specialized tools and technologies, such as **online analytical processing (OLAP)** and data mining, to extract insights and intelligence from data.

Data warehouses are typically used by large organizations that need to analyze and report on large amounts of data from multiple sources. They are commonly used in industries such as finance, retail, healthcare, and telecommunications, where there is a need to analyze data from many different sources and perform complex analyses and reporting. *Figure 4.2* shows examples of data warehouse functions:

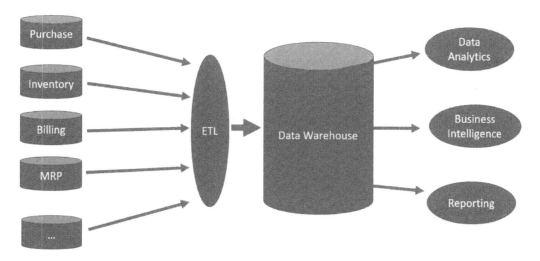

Figure 4.2 – Data warehouse functions

By **Extracting, Transforming, and Loading (ETL)** from various sources, data is ingested into the data warehouse, which is a large, centralized data repository, in a structured format that is optimized to conduct data analytics and business intelligence, and generate reporting. After we have briefed the different types of AWS cloud database services, we will now closely examine each of these services.

Amazon RDS

RDS is a fully managed relational database service provided by Amazon in the cloud. With RDS, AWS provides a few popular relational database management systems as a service, including MySQL, PostgreSQL, Oracle, SQL Server, and MariaDB.

Amazon RDS is a managed service. There are different ways to create a database, such as MySQL, in the cloud. One is provisioning an EC2 instance and installing a **database management system (DBMS)** on the instance, and then creating databases, tables, and so on. This is an unmanaged approach since you will have to take care of all the administrative tasks such as database scaling, high availability, disaster recovery, and so on. Another is using cloud-managed services to provision a database where AWS will handle the mundane and time-consuming tasks such as hardware provisioning, software installation, backup and recovery, patching, scaling, and so on. Managed services allow users to focus on their applications and data without worrying about the underlying infrastructure.

RDS is a managed service. It provides high availability and fault tolerance by replicating the database to multiple **AZs** and providing automatic failover in the event of a primary database failure. It also supports automated backups and point-in-time restores, ensuring data durability and recoverability. RDS allows users to scale databases vertically as needed with minimal downtime.

As an AWS cloud service, RDS integrates with other AWS services, such as Amazon CloudWatch, which provides monitoring, alarms, and AWS IAM, which allows users to control who can access their databases and what they can do with them.

Recall that an EC2 instance in the public subnet can send or receive traffic directly to and from the internet, whereas an instance in the private subnet can only access the internet via a NAT gateway in the public subnet. This holds true for the database instances in different subnets. A typical multi-tier design is to expose the web tier to the internet while hiding the app tier and database tier in the private subnets. *Figure 4.3* shows an architecture of multi-tiers including web, application, and RDS databases:

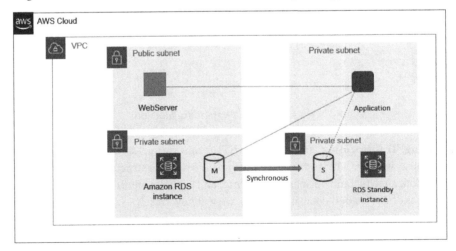

Figure 4.3 – Multi-tier architecture with a multi-AZ RDS

The web server instance is sitting in the public subnet, the application instance sits in the private subnet, and the RDS instance is configured as multi-AZ with a master server in one subnet and the slave server in another so that the slave can take charge when the master is down. We will now implement the RDS portion of the architecture and connect it from an EC2 instance, step by step (for simplicity, we use Zonal RDS):

1. **From the AWS Console | RDS | Create Database**: Fill in the details and click **Create Database**. *Figure 4.4* shows a summary of the database:

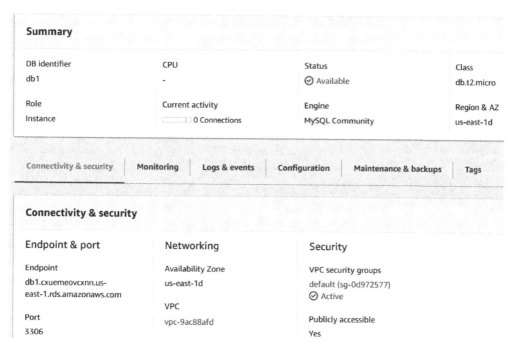

Figure 4.4 – RDS database

2. **Connect from an EC2 instance**: Using Putty to connect to a Linux instance, install mysql client pkg and connect to the RDS endpoint:

    ```
    sudo yum install mysql
    mysql --user admin --password --host db1.cxuemeovcxnn.us-east-1.
    rds.amazonaws.com
    ```

3. Once connected to the RDS instance, we will create a database and a table, insert entries into the table, and run some SQL queries, as shown in *Figure 4.5*:

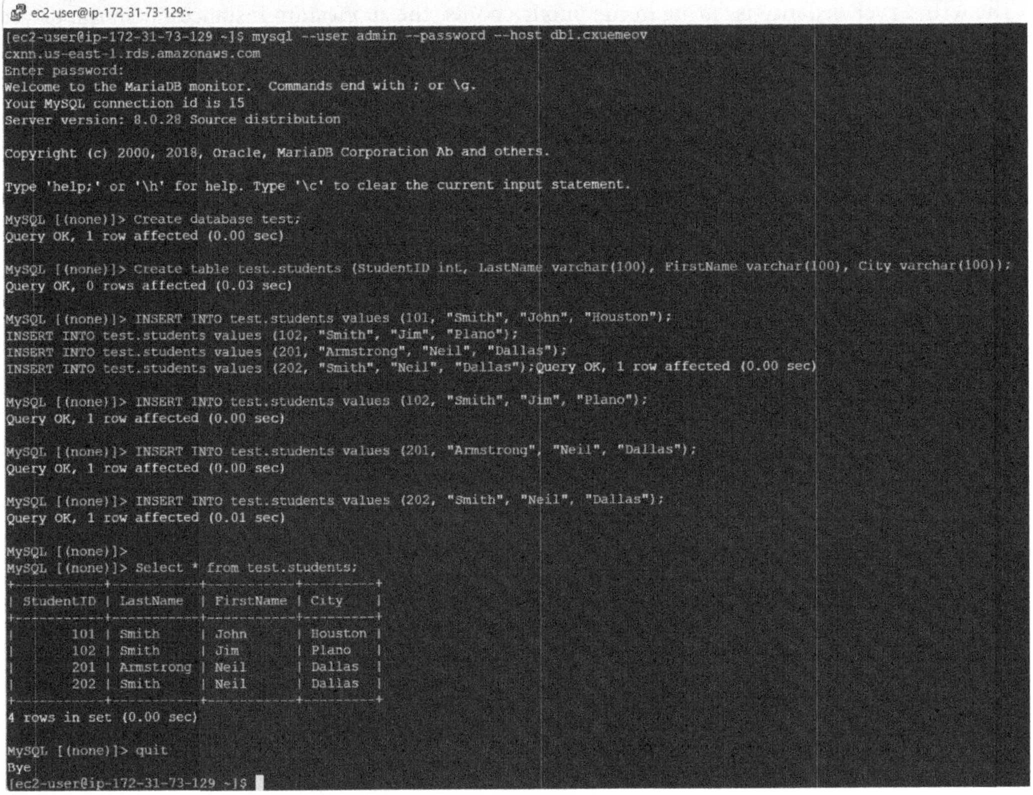

```
ec2-user@ip-172-31-73-129:~
[ec2-user@ip-172-31-73-129 ~]$ mysql --user admin --password --host db1.cxuemeov
cxnn.us-east-1.rds.amazonaws.com
Enter password:
Welcome to the MariaDB monitor.  Commands end with ; or \g.
Your MySQL connection id is 15
Server version: 8.0.28 Source distribution

Copyright (c) 2000, 2018, Oracle, MariaDB Corporation Ab and others.

Type 'help;' or '\h' for help. Type '\c' to clear the current input statement.

MySQL [(none)]> Create database test;
Query OK, 1 row affected (0.00 sec)

MySQL [(none)]> Create table test.students (StudentID int, LastName varchar(100), FirstName varchar(100), City varchar(100));
Query OK, 0 rows affected (0.03 sec)

MySQL [(none)]> INSERT INTO test.students values (101, "Smith", "John", "Houston");
INSERT INTO test.students values (102, "Smith", "Jim", "Plano");
INSERT INTO test.students values (201, "Armstrong", "Neil", "Dallas");
INSERT INTO test.students values (202, "Smith", "Neil", "Dallas");Query OK, 1 row affected (0.00 sec)

MySQL [(none)]> INSERT INTO test.students values (102, "Smith", "Jim", "Plano");
Query OK, 1 row affected (0.00 sec)

MySQL [(none)]> INSERT INTO test.students values (201, "Armstrong", "Neil", "Dallas");
Query OK, 1 row affected (0.00 sec)

MySQL [(none)]> INSERT INTO test.students values (202, "Smith", "Neil", "Dallas");
Query OK, 1 row affected (0.01 sec)

MySQL [(none)]>
MySQL [(none)]> Select * from test.students;
+-----------+-----------+-----------+---------+
| StudentID | LastName  | FirstName | City    |
+-----------+-----------+-----------+---------+
|       101 | Smith     | John      | Houston |
|       102 | Smith     | Jim       | Plano   |
|       201 | Armstrong | Neil      | Dallas  |
|       202 | Smith     | Neil      | Dallas  |
+-----------+-----------+-----------+---------+
4 rows in set (0.00 sec)

MySQL [(none)]> quit
Bye
[ec2-user@ip-172-31-73-129 ~]$
```

Figure 4.5 – Connect and operate the RDS database

AWS RDS provides an option that enables users to create one or more read-only copies of their database instance within the same AWS region or across different AWS regions, called `read- replicas`. By copying the data from the primary/source database instance to the replica instance, you can offload read traffic from the primary instance to the replica. Because a read replica is read-only, any write operations must still be performed on the primary instance. The read replica can be used to improve the performance of read-intensive workloads or to create a DR solution. In the case of DR, if the primary instance fails, the read replica can be promoted to the primary instance, reducing downtime.

AWS RDS read replicas can be created for various database engines, including MySQL, PostgreSQL, Oracle, and SQL Server. The replica instances can be resized, backed up, and deleted independently of the primary instance. Additionally, users can configure the replication settings, including the replication frequency and the source and destination databases.

In addition to cloud RDS, Amazon offers another powerful cloud relational database service, Amazon Aurora, which is highly available globally, highly scalable, durable, and performs great. Amazon Aurora has many features:

- It uses a distributed architecture that enables its scaling horizontally across multiple nodes, while maintaining low latency and high throughput

- It can automatically replicate data across multiple AZs for high availability and durability

- It supports both across-region read replicas and global databases

- It offers point-in-time recovery, allowing the database to restore to a specific point in time

- It's compatible with MySQL and PostgreSQL – existing applications and tools that use MySQL/PostgreSQL can be migrated to Aurora easily

- It offers advanced security features such as encryption at rest and in transit

Overall, AWS RDS and Aurora are powerful and flexible cloud relational database services that are highly available, scalable, and cost-effective. They are great choices for organizations of all sizes, from start-ups to enterprises that need to manage their relational databases in the cloud. While RDS suits small or medium-sized databases with relatively low cost, Aurora is a global petabyte-scale database for mission-critical applications and is thus more expensive than RDS. More details about AWS relational databases can be found at `https://aws.amazon.com/rds/pricing/` and `https://aws.amazon.com/rds/aurora/pricing/`.

In the next section, we will examine the NoSQL databases in the AWS cloud.

Amazon cloud NoSQL databases

DynamoDB is a fully managed NoSQL database service provided by Amazon in the cloud. It is a key-value and document database that can handle structured, semi-structured, and unstructured data, making it a versatile solution for a wide range of applications. It is also designed to be highly available, with automatic multi-AZ replication for built-in redundancy and durability.

DynamoDB can scale seamlessly with no downtime or disruption, allowing users to scale their databases up or down as needed, with pay-as-you-go pricing based on the amount of data stored and the number of requests made.

DynamoDB is designed for high performance with sub-millisecond latency for read and write operations, making it an ideal choice for real-time, low-latency applications. It is also highly secure, with support for encryption at rest and in transit, as well as fine-grained access control through AWS IAM. We will create a DynamoDB through AWS Cloudshell:

```
aws dynamodb create-table \
--table-name Music \
--attributedefinitions \
AttributeName=Artist, AttributeType=S \
```

```
AttributeName=SongTitle, AttributeType=S \
--key-schema \
AttributeName=Artist,KeyType=HASH \
AttributeName=SongTitle, KeyType=RANGE \
--provisionedthroughput \
ReadCapacityUnits=5,WriteCapacityUnits=5 \
--table-class STANDARD
```

As shown in *Figure 4.6*, the DynamoDB table `Music` is created:

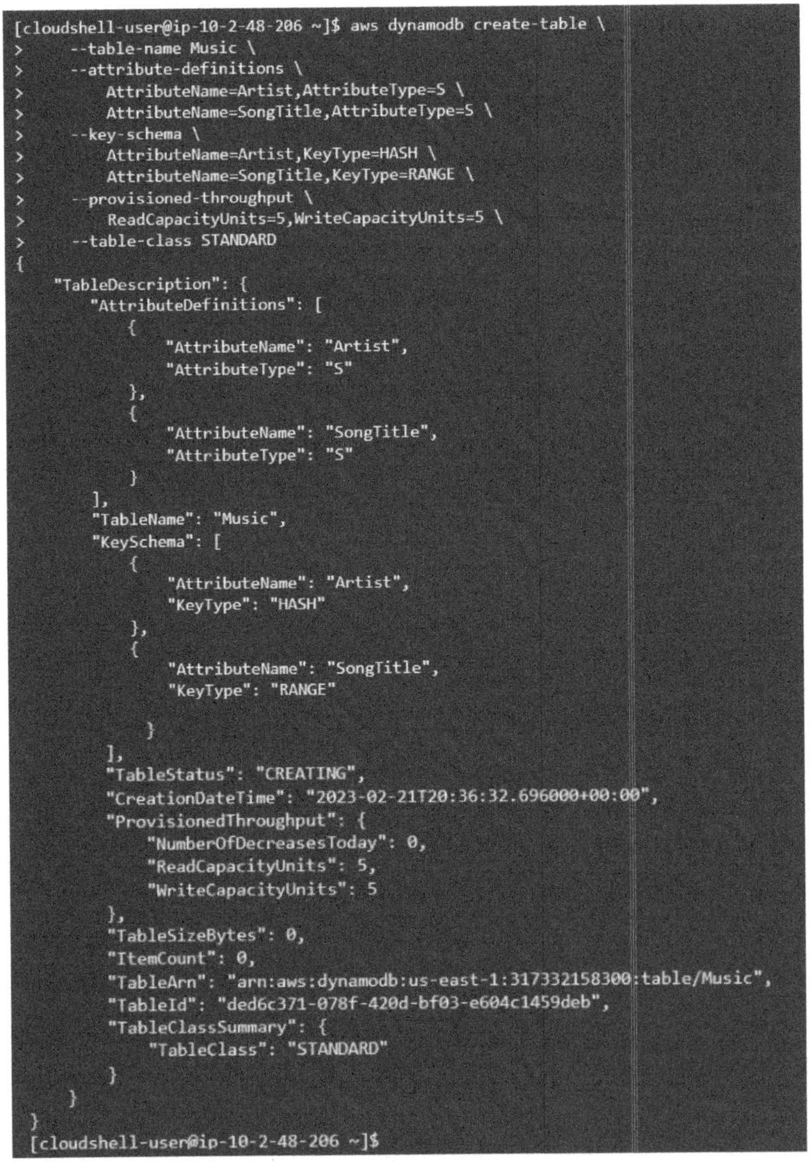

Figure 4.6 – Create a DynamoDB database

In the preceding DynamoDB table creation command, there are some concepts we need to understand:

- **Key schema**: A DynamoDB table has two types of keys:

  The **hash key**, also known as the **partition key**, is a required attribute that uniquely identifies items in a table. The hash key is used to partition the table's items across multiple physical storage partitions for scalability and performance. For example, for the `Music` table, we choose the `Artist` attribute as the hash key to ensure that all items for a given artist are stored in the same partition, which allows for fast access to that artist's data.

  The **range key**, also known as the **sort key**, is an optional attribute that is used in combination with the hash key to uniquely identify items in a table. The range key is used to further sort and organize items within a particular hash key partition. For example, for the `Music` table, we choose the `SongTitle` attribute as the range key to ensure that all items for a given artist are sorted by song titles within their partition.

  The combination of a hash key and a range key is called a **composite primary key**. This allows for efficient querying of items in a table based on both the hash key and range key values.

- **Provisioned throughput**: This is a setting that determines the amount of read and write capacity that is provisioned for a table or an index. Provisioned throughput is specified as two separate values: the **read capacity unit (RCU)** and the **write capacity unit (WCU)**. One RCU represents the capacity to read up to 4 KB of data per second, while one WCU represents the capacity to write up to 1 KB of data per second.

  Provisioned throughput is important because it determines the rate at which your application can read and write data to the table or index. If your application exceeds the provisioned throughput capacity, then DynamoDB may start returning throttling errors. On the other hand, if you provision more capacity than you need, you will be paying more for unused capacity. In the DynamoDB instance created earlier, we have set an RCU of 5 and a WCU of 5, now let's add some items to the table and run some queries against it:

1. **Add items to the DynamoDB table**:

```
aws dynamodb put-item --table-name Music --item \
'{"Artist": {"S": "Broadway"}, "SongTitle": {"S": "Call Me"},
"AlbumTitle": {"S": "Somewhat Famous"}}'

aws dynamodb put-item --table-name Music --item \
'{"Artist": {"S": "Broadway"}, "SongTitle": {"S": "Howdy"},
"AlbumTitle": {"S": "Famous"}, "Awards": {"N": "2"}}'

aws dynamodb put-item --table-name Music --item \
'{"Artist": {"S": "Acme Band"}, "SongTitle": {"S": "Happy"},
"AlbumTitle": {"S": "About Life"}, "Awards": {"N": "10"}}'
```

```
aws dynamodb put-item --table-name Music --item \
'{"Artist": {"S": "Acme Band"}, "SongTitle": {"S": "Rocks"},
"Awards": {"N": "8"}}'
```

2. **Query the table in the AWS console**:

Going to **AWS Console | DynamoDB | Tables**, we can see the table shown in *Figure 4.7*:

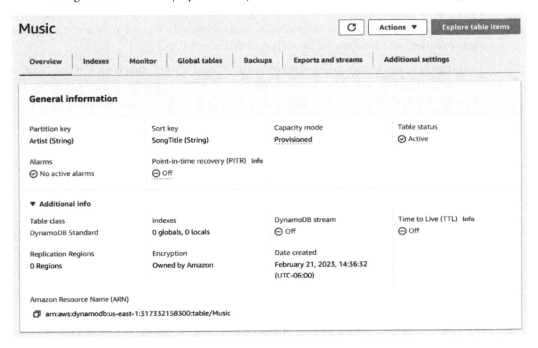

Figure 4.7 – DynamoDB "Music" table

Click **Explore table items**, and you can scan the table or run a query against the table. *Figure 4.8* shows the result of scanning the table:

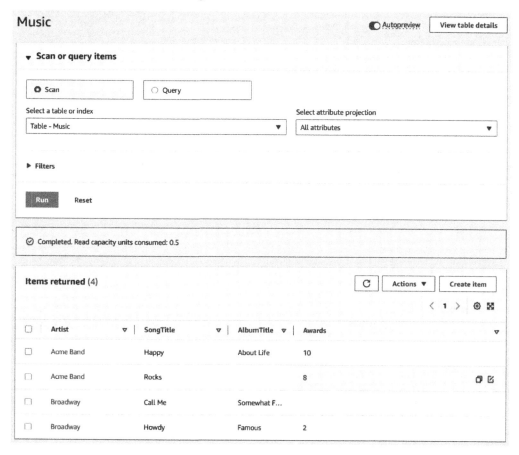

Figure 4.8 – Scan the "Music" table

Figure 4.9 shows the result of running a query by listing all the items for **Artist | Broadway**:

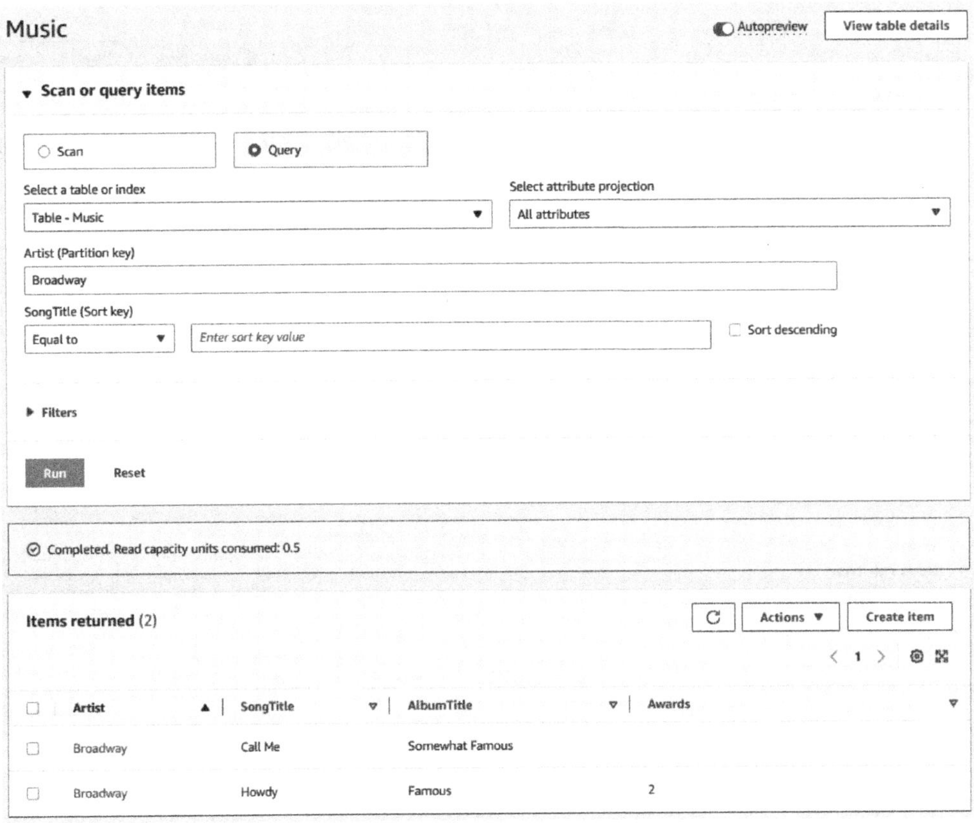

Figure 4.9 – Query the "Music" table

As we can see from *Figure 4.9*, DynamoDB provides a range of features for managing and querying data, including built-in support for indexing, filtering, and sorting, as well as a powerful query language called AWS Query and Scan. It also integrates with other AWS services, such as AWS Lambda and Amazon CloudWatch, for seamless integration with other parts of an AWS application stack. Overall, DynamoDB provides a scalable, flexible, and high-performance NoSQL database solution for a wide range of applications, from mobile and web applications to large-scale enterprise systems.

We have discussed Amazon RDS and DynamoDB. One of the issues with databases is performance, specifically when a table in the database is accessed by many users or applications and poses delays in responding to queries against it. One solution is caching the table into memory. This will lead us to the next section about Amazon ElastiCache.

Amazon ElastiCache

ElastiCache is a fully managed, in-memory data caching service provided by Amazon in the cloud. ElastiCache supports two popular in-memory data stores, Redis and Memcached, which can be used as caching layers for a wide range of applications, including web applications, mobile applications, and gaming applications.

ElastiCache provides automatic scaling and availability, with the ability to scale up or down based on the needs of the application. It also integrates with other AWS services, such as Amazon EC2, AWS Lambda, and Amazon RDS, for seamless integration with other parts of an AWS application stack. ElastiCache provides a range of features for managing and monitoring the caching environment, including automatic failover and automated backups.

ElastiCache also supports a range of use cases, including read-heavy workloads, session management, caching database queries, and real-time analytics. It also supports a range of data structures, including strings, hashes, sets, and lists, and provides a powerful query language for searching and manipulating data.

We will now create an ElastiCache instance and connect it to a client application:

1. **Create an EC2 instance with an SG**: This is to allow default SSH from the computer where you will access the ElastiCache cluster. Use the VPC/subnet for the EC2 instance, which we will name EC2-1, with an SG of allowing SSH from my computer so we can access the EC2 instance from our home computer. Save the key pair and the instance's public IP address. In our case, they are kp.pem and 3.238.218.212.

   Create an SG named **RedisSG** to allow SSH from the previous SG.

2. **Go to the Amazon ElastiCache service**: Click **Get started**, then click **Create cluster**. Choose **Create Redis cluster**. Choose **RedisSG** as the security group, and select **minimum configuration**. *Figure 4.10* shows the details after the cluster has been created:

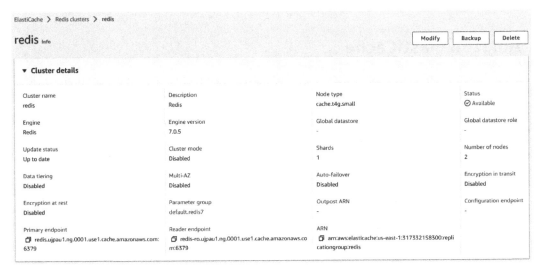

Figure 4.10 – Redis cluster details

3. **Access the Redis cluster from RedisInsight**: Just like the PUTTY tool we used to access Linux EC2 instances in the cloud, RedisInsight is a tool to access the Redis cluster remotely. After launching RedisInsight, click **Add Database**, then fill in the information for the cluster. Fill in **Host** using the primary endpoint copied from the Redis cluster details, leaving the default Redis port of 6379. Since we will use the EC2 instance as the SSH tunnel, check **Use SSH Tunnel** and enter the instance's public IP address for **Host**, leaving the SSH port 22. Check **Private Key** and copy the key from the kp.pem file as shown in *Figure 4.11*:

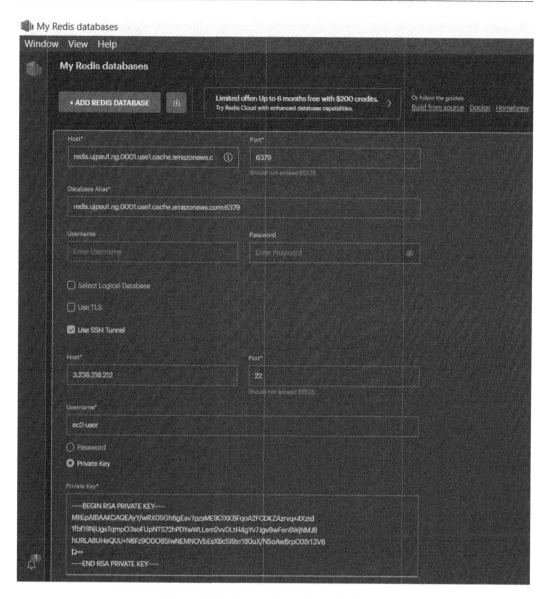

Figure 4.11 – Connecting to the Redis cluster

Once the Redis database is added, we can use **Browser**, **Workbench,** and the **Analysis** tools from the left side. More details are available at `https://redis.io/docs/ui/insight/`.

Amazon ElastiCache provides a highly scalable, fully managed in-memory data caching service that can improve application performance and reduce the need for expensive database queries. It is a popular choice for organizations of all sizes, from start-ups to enterprises that need to manage their caching environment in the cloud.

So far, we have learned about the Amazon cloud databases that support OLTP, including RDS, DynamoDB, and ElastiCache. There is another type of database that supports OLAP, which we refer to as data warehouses. Let's examine an AWS data warehouse: Redshift.

Amazon cloud data warehouse service

Amazon Redshift is a cloud-based data warehousing service that is designed to provide fast querying and analysis of large datasets. Redshift is a fully managed service where AWS handles the infrastructure and administration tasks, such as hardware provisioning, software installation, and backup and recovery, to allow users to focus on their data and analysis without worrying about the underlying infrastructure.

Redshift is based on a columnar storage format, which provides efficient storage and fast querying of large datasets. It can scale up or down as needed, with pay-as-you-go pricing based on the amount of data stored and the number of queries made. It also integrates with other AWS services, such as Amazon S3, Amazon EMR, and Amazon Kinesis, for seamless integration with other parts of an AWS application stack. Redshift supports standard SQL and BI tools such as Tableau, MicroStrategy, and Looker, allowing users to perform complex analytics and reporting on their data. It also provides a range of features for managing and optimizing queries, including query monitoring, query profiling, and automatic query optimization. Redshift is highly secure, with support for encryption at rest and in transit, as well as fine-grained access control through AWS IAM. It is also designed for high availability, with automatic replication of data to multi-AZs and automatic failover in the event of a node failure.

We will now create a Redshift instance and connect it to a client application:

1. **Create a security group**: This allows Redshift traffic from the computer where you will access the data warehouse, as shown in *Figure 4.12*:

Figure 4.12 – SG for Redshift access

2. Create a subnet group that is designated for the Redshift clusters running in the VPC environment. Create an IAM role that has permissions to copy, unload, and query data with Amazon Redshift, and to run SELECT statements for related services, such as Amazon S3, Amazon CloudWatch logs, and so on.

3. Navigate through **AWS Console | Amazon Redshift | Create Cluster**: Fill in the cluster configurations, including name, SG, subnet group, and role and choose the minimum requirements in monitoring, backup, and so on. Make sure the cluster is publicly available. When the cluster is created, copy its endpoint:

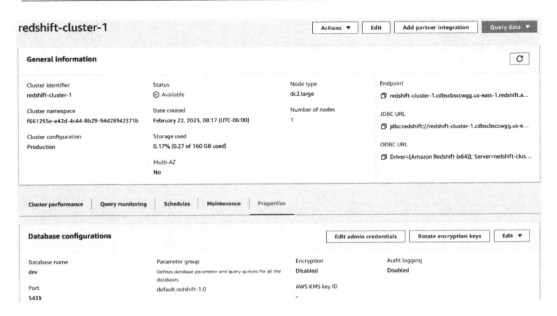

Figure 4.13 – Redshift cluster

4. **Access the Redshift database from DBeaver**: Just like the PUTTY tool we used to access Linux
    EC2 instances in the cloud, **Dbeaver** is a tool to access cloud databases remotely.

    Open **DBeaver | Database | New Database Connection**. In the new pop-up window, choose
    Redshift as the database type, and fill in the endpoint copied from the AWS Redshift dashboard,
    the **Database** name, **Username**, and **Password**, as shown in *Figure 4.14*:

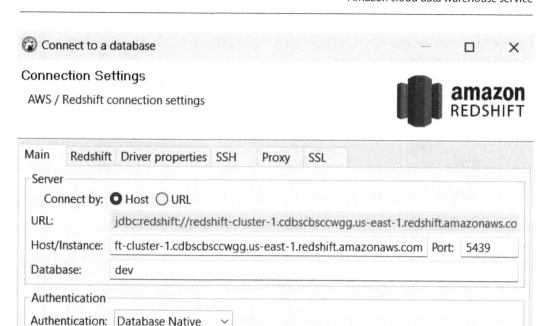

Figure 4.14 – Connect to Redshift cluster

Figure 4.15 shows the connection to the Redshift cluster. You can see the database schemas and use SQL Editor to compile and run queries again in the data warehouse:

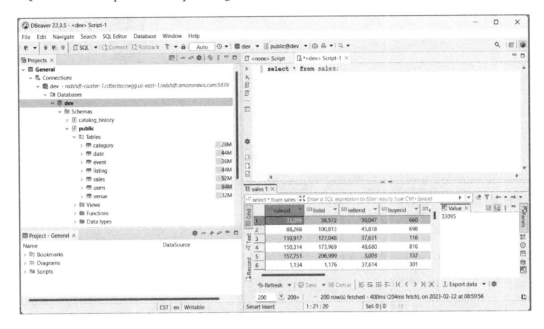

Figure 4.15 – Connection to Redshift cluster

Redshift provides a scalable, flexible, and high-performance data warehousing solution for a wide range of applications, from small data marts to large-scale enterprise data warehouses. More details are available at `https://docs.aws.amazon.com/redshift/`.

Summary

In this chapter, we discussed Amazon cloud databases including RDS, Aurora, DynamoDB, ElastiCache, and Redshift. We provisioned simple database instances and showed how to connect them and use the services. With all the different data schemas, business use cases, and application requirements such as size, scale, performance, and cost, selecting the right database is a critical step. More details are included at `https://aws.amazon.com/startups/start-building/how-to-choose-a-database/`.

In the next chapter, we will further explore Amazon's big data services.

Practice questions

Questions 1-10 are based on *Figure 4.16*:

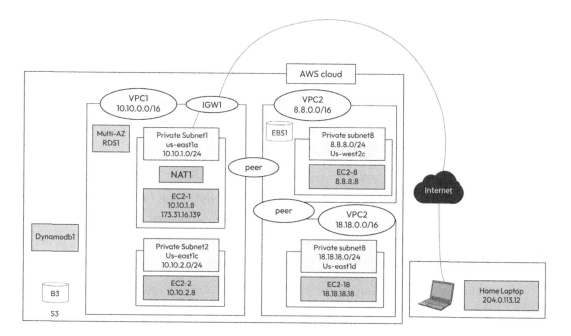

Figure 4.16 – Cloud architect diagram

1. RDS1 is created in VPC1. How would you configure it to be accessible from your home laptop?

    A. Configure SG for RDS1 and NACL for subnet1/subnet2.

    B. Configure SG for RDS1.

    C. Configure NACL for VPC1.

    D. Configure SG for VPC1.

2. Which of the following is not true?

    A. EC2-18 can access RDS1 via VPC peering.

    B. EC2-2 can access RDS1 within VPC1.

    C. EC2-8 can access RDS1 via VPC peering.

    D. EC2-1 can access RDS1 within VPC1.

3. An engineer is developing a web server W1 on EC2-18. W1 needs to access Dynamodb1. What is your recommendation?

    A. Create an EC2 role R1 for Dynamodb1 access, assign R1 to EC2-18, and create an endpoint for Dynamodb1 in VPC3.

    B. Create an EC2 role R1 for Dynamodb1 access, and assign R1 to EC2-18.

    C. Create an endpoint for Dynamodb1 in VPC3.

    D. Create an EC2 role R1 for Dynamodb1 access, assign R1 to EC2-18, create an endpoint for Dynamodb1 in VPC1, and create peering between VPC1 and VPC3.

4. RDS1 was created without encryption, but now encryption is required for compliance reasons. What is your recommendation?

    A. Back up RDS1 and enable encryption on the fly.

    B. Export RDS1. Create a new RDS2 with encryption and import from the RDS1 export.

    C. Snapshot RDS1. Create a new RDS2 and restore it from the RDS1 snapshot.

    D. Snapshot RDS1. Create an encrypted copy of the snapshot. Create a new RDS2 from the encrypted snapshot.

5. RDS1 is not configured with auto-scaling, and it ran out of storage space in the last hour. What is your recommendation?

    A. Add more space to RDS1 using the `ModifyDBInstance` option. Then, enable storage auto-scaling thereafter.

    B. Create a new RDS2 with more storage space. Import it from the latest backup.

    C. Enable storage auto-scaling for RDS1 immediately.

    D. Configure a new read replica of RDS1 with more storage space.

6. The master database for RDS1 is in `Subnet1`. Where shall the slave database be placed for RDS1?

    A. Subnet2

    B. Subnet8

    C. Subnet1

    D. VPC2

7. RDS1 has performance issues with table1, which is updated by many users. What's your recommendation?

    A. Use Elastic Cache.

    B. Use Read Replica for RDS1.

C. Create RDS2.

D. Separate table1 into multiple tables.

8. EC2-8 needs to access Dynamodb1 without trespassing the internet. What needs to be done?

A. Create a DynamoDB endpoint in VPC1 and access Dynamodb through VPC-peering.

B. Create a DynamoDB endpoint in VPC2 directly.

C. Create a DynamoDB endpoint in subnet2.

D. Create a DynamoDB endpoint in subnet8.

9. EC2-2 needs to add a new EBS volume. Where shall the new volume be created?

A. US-EAST1a

B. US-EAST1b

C. US-EAST1d

D. US-WEST1c

10. EC2-2 has a web application that needs to generate new reports from RDS1. Without impacting the database, what's your suggestion?

A. Create a read replica and allow the application to access the replica.

B. Upgrade RDS1 to Aurora.

C. Copy RDS1 to RDS2. Provide EC2-2 access to RDS2.

D. Load RDS1 to ElastiCache, and allow the application to access the cache.

Answers to the practice questions

1. A
2. A
3. A
4. D
5. A
6. A
7. A
8. A
9. D
10. A

Further reading

For further insights into what you've learned in this chapter, refer to the following links:

- `https://aws.amazon.com/products/databases/`
- `https://docs.aws.amazon.com/AmazonRDS/latest/UserGuide/Welcome.html`
- `https://docs.aws.amazon.com/amazondynamodb/latest/developerguide/Introduction.html`
- `https://docs.aws.amazon.com/AmazonRDS/latest/AuroraUserGuide/CHAP_GettingStartedAurora.html`
- `https://docs.aws.amazon.com/elasticache/`

5

Amazon Data Analytics Services

Amazon provides analytics tools and services for many forms of data. Continuing from the **Amazon Web Services (AWS)** database discussions in the previous chapter, we will focus on the AWS big data analytics services in this chapter.

What is big data? In a nutshell, **big data** refers to big and complex datasets that are difficult to process using traditional data analytics tools. Big data is typically characterized by its volume, velocity, and variety:

- **Volume**: Big data refers to datasets that are too large to be processed using traditional database management systems. The size of big data can range from terabytes to petabytes, and it is often generated in real time.

- **Velocity**: Big data is often generated at a high velocity, meaning that it is created and collected rapidly. This requires real-time or near-real-time processing and analysis to turn the data into meaningful insights.

- **Variety**: Big data comes in many different forms, including structured data, semi-structured data, and unstructured data. It can also include audio and video files, images, and sensor data.

Big data can be collected from a wide range of sources, including social media, online transactions, mobile devices, and sensors. It can provide valuable business insights and opportunities. However, it requires advanced tools and techniques to manage and process, including cloud-based storage, computing and other modern tools. AWS offers a range of data analytics services that can be used to manage big data. In this chapter, we will cover the following AWS big data analytics services:

- AWS Glue and data crawlers

- Amazon Athena

- The AWS Kinesis service family

- Amazon QuickSight

- Amazon **Elastic MapReduce** (**EMR**)

During our discussions in this chapter, we will use sample code to process big data. The examples shown in this chapter are also available in the GitHub repository for this book: `https://github.com/PacktPublishing/Self-Taught-Cloud-computing-Engineer`.

Let us start with the AWS big data pipeline and understand the data life cycle in the cloud, including the ingestion, storing, processing, and visualization steps.

Understanding the AWS big data pipeline

With the rise of big data and the increasing availability of data analytics tools and technologies, data analytics has become an essential component of modern business operations. Cloud-based technologies and services have been widely used to analyze and derive insights from big data, and provide the following benefits:

- **Scalability**: Cloud-based data analytics systems can scale up or down based on the input volume of data and traffic, allowing businesses to handle large-scale datasets without having to invest in expensive hardware and infrastructure

- **Cost-effectiveness**: Cloud-based data analytics systems are typically pay-as-you-go, allowing businesses to only pay for the resources they need and avoid extra investment in expensive hardware and infrastructure

- **Flexibility**: Cloud-based data analytics provides a flexible and agile environment for processing and analyzing data, allowing businesses to select the best from different techniques and algorithms

- **Accessibility**: Cloud-based data analytics can be accessed from anywhere with an internet connection, providing a globally accessible and collaborative environment for analyzing data

- **Security**: Cloud-based data analytics provides strong security features, such as encryption, access controls, and compliance with **General Data Protection Regulation** (**GDPR**) and other requirements

AWS provides a suite of data analytics services to manage big data life cycles:

- **Data ingestion**: In *Chapter 1*, we learned about Amazon Snowball and Snowmobile, which transfer large amounts of data from on-premises to the AWS cloud. In this chapter, we will discuss the following data ingestion services:

  - **AWS Glue**: A fully managed ETL service that can automate the process of discovering and cataloging metadata about data sources, generate ETL code to transform and load data, and schedule and run ETL jobs. As part of the AWS Glue service, an **AWS crawler** detects the schema and structure of data and enables users to automatically discover, categorize, and organize their data in various data stores.

- **Amazon Kinesis**: A fully managed service that enables real-time streaming data ingestion at scale. With Kinesis, organizations can easily collect, process, and analyze data from various sources, such as website clickstreams, IoT devices, and social media feeds.

- **Data storage**: In previous chapters, we introduced Amazon cloud storage services such as EBS, EFS, S3, and Glacier. We also discussed Amazon database services such as RDS, DynamoDB, ElastiCache, and Redshift.

- **Data processing**: We will cover the following AWS data processing services:

  - **Amazon EMR**: A managed Hadoop framework that allows you to process large amounts of data using distributed computing. It can also be used to run other distributed data processing frameworks, such as Apache Spark and Apache Hive.

  - **Amazon Athena**: A flexible, serverless, interactive service to analyze structured, semi-structured, or structured data stored in Amazon S3, using SQL or Python.

- **Data visualizing**: We will focus on **Amazon QuickSight**, a **business intelligence (BI)** service that allows users to create interactive visualizations, dashboards, and reports using a web-based interface. QuickSight supports a wide range of data sources, including AWS data services such as Amazon S3, Amazon Redshift, Amazon Athena, and Amazon RDS.

From data ingestion, storing, and processing to visualization, these Amazon cloud tools provide efficient big data management services. Let's start by looking at an Amazon data ingestion service – Amazon Glue and data crawlers.

AWS Glue

As we explained earlier, AWS Glue is an ETL process used to extract data from various sources, transform it into a consistent format and structure, and then load it into a target data repository, such as an S3 bucket or a data warehouse. In an ETL process such as the one used in AWS Glue, the data is typically transformed before it is loaded into the target database. AWS Glue has the following features:

- Automatically generate schemas from semi-structured data by using crawlers, which run on your data sources, derive a schema from them, and populate the Data Catalog. Crawlers can run on many data stores, including Amazon S3, Amazon Redshift, most relational databases, and DynamoDB. By using the metadata in the Data Catalog, you can also automatically generate scripts with AWS Glue extensions as the starting point of your AWS Glue jobs.

- Catalog data and get a unified view with the AWS Glue Data Catalog, which stores metadata including schema information about data sources and targets of your ETL jobs. When ingesting multiple data sources, the Data Catalog provides a centralized location to store and manage metadata about the various data assets across different AWS services.

- Use AWS Glue Studio to author ETL jobs that bring data in from different sources and load it into a target. AWS Glue Studio provides an easy-to-use graphical interface to author ETL jobs. With AWS Glue Studio, you can pull data from Amazon S3 or other sources, configure a transformation that joins or transforms source data, specify a target location for the transformed data, view the schema or a sample of the dataset, and run, monitor, and manage the ETL jobs.

- Perform serverless ETL processing in the AWS Glue Spark runtime engine, which is a serverless compute engine for running ETL jobs. Designed to be highly scalable to process large volumes of data quickly and efficiently, the AWS Glue runtime engine supports both Apache Spark-based jobs, which are heavy-duty and so for large datasets, and Python shell-based jobs, which are lightweight and so for smaller datasets or simple transformations.

- Orchestrate complex ETL tasks with interdependencies by using workflows.

After AWS Glue detects the data from the sources and generates metadata in the target, we can use AWS Athena to query and analyze. Let's look at the Athena service.

Amazon Athena

Amazon Athena is a serverless, interactive, query-managed service that allows users to analyze data stored in Amazon S3 by using standard SQL queries. With Athena, users can easily query data in S3 without the need to set up or manage any infrastructure. Athena is designed to work with a wide variety of data formats, including CSV, JSON, ORC, Parquet, and Avro. It also supports complex data types, such as arrays and maps, making it easy to query nested data structures. Athena has the following features:

- **Serverless architecture**: Athena is a serverless service, which means users don't need to form or manage any infrastructure. AWS takes care of all the underlying infrastructure management, including scaling, monitoring, and maintenance.

- **Standard SQL support**: Athena supports standard SQL, which makes it easy for users to get started and query data using their existing SQL skills.

- **Integration with AWS S3**: Athena integrates seamlessly with Amazon S3, making it easy to analyze data stored in S3 without the need to move the data.

- **Compatibility with popular BI tools**: Athena is compatible with a variety of popular BI tools, including Tableau, Amazon QuickSight, and Microsoft Power BI.

- **Cost-effective**: The service is cost-effective since users only pay for the queries they run.

Now, let's get our hands dirty and provision an AWS Glue service to ingest data from a CSV spreadsheet, and then use the Amazon Athena service to analyze the data with SQL queries:

1. Use S3 to set up **the source and target for the Glue service**, as in the following screenshot:

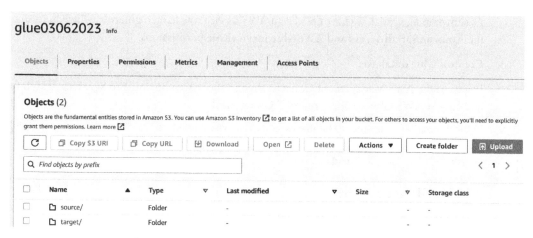

Figure 5.1 – Glue data ingestion source and target store

As shown in *Figure 5.1*, we have created an S3 bucket named **Glue03062023** and two folders underneath – **source**, which has the source data file uploaded from a client, and **target**, which will be the output destination of the AWS Glue crawler job.

2.   Use IAM to create a **role for Glue:**

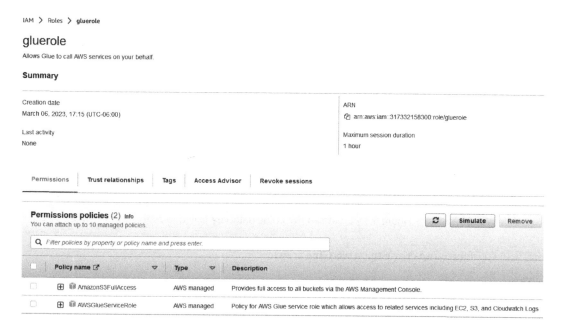

Figure 5.2 – IAM gluerole role in AWS Glue

As shown in *Figure 5.2*, we have created an AWS service role named **gluerole**, which is assigned the **AmazonS3FullAccess** and **AWSGlueServiceRole** permissions.

3. **Create a Glue database:**

    Log in to the AWS Management Console, then in the search box next to **Services**, search for and choose **AWS Glue** to open the AWS Glue console.

    In the navigation pane, under **Databases**, add a database named salesdb, as shown in *Figure 5.3*:

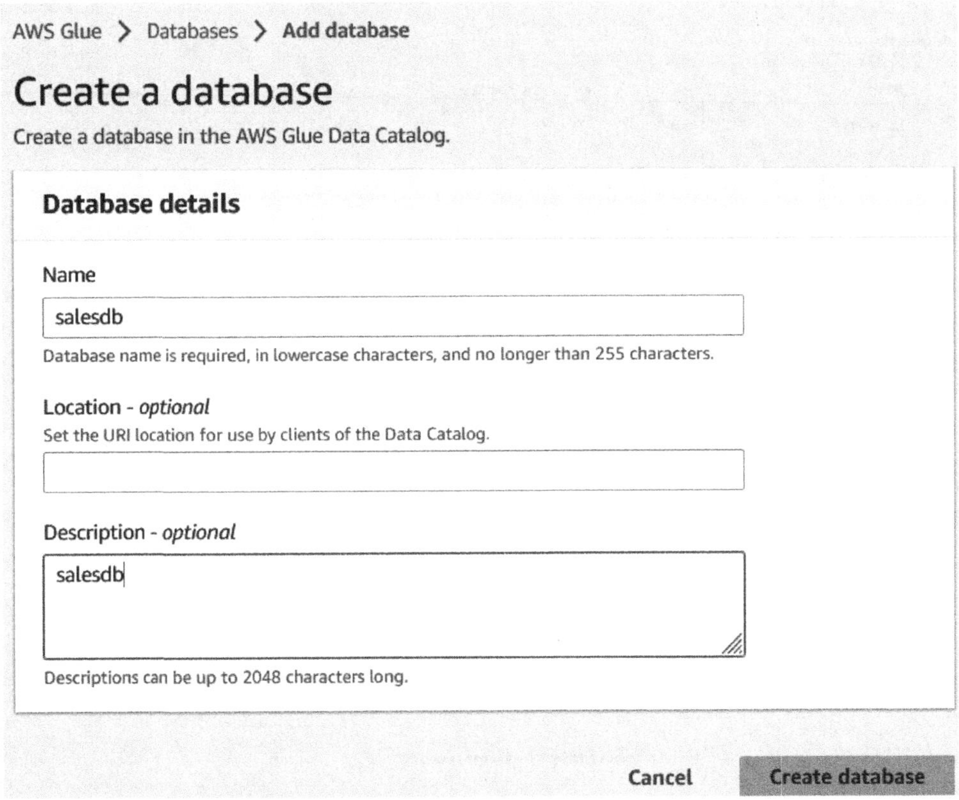

AWS Glue > Databases > **Add database**

Create a database

Create a database in the AWS Glue Data Catalog.

Database details

Name

> salesdb

Database name is required, in lowercase characters, and no longer than 255 characters.

Location - *optional*
Set the URI location for use by clients of the Data Catalog.

Description - *optional*

> salesdb

Descriptions can be up to 2048 characters long.

Cancel   **Create database**

Figure 5.3 – Create an AWS Glue database called salesdb

4. **Configure and create the AWS Glue crawler:**

Under the created database, select **Tables**. Then, click **Add tables using crawler**.

For **Name**, enter `sales`. Click **Next** at the bottom of the page. Select **Add a data source** and configure the following, as shown in *Figure 5.4*:

- **Data sources**: Choose **S3**

- **Location of S3 data**: Choose **in the same account**, and enter the source S3 bucket: `s3://glue03062023/source/`

- **Existing IAM role**: Choose **gluerole**, which we created earlier

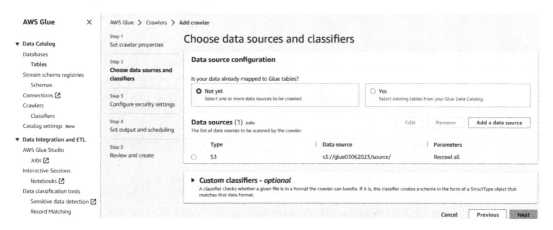

Figure 5.4 – Choose data sources for the Glue crawler

Click **Next**. In the **Output configuration** section, select **Add database**. For **Name**, enter `salesdb`. In the **Crawler schedule** section, for **Frequency**, keep the default **On demand**, as shown in *Figure 5.5*:

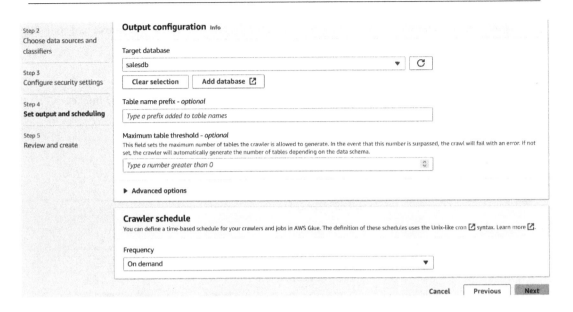

Figure 5.5 – Crawler output configuration

Click **Next** to go to the **Review and create crawler** page, as shown in *Figure 5.6*. Click **Create crawler**:

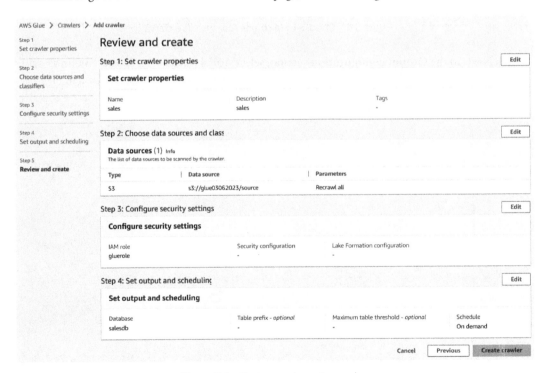

Figure 5.6 – Review and create crawler

5. **Run the crawler:**

After the crawler is created, select it and click **Run**.

The crawler state changes to **Running**, then to **Completed**, as shown in *Figure 5.7*:

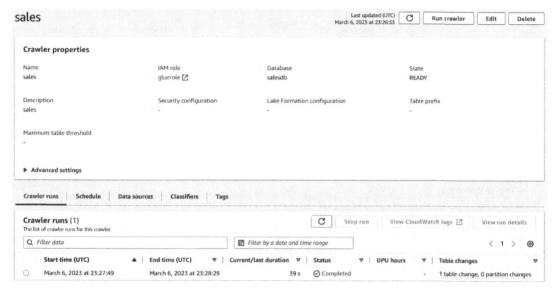

Figure 5.7 – Crawler job was run and completed

6. **Review the metadata that AWS Glue created:**

In the navigation pane, select **Databases**. Choose the link for the **salesdb** database. In the **Tables** section, click the **sales** link.

Review the metadata that the crawler has captured, as shown in *Figure 5.8*. The schema lists the columns that the crawler discovered from the source dataset.

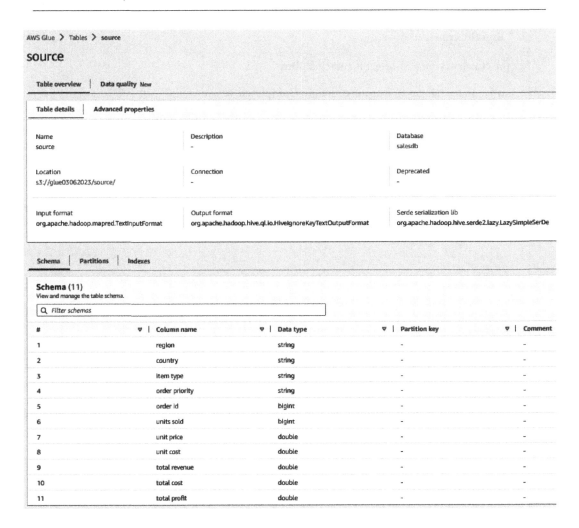

Figure 5.8 – Metadata crawler created

7.   **Edit the data schema:**

From the **Actions** menu in the upper-right corner of the page, choose **Edit schema**. Change the schema as needed and click **Update schema**. *Figure 5.9* shows the updated schema:

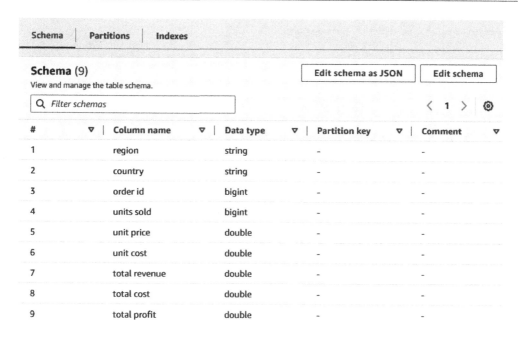

#	Column name	Data type	Partition key	Comment
1	region	string	-	-
2	country	string	-	-
3	order id	bigint	-	-
4	units sold	bigint	-	-
5	unit price	double	-	-
6	unit cost	double	-	-
7	total revenue	double	-	-
8	total cost	double	-	-
9	total profit	double	-	-

Figure 5.9 – Updated schema

8. **Configure an S3 bucket to store Athena query results**:

In the Glue navigation pane, under **Databases**, choose **Tables**. Choose the link for the sales table.

Select **Actions | View data**. When the popup appears to warn you that you will be taken to the Athena console, click **Proceed**.

The Athena console opens. Before you run a query in Athena, you need to specify an S3 bucket to hold the query results.

Click on the **Settings** tab. Choose **Manage**.

To the right of **Location of query result**, click on **Browse S3**. Choose the bucket name **s3://glue03062023/ target**. Select **Choose**. Fill in the **Expected bucket owner** section and then click **Save**, as shown in *Figure 5.10*:

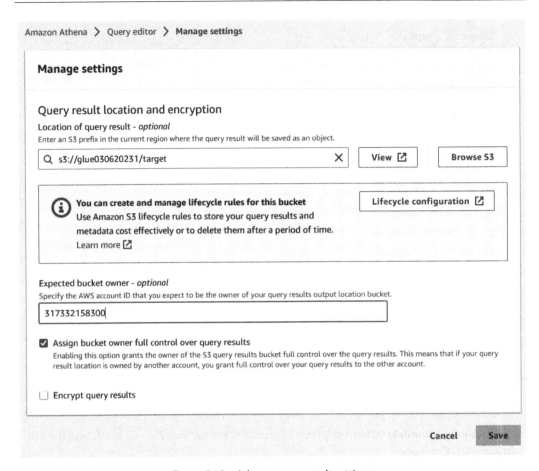

Figure 5.10 – Athena query result settings

9. **Preview a table in Athena**:

Return to the Athena query editor.

Click on the **Editor** tab. In the **Data** panel on the left, notice that the data source is **AwsDataCatalog**. For **Database**, choose **salesdb**.

In the **Tables** section, click the ellipsis (three-dot) icon for the **sales** table, and then select **Preview Table**. The first 10 records from the **sales** table will display.

10. **Create a table for the Europe region**:

In the Athena query editor, copy and paste the following query into a query tab:

```
CREATE table salesdb.region
WITH (
```

```
    format='PARQUET', external_location='s3://glue030620231/
target/'
) AS SELECT * FROM source
where region = 'Europe';
```

Click **Run**. The query and result are shown in *Figure 5.11*:

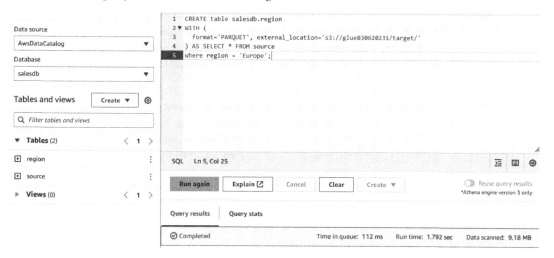

Figure 5.11 – Athena query and result

To preview the results, in the **Tables** section, to the right of the **region** table, click the ellipsis icon, and then select **Preview Table**.

Now that you have isolated the data that you are interested in, you can write queries for further analysis.

Through the preceding process, you learned how to use Athena to query tables in a database that an AWS Glue crawler created. You built a table called `salesdb.region` from the original dataset and store output to the target S3 bucket.

As we can see, AWS Glue created a crawler to ingest the original dataset from the S3 target folder into a database and infer the appropriate schema, which can be edited. Then, using Athena, we can develop queries and better understand the data. This integration reduces the time that it takes to derive insights from the raw data and apply these insights to make better decisions. With AWS Glue, we can batch-ingest data from various data sources.

In the next section, we will switch gears and discuss streaming data ingestion with Amazon Kinesis.

The Amazon Kinesis family

The **Amazon Kinesis** family is a set of fully managed services provided by AWS for streaming data processing and analysis. The family consists of the following main services:

- **Amazon Kinesis Data Streams**: This is a service for collecting and processing large amounts of data in real time from various sources, such as websites, mobile apps, IoT devices, and social media. Data is stored in shards and processed with custom applications. You can use Kinesis Data Streams to process data with Amazon Lambda and other custom applications. Kinesis Data Streams also offers the ability to store data in Amazon S3, enabling you to perform additional analysis on data stored in Amazon S3.

- **Amazon Kinesis Data Firehose**: This is a fully managed service that enables you to capture, transform, and load streaming data into various destinations. Firehose provides a simple and scalable way to capture and transform streaming data from various sources, such as IoT devices, clickstreams, social media feeds, and server logs. Kinesis Data Firehose supports a variety of destination options, including Amazon S3 for cost-effective and durable storage of raw data, Amazon Redshift for data warehousing and analytics, and Amazon Elasticsearch for full-text search and analysis. Kinesis Data Firehose also supports third-party destinations such as Splunk, Datadog, and New Relic.

- **Amazon Kinesis Data Analytics**: This is a fully managed service provided by AWS that enables you to perform real-time data analysis on streaming data using SQL queries. Kinesis Data Analytics provides a simple and scalable way to perform real-time data analysis on streaming data from various sources, such as Amazon Kinesis Data Streams, Amazon Kinesis Data Firehose, and Amazon S3. You can use Kinesis Data Analytics to query data from these sources, apply real-time transformations, and then output the results to a variety of destinations, such as Amazon S3, Amazon Kinesis Data Streams, and Amazon Elasticsearch.

The AWS Kinesis family provides powerful big data processing capacities, such as real-time analytics, machine learning, and security monitoring. *Figure 5.12* shows two paths for data streaming ingestion. In the top path, streaming data from various sources is ingested into **Kinesis Data Streams**, passed to **Kinesis Data Firehose**, and stored in **Amazon S3** for future use. In the second path, after data is ingested into **Kinesis Data Streams**, it is fed to **Kinesis Data Analytics** for real-time analytics:

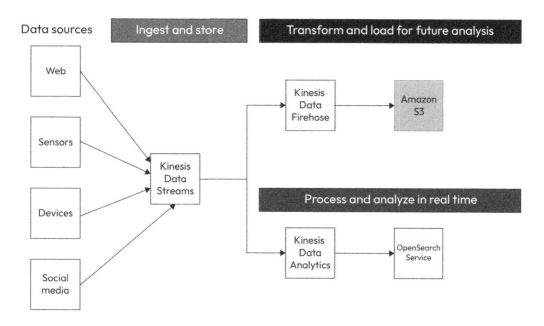

Figure 5.12 – Amazon Kinesis family

As shown in *Figure 5.13*, Kinesis Data Firehose can ingest streaming data and store it in an Amazon cloud storage service such as S3, Redshift, or OpenSearch:

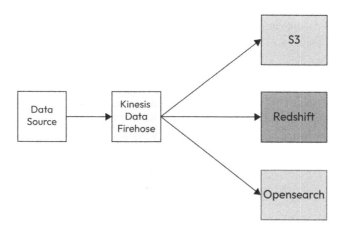

Figure 5.13 – Amazon Kinesis DataFirehose

After introducing the concepts, now let us show how to set Kinesis Firehose up to ingest data and store outputs to Amazon S3 buckets:

1. **Create a target for Kinesis Firehose:**

   Create a target S3 bucket for Firehose to store raw data, as shown in *Figure 5.14*:

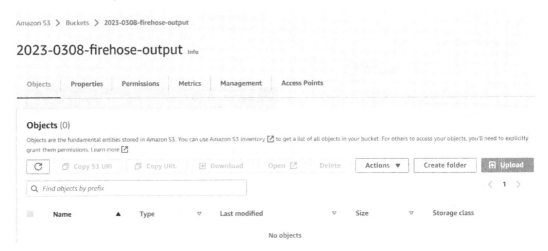

Figure 5.14 – Create a target S3 bucket

2. **Create a Kinesis delivery stream:**

Log in to the AWS console and navigate to **Kinesis**. Click **Create delivery stream**, then fill in the details as shown in *Figure 5.15*.

> **Note**
>
> We have used **Direct PUT** as the source – it means Kinesis Data Firehose will ingest data directly into the source. Also, note that we have used 2 MiB or 120 seconds as the buffer size, whichever comes first, and we have used all the default settings.

Click **Create delivery stream**:

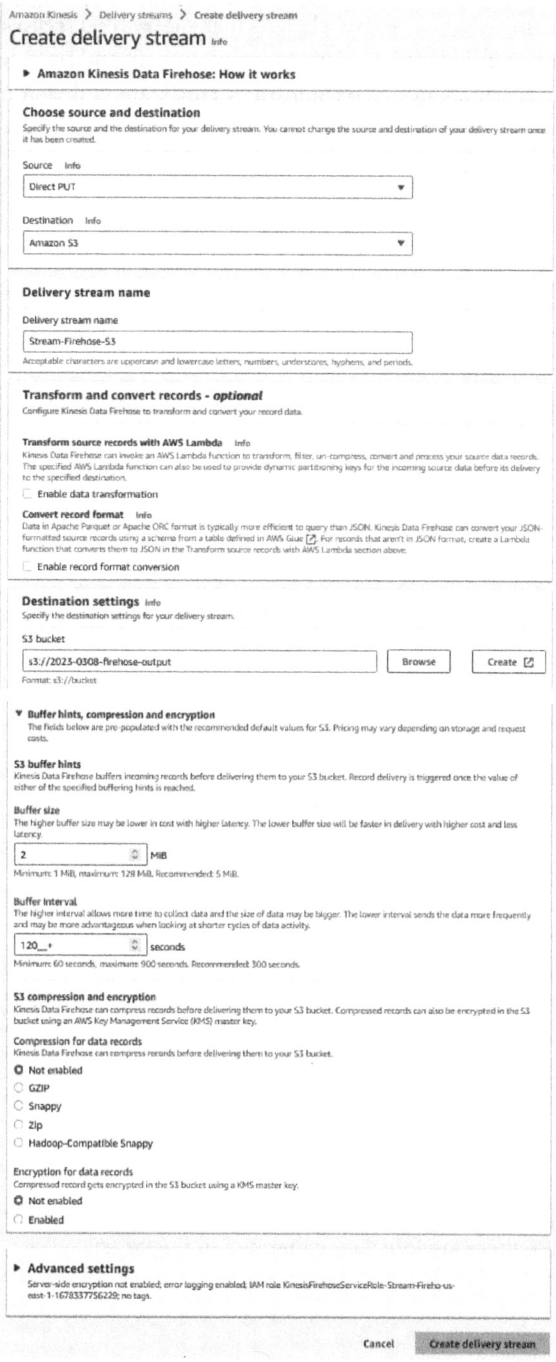

Figure 5.15 – Firehose delivery stream details

3.   **Test with demo data:**

When the delivery stream shows as **Active**, click its name, **Stream-Firehose-S3**, and then click **Test with demo data**, as shown in *Figure 5.16*. This test runs a script and puts demo data in your Kinesis Data Firehose delivery stream. Click **Start sending demo data** and wait for several minutes, then click **Stop sending demo data**:

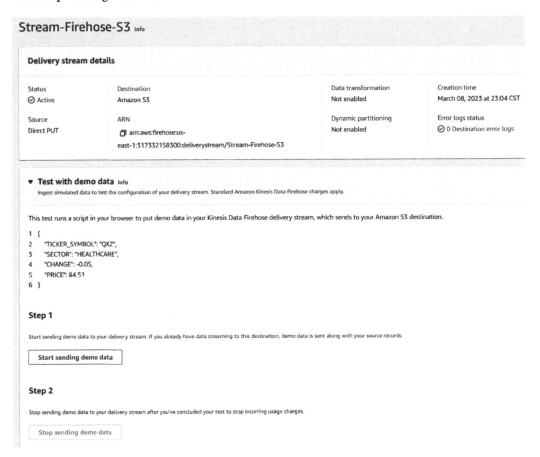

Figure 5.16 – Test with demo data

4.   **Examine the target output:**

Now, check the S3 target folder. You will see output files are generated in the target S3 bucket folder. As shown in *Figure 5.17*, there are four files generated in the target:

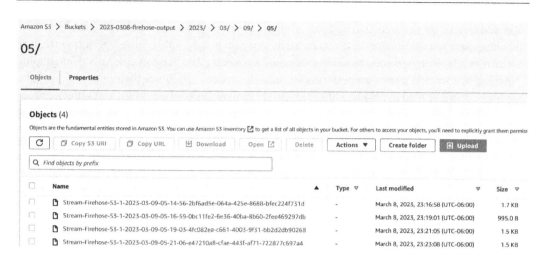

Figure 5.17 – Target output files

With the preceding steps, we have used Kinesis Firehose to directly ingest the demo data and output it into the target S3 folder. In the next section, we will introduce Amazon QuickSight and use it to visualize these output files.

Amazon QuickSight

Amazon QuickSight is a cloud-based BI and data visualization service. It enables users to easily create interactive dashboards, perform ad hoc data analysis, and share insights with others in their organization. Some of the key features of Amazon QuickSight include the following:

- **Data connectivity**: Amazon QuickSight can connect to a wide range of data sources, including AWS services such as Amazon S3, Amazon Redshift, and Amazon RDS, as well as other popular data sources, such as Salesforce, MySQL, and Microsoft Excel.

- **Data preparation**: Amazon QuickSight provides a simple, intuitive interface for preparing data for analysis, including features such as data cleaning, filtering, and aggregation.

- **Data visualization**: Amazon QuickSight offers a variety of visualization options, including charts, tables, and maps, allowing users to easily create interactive dashboards and reports.

- **Team collaboration**: Amazon QuickSight allows users to share dashboards and reports with others in their organization and provides access controls to ensure that data is shared only with authorized users.

- **Integration with other AWS services**: As a virtualization tool, QuickSight integrates seamlessly with the other Amazon data analytics services.

- **Leveraging Super-fast, Parallel, In-memory Calculation Engine (SPICE)**: This is an in-memory data caching service for faster querying and visualization of data.

Amazon QuickSight can be used in Business Intelligence to create dashboards and reports for BI purposes, allowing users to easily analyze and visualize data and gain insights into business performance. It can be used in sales and marketing to analyze sales and marketing data, such as customer demographics, purchase history, and campaign performance, allowing users to optimize their sales and marketing strategies. It can be used in finance and accounting to analyze financial data, such as revenue, expenses, and cash flow, allowing users to monitor financial performance and identify areas for improvement.

Amazon QuickSight is a powerful tool for data visualization and analysis and provides a wide range of features for data connectivity, preparation, and visualization. It is a great platform for businesses to gain insights from their data and make data-driven decisions.

Now we will show how to use QuickSight to visualize the data we generated from Amazon Kinesis Firehose in the previous section:

1. **Sign up for a QuickSight account**

Log in to the AWS console, then navigate to **QuickSight**. Sign up for a QuickSight account if you haven't done so already.

Generate the QuickSight manifest file.

We will use the data file generated by Kinesis Firehose earlier. We need to find the data file URL and create a manifest file named `manifest1`, as shown in *Figure 5.18*:

```
{
    "fileLocations": [
        {
            "URIs": [
                "s3://2023-0308-firehose-output/2023/03/09/05/Stream-Firehose-S3-1-2023-03-09-05-14-56-2bf6ad5e-064a-425e-8688-bfec224f731d"
            ]
        },
    ],
    "globalUploadSettings": {
        "format": "JSON",
        "delimiter": ",",
        "textqualifier": "'",
        "containsHeader": "true"
    }
}
```

Figure 5.18 – QuickSight manifest file

2. **Define the dataset:**

Log in to your QuickSight account, click **New dataset**, and then choose **s3**. Fill in the details in the pop-up window shown in *Figure 5.19*:

Figure 5.19 – Generate dataset

3. **Connect to the dataset:**

Click **Connect**. The new dataset is created, as shown in *Figure 5.20*. Click **Visualize**:

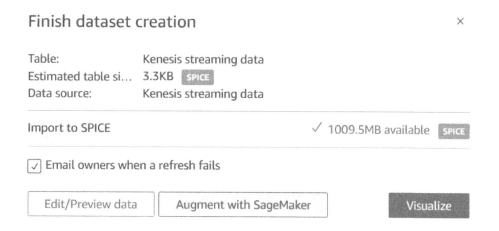

Figure 5.20 – Visualize dataset

4. **Create data visualization:**

There are four fields shown for the dataset. Choose **Bar chart** as the visual type, **Ticker symbol** as the *x* axis, and **Price(sum)** as the *y* axis. A graph will be generated, as shown in *Figure 5.21*:

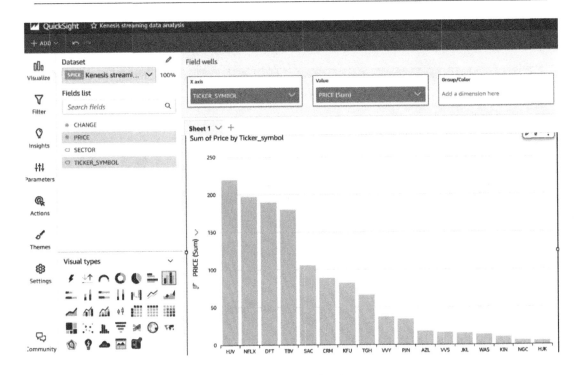

Figure 5.21 – Visualization

This concludes our hands-on exercises on data ingestion using Amazon Kinesis Firehose, storing data in S3, and visualizing data using QuickSight. In the next section, we will examine Amazon EMR, which is a powerful data processing platform.

Amazon EMR

Amazon EMR is a platform for leveraging many big data tools for data processing. We will start by looking at the concepts of MapReduce and Hadoop.

MapReduce and Hadoop

MapReduce and **Hadoop** are two related concepts in the field of distributed computing and big data processing.

The idea of MapReduce is "divide and conquer": decompose a big dataset into smaller ones to be processed in parallel on distributed computers. It was originally developed by Google for its search engine to handle the massive amounts of data generated by web crawling. The MapReduce programming model involves two functions: a map function that divides and processes in parallel the datasets and a map function that aggregates the map outputs.

Hadoop is an open source software framework that implements the MapReduce model. Hadoop consists of two core components: **Hadoop Distributed File System** (**HDFS**) and MapReduce. HDFS is a distributed filesystem that can rapidly transfer data between Hadoop cluster nodes. MapReduce can process big data on distributed nodes and scale massively.

In summary, MapReduce is a programming model that enables parallel processing of large datasets, while Hadoop is a software framework that implements MapReduce and provides a distributed filesystem for storing and managing large datasets.

AWS EMR

AWS EMR is a fully managed cloud service that allows you to easily process large amounts of data using open source tools such as Apache Hadoop, Spark, Hive, Presto, and Flink. With EMR, you can quickly and easily create and configure a Hadoop cluster on AWS infrastructure, allowing you to perform big data processing tasks without the need for upfront hardware investment or management. EMR also provides several useful features, including the following:

- **Pre-installed applications**: EMR comes pre-installed with many popular big data processing tools, allowing you to get started quickly

- **Autoscaling**: EMR automatically scales the cluster based on the workload, allowing you to efficiently use resources and reduce costs

- **Integration with AWS services**: EMR integrates with other AWS services, such as S3, EC2, and CloudWatch, making it easy to move data into and out of the cluster and monitor its performance

- **Security**: EMR provides several security features, including encryption at rest and in transit, secure network configuration, and integration with AWS IAM

- **Storage**: EMR provides different types of storage options, including HDFS and **EMR File System** (**EMRFS**, which extends HDFS to S3)

EMR is a powerful and flexible tool that allows you to easily process large amounts of data using open source tools on AWS infrastructure. The components of an EMR cluster can be classified into four categories: core components, optional components, data sources, and external interfaces.

EMR core components are the main components of an EMR cluster. They include the following:

- **Master nodes**, which act as the entry point to the cluster and manage HDFS, job scheduling, and coordination with other cluster nodes.

- **Core nodes**, which provide compute and storage resources for processing big data jobs. They store data in HDFS, which is the distributed filesystem of the cluster.

- **Task nodes**, which provide additional compute resources to run parallelized tasks in the cluster. Task nodes do not store data in HDFS and are used to offload processing from the core nodes. For cost saving, spot instances can be used for task nodes.

EMR optional components can be added to the cluster based on the use case. Example optional components are the following:

- **Apache HBase**: A distributed, scalable, and NoSQL database system on top of Hadoop
- **Hive**: A data warehousing and SQL-like query engine for Hadoop
- **Pig**: A high-level language for querying large datasets
- **Hue**: A web-based user interface for interacting with Hadoop services
- **Presto**: A distributed SQL query engine designed for interactive analytics
- **Flink**: A real-time streaming data processing framework
- **Spark**: An in-memory big data processing framework

Let's examine two optional EMR components: Apache Hive and Apache Spark.

Apache Hive

Apache Hive is a data warehousing and SQL-like query engine built on top of Hadoop. It provides a high-level abstraction of HDFS and MapReduce, allowing users to write SQL-like queries to analyze large datasets stored in HDFS. Hive is designed to make it easier for analysts and data scientists to work with large datasets without having to write low-level MapReduce code. It supports various data formats, including CSV, JSON, Avro, Parquet, and ORC. Some of the key features of Hive include the following:

- **Schema-on-read**: Hive supports schema-on-read, which means that it can read and interpret data stored in different formats
- **Partitioning**: Hive allows users to partition data based on specific columns, making it easy to query large datasets
- **Data processing**: Hive supports a wide range of data processing functions, such as filtering, sorting, joining, and aggregating
- **User-defined functions** (UDFs): Hive allows users to write custom UDFs to perform complex data processing tasks

Hive is a powerful tool for data analysis and processing, especially for SQL-literate users who are familiar with the SQL language. Hive enables users to work with large datasets stored in Hadoop, using a SQL-like language, which makes it an ideal tool for data warehousing and data analysis tasks.

Apache Spark

Apache Spark is an open source big data processing engine designed to perform fast, in-memory data processing. It is built on top of Hadoop and uses HDFS for distributed storage. Spark provides a programming model called **Resilient Distributed Dataset (RDD)**, which allows developers to perform distributed data processing in a fault-tolerant manner. RDD is an immutable distributed collection of objects that can be processed in parallel across a cluster of machines. Spark provides a wide range of libraries and APIs to perform various data processing tasks, including the following:

- **Spark Core**: Provides the basic functionality of Spark, including RDD and distributed task scheduling
- **Spark SQL**: A module for structured data processing
- **Spark Streaming**: A module for the real-time processing of streaming data
- **MLlib**: A library for machine learning and data mining tasks
- **GraphX**: A library for processing graph data

Some of the key features of Spark include the following:

- **In-memory processing**: Spark uses in-memory processing to speed up data processing tasks
- **Fault tolerance**: Spark provides fault tolerance through RDD, which can be reconstructed if a node fails
- **Scalability**: Spark can scale to thousands of nodes in a cluster, making it suitable for processing large datasets
- **Compatibility**: Spark can run on Hadoop YARN, Mesos, and standalone clusters

Apache Spark is a powerful big data processing engine that provides fast, in-memory processing of large datasets. It provides a wide range of libraries and APIs to perform various data processing tasks, making it an ideal tool for big data analytics, machine learning, and real-time processing of streaming data.

Now we will create an EMR cluster and submit a workload to an Amazon EMR cluster:

1. **Launch an EMR cluster**:

Log in to the AWS console and select the EMR service. From the left navigation pane, choose **Clusters | Create Cluster | Advanced Options**.

First, fill in the **Software and Steps** section, as shown in *Figure 5.22*:

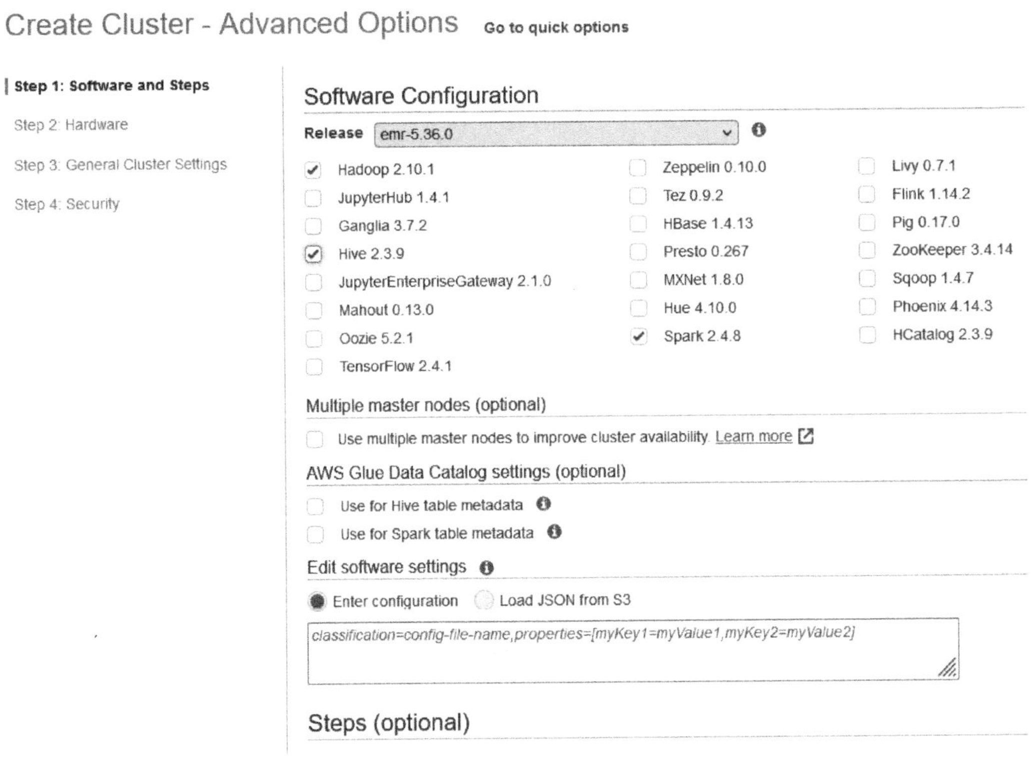

Create Cluster - Advanced Options   Go to quick options

| Step 1: Software and Steps

Step 2: Hardware

Step 3: General Cluster Settings

Step 4: Security

Software Configuration

Release [emr-5.36.0]

☑ Hadoop 2.10.1	☐ Zeppelin 0.10.0	☐ Livy 0.7.1
☐ JupyterHub 1.4.1	☐ Tez 0.9.2	☐ Flink 1.14.2
☐ Ganglia 3.7.2	☐ HBase 1.4.13	☐ Pig 0.17.0
☑ Hive 2.3.9	☐ Presto 0.267	☐ ZooKeeper 3.4.14
☐ JupyterEnterpriseGateway 2.1.0	☐ MXNet 1.8.0	☐ Sqoop 1.4.7
☐ Mahout 0.13.0	☐ Hue 4.10.0	☐ Phoenix 4.14.3
☐ Oozie 5.2.1	☑ Spark 2.4.8	☐ HCatalog 2.3.9
☐ TensorFlow 2.4.1		

Multiple master nodes (optional)

☐ Use multiple master nodes to improve cluster availability. Learn more ↗

AWS Glue Data Catalog settings (optional)

☐ Use for Hive table metadata ❶
☐ Use for Spark table metadata ❶

Edit software settings ❶

◉ Enter configuration   ◯ Load JSON from S3

```
classification=config-file-name,properties=[myKey1=myValue1,myKey2=myValue2]
```

Steps (optional)

Figure 5.22 – EMR cluster creation step 1

Then, move on to step 2, which is filling in the hardware details, as shown in *Figure 5.23*:

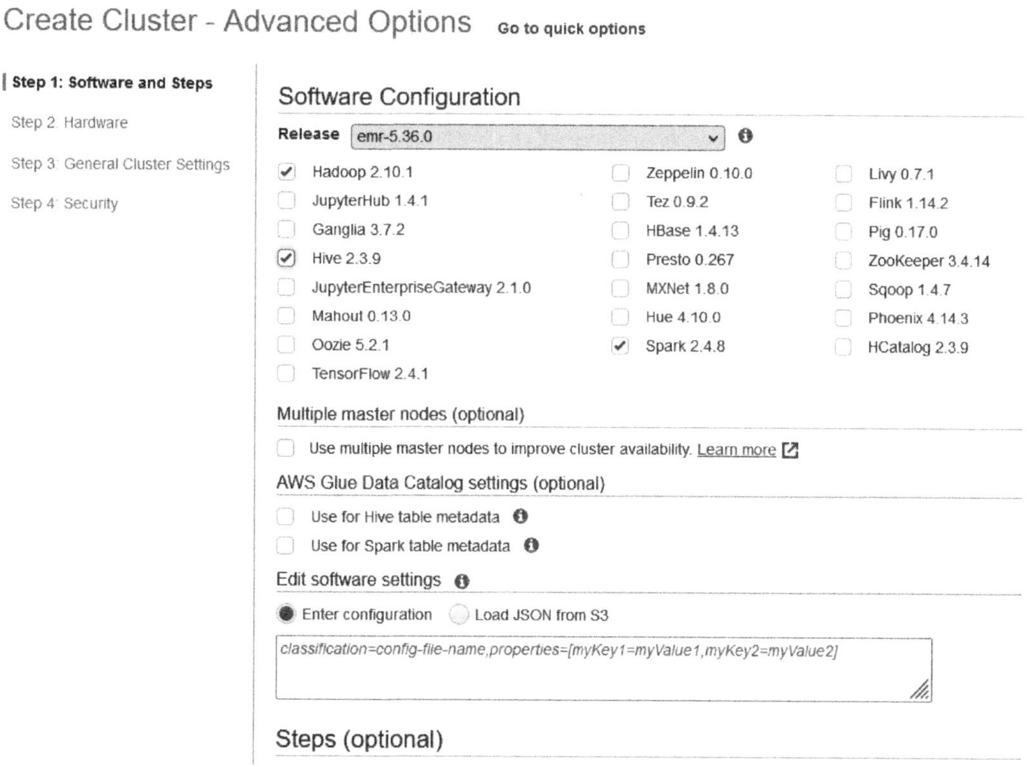

Create Cluster - Advanced Options   Go to quick options

| Step 1: Software and Steps

Step 2: Hardware

Step 3: General Cluster Settings

Step 4: Security

Software Configuration

Release   emr-5.36.0   ⌄   ⓘ

☑ Hadoop 2.10.1	☐ Zeppelin 0.10.0	☐ Livy 0.7.1
☐ JupyterHub 1.4.1	☐ Tez 0.9.2	☐ Flink 1.14.2
☐ Ganglia 3.7.2	☐ HBase 1.4.13	☐ Pig 0.17.0
☑ Hive 2.3.9	☐ Presto 0.267	☐ ZooKeeper 3.4.14
☐ JupyterEnterpriseGateway 2.1.0	☐ MXNet 1.8.0	☐ Sqoop 1.4.7
☐ Mahout 0.13.0	☐ Hue 4.10.0	☐ Phoenix 4.14.3
☐ Oozie 5.2.1	☑ Spark 2.4.8	☐ HCatalog 2.3.9
☐ TensorFlow 2.4.1		

Multiple master nodes (optional)

☐ Use multiple master nodes to improve cluster availability. Learn more ☐

AWS Glue Data Catalog settings (optional)

☐ Use for Hive table metadata   ⓘ
☐ Use for Spark table metadata   ⓘ

Edit software settings   ⓘ

● Enter configuration   ◯ Load JSON from S3

classification=config-file-name,properties=[myKey1=myValue1,myKey2=myValue2]

Steps (optional)

Figure 5.23 – EMR cluster creation step 2

For the third step, fill in the general cluster settings, as shown in *Figure 5.24*:

Figure 5.24 – EMR cluster creation step 3

For the fourth step, fill in the security options, as shown in *Figure 5.25*:

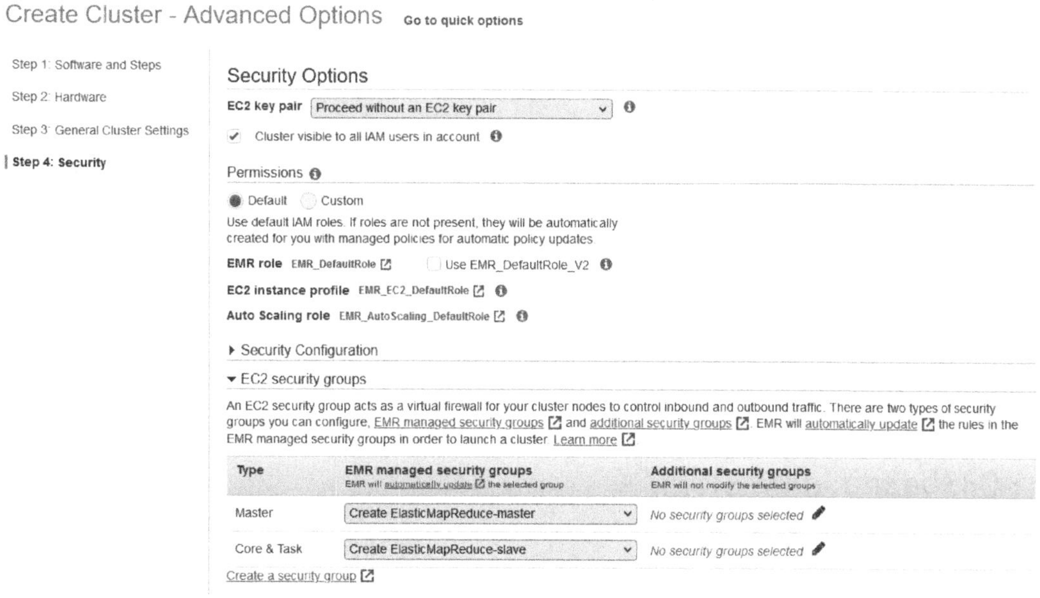

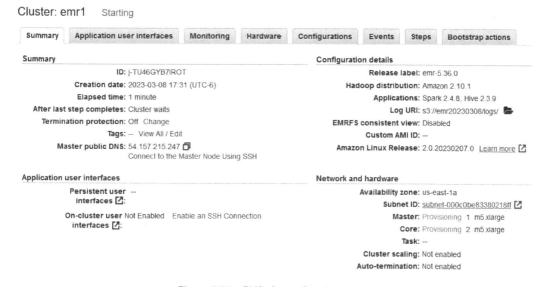

Figure 5.25 – EMR cluster creation step 4

Create the EMR cluster. It will show the state as **Starting**, as shown in *Figure 5.26*:

Figure 5.26 – EMR cluster Starting state

The nodes (EC2 instances) and S3 buckets will be created, as shown in *Figure 5.27*:

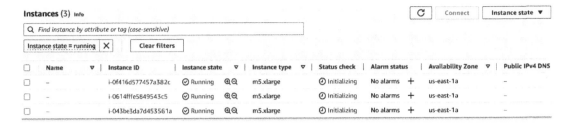

Figure 5.27 – EMR cluster nodes

The S3 buckets are created as the output locations for the cluster, as shown in *Figure 5.28*.

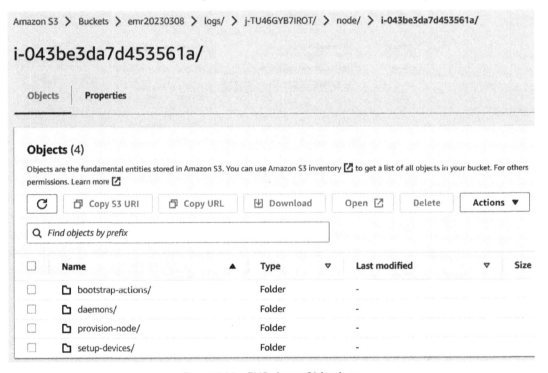

Figure 5.28 – EMR cluster S3 buckets

The cluster status changes from **Starting** to **Waiting** when the cluster is up, running, and ready to accept work, as shown in *Figure 5.29*:

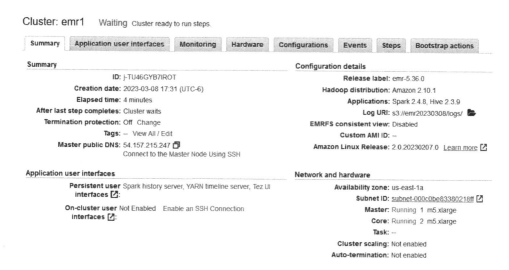

Figure 5.29 – EMR cluster in the Waiting state

2. **Submit Spark work to process food inspection data**

We will now use Apache Spark in the EMR cluster to process a big data CSV spreadsheet called
`food_inspection_data.csv`, which has 200,000 rows. We will find the top 10 names that
have the most violations. The table columns are shown in *Figure 5.30*:

name	inspection_ result	inspection_closed business	violation type	violation points
100 LB CLAM	Incomplete	FALSE		0
100 LB CLAM	Unsatisfactor	FALSE	BLUE	5
100 LB CLAM	Unsatisfactor	FALSE	RED	5
100 LB CLAM	Unsatisfactor	FALSE	RED	10
100 LB CLAM	Unsatisfactor	FALSE	RED	5
100 LB CLAM	Complete	FALSE		0
100 LB CLAM	Complete	FALSE		0
100 PERCENT NUTRICION	Unsatisfactor	FALSE	BLUE	5
100 PERCENT NUTRICION	Unsatisfactor	FALSE	BLUE	5
100 PERCENT NUTRICION	Unsatisfactor	FALSE	RED	10
100 PERCENT NUTRICION	Unsatisfactor	FALSE	RED	5
1000 SPIRITS	Satisfactory	FALSE	BLUE	5
1000 SPIRITS	Satisfactory	FALSE		0
1000 SPIRITS	Unsatisfactor	FALSE	RED	5
1000 SPIRITS	Complete	FALSE		0
1000 SPIRITS	Satisfactory	FALSE	BLUE	5
1000 SPIRITS	Satisfactory	FALSE		0
1000 SPIRITS	Unsatisfactor	FALSE	BLUE	5
1000 SPIRITS	Unsatisfactor	FALSE	BLUE	2
1000 SPIRITS	Unsatisfactor	FALSE	RED	25
1000 SPIRITS	Unsatisfactor	FALSE	RED	25
1000 SPIRITS	Unsatisfactor	FALSE	BLUE	5
1000 SPIRITS	Unsatisfactor	FALSE	RED	5

Figure 5.30 – Input big data spreadsheet

Since the EMR cluster is launched and ready, we will submit a Spark script to the cluster to process our data, as a step (EMR Step is a unit of work that contains instructions to manipulate data for processing in the EMR cluster).

The file `emr_process.py` Spark script is shown here:

```python
import argparse
from pyspark.sql import SparkSession
def calculate_red_violations(data_source, output_target):
    with SparkSession.builder.appName("Calculate Red Health
Violations").getOrCreate() as spark:
        # Load the violation CSV data
        if data_source is not None:
            restaurants_df = spark.read.option("header",
"true").csv(data_source)
        # Create an in-memory DataFrame to query
        restaurants_df.createOrReplaceTempView("restaurant_
violations")
        # Create a DataFrame of the top 10 restaurants with the
most Red violations
        top_red_violation_restaurants = spark.sql("""SELECT
name, count(*) AS total_red_violations
        FROM restaurant_violations
        WHERE violation_type = 'RED'
        GROUP BY name
        ORDER BY total_red_violations DESC LIMIT 10""")
        # Write the results to the specified target
        top_red_violation_restaurants.write.option("header",
"true").mode("overwrite").csv(output_target)
if __name__ == "__main__":
    parser = argparse.ArgumentParser()
    parser.add_argument(
        '--data_source', help="Data Source location.")
    parser.add_argument(
        '--output_target', help="Output target location.")
    args = parser.parse_args()

    calculate_red_violations(args.data_source, args.output_
target)
```

Upload the Spark script, `emr_process.py`, to the S3 bucket, `s3://emr20230308/`.

Upload the source spreadsheet, `s3://emr20230308/source/food_inspection_data.csv`, and create a target S3 folder, `s3://emr20230308/target`. We are now ready for the next step.

Click the cluster, click the **Steps** tab, and then select **Add step**. Fill in the step details as shown in *Figure 5.31*:

- For **Step type**, choose **Spark application**.

- For **Name**, enter Spark application.

- For **Deploy mode**, keep the default "**Cluster**".

- For **Application location**, enter the Spark script, s3://emr20230308/emr_process.py.

- In the **Arguments** field, enter the following arguments and values:

  - --data_source s3://emr20230308/source/food_inspection_data.csv

  - --output_target s3://emr20230308/target

This is shown in the following screenshot:

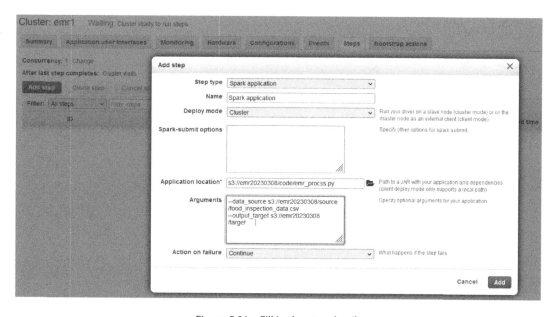

Figure 5.31 – Fill in the step details

Click **Add** to submit the Spark step. Initially, the status will show as **Pending**, but it will change to **Running** and then **Completed**, as shown in *Figure 5.32*:

Figure 5.32 – Spark step is complete

Now, you can view its output results in your Amazon S3 output folder. As shown in *Figure 5.33*, there are two files generated from the Spark step:

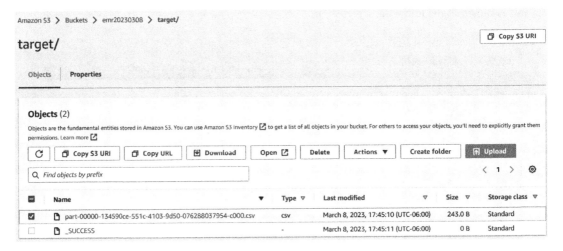

Figure 5.33 – Spark step target folder

Download the results to your local filesystem. *Figure 5.34* shows the content of the CSV spreadsheet – the EMR processing result of the submitted Spark step:

	A	B	C
1	name	total_red_violations	
2	PCC COMMUNITY MARKETS	251	
3	MCDONALD'S	177	
4	SAFEWAY INC #1508	143	
5	HIMITSU TERIYAKI	128	
6	NASAI TERIYAKI	119	
7	SAFEWAY # 1965	119	
8	SAFEWAY STORES INC #1550	118	
9	SAFEWAY STORE #1477	115	
10	SAFEWAY #1993	115	
11	FRED MEYER INC #179	111	
12			

Figure 5.34 – Spark step processing result

3. **Submit a Hive step to process CloudFront data**

With the same procedure, we submit a Hive step to process some CloudFront data, with the following code, source, target, and step submission shown in *Figure 5.35*:

```
s3://us-east-1.elasticmapreduce.samples/cloudfront/code/Hive_
CloudFront.q
```

```
s3://us-east-1.elasticmapreduce.samples
```

```
s3://emr20230308/hive/target
```

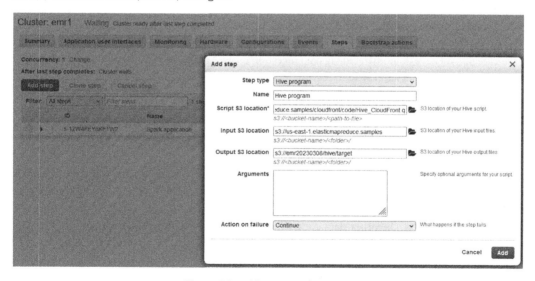

Figure 5.35 – Hive step submission

As shown in *Figure 5.36*, there are two files generated from the Hive step. Download them to your local filesystem. Please compare the source data and target processing results.

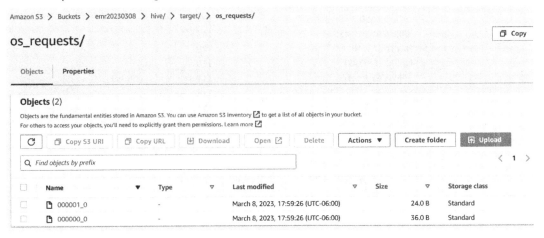

Figure 5.36 – Hive step output files

To recap, we have launched an EMR cluster and added two steps for the big data process: a Spark step and a Hive step. As you can see, both steps of big data processing takes less than a minute to process a big amount of data.

Summary

In this chapter, we explained big data analytics in the AWS cloud: ingestion, storing, processing, and visualization. We introduced AWS big data services including Glue, Kinesis, Athena, EMR, and QuickSight. We have demonstrated big data ingestion using AWS Glue and Kinesis, big data processing using Amazon Athena and EMR, and visualization using Quicksight, S3 stores the big datasets.

In the next chapter, we will discuss the Amazon machine learning services.

Practice questions

Questions 1-8 are based on the data analytics pipeline in the AWS cloud shown in *Figure 5.37*. An engineer is designing a pipeline that will ingest long-term, big-volume streaming data from the web using Kinesis Data Streams, then make two copies: one copy pass to Kinesis Firehose and stored in an Amazon S3 bucket, the other data copy will be processed with Amazon EMR and then queried by Athena and visualized using Amazon QuickSight. Performance and costs are the main factors to be taken into account.

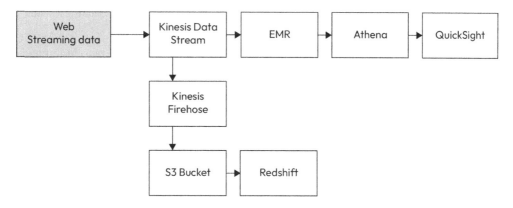

Figure 5.37 – Data analytics pipeline in the AWS cloud (redraw)

1. What instances would you recommend for the EMR cluster?

    A. Reserved Instances for the cluster

    B. Spot Instances for core and task nodes and a Reserved Instance for the master node

    C. Spot Instances for the cluster

    D. On-demand instances for the cluster

2. What filesystem would you recommend for the EMR cluster?

    A. HDFS with a consistent view

    B. EMRFS with a consistent view

    C. HDFS

    D. EBS on the cluster nodes

3. A senior manager needs to see the web data traffic trends for weekends from QuickSight. What is your recommendation?

    A. A line graph plotting traffic versus time

    B. A pie chart plotting traffic per day of the week

    C. A heatmap overlay to show the volume of traffic

    D. A bar graph plotting location versus web traffic

4. Several rows in a Redshift table were accidentally deleted. What is your recommendation to restore the rows from a snapshot?

    A. Restore from the snapshot to a new Redshift cluster. Truncate the table in the original cluster and copy the table from the new cluster.

B. Restore to a new table from the snapshot. Drop the original table and rename the new table to the original table name.

C. Restore from the snapshot to a new cluster. Create a link between the two clusters and copy the data from the new cluster.

D. Restore from the snapshot and overwrite the original table.

5. Right after the data is output from Kinesis Firehose to S3, it will be sent to Redshift, and the S3 data will be kept for 30 days before moving to the Infrequent Access tier and being deleted in a year. What's your recommendation for the S3 data storage?

A. Archive it in Glacier till deletion

B. Use standard S3 till it's deleted

C. Leverage S3 life cycle management

D. Enable S3 versioning

6. New regulation requires that only authorized staff can access customers' Social Security numbers in the data ingested from the social media.

What's your recommendation for handling this sensitive information?

A. Mask the Social Security numbers in Kinesis data stream ingestion

B. Store a cryptographic hash of the Social Security numbers

C. Encrypt the Social Security numbers with a key and share the key only with authorized staff

D. Encrypt the Social Security numbers with a key and give the decryption key only to authorized staff

7. A Spark step will be added to the EMR cluster for machine learning model training. What instances will you choose?

A. C instance types

B. R instance types

C. T instance types

D. D instance types

8. Senior management needs QuickSight visual reports every Monday morning, regarding the previous weekend's social media engagement. What's your recommendation for the EMR cluster?

A. Keep the EMR up and generate reports every Monday morning

B. Use a transient EMR cluster to generate reports every Monday morning

C. Use Spark Streaming on EMR to aggregate and generate reports every Monday morning

D. Use the EMR cluster to aggregate media data each night and use QuickSight to report on Monday morning

Answers to the practice questions

1. B

2. B

3. A

4. B

5. C

6. B

7. A

8. B

Further reading

For further insights into what you've learned in this chapter, refer to the following links:

- `https://aws.amazon.com/glue`

- `https://aws.amazon.com/kinesis/`

- `https://aws.amazon.com/athena/`

- `https://aws.amazon.com/emr/`

- `https://aws.amazon.com/quicksight/`

- `https://docs.aws.amazon.com/emr/index.html`

- `https://docs.aws.amazon.com/quicksight/index.html`

6
Amazon Machine Learning Services

We discussed cloud databases and big data analytics in previous chapters. Part of the data analytics spectrum, **machine learning** (**ML**) involves building models or algorithms that enable computers to analyze and learn from data, identify patterns, relationships, and trends that can be used to make predictions or decisions.

Cloud-based ML platforms provide a range of tools and services to support ML workflows of data preparation, feature engineering, model training, tuning, and deployment. Cloud ML can be used for **computer vision**, **natural language processing** (**NLP**), and many other predictive analytics tasks. The Amazon cloud provides platforms for engineers and data scientists to develop ML models from end to end. In this chapter, we will discuss the following topics:

- **ML basics**: What is ML? What are the objectives of ML? What problems can be solved using ML? What are some basic ML problems?

- **Amazon SageMaker**: A fully managed AWS ML service that allows users to build, train, and deploy ML models from end to end and at scale.

- **Deep learning (DL) basics**: What are neural networks and DL models? What are their components, and how do we construct and train a DL model?

- **Amazon computer vision** solutions using DL, mainly Amazon Rekognition – a DL-based image and video analysis service.

- **Amazon NLP solutions** using DL, including the following:

  - **Amazon Comprehend**, which uncovers valuable insights and connections in text

  - **Amazon Transcribe**, which is a speech-to-text service that can transcribe audio and video recordings into text

- **Amazon Polly**, which is a text-to-speech service

- **Amazon Translate**, which translates text between languages

- **Amazon Lex**, which can be used to build application interfaces that are based on voice and text

During our discussions, we will use some examples. The sample code is available in the GitHub repository for this book: `https://github.com/PacktPublishing/Self-Taught-Cloud-computing-Engineer`.

The AWS ML services can be used individually or in combination to build a wide range of ML applications, such as recommendation systems, chatbots, and predictive systems. Let's start with an introduction to ML basics and ML pipelines.

ML basics and ML pipelines

What is ML? ML is a subfield of **artificial intelligence** (**AI**) that focuses on building models and algorithms to learn patterns and relationships from data and make predictions or decisions. A typical ML project involves the following process – the so-called ML pipeline:

- **Problem framing**: Define ML problems from business projects

- **Data collection**: Collect data from various sources, which may involve data labeling

- **Data evaluation**: Examine the data using statistical tools

- **Feature engineering**: Select and extract model features and targets

- **Model training**: Train the model with the training dataset

- **Model verification**: Verify the model with the verification dataset

- **Model testing**: Test the model with the testing dataset

- **Model deployment**: Deploy the ML model to production

Figure 6.1 shows the ML pipeline, which is an iterative process to collect data and develop ML models for deployment:

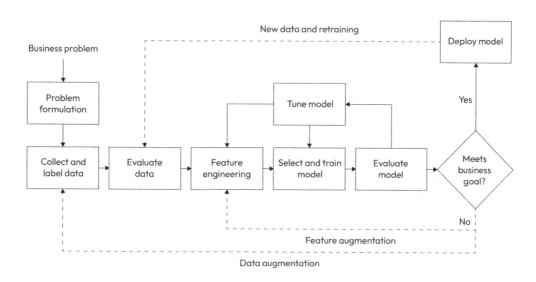

Figure 6.1 – ML pipeline

In the next subsections, we will examine the ML pipeline and discuss each stage of the pipeline in more detail.

ML problem framing

The first stage in the ML pipeline is defining the problem we need to solve and the goal we need to reach. Understanding the business goal of the problem is key in this stage since we will use the defined goal to measure the performance of our solution. During this stage, we will examine the problem and decide whether ML is the right approach to solve the problem. While ML is very useful for many business projects, it may not be the best solution for all problems. To decide whether ML is a good solution for a problem, we need to ask the following questions:

- What is the success measurement of the problem?
- What are the traditional ways of solving the problem?
- Is there enough quality data to solve the problem using ML?

After we have fully explored these questions and drawn the conclusion that ML is the best approach for the problem, we will further review the problem and data and see what type of ML problem it is. ML problems can be broadly classified into three categories:

- **Supervised learning** is training a model based on labeled data and then using the trained model to predict the output for new input data. For example, we can predict house prices based on historical sales data.

- **Unsupervised learning** involves training a model on unlabeled data to identify patterns and relationships.

- **Reinforcement learning** involves training a model based on feedback from the environment, where the algorithm learns to maximize a reward signal by taking steps toward the highest reward.

Once we have framed the ML problem and determined the ML model type, we will collect and prepare the dataset.

Data collection and preparation

The objective of this stage is to make sure that the datasets represent the real ML problem and are in the right format for ML model training. Since data usually comes from many different sources in different formats, we often use statistical techniques to sample, balance, and scale datasets and handle missing values and outliers in the datasets. Python data science libraries are powerful tools to manipulate data at this stage. This includes NumPy, Pandas, Matplotlib, and Seaborn:

- **NumPy** is a general-purpose array-processing Python library that is very good at carrying out array operations.

- **Pandas** is considered a powerful data analysis and manipulation library. It contains data structures for storing and manipulating multi-dimensional arrays.

- **Matplotlib** is a graphics Python library for data visualization. It is well integrated with NumPy and pandas.

- **Seaborn** is another data visualization library. It supports built-in Python types, such as lists and dictionaries, and objects from pandas and NumPy.

We will leverage these Python data science libraries in this chapter.

Feature engineering

After we have explored the data, we need to select and extract the model features, which are the columns of data that have the most impact on the model. **Feature selection** refers to selecting the *features* that are most relevant to the model *target*. We want to select a good number of features to avoid model underfitting or overfitting, and also build up valuable information by formatting, transforming, or combining features.

For example, **feature crossing** is a feature extraction method to synthesize two or more features into one, which will provide predictive abilities beyond what the original features can provide individually. *Figure 6.2* shows the relationship between the *target* and *features* (x and y) of a model. As we can see, it is difficult to build a model on these features, but if we synthesize a new feature from the original using a formula ($x^*x + y^*y$), then the model will be much easier to understand and process:

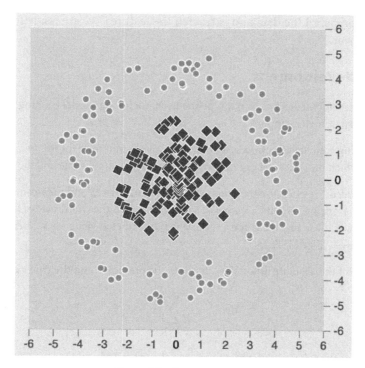

Figure 6.2 – Feature crossing

Another example is transforming categorical feature values into numerical, since computers only understand numbers. For ordinal categories such as cost, we can encode them using numbers, for example, *Low* to 1, *Medium* to 2, *High* to 3, and *Very High* to 4. But for non-ordinal categories, such as color, we need to use *one-hot encoding* to transform the different colors, as shown in *Figure 6.3*:

Color		Red	Blue	Green
Red	→	1	0	0
Blue		0	1	0
Green		0	0	1
Blue		0	1	0
Green		0	0	1

Figure 6.3 – One-hot encoding

There are also times when we need to handle missing values and outliers in the dataset. Depending on the case, we can either drop the missing values or impute them with the mean or median value for the feature. Outliers are values that lie far from other values, and we may need to delete, scale, or impute them based on the specific situation.

After we have prepared the data and extracted the features, we are ready for the next stage: model development.

ML model development

The ML model development process is a pipeline itself, including model training, model validation, and model hyperparameter tuning.

ML model training is an iterative process with the objective to minimize the *loss function* (also called the cost function), which measures the gap between the forecasted target value and the actual target value.

For regression models, we often use the **mean absolute error** (**MAE**) and **mean squared error** (**MSE**) as loss functions. Denote N is the number of samples. (x_i, y_i) is the coordinate of the ith sample data point; that is, if y_i is the actual value for x_i, and $\hat{y}$ is the predicted value for x_i, then the loss function can be defined as MAE or MSE.

MAE is the sum of the absolute differences between the predicted and the true values:

$$MAE = \frac{1}{N}\sum_{i=1}^{N}|y_i - \hat{y}_i\|$$

MSE is the sum of the squared differences between the predicted and the true values:

$$MSE = \frac{1}{N}\sum_{i=1}^{N}(y_i - \hat{y}_i)^2$$

For classification models, the cost function is the difference between the probability distributions for different classes. For binary classification models where the model outputs are binary (1 for yes or 0 for no), we use **binary cross-entropy**; for multi-class classification models, we use **categorical cross-entropy** or **sparse categorical cross-entropy**, based on the input dataset labels. More details are available at https://gombru.github.io/2018/05/23/cross_entropy_loss/.

To minimize the loss function, we leverage many ML algorithms, such as **linear regression**, **logistic regression**, **gradient descent**, **support vector machine**, **decision trees**, and **random forest**. For more details about these algorithms and how to choose the right one, please refer to https://learn.microsoft.com/en-us/azure/machine-learning/how-to-select-algorithms.

Among these ML algorithms, there is a popular one that we will use in this chapter – called **Extreme Gradient Boosting** (**XGBoost**). XGBoost is a class of boosting algorithms that iteratively adds weak learners to a model to improve its performance. Building on decision trees and using a gradient-boosting framework, XGBoost starts from a very general model and then refines it by adding weak learners using gradient descent methods. Over the years, XGBoost has become a popular choice in the ML community, and it is available in several programming languages, including Python, R, Java, and Scala.

For more details, please refer to `https://www.nvidia.com/en-us/glossary/data-science/xgboost/`.

ML model validation is the stage to verify the performance of the trained model. Typically, at the beginning of an ML model development process, we divide the dataset into training, validation, and testing datasets. These datasets are randomly split and are independent of each other. In the validation process, we also use the loss function to measure the gap between the predicted and actual target values for the validation dataset, and thus validate the model performance.

As we discussed earlier, the MAE and MSE can be used to validate regression models. For classification models, a **confusion matrix** is usually created to measure the model's performance. *Figure 6.4* shows a confusion matrix example for a binary classification problem of predicting whether an image is a cat. As you can see, **true positive** (**TP**) refers to cases where the image is predicted to be a cat and it is a cat; **false positive** (**FP**) refers to when the image is predicted to be a cat but it is not in fact a cat; **false negative** (**FN**) refers to when the image is predicted to not be a cat but it is a cat; and **true negative** (**TN**) is when the image is predicted not to be a cat and it is not a cat.

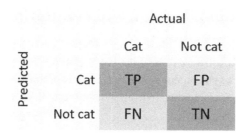

Figure 6.4 – Confusion matrix

Once we have created the confusion matrix, we can calculate the model performance stats for validation. The most used stats are as follows:

- **Recall** (**sensitivity**) measures the proportion of actual positives that were identified correctly:

  Recall = TP/(TP+FN)

- **Specificity** measures the proportion of actual negatives that were identified correctly:

  Specificity = TN/(FP+TN)

- **Precision** measures the proportion of positive identifications that are correct:

  Precision=TP/(TP+FP)

More details on model validation and the confusion matrix can be found at `https://www.sciencedirect.com/topics/engineering/confusion-matrix` and `https://towardsdatascience.com/supervised-machine-learning-model-validation-a-step-by-step-approach-771109ae0253`.

Many times during model training and validation, we come across model underfitting and overfitting. **Model underfitting** describes the situation where the prediction error is not minimized, and model overfitting is when the model fits the training dataset very well but does not fit the validation dataset. We want to avoid both underfitting and overfitting and make a good fit/robust model. There are many techniques we can use.

For more details, please refer to `https://www.geeksforgeeks.org/underfitting-and-overfitting-in-machine-learning/`.

ML model hyperparameter tuning is the process of selecting the best set of hyperparameters for an ML model to maximize its performance on a given dataset. Hyperparameters are not learned by the model during training but are specified by the user at the beginning of the training process, such as the learning rate, number of epochs, and batch size.

For more details, please refer to `https://cloud.google.com/ai-platform/training/docs/hyperparameter-tuning-overview`.

ML model deployment, testing, and monitoring

After the model is trained, tuned, and validated, we will deploy it in a production environment, with the necessary hardware and software to host the prediction service. Model testing means testing a model in a production-like environment and monitoring its performance to detect any issues. After the model is deployed to the production environment and tested, we still need to monitor the model performance and retrain it as needed.

Now that we have introduced the basic ML concepts and ML pipeline, let's take a look at Amazon SageMaker and go through the ML pipeline process under SageMaker.

Amazon SageMaker

Amazon SageMaker provides a fully managed cloud platform for users to develop ML models from end to end. Some of the key features of Amazon SageMaker are as follows:

- **Data preparation**: Amazon SageMaker provides various tools to preprocess and prepare data
- **Model training algorithms**: SageMaker provides built-in algorithms for supervised learning, unsupervised learning, and reinforcement learning
- **Model deployment**: After the ML model is trained and validated, SageMaker provides tools for model deployment, either as a batch transform job or a real-time endpoint
- **Scalability**: SageMaker is a fully managed service, which means that AWS takes care of all the infrastructure and scaling, so the data scientists can focus on building better models rather than worrying about infrastructure

- **Integration**: SageMaker integrates with other AWS services, such as S3, AWS Glue, and AWS Lambda, so data scientists can easily access and use datasets stored in AWS

Next, we will use Amazon SageMaker to solve a real-life problem. The details of the problem are as follows:

- **Problem definition**: A healthcare provider wants to improve the success rate of detecting abnormalities in orthopedic patients. The problem will be solved using ML. The dataset contains six biomechanical features and a target of normal or abnormal. We will use it to train an ML model and predict whether a patient will have an abnormality.

- **The dataset**: We will use the public vertebral column dataset from the UCI Machine Learning Repository (`https://archive.ics.uci.edu/ml/datasets/vertebral%2Bcolumn`).

- **The platform**: We will use Amazon SageMaker to collect and prepare the datasets, conduct model training and validation, deploy the model and perform batch transformation for the testing dataset, and fine-tune the model.

Are you ready? Let's get our hands dirty to develop an ML pipeline using Amazon SageMaker:

1. **Launch a Jupyter notebook**:

Log in to the AWS Management Console. From the **Services** menu, choose **Amazon SageMaker**. In the navigation menu on the left, expand the **Notebook** section and choose **Notebook instances**. Click **Create notebook instance**.

In the **Notebook instance name** box, enter a name for the notebook, such as `notebook1`. From the **Notebook instance type** drop-down list, choose **ml.t3.medium**. Set **Platform identifier type** to the latest one (**notebook-al2-v2**). Leave the remaining settings at their default values. Click **Create notebook instance**, as shown in *Figure 6.5*:

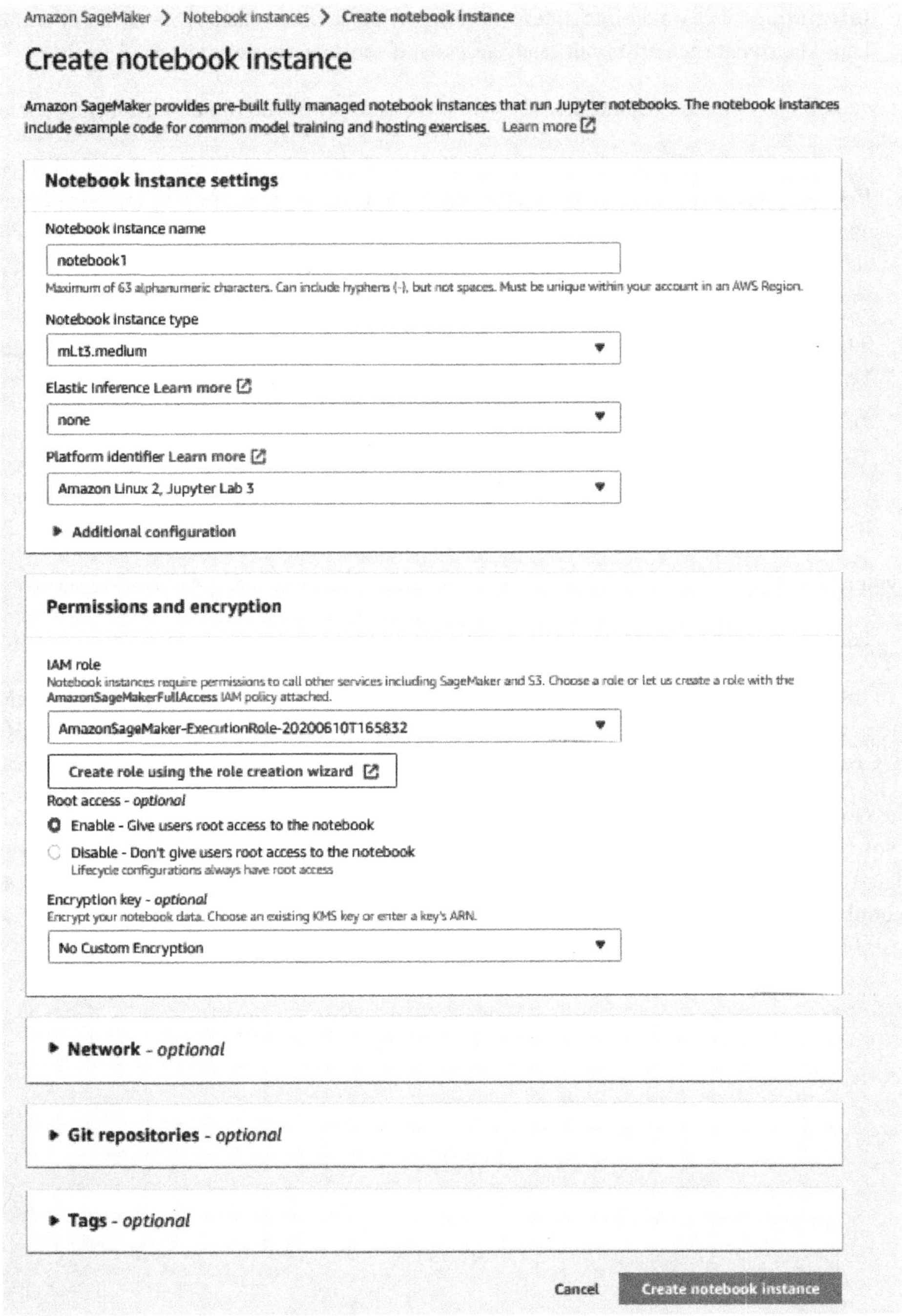

Amazon SageMaker 〉 Notebook instances 〉 **Create notebook instance**

Create notebook instance

Amazon SageMaker provides pre-built fully managed notebook instances that run Jupyter notebooks. The notebook instances include example code for common model training and hosting exercises.   Learn more ⧉

Notebook instance settings

Notebook instance name

```
notebook1
```

Maximum of 63 alphanumeric characters. Can include hyphens (-), but not spaces. Must be unique within your account in an AWS Region.

Notebook instance type

```
mL.t3.medium                                                          ▼
```

Elastic Inference Learn more ⧉

```
none                                                                  ▼
```

Platform identifier Learn more ⧉

```
Amazon Linux 2, Jupyter Lab 3                                         ▼
```

▶ Additional configuration

Permissions and encryption

IAM role

Notebook instances require permissions to call other services including SageMaker and S3. Choose a role or let us create a role with the **AmazonSageMakerFullAccess** IAM policy attached.

```
AmazonSageMaker-ExecutionRole-20200610T165832                         ▼
```

Create role using the role creation wizard ⧉

Root access - *optional*

⦿ Enable - Give users root access to the notebook

○ Disable - Don't give users root access to the notebook
   Lifecycle configurations always have root access

Encryption key - *optional*
Encrypt your notebook data. Choose an existing KMS key or enter a key's ARN.

```
No Custom Encryption                                                  ▼
```

▶ **Network** - *optional*

▶ **Git repositories** - *optional*

▶ **Tags** - *optional*

Cancel   Create notebook instance

Figure 6.5 – Launch a SageMaker notebook instance

When it's initially created, the new notebook instance will show as **Pending**. After it changes to **InService**, choose **Open JupyterLab** at the end of the row. A new window opens with the launcher. Choose **conda_python3**.

2. **Working in Jupyter Notebook**

   Now, the Jupyter notebook is ready to execute the ML pipeline process, using Python code. We will develop the pipeline step by step:

   I. **Import the Python data science libraries**:

```python
import warnings, requests, zipfile, io
warnings.simplefilter('ignore')
import pandas as pd
from scipy.io import arff
import boto3
```

   II. **Import the dataset and load data into a pandas DataFrame**:

```python
f_zip=
'http://archive.ics.uci.edu/ml/machine-learning-databases/00212/
vertebral_column_data.zip'
r=requests.get(f_zip, stream=True)
Vertebral_zip=zipfile.ZipFile(io.BytesIO(r.content))
Vertebral_zip.extractall()
```

The data is imported and ready for use, and you will see four files show up on the left panel, as shown in *Figure 6.6*. We can load them into pandas DataFrames:

```python
data = arff.loadarff('column_2C_weka.arff')
df = pd.DataFrame(data[0])
class_mapper = {b'Abnormal':1,b'Normal':0}
df['class']=df['class'].replace(class_mapper)
```

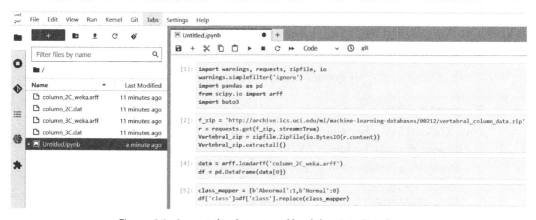

Figure 6.6 – Import the dataset and load data into DataFrames

III. **Explore the data**

Use df.shape to examine the number of rows and columns and df.columns to list the six biomechanical features. The target column is named class.

IV. **Prepare the data**

Since XGBoost requires the training data to be in a single file with the first column as the target value, we need to move the target column to the first position. Then, we split the dataset into training, validate, and test datasets and examine the three datasets.

Figure 6.7 shows the execution results of steps III and IV:

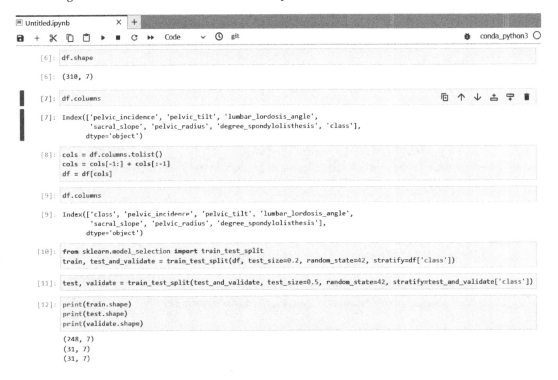

Figure 6.7 – Explore and prepare data

V. **Upload the data to Amazon S3**

Since XGBoost loads the training data from S3, we need to create an S3 bucket, write the data to a **comma-separated values (CSV)** file, and then upload the file to Amazon S3:

```
bucket='arn:aws:s3:::juyper03172023'
prefix='lab'
train_file='vertebral_train.csv'
test_file='vertebral_test.csv'
validate_file='vertebral_validate.csv'
```

```
import os
s3_resource = boto3.Session().resource('s3')
def upload_s3_csv(filename, folder, dataframe):
    csv_buffer = io.StringIO()
    dataframe.to_csv(csv_buffer, header=False, index=False)
    s3_resource.Bucket(bucket).Object(os.path.join(prefix,
folder, filename)).put(Body=csv_buffer.getvalue())
```

Figure 6.8 shows the execution results of step V:

```
[23]: bucket='juyper03172023'
      prefix='lab'

      train_file='vertebral_train.csv'
      test_file='vertebral_test.csv'
      validate_file='vertebral_validate.csv'
```

```
[24]: import os
      s3_resource = boto3.Session().resource('s3')
```

```
[25]: def upload_s3_csv(filename, folder, dataframe):
          csv_buffer = io.StringIO()
          dataframe.to_csv(csv_buffer, header=False, index=False)
          s3_resource.Bucket(bucket).Object(os.path.join(prefix, folder, filename)).put(Body=csv_buffer.getvalue())
```

```
[26]: upload_s3_csv(train_file, 'train', train)
      upload_s3_csv(test_file, 'test', test)
      upload_s3_csv(validate_file, 'validate', validate)
```

Figure 6.8 – Upload data to S3

Now we are ready to train the model!

VI. **Train the model using XGBoost**

The first step is to get the XGBoost container URL:

```
import boto3
from sagemaker.image_uris import retrieve
container = retrieve('xgboost',boto3.Session().region_name,'1.0-
1')
```

Set initial hyperparameters for the model and use the estimator function to set the model up:

```
hyperparams={"num_round":"42",
             "eval_metric": "auc",
             "objective": "binary:logistic"}

import sagemaker
s3_output_location="s3://{}/{}/output/".format(bucket,prefix)
xgb_model=sagemaker.estimator.Estimator(container,
                                        sagemaker.get_execution_
role(),
instance_count=1,
```

```
                                               instance_type='ml
.m4.xlarge',
                                               output_path=s3_
output_location,
                                                hyperparameters=
hyperparams,
                                               sagemaker_session=
sagemaker.Session())
```

The estimator needs **channels** to feed data into the model. We will use `train_channel` and `validate_channel`:

```
train_channel = sagemaker.inputs.TrainingInput(
    "s3://{}/{}/train/".format(bucket,prefix,train_file),
    content_type='text/csv')

validate_channel = sagemaker.inputs.TrainingInput(
    "s3://{}/{}/validate/".format(bucket,prefix,validate_file),
    content_type='text/csv')

data_channels = {'train': train_channel, 'validation':
validate_channel}
```

Figure 6.9 shows the execution in the notebook of these steps.

```
[27]:  import boto3
       from sagemaker.image_uris import retrieve
       container = retrieve('xgboost',boto3.Session().region_name,'1.0-1')
```

```
[28]:  hyperparams={"num_round":"42",
                    "eval_metric": "auc",
                    "objective": "binary:logistic"}
```

```
[29]:  import sagemaker
       s3_output_location="s3://{}/{}/output/".format(bucket,prefix)
       xgb_model=sagemaker.estimator.Estimator(container,
                                        sagemaker.get_execution_role(),
                                        instance_count=1,
                                        instance_type='ml.m4.xlarge',
                                        output_path=s3_output_location,
                                         hyperparameters=hyperparams,
                                         sagemaker_session=sagemaker.Session())
```

```
[30]:  train_channel = sagemaker.inputs.TrainingInput(
           "s3://{}/{}/train/".format(bucket,prefix,train_file),
           content_type='text/csv')

       validate_channel = sagemaker.inputs.TrainingInput(
           "s3://{}/{}/validate/".format(bucket,prefix,validate_file),
           content_type='text/csv')

       data_channels = {'train': train_channel, 'validation': validate_channel}
```

Figure 6.9 – Split dataset and define estimator

Now, train the model:

```
xgb_model.fit(inputs=data_channels, logs=False)
```

Figure 6.10 shows a screenshot of the model training:

```
[31]:  xgb_model.fit(inputs=data_channels, logs=False)

       INFO:sagemaker:Creating training-job with name: sagemaker-xgboost-2023-03-17-22-16-09-934

       2023-03-17 22:16:10 Starting - Starting the training job.......
       2023-03-17 22:16:50 Starting - Preparing the instances for training...........
       2023-03-17 22:17:53 Downloading - Downloading input data.....
       2023-03-17 22:18:23 Training - Downloading the training image........
       2023-03-17 22:19:09 Training - Training image download completed. Training in progress....
       2023-03-17 22:19:29 Uploading - Uploading generated training model..
       2023-03-17 22:19:45 Completed - Training job completed
```

Figure 6.10 – Model training

We can see that the model training has completed.

VII. **Conduct a batch transform on the testing dataset**

We will now construct a batch transformation, as seen in *Figure 6.11*.

```
batch_X = test.iloc[:,1:];

batch_X_file='batch-in.csv'
upload_s3_csv(batch_X_file, 'batch-in', batch_X)

batch_output = "s3://{}/{}/batch-out/".format(bucket,prefix)
batch_input = "s3://{}/{}/batch-in/{}".format(bucket,prefix,batch_X_file)

xgb_transformer = xgb_model.transformer(instance_count=1,
                                        instance_type='ml.m4.xlarge',
                                        strategy='MultiRecord',
                                        assemble_with='Line',
                                        output_path=batch_output)

xgb_transformer.transform(data=batch_input,
                          data_type='S3Prefix',
                          content_type='text/csv',
                          split_type='Line')
xgb_transformer.wait()

s3 = boto3.client('s3')
obj = s3.get_object(Bucket=bucket, Key="{}/batch-out/{}".format(prefix,'batch-in.csv.out'))
target_predicted = pd.read_csv(io.BytesIO(obj['Body'].read()),',',names=['class'])
```

```
INFO:sagemaker:Creating model with name: sagemaker-xgboost-2023-03-18-04-02-54-790
```

```
INFO:sagemaker:Creating transform job with name: sagemaker-xgboost-2023-03-18-04-02-55-529
```

```
2023-03-18T04:08:52.134:[sagemaker logs]: MaxConcurrentTransforms=4, MaxPayloadInMB=6, BatchStrategy=MULTI_RECORD
```

Figure 6.11 – Batch transformation

After the batch transformation step, we can build a confusion matrix.

VIII. **Create a confusion matrix**

Build a function to convert the positive probability into binary (0 or 1):

```
def binary_convert(x):
    threshold = 0.3
    if x > threshold:
        return 1
    else:
        return 0

target_predicted_binary = target_predicted['class'].
apply(binary_convert)

print(target_predicted_binary.head(5))
test.head(5)
```

Figure 6.12 shows the execution in a notebook.

```
[5]: def binary_convert(x):
         threshold = 0.3
         if x > threshold:
             return 1
         else:
             return 0

     target_predicted_binary = target_predicted['class'].apply(binary_convert)

     print(target_predicted_binary.head(5))
     test.head(5)

     0    1
     1    1
     2    1
     3    1
     4    1
     Name: class, dtype: int64
```

[5]:	class	pelvic_incidence	pelvic_tilt	lumbar_lordosis_angle	sacral_slope	pelvic_radius	degree_spondylolisthesis
136	1	88.024499	39.844669	81.774473	48.179830	116.601538	56.766083
230	0	65.611802	23.137919	62.582179	42.473883	124.128001	-4.083298
134	1	52.204693	17.212673	78.094969	34.992020	136.972517	54.939134
130	1	50.066786	9.120340	32.168463	40.946446	99.712453	26.766697
47	1	41.352504	16.577364	30.706191	24.775141	113.266675	-4.497958

Figure 6.12 – Forecast testing dataset

Then, create a confusion matrix using the target values from the test dataset and the predicted value:

```
test_labels = test.iloc[:,0]
test_labels.head()
from sklearn.metrics import confusion_matrix
matrix = confusion_matrix(test_labels, target_predicted_binary)
df_confusion = pd.DataFrame(matrix,
index=['Normal','Abnormal'],columns=['Normal','Abnormal'])
df_confusion
```

Figure 6.13 shows the execution in a notebook:

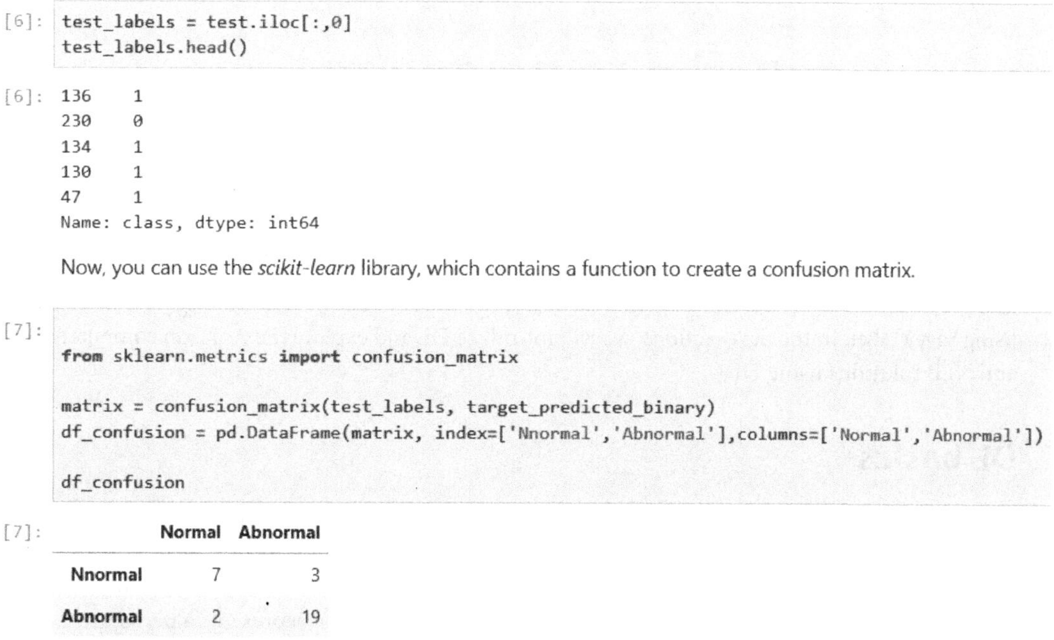

```
[6]: test_labels = test.iloc[:,0]
     test_labels.head()
```

```
[6]: 136    1
     230    0
     134    1
     130    1
     47     1
     Name: class, dtype: int64
```

Now, you can use the *scikit-learn* library, which contains a function to create a confusion matrix.

```
[7]:
from sklearn.metrics import confusion_matrix

matrix = confusion_matrix(test_labels, target_predicted_binary)
df_confusion = pd.DataFrame(matrix, index=['Nnormal','Abnormal'],columns=['Normal','Abnormal'])

df_confusion
```

[7]:	Normal	Abnormal
Nnormal	7	3
Abnormal	2	19

Figure 6.13 – Create a confusion matrix

Now, we can calculate the performance stats for the model.

IX. **Calculate the performance stats**

Now calculate the stats:

```
Sensitivity  = float(TP)/(TP+FN)*100
print(f"Sensitivity or TPR: {Sensitivity}%")
Specificity  = float(TN)/(TN+FP)*100
print(f"Specificity or TNR: {Specificity}%")
```

```
Precision = float(TP)/(TP+FP)*100
print(f"Precision: {Precision}%")
```

Figure 6.14 shows the execution in a notebook.

```
[21]: Sensitivity  = float(TP)/(TP+FN)*100
      print(f"Sensitivity or TPR: {Sensitivity}%")
      Specificity  = float(TN)/(TN+FP)*100
      print(f"Specificity or TNR: {Specificity}%")
      Precision = float(TP)/(TP+FP)*100
      print(f"Precision: {Precision}%")
```

```
Sensitivity or TPR: 90.47619047619048%
Specificity or TNR: 70.0%
Precision: 86.36363636363636%
```

Figure 6.14 – Performance stats

In this section, we introduced Amazon SageMaker and showed the ML pipeline, from data collection and preparation, to model training and validation, to model deployment, testing, and fine-tuning, using SageMaker. In the next sections, we will introduce DL and explore the Amazon computer vision and NLP solutions using DL.

DL basics

DL was introduced in 2012. The basic idea is to mimic the human brain and construct **artificial neural networks** (**ANNs**) to train models. A typical multi-layer ANN has three types of layers: an **input layer**, one or more **hidden layers**, and an **output layer**. *Figure 6.15* shows an ANN that has one input layer, two hidden layers, and an output layer. In the ANN, a circular node represents a perceptron, and a line represents the connection from the output of one perceptron to the input of another.

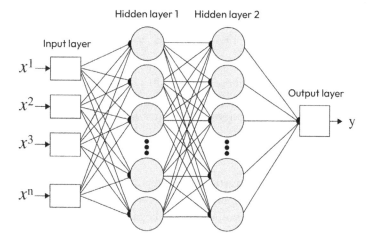

Figure 6.15 – A multi-layer ANN

The objective of DL model training is the same as ML: minimize the loss function, which is defined as the gap between the model's predicted value and the actual value. Different from traditional ML algorithms, DL uses the activation function to add nonlinearity to the model training process.

In a typical DL model, we define the following to construct a neural network:

- The **layers of the model** (input layer, hidden layers, and output layers)

- The **activation function** for each layer (such as ReLU or softmax)

- The **optimizer**, which is the DL algorithm used to train the model

- The **loss function** (such as MAE, MSE, and `categorical_crossentropy`)

- The **dropout rate**, which is the percentage of nodes and their incoming/outgoing connections to be temporarily removed from the network – to avoid model overfitting

The following code snippet shows an example of building and training a DL model using **Keras**, which is a software library for constructing DL models. As we can see, it builds a neural network of three layers: the input layer with 16 nodes, 2 hidden layers with 128 and 24 nodes (`0.25` dropout), and an output layer of 3 nodes (softmax activation). The optimizer algorithm is **stochastic gradient descent (SGD)**, and the loss function is `categorical_crossentropy`, which fits multi-classification models:

```
#Import keras
model = keras.sequential
model.add(layers.Dense(128,activation='relu',input_shape=(16,
)))
model.add(layers.Dense(24,activation='relu'))
model.add(layers.Dropout(rate=0.25))
model.add(layers.Dense(3,activation='softmax'))
```

```
model.compile(sgd(lr=0.5), loss='categorical_crossentropy',
metrics=['accuracy'])
model.fit(train_set, train_label, batch_size=20, epochs=30,
shuffle=True)
```

Since DL was introduced, it has made breakthroughs in a lot of AI areas, including computer vision and NLP. Many applications are developed using pretrained neural DL models. In the next section, we will introduce the Amazon DL solutions in computer vision and NLP.

Amazon computer vision solutions

Computer vision is the automated extraction of information from digital images. To solve computer vision problems, Amazon provides **Rekognition** – a fully managed service using DL to analyze images and videos. Here are some key features of Amazon Rekognition:

- **Object and scene detection**: Rekognition can identify objects and scenes within an image or video frame, including vehicles, buildings, animals, and landscapes.

- **Facial analysis and facial comparison**: Rekognition can detect faces in images and videos and perform facial analysis, including facial recognition, gender identification, age estimation, and facial expression analysis. It can compare and match faces from different images.

- **Text detection**: Rekognition can detect and extract text in images and videos, including printed and handwritten text.

- **Custom labels**: Rekognition also allows you to create custom labels for specific objects or scenes that are important to your business or use case.

- **Video analysis**: Rekognition can analyze videos and extract specific frames or segments based on your criteria, such as facial recognition or object detection.

Amazon Rekognition provides a powerful set of image and video analysis capabilities that can be used in a variety of applications, such as security, media analysis, customer engagement, and content moderation. Next, we will show two of its functions: label detection and facial recognition and matching.

Label detection

In the AWS Management Console, select **Amazon Rekognition** and go to the **Rekognition** console. Select **Demos | Label detection**. When you upload an image, it analyzes the content and returns a list of labels that describe the visual elements of the content. *Figure 6.16* shows the label detection results:

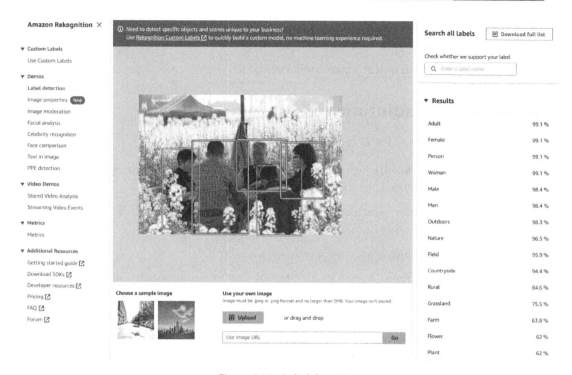

Figure 6.16 – Label detection

Facial recognition and matching

In the AWS Management Console, select **Amazon Rekognition** and go to the **Rekognition** console. Select **Demos | Face comparison**. Upload an image as a reference face and another image for the comparison faces. Rekognition compares the reference face with each of the comparison faces and returns the results. *Figure 6.17* shows the face comparison results:

Figure 6.17 – Face comparison

Due to space limits, we have only shown some Amazon Rekognition features. Please feel free to explore more computer vision solutions and have fun!

In the next section, we will look at Amazon's NLP services.

Amazon's NLP solutions

Amazon offers a range of NLP solutions:

- **Amazon Comprehend**, which is a service to perform sentiment analysis, entity recognition, and topic modeling on large volumes of unstructured text
- **Amazon Transcribe**, which converts speech to text and supports multiple languages and a variety of audio formats
- **Amazon Polly**, which is a text-to-speech service
- **Amazon Translate**, which provides high-quality translations for a variety of languages
- **Amazon Lex**, which is a service for building chatbots and conversational interfaces

Amazon Comprehend

Amazon Comprehend uses DL algorithms to analyze and understand text data in multiple languages. Amazon Comprehend can perform the following functions:

- **Language detection**: Automatically detect the language of the text data, which is useful in multilingual applications
- **Sentiment analysis**: Determine the sentiment of text data: positive, negative, or neutral
- **Entity recognition**: Identify and extract entities from text data, such as people, organizations, locations, and dates
- **Key phrase extraction**: Extract key phrases from text data, such as important topics or keywords
- **Topic modeling**: Identify topics in text data and group them based on their similarity
- **Custom classification**: Allows users to create custom classifiers for specific use cases, such as categorizing customer feedback into different categories

Amazon Comprehend provides a powerful set of NLP capabilities that can be used in a variety of applications, such as customer service, social media monitoring, content analysis, and compliance monitoring.

Amazon Transcribe

Amazon Transcribe is a speech recognition service that uses advanced ML algorithms to convert audio and video files into text transcripts in real time or asynchronously. Here are some key features of Amazon Transcribe:

- **Speech-to-text conversion**: It can transcribe audio and video files into text transcripts, with support for multiple languages and dialects

- **Real-time transcription**: It can transcribe live audio and video streams in real time, making it useful for applications such as call centers and live events

- **Speaker identification**: It can identify individual speakers in a multi-speaker audio or video file and label each spoken word with the corresponding speaker ID

- **Automatic punctuation**: It can add appropriate punctuation to the transcribed text, making it easier to read and understand

- **Custom vocabulary**: It allows you to upload custom vocabularies that can be used to improve the accuracy of the transcription for a domain-specific language

- **Compliance and security**: It is designed with strong security and compliance features, such as encryption, access controls, and compliance with GDPR and other regulations

Amazon Transcribe provides powerful speech-to-text capabilities that can be used in a variety of applications, such as call transcription, captioning, subtitling, and voice search.

Amazon Polly

Amazon Polly is a text-to-speech service that uses advanced DL technologies to create natural-sounding speech from text. Amazon Polly supports a wide range of languages and voices, including male and female voices with different accents and styles. The service can generate speech in real time, allowing applications to provide dynamic and responsive voice output. Amazon Polly also supports the use of **Speech Synthesis Markup Language** (**SSML**), which allows developers to fine-tune the pronunciation and intonation of the generated speech. Some of the key benefits of using Amazon Polly include the following:

- **High-quality speech output**: Amazon Polly uses advanced neural text-to-speech technology to create natural-sounding speech with lifelike intonation and pronunciation.

- **Customizability**: Developers can control various aspects of the speech output, such as voice, intonation, and pronunciation, to create a more personalized and engaging experience.

- **Cost-effectiveness**: Amazon Polly offers pay-as-you-go pricing, which means that you only pay for what you use.

- **Easy integration**: Amazon Polly provides a simple API that developers can use to integrate speech capabilities into their applications. The service can be used with a variety of programming languages and platforms, including Java, Python, and .NET.

Amazon Polly can be used in e-learning, gaming, accessibility, and more. It can also be used in conjunction with other AWS services, such as Amazon Lex and Amazon Comprehend, to create more sophisticated and intelligent voice-based applications.

Amazon Translate

Amazon Translate is a fully managed machine translation service that translates text in multiple languages. Some key features of Amazon Translate are as follows:

- **Language translation**: Translate can translate text from one language to another, with support for over 70 languages

- **Real-time translation**: Translate can translate text in real time, making it useful for applications such as chatbots and customer support

- **Batch translation**: Translate can translate large volumes of text in batches, making it useful for tasks such as website localization

- **Custom terminology**: Translate allows you to upload custom terminology that can be used to improve the accuracy of the translation for a domain-specific language

- **Neural machine translation**: Translate uses a neural machine translation engine that provides high-quality translations that are more accurate and natural sounding than traditional machine translation methods

- **Automatic language detection**: Translate can automatically detect the language of the input text, making it easier to use in multilingual applications

- **Compliance and security**: Translate is designed with strong security and compliance features, such as encryption, access controls, and compliance with GDPR and other regulations

Amazon Translate provides a powerful set of machine translation capabilities that can be used in a variety of applications, such as e-commerce, customer service, and content localization. It allows businesses to expand their reach globally by providing quick and accurate translations of their content in multiple languages.

Amazon Lex

Amazon Lex is a service that enables developers to build conversational interfaces and chatbots using NLP and **automatic speech recognition** (**ASR**) technologies. Amazon Lex can be used to create chatbots for a wide range of applications, including customer service, e-commerce, and education. Some of the key features of Amazon Lex include the following:

- **Natural language understanding**: Amazon Lex uses advanced NLP technology to understand natural language input and map it to intents and slots

- **Automatic speech recognition**: Amazon Lex can process spoken language and convert it into text, enabling users to interact with chatbots through voice commands

- **Multi-platform support**: Amazon Lex provides SDKs for several popular platforms, including iOS, Android, and JavaScript, enabling developers to build chatbots for web and mobile applications

- **Integration with other AWS services**: Amazon Lex can be integrated with other AWS services, such as Amazon Lambda, Amazon DynamoDB, and Amazon S3, to create more sophisticated chatbots

- **Scalability**: Amazon Lex is designed to handle large volumes of requests and can scale automatically based on demand

Using Amazon Lex, developers can create chatbots that can handle simple and complex interactions with users, such as answering questions, providing recommendations, and processing transactions. Chatbots built with Amazon Lex can be deployed across multiple channels, including web, mobile, and messaging platforms, providing a seamless and consistent user experience.

These AWS NLP services are easy to access and set up from the console or CLI. We will not show any hands-on examples here. Please feel free to explore these services by yourself.

Summary

In this chapter, we have discussed AWS ML services. We started by introducing ML concepts and the ML pipeline, then dove into Amazon SageMaker, which provides fully managed end-to-end ML services. We then introduce DL concepts and examined the AWS computer vision and NLP solutions using DL pretrained models.

So far, we have explored AWS cloud services such as compute, storage, networking, databases, big data, and ML. In the next chapter, we will discuss another important cloud topic: Amazon cloud security.

Practice questions

Questions 1-4 are based on the following use case.

ML case #1

An engineer is training an Amazon SageMaker model to detect as many true **malignant tumors** (MTs) from MRI images as possible. The model features are shown in *Figure 6.18*.

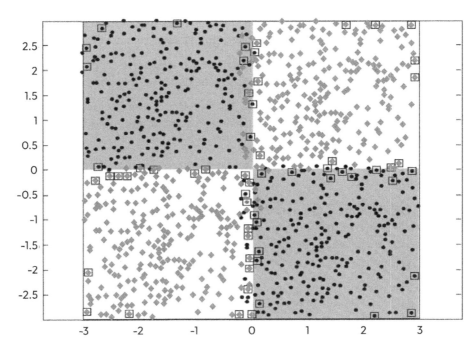

Figure 6.18 – Model features: x and y

The initial models were underfitting, so they put in a lot of effort and finally got two models working. Their confusion matrixes are shown in *Figure 6.19*:

Model A

		Actual	
		MT	Not MT
Predicted	MT	107	23
	Not MT	69	42

Model B

		Actual	
		MT	Not MT
Predicted	MT	148	53
	Not MT	28	12

Figure 6.19 – Confusion matrixes for models A and B

1. How should they synthesize the two features, x and y?

    A. $x^*x + y^*y$

    B. $x+y$

    C. x^*y

    D. $x^*10 + y^*10$

2. What is the precision for model B?

    A. 74%

    B. 84%

    C. 18%

    D. 50%

3. What may have helped them improve the initial model?

    A. Add more features to the model

    B. Add L1 regularization

    C. Add L2 regularization

    D. Increase the learning rate

4. Which of the following statements is true?

    A. Model B is better

    B. Model A is better

    C. We need an ROC curve to decide

    D. We need an F1 core to decide

Questions 5-10 are based on the following use case.

ML case #2

An engineer is building a DL model to predict whether images contain a driver's license, passport, or credit card. The code and initial training results are shown in *Figure 6.20*:

```
#Import keras
model = keras.sequential
model.add(layers.Dense(128,activation='relu',input_shape=(16,
)))
model.add(layers.Dense(24,activation='relu'))
model.add(layers.Dropout(rate=0.25))
model.add(layers.Dense(3,activation='softmax'))
model.compile(sgd(lr=0.5), loss='categorical_crossentropy',
metrics=['accuracy'])
model.fit(train_set, train_label, batch_size=20, epochs=30,
shuffle=True)
```

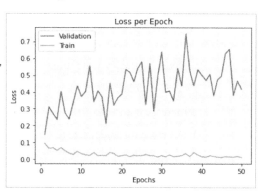

Figure 6.20 – DL model and initial training results

5. What optimizer did they use?

    a. Sequential

    b. ReLU

    C. Softmax

    D. Stochastic gradient descent

6: What kind of problem are they likely to solve?

    A. Binary classification

    B. Regression

    C. Multi-classification of three: a dog, a cat, or a giraffe

    D. Multi-classification of "a combination of three": a dog, a cat, and a giraffe

7: How many trainable weights does the model have?

    A. 16x128+128x24x0.25+24x3

    B. 16x128x24x3

    C. 16+128+24x0.25+3

    D. 16x128+128x24+24x3

8: How can they improve the model generality?

    A. Decrease the learning rate to 0.2

    B. Apply regularization

    C. Increase epochs to 60

    D. Decrease the batch size to 10

9. How can they make the model converge?

    A. Decrease the learning rate to 0.2

    B. Apply regularization

    C. Increase epochs to 60

    D. Decrease the batch size to 10

10. Which of the following is likely a label for the training dataset?

    A. drivers_license

    B. passport

    C. credit_card

    D. [drivers_license, passport, credit_card]

Questions 11-14 are based on the use case and diagrams shown in *Figure 6.21*:

An engineer **is working in a data science company that has collected a large amount of data to be analyzed using AWS ML services. There is one .CSV dataset in S3 bucket B1, one voice .MP3 dataset in B2, and another dataset in an RDS database db1.**
John has created SageMaker notebook instances ml-instance1 and ml-instance2.

Figure 6.21 – DL model training architecture

11. They are using `ml-instance1` to train ML models using `.csv` files in B1. It has taken a long time and they want to improve the performance. What is your suggestion?

  A. Use SageMaker Pipe mode

  B. Copy the `.csv` files to `ml-instance1`

  C. Use Amazon Kinesis to stream data from B1 to `ml-instance1`

  D. Use AWS Glue to transform the CSV dataset to JSON format first

12. They want to analyze the voice recordings in B2 to understand the topics with minimum effort. What is your suggestion?

  A. Amazon Transcribe + a custom NLP algorithm with Amazon SageMaker

  B. SageMaker BlazingText algorithm + Amazon Transcribe

  C. A custom NLP algorithm with Amazon SageMaker + Amazon Transcribe

  D. Amazon Transcribe + Amazon Comprehend

13. They and their coworkers have deployed many SageMaker notebook instances, and each team member only needs access to their personal instances. What is your recommendation?

  A. Create an IAM policy for each member and grant access to their personal instances only

  B. Use port forwarding to prevent all internet traffic from being forwarded to the notebook instances

C. Use Amazon CloudWatch to monitor and restrict unauthorized access

D. Attach an Amazon S3 bucket policy to restrict access to the buckets that contain other users' notebook instances

14. They checked all the VPCs and could not find `ml-instance1`. What is the reason?

   A. `ml-instance1` is hidden in the VPCs of John's account

   B. `ml-instance1` is run in the ECS service of John's account

   C. `ml-instance1` is run in SageMaker-managed VPCs

   D. `ml-instance1` is run in the root user's VPCs

15. They wants to use the dataset in `db1` to train a model on `ml-instance2`. What is your recommendation?

   A. Build a connection from `db1` to `ml-instance2`

   B. Transform data from `db1` to S3 and provide the S3 location to `ml-instance2`

   C. Move data to Amazon Redshift and build a connection between Redshift and `ml-instance2`

   D. Move data to `ml-instance2` directly from `db1`

Answers to the practice questions

1. C

2. A

3. A

4. A

5. D

6. D

7. A

8. B

9. A

10. D

11. A

12. D

13. A

14. C

15. B

Further reading

For further insights into what you've learned in this chapter, refer to the following links:

- `https://aws.amazon.com/sagemaker/`
- `https://docs.aws.amazon.com/sagemaker/index.html`
- `https://aws.amazon.com/rekognition/`
- `https://aws.amazon.com/comprehend/`
- `https://aws.amazon.com/transcribe/`
- `https://aws.amazon.com/polly/`
- `https://aws.amazon.com/translate/`
- `https://aws.amazon.com/lex/`

7

Amazon Cloud Security Services

Information security is protecting data and resources including sensitive information, computer systems, networks, and so on from unauthorized access, disruption, theft, or damage. Security also prevents attacks with a quick and effective response if an attack does occur. Effective security requires a combination of people, technologies, and processes.

Amazon Cloud Security protects data and resources on the AWS cloud platform. AWS provides a comprehensive cloud security model and a set of services to help customers secure their cloud-based applications and infrastructure. In this chapter, we will discuss the following topics:

- **AWS cloud security model**: The customer is responsible for the security of the cloud, and the provider is responsibility for security in the cloud.

- **AWS Identity and Access Management**: A cloud security service that enables customers to centrally manage access to AWS resources and services. Access is the first line of security defense, and this is where we practice the *least privilege* and *minimum attack surface* security principles.

- **AWS infrastructure security**: The security of Amazon cloud infrastructure, including cloud *endpoint* resources such as EC2, RDS, S3, and cloud *network* resources such as VPCs and subnets. This is where we practice the *zero-trust* security principle and the *multi-layer protection* security principle.

- **AWS data security**: Cloud data protection, including data encryption at rest and in transit, and encryption key management. This is where we enforce the *most encryption* security principle.

- **AWS cloud logging and monitoring**: Tracing all cloud assets and activities, all the time. This is where we enforce the *traceability* security principle.

- **AWS cloud threat detection and remediation**: Threat detection and remediation in the cloud. We will conduct a case study about *a threat auto-detection and auto-remediation ecosystem*.

We will start our journey with the AWS cloud security model.

Amazon cloud security model

The **AWS shared responsibility model** is about the responsibilities of AWS and its customers. AWS is responsible for the *security of the cloud*, including the physical infrastructure, network, hypervisor, and so on that supports the customer's applications and data. The customer is responsible for *security in the cloud*, including customers' data, applications, and other configurations that are hosted on the AWS infrastructure, such as access management, firewall configurations, data encryptions, and so on.

Based on the shared responsibilities, AWS provides a multi-layered security model to protect customer data and resources in the cloud, including the following layers:

- **Physical/hardware**: AWS data centers are designed and managed to comply with security standards and regulations by employing physical security equipment such as access control systems, surveillance cameras, and perimeter fencing to prevent unauthorized access. These are Amazon's responsibility and AWS provides an on-demand service called **AWS Artifact** that offers access to a central repository of physical security and compliance reports audited by third parties.

- **IAM**: AWS gives customers the ability to manage user access and permissions to AWS services and resources. With IAM, customers can create and manage IAM users, groups, and roles to control access to AWS services.

- **Network security**: AWS provides network security measures such as VPCs, SGs, and NACLs to ensure that data traffic between resources is protected and controlled. Customers are responsible for configuring the cloud VPCs, SGs, and NACLs.

- **Data encryption**: AWS offers multiple encryption options, including server-side encryption, client-side encryption, and **Key Management Service (KMS)**, to protect data at rest and in transit.

- **Compliance and auditing**: AWS provides compliance and auditing capabilities to meet various industrial regulatory requirements and standards, such as HIPAA, SOC 2, PCI DSS, and ISO 27001.

- **Application security**: AWS offers security tools and services, such as **AWS Web Application Firewall (WAF)** to protect against web application attacks, and **AWS Shield** to protect against **Distributed Denial of Service (DDoS)** attacks.

AWS's multi-layered cloud security model provides a comprehensive approach to securing cloud resources and allows customers to build and deploy applications securely in the cloud. Let's explore Amazon IAM first.

Amazon IAM

IAM manages resource identity and accessibility, including authentication, authorization, and accounting.

Authentication is authenticating an identity to access an information system. One of the important security features of IAM is that it supports **Multi-Factor Authentication** (**MFA**), which requires users to provide a second form of authentication, such as a one-time token, or biometric identity, in addition to their username and password. IAM also supports *identity federation*, which allows customers to integrate their existing identity management systems with AWS, enabling users to sign into AWS using their existing credentials, such as Google or Meta logins, and so on.

Authorization is the user's permission once they are authenticated in the system. With IAM, customers can create and manage AWS users and groups, and define permissions that grant or restrict access to specific AWS resources. Authentication defines who can perform which actions on what resources. The *Who* can be a user, a group, or a role. IAM supports **Role-Based Access Control** (**RBAC**), which allows customers to assign permissions to roles rather than individual users. The *What* is cloud resources including EC2, EBS, EFS, S3, VPC, and so on, and the *Which* is the actions that the *Who* can take on *What*.

Auditing is logging and tracking user activities in the AWS cloud. We will explore more about AWS auditing in the *Monitoring and logging* portion of this chapter.

IAM policies

In AWS IAM, *every permission is a policy*. IAM permissions are defined with an AWS policy – a JSON document. The following is a sample policy:

```
{
    "Version": "2012-10-17",
    "Statement": [
        {
            "Sid": "AllowReadAccess",
            "Effect": "Allow",
            "Action": [
                "s3:*"
            ],
            "Resource": [
                "arn:aws:s3:::bucket1",
                "arn:aws:s3:::bucket1/*"
            ]
        }
    ]
}
```

The preceding policy defines the permissions as *"any S3 actions against an S3 bucket named bucket1."* If we attach this policy to a user, then the user will have all the permissions to act against *bucket1*. Since this policy defines permissions on specific resources, it is a *resource-based IAM policy*. There is another type of policy that defines permissions on the principal (user, group, role, identities), and we call it an *identity-based IAM policy*. The following example shows an identity-based IAM policy:

```
{
    "Version": "2012-10-17",
    "Statement": {
        "Effect": "Deny",
        "Action": "*",
        "Resource": "*",
        "Condition": {
            "NotIpAddress": {
                "aws:SourceIp": [
                    "10.10.0.0/16",
                    "8.8.0.0/16"
                ]
            }
        }
    }
}
```

We will create several IAM policies and see how they are used in managing S3 objects

1.   Log in to the AWS console as an admin, and create the following four policies:

•   **Policy A "userjohn"**: This policy defines read-only resource permissions and assume-role permissions:

```
{
    "Version": "2012-10-17",
    "Statement": [
        {
            "Action": [
                "iam:Describe*",
                "iam:GetAccountAuthorizationDetails",
                "iam:GetPolicy",
                "iam:GetRole",
                "iam:GetRolePolicy",
                "iam:GetUser",
                "iam:GetUserPolicy",
                "iam:List*",
                "logs:Desc*",
                "logs:Get*",
                "logs:List*",
```

```
                "s3:ListAllMyBuckets",
                "s3:ListBucket",
                "s3:PutAccountPublicAccessBlock",
                "s3:PutBucketOwnershipControls",
                "s3:PutBucketPublicAccessBlock",
                "sts:AssumeRole"
            ],
            "Resource": "*",
            "Effect": "Allow"
        }
    ]
}
```

- **Policy B "switchrole"**: This policy defines `list bucket` and `get bucket` permissions for all S3 buckets, and `list, get (download) objects` permissions for an S3 bucket named `03252023-bucket1`:

```
{
    "Version": "2012-10-17",
    "Statement": [
        {
            "Action": [
                "s3:GetBucketPolicy",
                "s3:ListBucket"
            ],
            "Resource": "*",
            "Effect": "Allow"
        },
        {
            "Action": [
                "s3:GetObject",
                "s3:ListObjects",
                "s3:ListBucket"
            ],
            "Resource": [
                "arn:aws:s3:::03252023-bucket1",
                "arn:aws:s3:::03252023-bucket1/*"
            ],
            "Effect": "Allow"
        }
    ]
}
```

- **Policy C "trustpolicy"**: This allows the user `userjohn` to assume the role assigned to it:

```
{
    "Version": "2012-10-17",
```

```
        "Statement": [
            {
                "Effect": "Allow",
                "Principal": {
                    "AWS": "arn:aws:iam::317332158300:root"
                },
                "Action": "sts:AssumeRole",
                "Condition": {}
            },
            {
                "Effect": "Allow",
                "Principal": {
                    "AWS": "arn:aws:iam::317332158300:user/userjohn"
                },
                "Action": "sts:AssumeRole"
            }
        ]
    }
```

- **Policy D "bucket2-permission"**: This gives the `switchrole` role `list bucket` and `get/put objects` permissions on `03252023-bucket2`:

```
    {
        "Version": "2008-10-17",
        "Statement": [
            {
                "Sid": "S3Write",
                "Effect": "Allow",
                "Principal": {
                    "AWS": "arn:aws:iam::317332158300:role/
switchrole"
                },
                "Action": [
                    "s3:GetObject",
                    "s3:PutObject"
                ],
                "Resource": "arn:aws:s3:::03252023-bucket2/*"
            },
            {
                "Sid": "ListBucket",
                "Effect": "Allow",
                "Principal": {
                    "AWS": "arn:aws:iam::317332158300:role/
switchrole"
                },
                "Action": "s3:ListBucket",
```

```
                    "Resource": "arn:aws:s3:::03252023-bucket2"
           }
        ]}
```

2. As the AWS account admin, create a user, a role, and some S3 buckets:

    I.   Under IAM, create a user named `userjohn` with AWS console access, and assign permission policy A, `userjohn`, to the `userjohn` user.

    II.   Create a role named `switchrole` with permission policy B, `switchrole`, and trust policy C, `trustpolicy`, as shown in *Figure 7.1*.

    III. Under the S3 console, create two buckets named `03252023-bucket1` and `03252023-bucket2`:

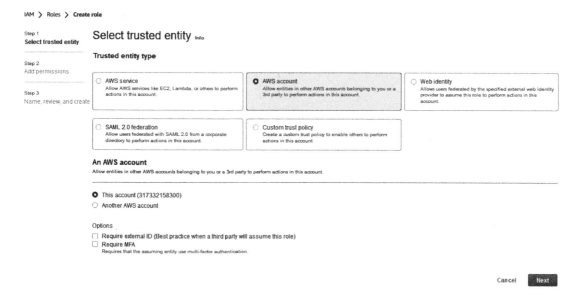

Figure 7.1 – Create an IAM role called "switchrole"

3. **Log in to the AWS console as the userjohn user**:

Based on the authorization defined in the policy, `userjohn` will have read-only permission in the EC2 dashboard or S3 console, as shown in *Figure 7.2*:

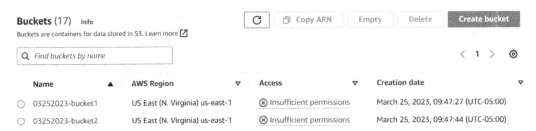

Figure 7.2 – userjohn has read-only permissions

Go to the S3 console and try to upload an object to the two S3 buckets. It will fail since the user has read-only permissions to the S3 bucket. This is shown in *Figure 7.3*:

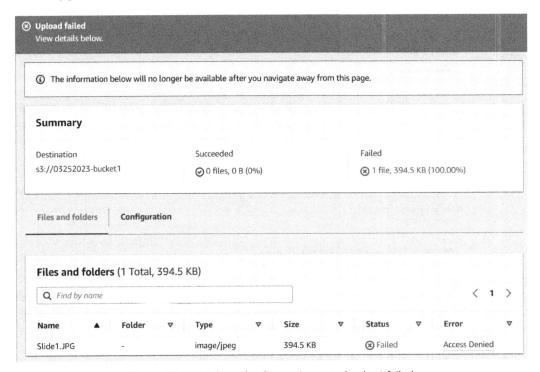

Figure 7.3 – userjohn uploading an image to bucket1 failed

4. Switch role and upload the object to **bucket1**:

Go to the AWS console and click **userid** in the top-right corner; select **Switch Role**. Fill in the AWS account number and enter `switchrole` as the role name, as shown in *Figure 7.4*:

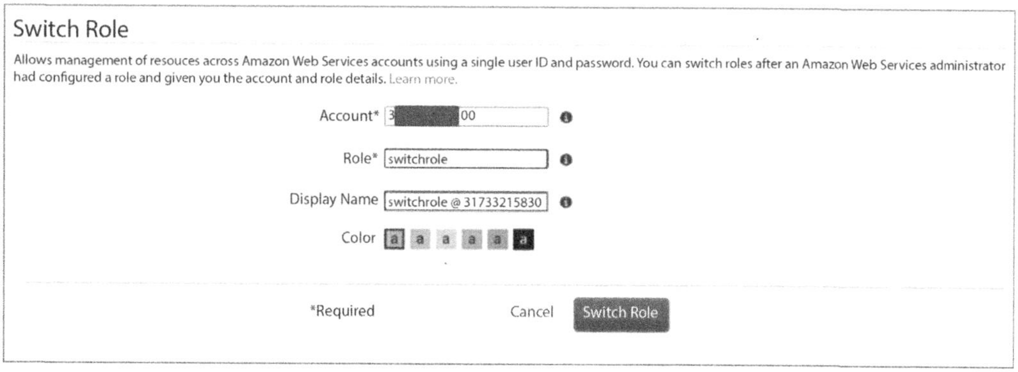

Figure 7.4 – Switch role from userjohn to switchrole

After switching to the role, you will be able to upload objects to the `03252023-bucket1` S3 bucket since `switchrole` has the right permissions assigned to it. However, you still cannot upload objects to the `03252023-bucket2` S3 bucket since no permissions are granted to it. We will fix that with the admin account.

Open another window, log in to the AWS console as `admin`. Go to bucket `03252023-bucket2`, and add policy D, `bucket2-permission`, to it

• Go back to the AWS console window where you're logged in as `userjohn`.

Upload an object to bucket `03252023-bucket2` again, and now it succeeds since `03252023-bucket2` is assigned the `bucket2-permission` policy, which permits `switchrole` to put objects. This is shown in *Figure 7.5*:

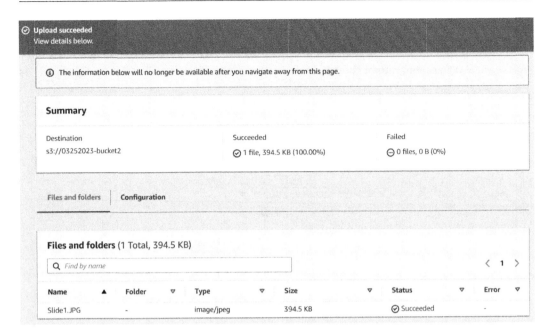

Figure 7.5 – userjohn uploading to bucket2 succeeds

From the preceding process, we can see that all the IAM permissions are defined as policies, so we can assign permissions to users, groups, roles, and S3 buckets, and we can switch roles to get different permissions for AWS resources.

In summary, AWS IAM provides customers with a powerful set of tools for managing AWS cloud resources. In the next section, we will further explore AWS infrastructure security.

AWS infrastructure security

The basic unit of AWS infrastructure is the *12-digit AWS account* that we have been logging in to and configuring our cloud services with. When you have many AWS accounts, it is necessary to have an infrastructure hierarchy – called **AWS Organizations** – to manage these accounts. In this section, we will first discuss the AWS resource organization hierarchy and security policies, and then inspect security for the AWS basic infrastructure components: EC2, S3, VPC, databases, and many others.

AWS Organizations

AWS Organizations consolidates multiple accounts into a central management unit, to manage business budgets, security, and compliance. With AWS Organizations, you can do the following:

- Automate AWS account creation and management using AWS APIs

- Consolidate billing and perform cost management across many AWS accounts, at various levels of your organization

With IAM policies, you can manage permissions for AWS users, groups, or roles, but you cannot restrict the AWS account root user. However, with Organizations, you can use **service control policies** (**SCPs**) to manage access to AWS services for individual AWS accounts, or for groups of accounts in an **Organization Unit** (**OU**), as shown in *Figure 7.6*:

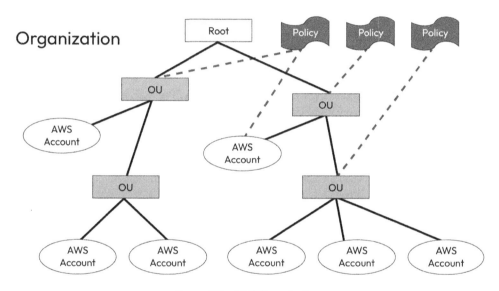

Figure 7.6 – AWS Organizations

Having reviewed security at the OU and account levels, now let's look at security management at the resource and service levels.

AWS resource security

We will discuss AWS resource security in the following basic domains:

- AWS compute security, mainly EC2

- AWS storage security, mainly S3

- AWS network security (VPC)

- AWS data security, including databases, big data, and machine learning

Amazon compute security

We discussed EC2 in *Chapter 1*. EC2 instances are virtual machines that customers can launch in the AWS cloud to run applications and services. The key security features of AWS EC2 include the following:

- **Instance isolation**: EC2 instances are isolated from each other using virtualization technology. This ensures that a security breach in one instance does not affect other instances running on the same host.

- **EBS encryption**: EBS is a block-level storage service used by EC2 instances. EBS volumes can be encrypted to ensure that data is protected at rest.

- **AMIs**: AMIs are pre-configured templates for EC2 instances that include operating systems, applications, and other software. Customers can create their own custom AMIs to ensure that their instances are pre-configured with the necessary security settings.

- **IAM**: IAM enables customers to create IAM policies that control who can launch and terminate instances, as well as access their instances using the AWS Management Console.

- **SGs**: EC2 instances are secured using security groups, which act as virtual firewalls. Customers can define inbound and outbound rules for each security group to control access to their instances.

- **Key pairs**: EC2 instances are accessed using key pairs, which consist of a public and private key. Customers can use key pairs to securely log in to their instances.

By following best practices and using these features, customers can secure and protect compute resources from unauthorized access.

Amazon storage security

We discussed S3 in *Chapter 2*. Amazon S3 is a cloud-based storage service that is designed to provide secure and scalable storage for businesses and developers. The key security features of AWS S3 are as follows:

- **Access controls**: S3 enables customers to set access controls on their buckets, including bucket policies and access control lists. We discussed bucket-level permission policies earlier in this chapter.

- **MFA delete**: This requires an authentication code from an MFA device before allowing the deletion of objects in an S3 bucket.

- **Versioning**: This supports multiple versions of objects to protect against the accidental deletion or modification of objects.

- **Encryption**: S3 supports server-side encryption for data at rest. Customers can choose to encrypt their data using different encryption methods.

- **Access logging**: S3 provides access logging, which enables customers to log all requests made to their buckets, to help with audit and compliance requirements.

- **Cross-region replication**: S3 provides cross-region replication, which enables customers to replicate their data across multiple regions. This can help with disaster recovery and data resilience.

Amazon storage provides a range of security features and controls to secure cloud storage from unauthorized access.

Amazon network security

We discussed VPC in *Chapter 3*. Amazon VPC is a cloud network service that allows customers to create an isolated network within the AWS cloud, to deploy cloud resources such as Amazon EC2 instances, databases, and so on. Here are some of the key security features of AWS VPC:

- **Network isolation**: VPC enables customers to create a private network within the AWS cloud. This network is isolated from the public internet and other VPCs, providing an additional layer of security.

- **Private subnets**: VPC allows customers to create private subnets within their VPC that have no direct access to the internet. Resources in private subnets can only communicate with other resources within the VPC.

- **Network ACLs**: VPC provides network **Access Control Lists** (**ACLs**), which are stateless and allow customers to control inbound and outbound traffic at the subnet level. Network ACLs can be used in conjunction with security groups to provide layered security.

- **VPN connections**: VPC provides the ability to establish VPN connections between the customer's on-premises network and their VPCs, to securely access resources within their VPC from their on-premises network.

- **VPC Flow Logs**: This enables you to record the traffic flowing to and from resources in VPCs, to analyze, troubleshoot, and audit network traffic flows.

AWS VPC and VPC peering secure cloud networks in multiple layers, including VPC routers and routing tables, firewalls (NACLs and SGs), and monitoring and logging tools (such as Flow Logs). Third-party tools such as Palo Alto virtual firewall appliances can also be deployed into VPCs for secure traffic management.

Amazon data security

We discussed AWS databases in *Chapter 4*, data analytics in *Chapter 5*, and ML in *Chapter 6*. These data services provide built-in security features to help customers protect their data stored in the cloud, including the following:

- **Encryption**: AWS provides various encryption options to help customers protect their data at rest and in transit. For example, RDS supports encryption at rest using **AWS Key Management Service** (**KMS**), DynamoDB supports server-side encryption, and Kinesis supports the encryption of data in transit using SSL/TLS, and also provides the option to encrypt data at rest using server-side encryption or customer-managed keys with AWS KMS.

- **Access controls**: AWS database services provide various access control mechanisms, such as IAM policies, database-specific access controls, and VPC security groups. IAM policies can be used to restrict access to Glue, EMR, Athena, and other resources. These access controls enable customers to restrict access to their databases and data.

- **Auditing and logging**: AWS database and data analytics services provide various auditing and logging features, such as AWS CloudWatch, CloudTrail, RDS audit logs, DynamoDB streams, and EMR logs. These features allow customers to track and monitor database activity and can be used for compliance and auditing purposes.

- **Backup and recovery**: AWS database and data analytics services provide backup and recovery features to help customers protect against data loss. For example, Amazon RDS provides automated backups and snapshots, and Amazon DynamoDB provides point-in-time recovery.

- **Data replication**: AWS database and data analytics services provide various data replication options, such as multi-AZ deployments, read replicas, and global tables. These replication features can help improve database performance and availability while also providing data redundancy and disaster recovery capabilities.

- **Compliance**: AWS database services comply with various industry standards and regulations, such as HIPAA, PCI DSS, and GDPR. Customers can use these services to help meet their compliance requirements.

Overall, AWS database services provide a range of security features and controls to help customers protect their data stored in the cloud. In the next section, we will discuss data encryption.

Amazon data encryption

Data encryption is a must for securing sensitive data in the cloud. As we have discussed, almost all the AWS cloud data services provide data encryption. In this section, we will spend time introducing AWS KMS and explain how it is leveraged in S3 object encryption using an example.

KMS is a fully managed service to manage encryption keys. It is designed to simplify the process of creating and managing encryption keys, whether they are stored in Amazon S3, EBS, RDS, or other services. AWS KMS provides the following:

- **Centralized key management**: With AWS KMS, you can centrally manage encryption keys used to protect your data across multiple AWS services and applications.

- **Customizable key policies**: You can set fine-grained access controls on your encryption keys to define who can use them and under what conditions.

- **Encryption key creation**: AWS KMS enables you to create new encryption keys, import your own keys, and manage the lifecycle of your keys.

- **Integration with other AWS services**: AWS KMS is tightly integrated with other AWS services, making it easy to use encryption to protect your data across your entire cloud environment.

- **Auditing and compliance**: The AWS KMS service provides detailed logging and auditing capabilities that help you meet regulatory and compliance requirements.

Now let us dive into the encryption process of an S3 object, to understand how KMS is leveraged in securing AWS data in the cloud:

1. **Create a KMS key**:

   The *AWS KMS master key* is used to generate, encrypt, and decrypt *data keys* that will be shared with other AWS services, such as S3 and EC2, to encrypt the actual data stored in an S3 bucket and on EBS volumes.

   Log in to the AWS Management Console, use the IAM service to add the user group `keyadmin` as key administrators who will *manage access* to the encryption key, and add another group, `keyusers`, for key users who will *use the key* to encrypt and decrypt data.

   Go to the AWS KMS console and then **Customer Managed Keys | Create Key**:

- For **Key type**, choose **Symmetric**.

- For **Alias**, enter the name of the master key, mk.

- For **Key administrators**, select **keyadmin**.

- For **Define key usage permissions**, select **keyusers**.

- At the bottom of the **Review** page, choose **Finish**.

2. **Create an S3 bucket and upload an encrypted object**:

    Go to the S3 console and create a bucket named `data`. Click the bucket and choose the **Properties** tab. In the **Default encryption** section, notice that the setting is currently disabled for the bucket. We will upload a file to the bucket and store it as an encrypted object:

    i.   At the top of the page, go to the **Objects** tab. Choose **Upload**, then **Add files**.

    ii. Browse to and select the `IMG2.jpg` file on your computer.

    iii. Expand the **Properties** section, and configure the following:

    *   In the **Server-side encryption settings** section, choose **Specify an encryption key**.

    *   For **Encryption key type**, choose **AWS Key Management Service key (SSE-KMS)**.

    *   For **AWS KMS key**, select **Choose from your AWS KMS keys**.

    *   From the **Available AWS KMS keys** drop-down menu, choose `mk`.

Figure 7.7 shows the encryption options:

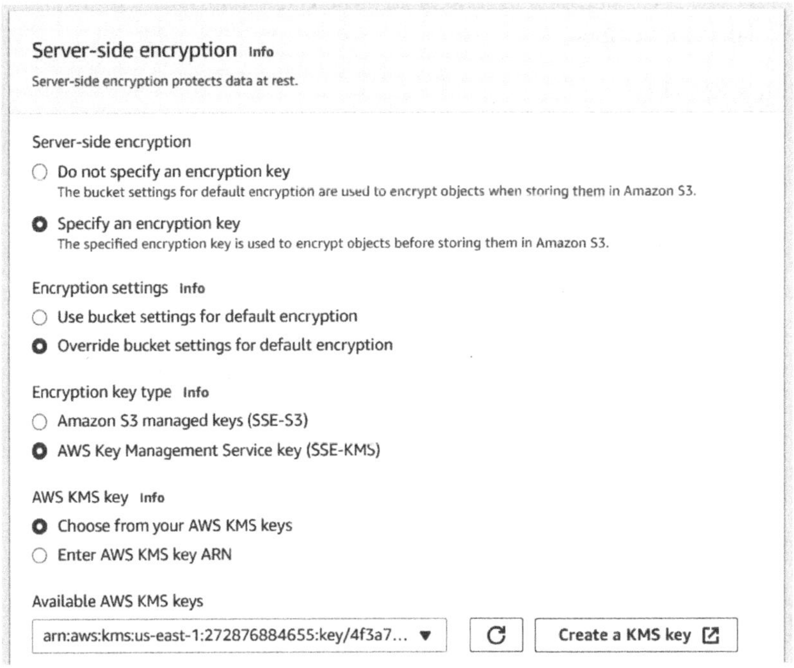

Figure 7.7 – Server side encryption

At the bottom of the page, choose **Upload**. Then click **Close** in the upper-right corner. Now, `IMG2.jpg` is listed as an object in the `data` bucket. Examine the object property and you will notice that server-side encryption using SSE-KMS is enabled on this object:

The following steps explain what transpired in the process of loading IMG2.jpg to data:

- The user requested to upload and store the IMG2.jpg file as an encrypted object in the data bucket.

- Amazon S3 requested a data key from AWS KMS to use to encrypt the file.

- AWS KMS generated a plaintext data key and encrypted the data key by using the customer-managed key mk.

- AWS KMS sent both copies of the data key to Amazon S3.

- Amazon S3 encrypted the object by using the plaintext data key, stored the object, and then deleted the plaintext data key. The encrypted key was kept in the object metadata.

When an object is stored in S3, the data key and the encrypted data (object) are both stored in S3. *Figure 7.8* gives an illustration.

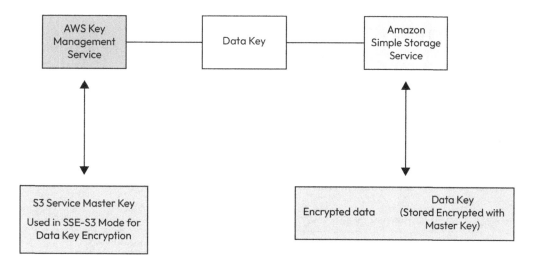

Figure 7.8 – Both data key and encrypted data are stored in S3

3. **Try to access the encrypted object**:

In the **Object overview** section at the top of the page, copy the object URL to your clipboard. Paste the object URL into a new browser tab and attempt to load the page. You will receive an **Access Denied** error, as shown in *Figure 7.9*:

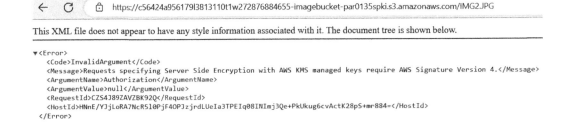

← C 🔒 https://c56424a956179l3813110t1w272876884655-imagebucket-par0135spki.s3.amazonaws.com/IMG2.JPG

This XML file does not appear to have any style information associated with it. The document tree is shown below.

```
▼<Error>
    <Code>AccessDenied</Code>
    <Message>Access Denied</Message>
    <RequestId>YNNNJ4AZ7SVX1K4C</RequestId>
    <HostId>nLMrxP/Wg7CV4UMbAvUwQXMG/WYn6V4O13gQZI5GYSCVvrZQVZOz2IXC7Br2fvdMHMrnwvISqw4=</HostId>
</Error>
```

Figure 7.9 – Access Denied due to S3 bucket permissions

Now let's try to fix the problem by opening the S3 bucket and object permissions:

I.Go back to the S3 bucket and modify the public access permissions `bucket data`:

i.Choose the **Permissions** tab.

ii. In the **Block public access** section, choose **Edit**.

iii.Clear **Block all public access** and click **Save changes**.

iv.Also modify the access settings for the `IMG2.jpg` object:

- Choose the **Objects** tab and then select **IMG2.jpg**.

- Choose **Actions | Make public using ACL**.

- Choose **Make public**.

II.Return to the browser tab that you opened earlier and attempt to load the S3 object URL and refresh the page. You'll now see a different error as shown in *Figure 7.10*:

← C 🔒 https://c56424a956179l3813110t1w272876884655-imagebucket-par0135spki.s3.amazonaws.com/IMG2.JPG

This XML file does not appear to have any style information associated with it. The document tree is shown below.

```
▼<Error>
    <Code>InvalidArgument</Code>
    <Message>Requests specifying Server Side Encryption with AWS KMS managed keys require AWS Signature Version 4.</Message>
    <ArgumentName>Authorization</ArgumentName>
    <ArgumentValue>null</ArgumentValue>
    <RequestId>CZS4J89ZAVZBK92Q</RequestId>
    <HostId>HNnE/YJjLoRA7NcR5l0PjF4OPJzjrdLUeIa3TPEIq08INImj3Qe+PkUkug6cvActK28pS+mr884=</HostId>
</Error>
```

Figure 7.10 – Access Denied due to object encryption

4. **Access the encrypted object URL:**

In the Amazon S3 console, go to bucket `data`. On the **Objects** tab, select `IMG2.jpg`, and then choose **Open**. The image opens in a new tab or window. Why is that? If you analyze the URL that was used to successfully open the object, you will notice the format is something similar to the following:

```
https://c56424a95617913813110t1w272876884655-imagebucket-
par0135spki.s3.us-east-1.amazonaws.com/IMG2.JPG?response-content
-disposition=inline&X-Amz-Security-Token=IQoJb3JpZ2luX2VjECOaCXV
zLWVhc3QtMiJGMEQCIFlnR7JdNb%2BzVYg6onN9TAJnJbuBzkjTolw%2Frf%2BAA
4v8AiByWi%2BoCDH4NjN3kscEngRdMhS8PEQQxs6yWTEcMZFPair0Agj2%2F%2F%
2F%2F%2F%2F%2F%2F%2F%2F8BEAAaDDI3Mjg3Njg4NDY1NSIM%2BOXEy7qW4Ltud
kqZKSgCUDjCFWSoYDnEsuVFS3YzlARzGQnX%2FSNdy3EBYpXCw9cCsLuivYap9nn
f8FpYhTQpjw4Q5iHd7XZxBjsIFxwxWxftmM7GFR8pr3Bj33NCRckPshQ7%2FopYJ
%2FDulh5q3XOaXz5laSv6BzAfm1LTsXCRabgDwv0HKmsDvVcOfClt6%2BdJAuw2k
p5ipPNh1nA8F0GUyQly6w297lsF%2Bd8nblSqru4GFkuXQ90ioEm5B%2Fo3tDxDD
nOrzEXIXXfntnlcknr3Fovle5TtrUKgln1BfOCnO0AdZvzgIncDTxsmpRonWWqK%
2FfWe7pMIX%2FxrSEpMZfHv5U6oACkEsm0nu6nfU2uOdXqbMfV1ijKowKY4DAdD0
goFJ1KBk%2BKi%2Fc86YIHndWjij%2BJlJe3Wxcf9sl%2F7fLpV5c3L9zM4sf1yb
rXZgiqRY7VB2PJzB3QTbzDuvv2gBjqIArm8e4LAAdY14psHogc%2FzaoF7xGd0Wy
9mLB9gWPru9wUmuDeP%2BS0737GQZXe50SvPGPuAUNOw11xyAq87G04p62oKvkcF
n4j%2FEGKGHwVbdmtToVM%2BqlxtBbDBq%2BNoydhvBnUroXLx2fF2JyViodFPvM
YVJCvuAIRox9KKSvLH7oP8%2FuC2bm6cwjPGL04OhcftmKS%2BaRK0%2BcYOc9vN
%2FvkkNUswKsLoBoMDuso7TSBfXMEdxK5iW%2BQqORNKTs1Io051QyCqO0dvJ%2F
rJz5q0iki%2FqCNVUqP%2FQNPlUVrXvFtZVNJHh792jTVbE8KyUbBsu240uYPzr9
dbF%2FfKQlF%2FSgPey6rPbifBpnWuA%3D%3D&X-Amz-Algorithm=AWS4-HMAC-
SHA256&X-Amz-Date=20230325T212511Z&X-Amz-SignedHeaders=host&X-Amz
-Expires=300&X-Amz-Credential=ASIAT7CF22KX7N6F64VX%2F20230325%2
Fus-east-1%2Fs3%2Faws4_request&X-Amz-Signature=b8cbcea71f497aa8
9222025e7135026e6fc62d35e38bca020e479718fcc20624
```

The following steps explain what transpired in the preceding process of accessing `IMG2.jpg`:

*   You requested to open an object.

*   Next, Amazon S3 noticed that the requested object was encrypted. Because you were authenticated to the AWS account when using the Amazon S3 console, the signature version 4 authentication information was automatically included in the request.

*   Amazon S3 then sent the encrypted copy of the data key that the object was encrypted with to AWS KMS.

*   AWS KMS then decrypted the data key by using the AWS KMS key (which never leaves the AWS KMS service).

*   AWS KMS then sent the plaintext data key back to Amazon S3.

Finally, Amazon S3 decrypted the ciphertext of the data object, allowed you to open the object, and deleted the plaintext copy of the data key.

5. **Verify the events from the CloudTrail event history**:

CloudTrail provides an audit log of API calls that are made in the AWS account, and its event history provides access to events from the last 90 days of account activity. Each time an API call is made to an AWS service within the Region that you have selected, if that service reports such events to CloudTrail, then the event and the AWS service that reported the event are listed.

In the search box to the right of **Services**, search for and choose **CloudTrail** to open the CloudTrail console. In the navigation pane, choose **Event history**.

Click on the drop-down menu on the left that currently displays **Read-only** and choose **Event source**. In the **Enter an event source** search box, search for kms and choose **kms.amazonaws.com**, as shown in *Figure 7.11*:

CloudTrail ×	CloudTrail > Event history					
Dashboard						
Event history	Event name	Event time	User name	Event source	Resource type	Resource name
Insights	PutBucketPublicAcce...	March 25, 2023, 16:22:14 (UTC-...	user1006062=Log...	s3.amazonaws.com	AWS::S3::Bucket	c56424a9561791381
Lake	PutAccountPublicAcc...	March 25, 2023, 16:19:17 (UTC-...	user1006062=Log...	s3.amazonaws.com	AWS::S3::AccountPubli...	272876884655.s3-c
Query						
Event data stores	PutBucketEncryption	March 25, 2023, 16:05:25 (UTC-...	user1006062=Log...	s3.amazonaws.com	AWS::S3::Bucket	c56424a9561791381
Integrations New	PutBucketEncryption	March 25, 2023, 16:05:11 (UTC-...	user1006062=Log...	s3.amazonaws.com	AWS::S3::Bucket	c56424a9561791381
Trails	CreateAlias	March 25, 2023, 15:59:43 (UTC-...	user1006062=Log...	kms.amazonaws.com	AWS::KMS::Key, AWS::K...	arn:aws:kms:us-east-
	CreateKey	March 25, 2023, 15:59:43 (UTC-...	user1006062=Log...	kms.amazonaws.com	AWS::KMS::Key, AWS::K...	arn:aws:kms:us-east-
Settings	ConsoleLogin	March 25, 2023, 15:55:47 (UTC-...	user1006062=Log...	signin.amazonaws.com	-	-

Figure 7.11 – CloudTrail event history

Analyze the GenerateDataKey event by choosing the **GenerateDataKey** link. In the **Event record** section, observe the details of the event, as shown in *Figure 7.12*:

```
                 }
             },
             "invokedBy": "AWS Internal"
         },
         "eventTime": "2023-03-25T21:17:58Z",
         "eventSource": "kms.amazonaws.com",
         "eventName": "GenerateDataKey",
         "awsRegion": "us-east-1",
         "sourceIPAddress": "AWS Internal",
         "userAgent": "AWS Internal",
         "requestParameters": {
             "encryptionContext": {
                 "aws:s3:arn": "arn:aws:s3:::c56424a956179l3813110t1w272876884655-imagebucket-par0135spki/IMG2.JPG"
             },
             "keyId": "arn:aws:kms:us-east-1:272876884655:key/4f3a702d-8a2d-4ba3-a5cd-5d5c0485622c",
             "keySpec": "AES_256"
         },
         "responseElements": null,
         "requestID": "a732d1df-72a6-4f9c-af50-aabb86325a4b",
         "eventID": "87c8c68f-b7ca-4e50-a479-803c7470097c",
         "readOnly": true,
         "resources": [
             {
                 "accountId": "272876884655",
                 "type": "AWS::KMS::Key",
                 "ARN": "arn:aws:kms:us-east-1:272876884655:key/4f3a702d-8a2d-4ba3-a5cd-5d5c0485622c"
             }
         ],
         "eventType": "AwsApiCall",
         "managementEvent": true,
         "recipientAccountId": "272876884655",
         "eventCategory": "Management",
```

CloudTrail ✕

Dashboard
Event history
Insights
Lake
  Query
  Event data stores
  Integrations New
Trails

Settings

Pricing
Documentation
Forums
FAQs

Figure 7.12 – CloudTrail GenerateDataKey event

Use the same steps and analyze the **Decrypt** event by choosing the link for the **Decrypt** event name, as shown in *Figure 7.13*:

Analysis: This event was generated when you successfully opened the img2.jpg file from the Amazon S3 console. Notice that the record again details who made the request, which AWS KMS key provided the unencrypted data key back to Amazon S3, and which S3 object was decrypted with the plaintext data key.

Figure 7.13 – CloudTrail Decrypt event

In this section, we have dived into the encryption process of S3 object uploading and the decryption process of object opening. CloudTrail logs all AWS KMS API activity and helps to examine the past usage of AWS KMS keys.

In the next section, we will closely look at AWS logging and monitoring services, including AWS CloudTrail and others.

AWS logging, monitoring, and incident handling

Logging and monitoring are everywhere in the AWS cloud. As we discussed earlier, the third A in AWS cloud's AAA provides traceability of all activities in the cloud. We also introduced CloudTrail and analyzed the CloudTrail logs generated in the encryption and decryption process. In this section, we will explore further the AWS security services related to cloud resource logging and monitoring.

While **CloudTrail** provides a record of API calls made within a customer's AWS account, thus enabling customers to monitor and audit activity within their accounts, Amazon CloudWatch is a managed service that enables customers to monitor, store, access, and analyze log files from AWS services and their own applications, such as EC2 instances, RDS databases, Lambda functions, and more, to gain insights into the health and performance of their applications and infrastructure. Some of the most important features of the AWS cloud are elasticity and auto-scaling, and **CloudWatch** is the service that monitors unit utilization, sets threshold alarms, and integrates with other AWS services such as AWS Lambda and AWS EC2 to enable automatic scaling of resources based on application demand.

AWS Config is a service that allows users to assess, audit, and evaluate the configurations of their AWS resources. It provides a historical record of configuration changes to AWS resources and can be used to simplify compliance auditing and reporting. It can also be integrated with other AWS services such as AWS CloudTrail and AWS Lambda to enable automated remediation of non-compliant resources. AWS Config can be used to track changes to resource configurations over time and to troubleshoot issues by pinpointing the root cause of changes or issues.

AWS Trusted Advisor checks four cloud infrastructure pillars, including security, performance, resilience, and cost. These checks analyze a user's AWS infrastructure and provide recommendations for improving resource utilization, security, and cost efficiency. For example, Trusted Advisor can identify security vulnerabilities in AWS S3 configurations and suggest ways to improve security settings for S3 buckets and objects. In addition, Trusted Advisor detects AWS service limits in users' environments, such as the number of instances that can be launched in a region, and provides users with direct access to AWS technical support to increase the limit. It can also be configured to provide automatic notifications when changes or issues are detected in a user's AWS environment.

Amazon Inspector is a security assessment service used to scan vulnerabilities, by providing a list of security findings and recommendations to help customers remediate potential vulnerabilities. Amazon Inspector supports a wide range of assessments, including checks for common security issues such as insecure communication protocols, vulnerabilities in software libraries, and misconfigurations in network and application components. It also supports assessments for compliance with industry standards such as the **Payment Card Industry Data Security Standard** (**PCI DSS**) and the **Health Insurance Portability and Accountability Act** (**HIPAA**). For example, when an EC2 instance is compromised, we can isolate the instance and run Inspector against it to assess the vulnerability and security risks.

Amazon Macie scans storage to detect personal information such as Social Security numbers, including Amazon S3, Amazon RDS, and Amazon Redshift. It can also provide users with a detailed inventory of their data assets, including the location and risk level of sensitive data. Macie can also monitor data access patterns and alert users to potential data breaches or unauthorized access to sensitive data. It can also provide recommendations for improving data security, such as access control policies, encryption, and data retention policies.

AWS Shield is a managed service that provides protection against **Distributed Denial of Service** (**DDoS**) attacks. While AWS Shield Standard is a free service that is automatically enabled for all AWS customers and provides protection against most common network and transport layer DDoS attacks, including SYN/ACK floods, UDP floods, and reflection attacks, Shield Advanced is a paid service that provides additional protection against more sophisticated DDoS attacks, including application layer attacks. AWS Shield Advanced includes 24/7 access to the AWS **DDoS Response Team** (**DRT**), for assistance in mitigating DDoS attacks.

Amazon GuardDuty is a threat detection service that uses ML technology to continuously monitor customers' AWS accounts for malicious activity and unauthorized behavior. In the next section, we will fully discuss GuardDuty and see how it can be integrated and built into a security ecosystem for security hardening.

Case study – an AWS threat detection and incident handling ecosystem

After the introduction of Amazon logging and monitoring services in the last section, we will conduct a case study on an actual security incident and details on how it was handled, by introducing an **automatic threat detection and remediation system** that the author developed for an AWS customer.

CloudSpace is an Amazon enterprise customer that functions as a reseller of AWS services to end customers, with over 4,000 AWS accounts in total. During 2017-2018, CloudSpace experienced three cases of account compromise. Three accounts were compromised in the first attack in November 2017, and four more in the second attack in March 2018. The third incident occurred in August 2018, when another five accounts were compromised. These incidents led to about $200,000 in losses. Investigations thereafter revealed that no threat-detection services were enabled and the Amazon fraud detection team's customer notifications went to their company emails and voice mails manually and thus were not acted upon in a timely manner.

To defend against these attacks, we have developed an automated threat detection and remediation ecosystem. The architecture of the system is shown in *Figure 7.14*:

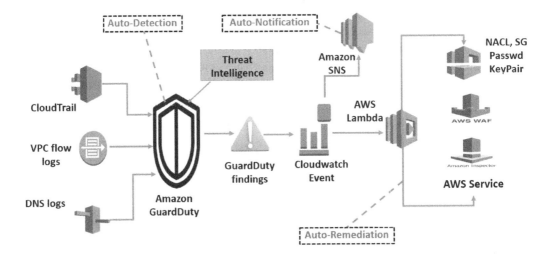

Figure 7.14 – Architecture of the threat detection and remediation ecosystem

The ecosystem has the following functions.

Automatic threat detection

Enabling Amazon GuardDuty is the first step for the ecosystem to work. As we discussed earlier, GuardDuty uses machine learning to monitor and generate the activity patterns of the AWS account, such as the normal and peak times and scope, and leverages threat intelligence to analyze and correlate data from various sources, such as AWS CloudTrail, Amazon VPC Flow Logs, and DNS logs, to detect and prioritize potential security threats. Once GuardDuty is enabled, it will continuously monitor the AWS accounts for malicious activity and unauthorized access automatically. GuardDuty can detect a variety of threats, including botnets, port scanning, cryptocurrency mining, and unauthorized API access. It can also provide users with detailed information about the nature of the threat, including the source IP address and the affected AWS resources.

Automatic notification

When GuardDuty detects a threat, it generates a finding in the GuardDuty console and creates a Cloudwatch event, which can be used to automatically notify the customer. In the ecosystem, GuardDuty integrates with **Simple Notification Service** (**SNS**) and some third-party tools, enables timely notifications about possible threats, and facilitates notifications to multiple parties, via Slack and its ticketing system.

Automatic remediation

In addition to notifications, CloudWatch events can trigger Lambda functions that serve as the basis for remediation. Depending on the attack, a customer can choose to automatically terminate a compromised instance if it is part of a non-critical development sandbox account, or to be notified only if the instance is part of a production workload. Following are some remediation actions we explored in the ecosystem:

- Blocking bad actor access with NACL and SG modifications

- Enabling MFA for accounts if not yet done

- Changing account user passwords

- Deleting and rotating account access keys (while being cautious about production accounts and ensuring applications are not using the keys before rotating them)

- Snapshotting compromised EC2 instances for forensic investigation

- Running Amazon Inspector assessments on compromised EC2 instances (or forensic instances launched based on snapshots)

- Terminating compromised EC2 instances (be cautious with production instances, termination is best suited for stateless applications that are deployed using Auto Scaling)

- Deleting all images (AMIs) created during the compromise

- Deleting all snapshots created during the compromise

The ecosystem was deployed successfully in the customer's environment. It guard-railed the customer against several successive attacks, and the customer loves the ecosystem and became one of the top 10 GuardDuty consumers in 2018.

Summary

In this chapter, we started with the Amazon cloud security model, then discussed IAM, which manages authentication, authorization, and auditing. We dived into AWS cloud infrastructure security, which protects cloud resources such as EC2, S3, and RDS, and data security, which is about data encryption and key management. We further explored the AWS data encryptions, cloud monitoring and logging services, and ended with a case study about an AWS automatic cloud threat detection and remediation ecosystem.

We have now concluded *Part 1* of the book: *Learning the Amazon Cloud*. In the next part, we will explore Google Cloud Platform.

Practice questions

Questions 1-10 are based on the AWS architecture shown in *Figure 7.15*. There is a cloud admin in company ABC, which has 10,000 EC2 instances in its AWS cloud. The diagram shows the three VPCs in the cloud admin account. All networks are configured correctly. The cloud admin created an EC2 role, R3, that can access the S3 bucket named B3 in us-east-1. EC2-1 has a security group named sg. Subnet1 has a network access control list named nacl:

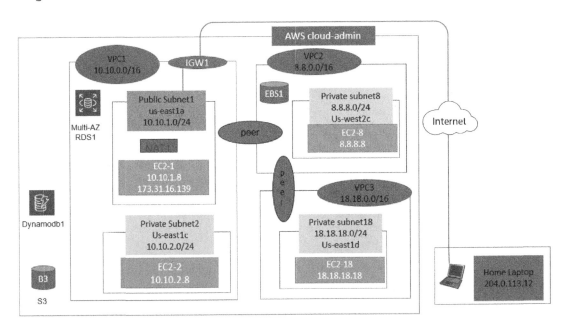

Figure 7.15 – AWS Networking Architecture

1. They are looking for a place to securely store a connection string to RDS1. What do you suggest?

    A. EBS

    B. Parameter store

    C. DynamoDB

    D. RDS

2. They couldn't ping EC2-1 from their home laptop, and he found the following in the AWS VPC flow log:

```
2 123456789010 eni-1235b8ca123456789 204.0.113.12 173.31.16.139
0 0 1 4 336 1432917027 1432917142 ACCEPT OK

2 123456789010 eni-1235b8ca123456789 173.31.16.139 204.0.113.12
0 0 1 4 336 1432917094 1432917142 REJECT OK
```

What is the likely reason the "ping" did not work?

    A. NACL outbound rule blocked the traffic

    B. SG inbound rule blocked the traffic

    C. NACL inbound rule blocked the traffic

    D. SG outbound rule blocked the traffic

3. How can they block the contractors/developers from accessing the EC2-18 instance's metadata?

    A. Modify EC2-18's GuestOS route table

    B. Modify Subnet18's NACLs

    C. Modify EC2-18's SG

    D. Modify EC2-18's GuestOS /etc/passwd file

4. How can they set the correct date/time on all 10,000 EC2 instances?

    A. Use AWS Systems Manager

    B. Use AWS Security Center

    C. Use AWS Config

    D. Use AWS Inspector

5. No one in the company can access the Linux instance EC2-8. What can they do to log into it?

    A. Generate a new keypair and utilize EC2-8's user data to copy the public key to EC2-8

    B. Generate a new keypair and utilize EC2-8's metadata to copy the key to EC2-8

    C. Generate a new keypair and scp the public key to EC2-8 to ssh into it

    D. ssh into a third Linux instance, EC2-1, and break into EC2-8 from there

6. Which of the following is not true?

   A. EC2-1 can ping EC2-8

   B. EC2-8 can ping EC2-18

   C. EC2-1 can ping EC2-18

   D. EC2-2 can ping EC2-8

7. C2-18 needs to access the internet for patching. Which one of these options is true?

   A. It can be done via IGW1

   B. It can be done via NAT1

   C. It cannot be done via IGW1 or NAT1

   D. It can be done via IGW1 and NAT1

8. They want to allow EC2-18 access to B3. What is your suggestion?

   A. Assign R3 to EC2-18. Create an S3 endpoint in VPC3

   B. Assign R3 to EC2-18

   C. Create an S3 endpoint in VPC3

   D. Assign R3 to EC2-18, then create an S3 endpoint in VPC1

9. EC-1 needs to access an external web server via port 888 with minimum exposure to the internet. How can it be done? (Choose two answers.)

   A. NACL needs a rule that allows outgoing traffic on port 888

   B. NACL needs rules that allow outgoing traffic on port 888 and incoming traffic on ephemeral ports

   C. SG needs a rule that allows outgoing traffic on port 888

   D. SG needs rules that allow outgoing traffic on port 888 and incoming traffic on ephemeral ports

   E. SG needs rules that allow outgoing traffic on port 888 and incoming traffic on port 888

10. Which one of these options is not recommended to protect the data in DynamoDB1?

   A. Data encryption

   B. SG

   C. IAM users/roles

   D. VPC endpoint

Answers to the practice questions

1. B

2. A

3. A

4. A

5. A

6. C

7. C

8. A

9. B and C

10. B

Further reading

For further insights into what you've learned about in this chapter, refer to the following links:

- `https://docs.aws.amazon.com/security/`

- `https://aws.amazon.com/iam/`

- `https://aws.amazon.com/guardduty/`

- `https://aws.amazon.com/inspector/`

- `https://aws.amazon.com/config/`

- `https://aws.amazon.com/premiumsupport/technology/trusted-advisor/`

- `https://docs.aws.amazon.com/whitepapers/latest/introduction-aws-security/data-encryption.html`

- `https://docs.aws.amazon.com/whitepapers/latest/introduction-aws-security/security-of-the-aws-infrastructure.html`

- `https://docs.aws.amazon.com/whitepapers/latest/introduction-aws-security/monitoring-and-logging.html`

- `https://aws.amazon.com/security/continuous-monitoring-threat-detection/`

Part 2:
Comprehending
GCP Cloud Services

This second part of the book dives into **Google Cloud Platform** (**GCP**). We will compare GCP cloud services with AWS cloud services. Starting with foundational discussions of the GCP services, we will then explore the GCP data services, including managed database services and big data services. We will then examine the GCP ML services, including Vertex AI, ML APIs, and the recently emerged Google generative AI services. This part ends by looking at Google Cloud security services, with a focus on GCP **Security Command Center** (**SCC**).

This part comprises the following chapters:

- *Chapter 8, Google Cloud Foundation Services*
- *Chapter 9, Google Cloud Data Services*
- *Chapter 10, Google Cloud AI Services*
- *Chapter 11, Google Cloud Security Services*

8

Google Cloud Foundation Services

In *Part 1* of the book, we dived into the Amazon cloud, explored and provisioned cloud services for compute, storage, networking, databases, big data, and machine learning. Now, in this second part, we are switching to another cloud platform: **Google Cloud Platform** (**GCP**). GCP has many similarities with AWS but also has many of its own features. Finding the similarities and examining the differences are what we will do in the second part of the book. In this chapter, we will focus on GCP's foundation services, including the following:

- Google Cloud resource hierarchy – organization, folders, projects, and resources

- Google compute services – **Google Compute Engine** (**GCE**), **Google App Engine** (**GAE**), **Google Kubernetes Engine** (**GKE**), and Google Cloud Functions (serverless)

- Google storage services – **Persistent Disk** (**PD**), **Filestore**, and **Google Cloud Storage** (**GCS**)

- Google Cloud networking services – **Virtual Private Cloud** (**VPC**), firewalls, etc.

During our discussions, we will use some examples. The sample code is available in the GitHub repository for this book: `https://github.com/PacktPublishing/Self-Taught-Cloud-computing-Engineer`.

Cloud Shell is an extremely useful tool for running cloud command lines to provision and manage cloud resources. It has a wide range of resource-managing commands and also an editor to write/edit files. In the first part of the book, we introduced and used AWS Cloud Shell for many use cases. In this part of the book, we will leverage the Cloud Shell tool heavily. In this chapter, we will use Google Cloud Shell to create and manage resources including compute, storage, and networking.

We will start by looking at the Google Cloud resource hierarchy.

Google Cloud resource hierarchy

Very similar to AWS's global infrastructure, **Google Cloud** has global data centers where the physical facilities and data resides. Each data center has redundant power, networking, and connectivity, and there are Google backbone networks connecting them. These data centers compose the Google Cloud, which is divided into **regions** and **zones**, like AWS Regions and AZs. *Figure 8.1* shows the Google global regions at the time of writing this book:

Region	City	Region	City	Region	City
asia-east1	Changhua County, Taiwan, APAC	europe-central2	Warsaw, Poland, Europe	northamerica-northeast1	Montreal, Quebec, North America
asia-east2	Hong Kong, APAC	europe-north1	Hamina, Finland, Europe	northamerica-northeast2	Toronto, Ontario, North America
asia-northeast1	Tokyo, Japan, APAC	europe-west1	St. Ghislain, Belgian, Europe	southamerica-east1	Osasco, Sao Paulo, Brazil, South America
asia-northeast2	Osaka, Japan, APAC	europe-west2	London, England, Europe	us-central1	Council Bluffs, Iowa, North America
asia-northeast3	Seoul, South Korea, APAC	europe-west3	Frankfurt, Germany, Europe	us-east1	Moncks Corner, South Carolina, North America
asia-south1	Mumbai, India APAC	europe-west4	Eemshaven, Netherlands, Europe	us-east4	Ashburn, Virginia, North America
asia-south2	Delhi, India APAC	europe-west6	Zurich, Switzerland, Europe	us-west1	The Dalles, Oregon, North America
asia-southeast1	Jurong West, Singapore, APAC			us-west2	Los Angeles, California, North America
asia-southeast2	Jakarta, Indonesia, APAC			us-west3	Salt Lake City, Utah, North America
australia-southeast1	Sydney, Australia, APAC			us-west4	Las Vegas, Nevada, North America
australia-southeast2	Hong Kong, APAC				

Figure 8.1 – Google global regions

In the cloud, there are **Cloud Service Consumers** (**CSCs**), each having their own resource hierarchy. The GCP resource hierarchy structure is quite different from AWS's.

In the previous chapter, we discussed the AWS resource hierarchy, which consists of a root organization, **Organization Units** (**OUs**), and AWS accounts, from top to bottom. In GCP, the resource hierarchy consists of four main layers, as shown in *Figure 8.2*:

- **Organization (Org Node)**: This is the top level of the hierarchy and represents a company. The organization provides centralized control over billing, resource management, and access control.

- **Folders**: These represent departments or divisions in a company. Folders can be used to organize resources based on departments or divisions within an organization, with policies applied to all resources within them.

- **Projects**: These are the lowest layers in the hierarchy that manage GCP resources, such as **Virtual Machines** (**VMs**), storage, and databases. Projects are used to isolate and manage access to resources.

- **Resources**: These are the services and tools provided by GCP, such as VMs, storage buckets, databases, and APIs.

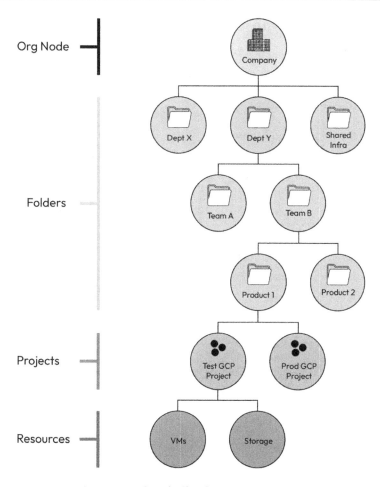

Figure 8.2 – Google Cloud resource hierarchy

In the GCP organization hierarchy, projects are managed and billed separately, although multiple projects may be associated with the same billing account. Each project is a separate partition and is isolated from other projects. Each resource belongs to exactly one project. We will start with our first GCP resource, GCE, which is part of the Google Cloud compute services.

Google Cloud compute

We learned about EC2 instances in *Chapter 1*, which was about Amazon cloud compute services. Switching to Google Cloud, we will first discuss GCE VMs, which are like the EC2 instances in AWS, and then GKE, which was originally developed at Google and released as open source in 2014.

Google Compute Engine

GCE offers VMs running in Google's cloud as a computing resource. Just like provisioning an AWS EC2 instance, we need to make choices about the computer hardware and software when provisioning a GCE VM in Google Cloud. Let us go to the Google Cloud console, provision a GCE instance, and add some cloud storage to it:

1. Log in to the Google Cloud console.

2. Go to the Google Cloud console: `https://console.cloud.google.com`. As we mentioned in an earlier section, each GCP resource belongs to a project, so you need to create a project first:

Figure 8.3 – Google Cloud console welcome page

Once a project is created, in this case, **project 11222020**, you will land on the welcome page, as shown in *Figure 8.3*.

3. Create a VM in the cloud:

   From the welcome page, select **Create a VM**. Fill in the following details, as shown in *Figure 8.4*:

   • **Name**: This is the VM's name, whatever you may want to call it.

   • **Labels**: This is a key-value tag for the VM, such as `Name: "vm1"` or `Department: "math"`.

   • **Region** and **Zone**: This is the location where you want to create the VM, such as `US-east1d`.

   • **Machine type**: This determines the VM's hardware. *Figure 8.4* shows our choice of the N1 series f1-micro machine type. You can also customize the hardware configurations.

   • **Boot disk | Image**: This determines the VM's software, including the operating system and applications.

In our case, we chose **f1.micro** in the **N1** family as the machine type, **centOS** as the disk image (the Figure below shows Debian which is another Linux OS), and take the **default** for the rest. Click **Create** to provision a VM in Google Cloud:

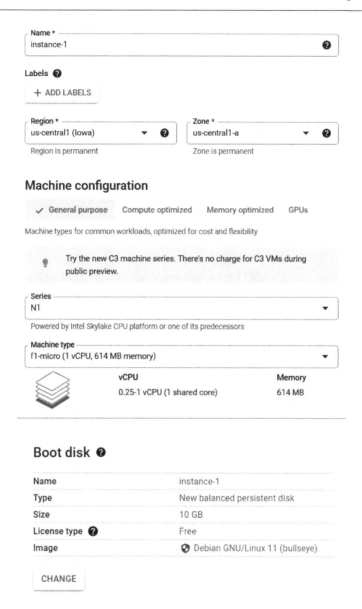

Figure 8.4 – Create a Google Cloud VM

The VM instance is created, showing a green status and the available actions you can take, as shown in *Figure 8.5*:

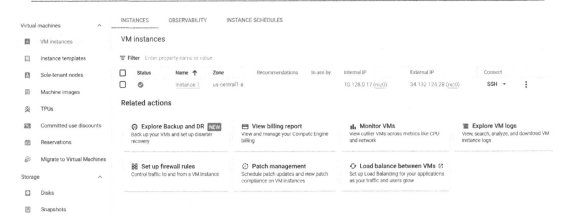

Figure 8.5 – A VM is created

To connect to the VM, click the **SSH** button and a new ssh session window pops up:

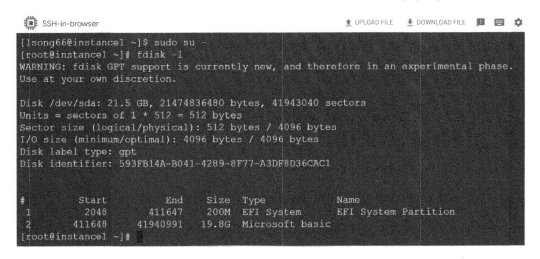

Figure 8.6 – SSH into the VM instance and check disks

Within the ssh session window, switch to the root super user and run fdisk -l. We can see there is one disk with a size of 20 GB in this Linux VM, as shown in *Figure 8.6*.

4.   Add a disk (block storage) to the VM:

Just as we added an EFS to an EC2 instance in *Chapter 1*, we can add block storage to the Google Cloud VM. The block storage volume here is called a PD.

I.   Create a PD:

Click **Disks** under **Storage** on the VM dashboard (as shown in *Figure 8.5*), then select **CREATE DISK**. Fill in the details as shown in *Figure 8.7*. In our case, we have chosen a **Single zone** disk that is 10 GB in size:

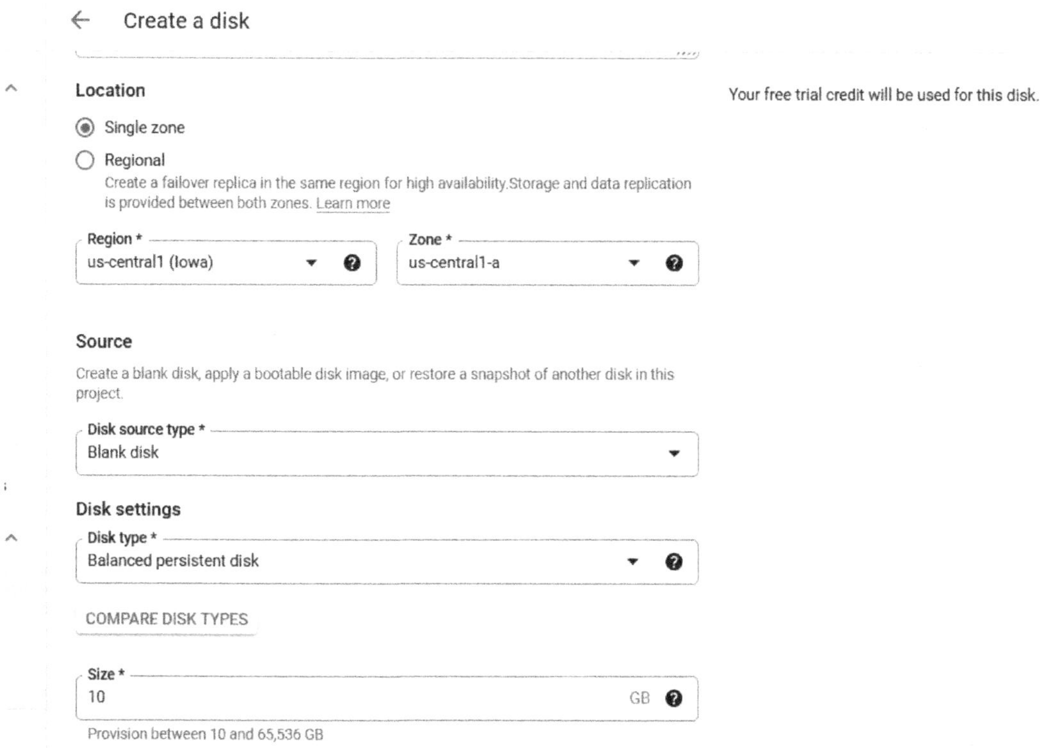

←   Create a disk

Location   Your free trial credit will be used for this disk.

◉ Single zone

○ Regional
Create a failover replica in the same region for high availability.Storage and data replication is provided between both zones. Learn more

Region *
us-central1 (Iowa)   ▼ ❷

Zone *
us-central1-a   ▼ ❷

Source

Create a blank disk, apply a bootable disk image, or restore a snapshot of another disk in this project.

Disk source type *
Blank disk   ▼

Disk settings

Disk type *
Balanced persistent disk   ▼ ❷

COMPARE DISK TYPES

Size *
10   GB ❷

Provision between 10 and 65,536 GB

Figure 8.7 – Create a persistent disk

Click **Create**. Now, it will show two PDs (20 GB for the root disk and 10 GB for the one just created).

    II.   Attach the PD to the VM:

Go back to the instance dashboard and click the instance name to edit the instance. Scroll down and click **ATTACH EXISTING DISK**. Choose the **disk-1** PD, which we created earlier, as shown in *Figure 8.8*. Then, click **SAVE** and then **SAVE** again:

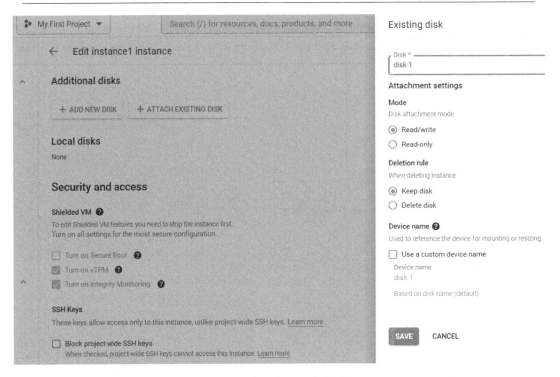

Figure 8.8 – Attach Disk-1 to the VM instance

Now, go back to the SSH session. Run `fdisk -l` again and we can see that `disk-1` (10 GB) is added to the instance, as shown in *Figure 8.9*. Now, you can use the `mkfs` and `mount` Linux commands to format the disk and make it available for the operating system to read/write:

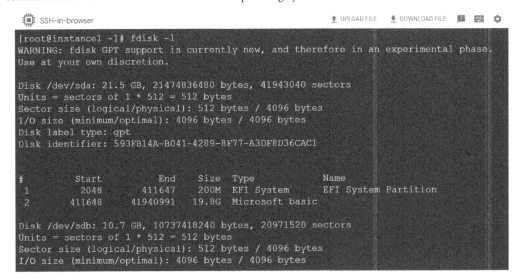

Figure 8.9 – Disk1 is added to the VM instance and visible to the operating system

In addition to PDs, which are block storage, we can also add network filesystems to Google Cloud VM instances. Like EFS in the AWS cloud, there is fully managed filesystem storage in Google Cloud, called **Filestore**, which can be created and shared by many VMs. More details are available at `https://cloud.google.com/filestore`.

From the preceding process of provisioning a GCE VM instance and adding a PD to the instance, we can see that the concepts and operations are very similar to that of the AWS EC2 instance and adding an EFS. *Figure 8.10* shows a comparison of GCE and Amazon EC2:

Features	Google GCE	Amazon EC2
Hardware (RAM,CPU,Disk)	Machine Types	Instance Types
Software (VM Images)	Disk Images	AMI
Local attached disk	Local SSD	Instance Store
Block Storage	PD (Persistent Disks)	EBS (Elastic Block Storage)
Network File System	FileStore	EFS (Elastic File System)

Figure 8.10 – Comparison of GCE and Amazon EC2

Within GCP, there are also the concepts of load balancing and scaling groups. GCP load balancing accepts the load and balances them among the instances in the group, which can be set up for autoscaling.

More details are available at `https://cloud.google.com/load-balancing` and `https://cloud.google.com/compute/docs/instance-groups`.

Having learned about GCE, we will now introduce GKE, a fully managed container orchestration service in the Google Cloud compute service spectrum.

Google Kubernetes Engine

First, let us recap some basic computing platform concepts, from physical computers to VMs, to containers, to serverless:

- **Physical computers**: These are physical machines with their own hardware components, such as CPUs, memory, storage, and network interfaces. Each physical computer runs a single operating system, and applications are installed and run directly on the hardware.

- **VMs**: These are virtual computers that emulate a physical computer. The virtualization technology makes it possible to create and run multiple VMs on the same physical host and share the hardware resources. Each VM is isolated from other VMs running on the same host, and the operating system running inside the VM has no knowledge of the underlying hardware.

- **Container**: This is a lightweight, standalone executable application software package that includes the application code, runtime, system tools, libraries, and settings. Containers provide an isolated environment for running applications, but they share the same operating system kernel as the host, which allows them to be more lightweight and faster to start up and shut down than VMs. Containers also consume fewer system resources and are easier to manage than VMs. To run and manage containers, you need to have **Docker**, which is a tool that provides a container runtime, an image format, and a set of tools to manage containers. With Docker, developers can build container images and run them on any system that supports Docker.

- **Serverless**: This refers to the practice of running applications and code without the underlying infrastructure or servers. In a serverless environment, the cloud provider manages the infrastructure and automatically scales resources up or down based on demand, so developers can focus on writing and submitting code without worrying about the underlying infrastructure.

- A container is a running instance of a Docker image, and it runs the same way on different machines. GKE is a container orchestration and management system. A GKE cluster is a group of GCE VM nodes working together to deploy applications by running containers on the cluster nodes. Some of the key features of GKE include the following:

  - **Automatic scaling**: GKE can automatically scale applications based on demand, ensuring that they have the resources they need to handle traffic spikes and scale down when traffic decreases

  - **Automatic upgrades**: GKE can automatically upgrade Kubernetes clusters to the latest version, ensuring that applications are running on the most up-to-date platform

  - **Built-in security**: GKE provides built-in security features, such as network policies, automatic encryption, and **Identity and Access Management** (**IAM**), to help protect applications and data

  - **Integrated monitoring**: GKE provides integrated monitoring and logging features, allowing developers to monitor the health and performance of their applications in real time

  - **Hybrid and multi-cloud support**: GKE can run applications in hybrid or multi-cloud environments, enabling developers to run their applications on-premises or in other cloud environments

Now that we understand the key GKE concepts, let us build a Docker image for a simple web server that will display a greeting message, create a GKE cluster, deploy the image to the cluster, and serve the web server on the internet:

1. Clone the source code from GitHub:

Open Google Cloud Shell and run the following command to clone the code from GitHub:

```
git clone https://github.com/PacktPublishing/Self-Taught-Cloud-
computing-Engineer.git
```

Change the directory to `gke-lab-01` and list the files in the directory:

```
cd chapter8; ls
```

There are three files in the directory:

- `requirement.txt` is a Python file that stores information about all the libraries, modules, and packages that are needed to build the Docker image.

- `app.py` is a Python file that defines the `webserver1` containerized application. More details about `webserver1` are available in the book's GitHub repository.

- `dockerfile` provides step-by-step instructions for building a Docker image for the application.

These files will be used in the following steps:

2. Containerize the application – build the Docker image and push it to **Google Container Registry (GCR)**:

```
docker build -t gcr.io/$DEVSHELL_PROJECT_ID/webserver1 .
docker images
docker push gcr.io/$DEVSHELL_PROJECT_ID/webserver1
```

3. Create a two-node GKE cluster and deploy the containerized `webserver1`:

   I.   Set up the environment:

```
gcloud config set compute/zone us-central1-a
gcloud services enable container.googleapis.com
```

   II. Create the GKE cluster:

```
gcloud container clusters create hello-cluster --num-nodes=2
```

   III. Deploy the container application (`webserver1`) to listen on port 80:

```
kubectl create deployment hello-web --image=gcr.io/$DEVSHELL_
PROJECT_ID/webserver1 --port 80
kubectl get deployments hello-web
```

   IV. Check out our Pods on the nodes:

```
kubectl get pods
```

4. Create a load balancer and expose the service to the internet:

   Create a load balancer and expose the application to the internet on port 8080:

```
kubectl expose deployment hello-web --type=LoadBalancer --port
8080 --target-port 80
```

> **Note**
>
> At this point, you can verify, from the Google Cloud console, the following resources are provisioned:
>
> GCE (two VMs; they are the cluster nodes), instance groups (one instance group that has the two VMs), and the load balancer.

5. Find the load balancer's public IP address and port:

```
kubectl get service
```

Open a new browser to access the service/web server.

6. Set up autoscaling for the cluster pods and nodes now:

> **Note**
>
> A Kubernetes pod is the smallest execution unit in a cluster. It groups the containers of an application. For example, a web service application pod may have two containers – a web server and web server logging.

    I.   Set up autoscaling for the application Pods:

```
kubectl autoscale deployment hello-1a --max 6 --min 4
--cpu-percent 50
```

    II.   Enable autoscaling for the cluster nodes:

```
gcloud container clusters update hello-cluster --enable-
autoscaling --min-nodes 2 --max-nodes 8
```

7. Clean up the resources we have provisioned earlier:

    I.   Delete the GKE cluster:

```
gcloud container clusters delete hello-cluster
```

    II.   Delete the container images in GCR:

```
gcloud container images delete gcr.io/$DEVSHELL_PROJECT_ID/
webserver1
```

In this example, we have built a Docker image, created a GKE cluster, and deployed the image to run on the GKE cluster as a container, and then created a global load balancer service pointing to the container. We then enabled the cluster for autoscaling.

GCP offers other cloud compute services apart from GCE and GKE, including GAE and Google Cloud Functions. GAE is a fully managed, serverless cloud platform for developing and hosting web applications at scale. After you develop an application with a program language, libraries and frameworks, GAE will deploy the apps by provisioning and scaling compute services, based on the workload demand. More details are available at `https://cloud.google.com/appengine`. Like AWS Lambda, Google Cloud Functions is a serverless compute service in which users only define and deploy the source function code to be triggered by certain events/conditions and executed at the backend. We will explore this in later chapters of the book, and more details are available at `https://cloud.google.com/functions`.

In this section, we examined the GCP compute services. We explored GCE and GKE and briefly discussed GAE and Google Cloud Functions. We launched GCE VM instances and a GKE cluster that deployed a load-balancing web server based on container deployment. We also enabled autoscaling for the GKE cluster. In the next section, we will discuss the GCS service.

Google Cloud Storage

Like Amazon S3, GCS offers multiple tiers for different cloud storage use cases, depending on the access frequency and durability requirements. *Figure 8.11*shows the comparison of GCS and S3:

Storage Features	Google Cloud Storage (GCS)	Amazon Simple Storage Service (S3)
Standard Storage	**GCS Standard** (Regional, Dual-regional, Multi-regional)	**S3 Standard** (Regional)
Cool Storage	**GCS Nearline** (Regional, Dual-reginal, Multi-regional, 30-days minimum duration)	**S3 Standard-IA** (Regional, 30-days minimum duration
	GCS Coldline (Regional, Dual-reginal, Multi-regional, 90-days minimum duration)	**S3 Standard One-zone-IA** (Zonal, 30-days minimum duration)
Cold/Archival Storage	**GCS Archieve** (Regional, Dual-reginal, Multi-regional, 365-days minimum duration, millisecond retrieval time)	**Glacier** (Regional, 90-days minimum duration, minutes to hours retrieval time)
Move to the cloud	**Data Transfer Appliance**	**Snowball and Snow Mobile**

Figure 8.11 – GCS tiers

In the AWS cloud, we have the concept of an IAM EC2 role, which, when attached to an EC2 instance, will entail the applications running on EC2 to have the same permission as assigned to the role. In GCP, we have a similar concept called a service account. Each GCE VM has a default service account, which is created at the same time as the VM to define GCP service permissions of the vm. As shown in *Figure 8.12*, the default permission for GCS is **Read Only** for a GCP VM instance, and we can change it to **Read and Write** at instance creation time or after it is created. For the latter, we need to shut down the instance in order to modify its permissions and restart it:

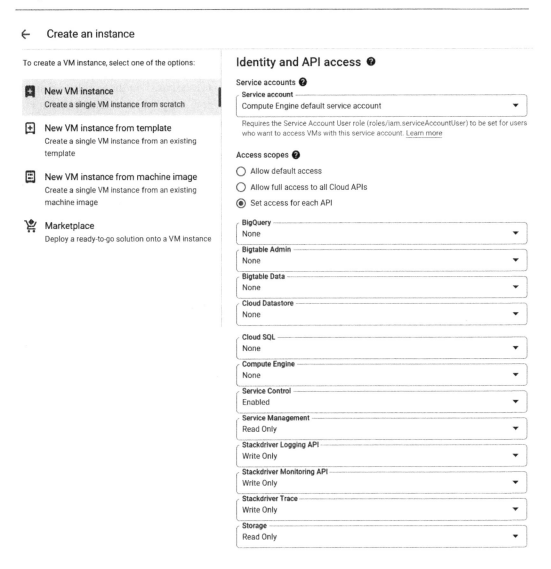

Figure 8.12 – Fill in the Identity and API access settings for a VM

We can use the Cloud Shell gsutil command to create a GCS bucket, copy files into it, and delete it. gsutil is a Python application that lets you access and manage GCS resources from the command line, such as creating and deleting GCS buckets, listing buckets and objects, uploading, downloading, and deleting GCS objects, and moving, copying, and renaming these objects. *Figure 8.13* shows several gsutil commands and their executions:

```
logan_song@cloudshell:~/GCP/gke-lab-01 (dito-contact-center-ai-sandbox)$
logan_song@cloudshell:~/GCP/gke-lab-01 (dito-contact-center-ai-sandbox)$ gsutil mb gs://z04092023-unsafe
Creating gs://z04092023-unsafe/...
logan_song@cloudshell:~/GCP/gke-lab-01 (dito-contact-center-ai-sandbox)$ gsutil cp /etc/hosts gs://z04092023-unsafe
Copying file:///etc/hosts [Content-Type=application/octet-stream]...
/ [1 files][  218.0 B/  218.0 B]
Operation completed over 1 objects/218.0 B.
logan_song@cloudshell:~/GCP/gke-lab-01 (dito-contact-center-ai-sandbox)$ gsutil ls gs://z04092023-unsafe
gs://z04092023-unsafe/hosts
logan_song@cloudshell:~/GCP/gke-lab-01 (dito-contact-center-ai-sandbox)$ gsutil rm gs://z04092023-unsafe/*
Removing gs://z04092023-unsafe/hosts...
/ [1 objects]
Operation completed over 1 objects.
logan_song@cloudshell:~/GCP/gke-lab-01 (dito-contact-center-ai-sandbox)$ gsutil rb gs://z04092023-unsafe/
Removing gs://z04092023-unsafe/...
logan_song@cloudshell:~/GCP/gke-lab-01 (dito-contact-center-ai-sandbox)$
```

Figure 8.13 – Cloud Shell commands for GCS

After the compute and storage discussions, let us switch to the GCP networking topic. We will use Google Cloud Shell commands to implement and manage GCP networking resources.

Google Cloud networking

Like AWS VPC, Google VPC provides network traffic management, segmentation, and isolation. The difference between them is that AWS VPC is regional and thus subnets in the same VPC are in the same region, while GCP VPC is global and thus subnets in the same VPC may be in different regions. In this section, we will use Cloud Shell to build up a GCP network. *Figure 8.14* shows the architecture of the network:

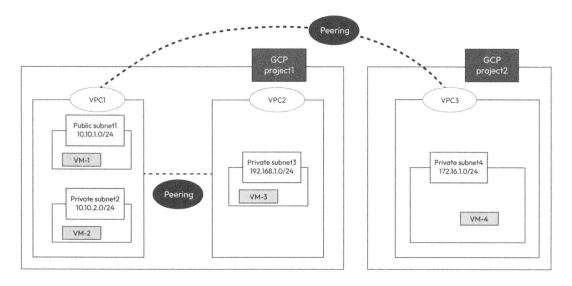

Figure 8.14 – GCP networking infrastructure

We will implement the preceding infrastructure next:

1. Create projects, networks and VMs.

> Go to the Google Cloud console, `console.cloud.google.com`, and go to **IAM | Manage Resources | Create or Delete projects**. Create two projects: `project1` and `project2`.

I.   Launch Cloud Shell and build up the Google Cloud networks:

> List the created projects (you will need to replace `project1` and `project2` with their actual project IDs):

```
gcloud projects list
```

II. Create the VPC and subnets.

```
gcloud compute networks create vpc1 --project
project1  --subnet-mode=custom
gcloud compute networks subnets create subnet1 --network=vpc1
--range=10.10.1.0/24 --project project1 --region us-west1
gcloud compute networks subnets create subnet2 --network=vpc1
--range=10.10.2.0/24 --project project1 --region us-east1
gcloud compute networks create vpc2 --project project1 --subnet-
mode=custom
gcloud compute networks subnets create subnet3 --network=vpc2
--range=192.168.1.0/24 --project project1 --region us-central1
gcloud compute networks create vpc3 --project
project2  --subnet-mode=custom
gcloud compute networks subnets create subnet4 --network=vpc3
--range=172.16.1.0/24 --project project2 --region us-central1
gcloud projects list
```

III. Create VMs in the VPC/subnets and record their information:

```
gcloud compute instances create vm-1 --project project1
--machine-type=f1-micro --zone=us-west1-a --subnet=subnet1
gcloud compute instances create vm-2 --project project1
--machine-type=f1-micro --network-interface=subnet=subnet2,no-
address  --zone=us-east1-b
gcloud compute instances create vm-3 --project project1
--machine-type=f1-micro --network-interface=subnet=subnet3,no-
address  --zone=us-central1-b
gcloud compute instances create vm-4 --project project2
--machine-type=f1-micro --network-interface=subnet=subnet4,no-
address --zone=us-central1-b
gcloud compute instances list --project project1
gcloud compute instances list --project project2
```

IV. Open a firewall for vpc1:

```
gcloud compute firewall-rules create fw1 --network vpc1 --allow
tcp:22,icmp --source-ranges 0.0.0.0/0 --project project1
```

2. Now, we can SSH to vm-1. From vm-1, you will be able to ping vm-2 since they are in the same VPC, but not vm-3, which is in a different VPC. How can we enable pinging from vm-1 to vm-3?

I. Peering vpc1 and vpc2 (in the same project) and open a firewall for vpc2:

```
gcloud compute networks peerings create peer12
--project=project1  --network=vpc1 --peer-project=project1
--peer-network=vpc2
gcloud compute networks peerings create peer21 --peer-
project=project1  --network=vpc2 --project=project1 --peer-
network=vpc1
gcloud compute networks peerings list --project=project1
gcloud compute firewall-rules create fw2 --network vpc2 --allow
tcp:22,icmp --source-ranges 0.0.0.0/0 --project project1
```

Now, you will be able to ping vm-3 from vm-1. With the same procedure, we can also enable pinging from vm-1 to vm-4:

II. Peering vpc1-vpc3 (a different project) and open a firewall for vpc3:

```
gcloud compute networks peerings create peer13
--project=project1  --network=vpc1 --peer-project=project2
--peer-network=vpc3
gcloud compute networks peerings create peer31
--project=project2 --network=vpc3 --peer-project=project1
--peer-network=vpc1
gcloud compute networks peerings list --project=project1
gcloud compute firewall-rules create fw3 --network vpc3 --allow
tcp:22,icmp --source-ranges 10.10.1.0/24 --project project2
```

3. Clean up the cloud resources we have provisioned.

I. Clean VPC peering:

```
gcloud compute networks peerings delete peer13
--project=project1  --network=vpc1
gcloud compute networks peerings delete peer31
--project=project2 --network=vpc3
gcloud compute networks peerings delete peer12
--project=project1  --network=vpc1
gcloud compute networks peerings delete peer21
--project=project1  --network=vpc2
```

II. Clean the VMs:

```
gcloud compute instances delete vm-1 --project project1
gcloud compute instances delete vm-2 --project project1
gcloud compute instances delete vm-3 --project project1
gcloud compute instances delete vm-4 --project project2
```

In the preceding example, we used GCP Cloud Shell commands to create VPCs, subnets, and VM instances, peer VPCs, and configure VPC firewall rules. Practicing these commands will help us understand the GCP networking concepts.

During our AWS cloud discussions, we examined the *VPC endpoint for S3 storage*. There is also a comparable situation in Google Cloud, where security requirements demand that the VM instances in a VPC access GCS buckets/objects without trespassing the internet. This time, we enable **private Google access** to a subnet in a VPC, so the VMs there will be able to access the other GCP services, such as GCS, within Google's internal network. More details about private Google access are available at https://cloud.google.com/vpc/docs/private-google-access.

Summary

In this chapter, we learned about GCP's foundation services: compute, storage, and networking. We launched GCE VM instances, GKE clusters, and VPC networks. We also explored service accounts, containers, and their deployments in GKE clusters. We compared GCP's foundations with AWS's to understand their similarities and differences. We hope you enjoyed it!

In the next chapter, we will examine the GCP data analytics services, including databases and big data. It is a very interesting chapter. Let's get ready to explore these services!

Practice questions

Questions 1-8 are based on the GCP foundation architecture shown in *Figure 8.15*. Default configurations are used:

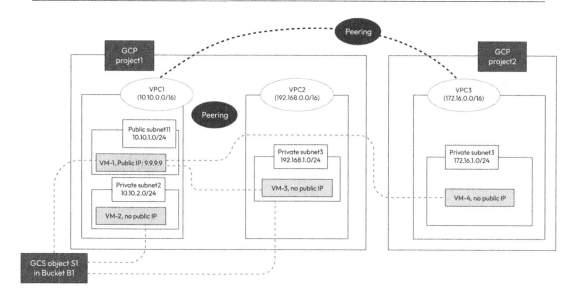

Figure 8.15 – GCP foundation infrastructure

1. How many VMs (with at least one IP address for each VM) can you create in a VPC1 subnet1 in GCP?

    A. 252

    B. 255

    C. 256

    D. 24

2. How many IP addresses are there in subnet3?

    A. 256

    B. 252

    C. 255

    D. 24

3. Which of the following statements is not true?

    A. **VM1** can ping VM3

    B. **VM1** can ping VM4

C. **VM2** can ping VM4

D. **VM3** can ping VM4

4. What needs to be done for VM1 to process (read/write) objects in B1?

   A. Nothing

   B. VM1's service account needs read/write access to B1

   C. VM1 needs to have a public IP address

   D. VM1 needs to have a private IP address and its service account needs read/write access to B1

5. VM1 needs to read object S1. What needs to be done?

   A. Nothing

   B. Enable Google private access for `subnet11`

   C. Enable Google private access for `subnet12`

   D. Enable Google private access for `subnet2`

6. VM2 needs to read object S1. What needs to be done?

   A. Nothing

   B. Enable Google private access for `subnet11`

   C. Enable Google private access for `subnet12`

   D. Enable Google private access for `subnet2`

   E. Peer VPC1 with VPC2

7. VM3 needs to read object S1. What needs to be done?

   A. Nothing

   B. Enable Google private access for `subnet11`

   C. Enable Google private access for `subnet12`

   D. Enable Google private access for `subnet2`

8. VM4 needs to read object S1. What needs to be done? (Choose two)

   A. Enable Google private access for `subnet3`

   B. Grant `project2`'s compute service account access to bucket B1

   C. Grant `project1`'s compute service account access to bucket B1

   D. Peer VPC1 with VPC3

   E. Enable Google private access for `project2`

Answers to the practice questions

1. A

2. A

3. D

4. B

5. A

6. C

7. D

8. A, B

Further reading

- For further insights into what you've learned in this chapter, refer to the following links:

- `https://cloud.google.com/compute`

- `https://cloud.google.com/load-balancing`

- `https://cloud.google.com/compute/docs/instance-groups`

- `https://cloud.google.com/kubernetes-engine`

- `https://cloud.google.com/storage`

- `https://cloud.google.com/vpc`

- `https://cloud.google.com/vpc/docs/private-google-access`

Google Cloud's Database and Big Data Services

Data plays a very important role in modern industry. Just as petroleum oil has been a primary energy resource for almost all industries, data has become a primary digital asset in modern companies. As more and more of our lives are lived online, more and more businesses are conducted online, and our interactions with technology generate more and more data, companies have realized the power of data in making informed business decisions, improving products and services, and ultimately adding value to businesses.

As a data company, Google provides varied data services on its cloud platform, from data ingestion, data storing, data processing, to data visualization. In this chapter, we will focus on the following topics:

- **Google Cloud's database services**, including Cloud SQL, Cloud Spanner, Cloud Firestore, Cloud Bigtable, and Cloud Memorystore
- **Google Cloud's big data services**, including Cloud Pub/Sub, Cloud Dataflow, Cloud BigQuery, Cloud Dataproc, and Looker

During our discussions, we will use some examples and the sample code is available in the GitHub repository for this book: `https://github.com/PacktPublishing/Self-Taught-Cloud-computing-Engineer`. Let us start our GCP data journey with Google Cloud database services.

Google Cloud database services

We have discussed Amazon's cloud database services, mainly the AWS RDS, and DynamoDB. Now switching to Google Cloud, we will also focus on the relational Cloud SQL service and the NoSQL Cloud Firestore service.

Google Cloud SQL

Google Cloud SQL is a fully managed service that allows users to create, manage, and administer relational databases in Google Cloud. It is a MySQL- and PostgreSQL-compatible database service and includes key managed database features such as automated backups, data replication, flexible pricing, and integration with other GCP services. Cloud SQL provides strong security measures such as encryption at rest and in transit, and role-based access control. It is a powerful tool for managing and storing data in Google Cloud. To make it simple, here we will demonstrate how to use GCP Cloud Shell to create a MySQL database, connect to it, and use it:

1. Launching Google Cloud Shell and creating a Cloud SQL instance:

   From the Google Cloud console, launch Cloud Shell and execute the following commands:

   ```
   gcloud config set compute/region us-central1
   gcloud sql instances create cloudsql1 --database-
   version=MYSQL_5_7 --cpu=1 --memory=4GB --region=us-central1
   --root-password=password123
   ```

2. Connecting to the MySQL instance:

   Use the following command to connect to the Cloud SQL instance from Cloud Shell:

   ```
   gcloud sql connect cloudsql1 --user=root --quiet
   ```

   As shown in *Figure 9.1*, we have created a SQL instance and logged in to it:

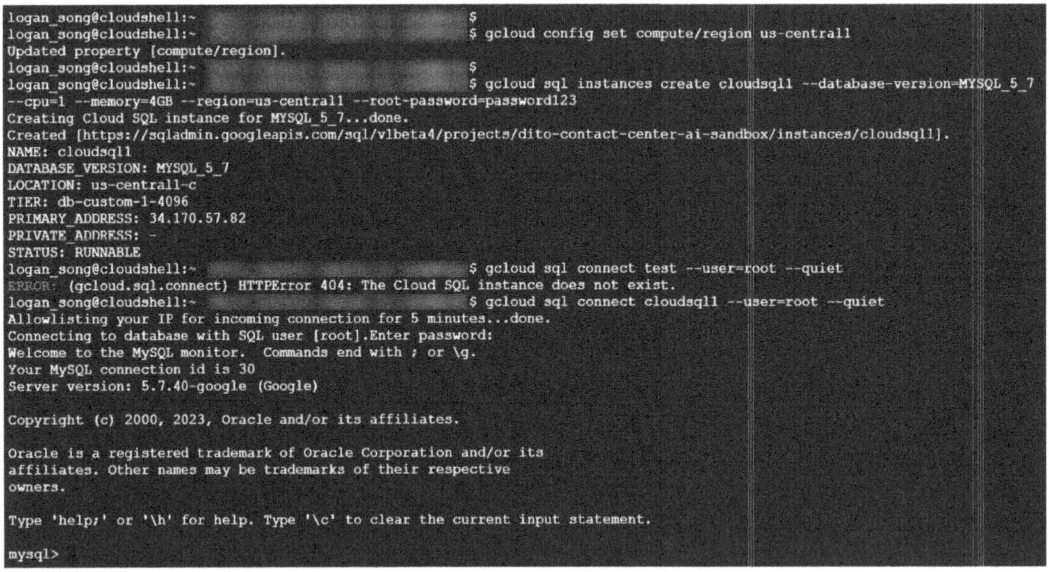

Figure 9.1 – Create and log in to the Cloud SQL instance

3. Creating a database and a table:

    After logging in to the MySQL database, run the following SQL statements:

    ```
    Create database test;
    Create table test.students (StudentID int,
        LastName varchar(100),
        FirstName varchar(100),
        City varchar(100)   );
    INSERT INTO test.students values (101, "Smith", "John",
    "Houston");
    INSERT INTO test.students values (102, "Smith", "Jim", "Plano");
    INSERT INTO test.students values (201, "Armstrong", "Neil",
    "Dallas");
    INSERT INTO test.students values (202, "Smith", "Neil",
    "Dallas");
    Select * from test.students;
    ```

Figure 9.2 shows the query execution in the SQL instance:

```
mysql> Create database test;
Query OK, 1 row affected (0.00 sec)

mysql> Create table test.students (
    ->     StudentID int,
    ->     LastName varchar(100),
    ->     FirstName varchar(100),
    ->     City varchar(100)   );
Query OK, 0 rows affected (0.03 sec)

mysql> INSERT INTO test.students values (101, "Smith", "John", "Houston");
Query OK, 1 row affected (0.01 sec)

mysql> INSERT INTO test.students values (102, "Smith", "Jim", "Plano");
Query OK, 1 row affected (0.00 sec)

mysql> INSERT INTO test.students values (201, "Armstrong", "Neil", "Dallas");
Query OK, 1 row affected (0.01 sec)

mysql> INSERT INTO test.students values (202, "Smith", "Neil", "Dallas");
Query OK, 1 row affected (0.00 sec)

mysql> Select * from test.students;
+-----------+-----------+-----------+---------+
| StudentID | LastName  | FirstName | City    |
+-----------+-----------+-----------+---------+
|       101 | Smith     | John      | Houston |
|       102 | Smith     | Jim       | Plano   |
|       201 | Armstrong | Neil      | Dallas  |
|       202 | Smith     | Neil      | Dallas  |
+-----------+-----------+-----------+---------+
4 rows in set (0.00 sec)

mysql>
```

Figure 9.2 – Executing SQL statements in the Cloud SQL instance

While Cloud SQL is a popular relational database service, it has limitations in size and horizontal scaling. To meet high-end relational database requirements, Google provides Cloud Spanner.

Google Cloud Spanner

Google Cloud Spanner is a fully managed, globally distributed, and strongly consistent relational database management system. It is designed to provide users with a scalable, reliable, and high-performance database solution that can support mission-critical applications.

Cloud Spanner combines the benefits of traditional relational database systems with the advantages of NoSQL databases and provides automatic scaling and rebalancing, high availability, fault tolerance, automatic backups, and point-in-time recovery. It supports SQL queries and ACID transactions. Cloud Spanner integrates seamlessly with other GCP services such as BigQuery, Dataflow, Cloud Functions, and so on.

Cloud Spanner fits well with applications that require low latency, big datasets, and global scaling. As a high-end Google Cloud database, it is for large, mission-critical business use cases and is pricey compared to Cloud SQL. We will not create a sample Cloud Spanner database here. For more details on Spanner and its prices, please refer to `https://cloud.google.com/spanner`.

After our discussion of Cloud SQL and Cloud Spanner, we will now look at the GCP NoSQL database services, starting with Google Cloud Firestore.

Google Cloud Firestore

Google Cloud Firestore is a fully managed, NoSQL document database that is designed to store, synchronize, and query data for mobile, web, and IoT applications. Firestore stores data in documents, using `JSON`-like structures, with the following features:

- It provides real-time updates for data changes across multiple devices and platforms, fitting for real-time collaborative application development
- It provides a serverless service where Google handles scaling, patching, and infrastructure management
- It provides many security features, such as SSL/TLS encryption and OAuth and Firebase authentication for user authentication and authorization
- It scales automatically for large data and high traffic volumes
- It supports multiple platforms such as Android, iOS, web, and many programming languages such as Node.js, Java, Python, and so on

Firestore fits well for small to medium-sized applications that require real-time data synchronization, offline data access, and scalability. Firestore supports two modes for its database: Native mode and Datastore mode:

- **Native mode** – In this mode, Firestore provides a more flexible data model, richer queries, and real-time updates. Along with API and client libraries, Firestore Native mode provides offline data access and real-time synchronization.

- **Datastore mode** – This mode is compatible with Cloud Datastore, which is a NoSQL document database built for automatic scaling, high performance, and ease of application development, so you can migrate applications from Cloud Datastore to Firestore without code changes.

We recommend enabling Firestore Native mode for more features and flexibility unless your existing applications use Cloud Datastore and have compatibility requirements.

To get you more familiar with the Cloud Firestore database, we will now create a Google Cloud Firestore instance from the Google Cloud console:

1. Choosing the Cloud Firestore mode:

    Navigate to **Google cloud console | Databases | Datastore | Entities**, and you will land on the starting page explaining the two Firestore modes, as shown in *Figure 9.3*. We will select **Datastore mode** in this lab:

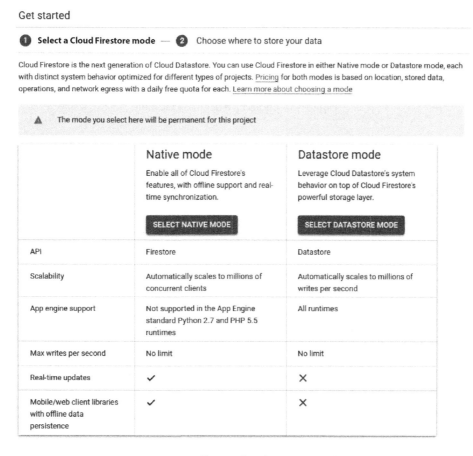

Figure 9.3 – Choose Cloud Firestore modes

Note the warning: **The mode you select here will be permanent for this project**.

2.   Choosing where to store data:

We select the **us-west1 (Oregon)** region and then **CREATE DATABASE**, as shown in *Figure 9.4*:

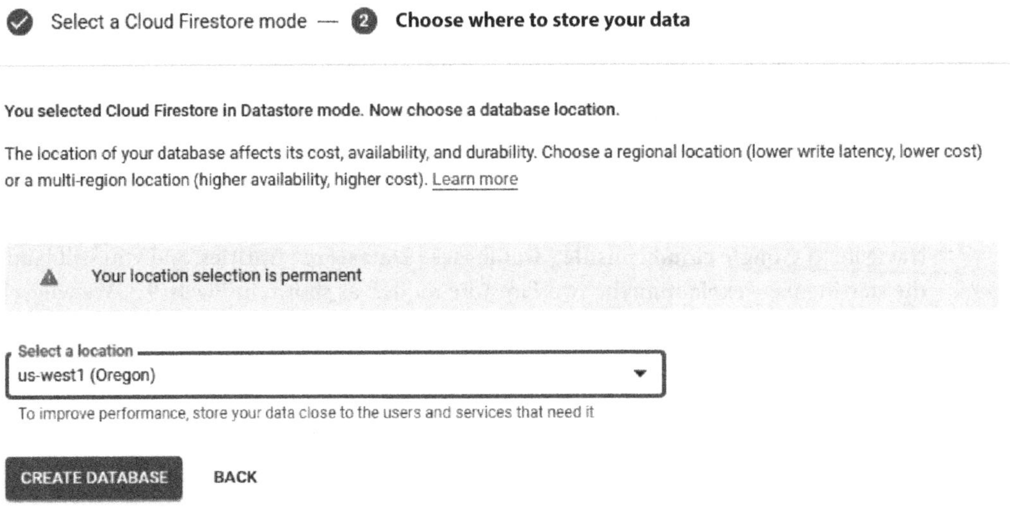

✓ Select a Cloud Firestore mode — ② **Choose where to store your data**

You selected Cloud Firestore in Datastore mode. Now choose a database location.

The location of your database affects its cost, availability, and durability. Choose a regional location (lower write latency, lower cost) or a multi-region location (higher availability, higher cost). Learn more

⚠ Your location selection is permanent

Select a location
us-west1 (Oregon)   ▼

To improve performance, store your data close to the users and services that need it

CREATE DATABASE   BACK

Figure 9.4 – Choosing a database location

3.   Creating entities:

The next step is to create entities. In a Cloud datastore, a **namespace** is like a partition; a **kind** is like a table; an **entity** is like an item in the table; and the **properties** are like table columns. Fill in **Properties** for an entity and click **CREATE**, as shown in *Figure 9.5*:

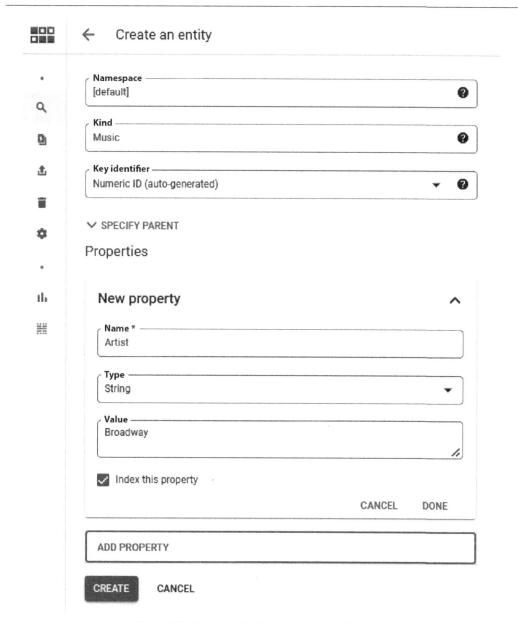

Figure 9.5 – Creating the Datastore kind and entities

More entities can be created in the same kind, and you have the flexibility to add more properties when adding new entities.

Figure 9.6 shows the two entities created for a kind called **Music**. With more entities added, you can query the kind using **QUERY BY KIND**, or **QUERY BY GQL**, which is a limited SQL-like query language – details about it can be found at `https://cloud.google.com/datastore/docs/concepts/queries`:

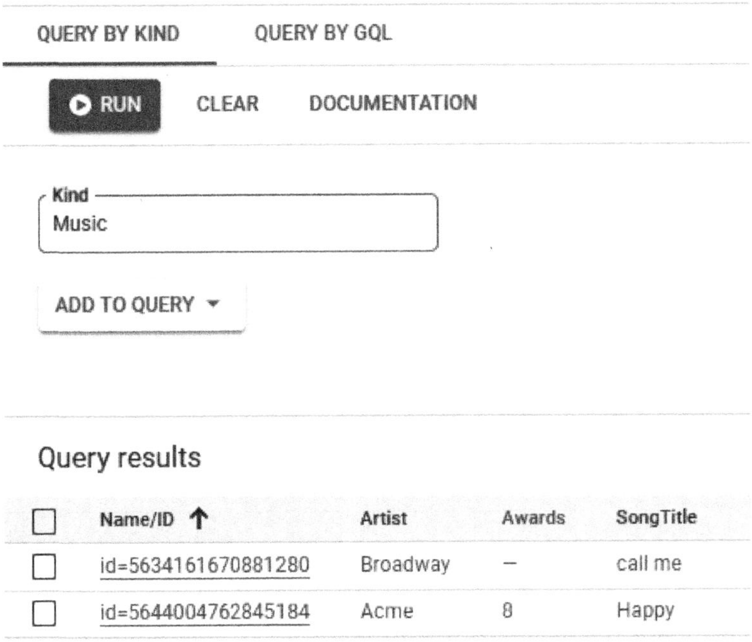

Figure 9.6 – Entities of a kind in Datastore

As we discussed earlier, the Firestore Native mode provides real-time updates. In the next example, we will create a sample three-tier web application. The frontend is the web tier, which accepts images from web users; at the backend, the app tier will move the images into a cloud storage bucket; and the database tier is a Firestore database in Native mode, which will update the image metadata in real time. We will use **Google Cloud Run** and **Google Cloud Firestore** to implement this sample application. Google Cloud Run is a serverless computing platform that allows developers to build application containers, run them based on triggers, and scale them based on workloads/traffic. Cloud Run only charges for the actual usage time, and more details about it are available at `https://cloud.google.com/run`. We will build the application and show its usage in five steps:

1. Enabling Firestore Native mode, and creating a GCS bucket in Google Cloud Shell:

    Choose Native mode from the Firestore starting page, and run the following Cloud Shell command to create a new GCS bucket:

    ```
    gsutil mb gs://04092023-target
    ```

2. Cloning the source code from GitHub:

Execute the following command to copy the application code from GitHub:

```
git clone https://github.com/PacktPublishing/Self-Taught-Cloud-
computing-Engineer.git
```

The cloned source code directory has the following three files:

I.   requirements.txt defines the software needed for the application. In our case, it reads as follows:

```
Flask
google-cloud-storage
google-cloud-firestore
```

II. app.py is a Python file that defines the web application process: it takes web user uploads and moves them into the bucket defined by the BUCKET_NAME variable – in our case, it is the bucket we created earlier. So, we need to modify the app.py file and replace BUCKET_NAME with the following:

```
BUCKET_NAME = "04092023-target"
```

III. Dockerfile is the instruction file for generating the Docker image.

3. Building the application (webserver2) container image:

In the previous chapter, we built the webserver1 container image with docker build. Now, we will use Google **Cloud Build** to create another web server container image: webserver2. Cloud Build is a service that produces artifacts such as Docker containers or Java archives.

Execute the following command in Cloud Shell to build the webserver2 container image:

```
gcloud builds submit --tag gcr.io/$DEVSHELL_PROJECT_ID/
webserver2
```

4. Deploying webserver2:

Execute the following command in Cloud Shell to set up the environment and deploy the container with Google Cloud Run:

```
gcloud config set run/platform managed
gcloud config set run/region us-west1
gcloud run deploy webserver2 --image gcr.io/$DEVSHELL_PROJECT_
ID/webserver2
```

Figure 9.7 shows the execution results for *steps 3* and *4* in Google Cloud Shell.

```
logan_song@cloudshell:~/Firestore/content-google-cloud-run-deep-dive/image-gallery/3-firestore
$ gcloud builds submit --tag gcr.io/$DEVSHELL_PROJECT_ID/webserver2 .
Creating temporary tarball archive of 4 file(s) totalling 2.4 KiB before compression.
Uploading tarball of [.] to [gs://dito-contact-center-ai-sandbox_cloudbuild/source/1681928847.260641-51c20b989fc24f9f96ef52ef0c
66b204.tgz]
Created [https://cloudbuild.googleapis.com/v1/projects/dito-contact-center-ai-sandbox/locations/global/builds/36dea169-fce9-445
7-bf03-504d742738e7].
Logs are available at [ https://console.cloud.google.com/cloud-build/builds/36dea169-fce9-4457-bf03-504d742738e7?project=254979
162583 ].
--------------------------------------------------------------------- REMOTE BUILD OUTPUT ---------------------------------------------------------------------
starting build "36dea169-fce9-4457-bf03-504d742738e7"


ID: 36dea169-fce9-4457-bf03-504d742738e7
CREATE_TIME: 2023-04-19T18:27:28+00:00
DURATION: 37S
SOURCE: gs://dito-contact-center-ai-sandbox_cloudbuild/source/1681928847.260641-51c20b989fc24f9f96ef52ef0c66b204.tgz
IMAGES: gcr.io/dito-contact-center-ai-sandbox/webserver2 (+1 more)
STATUS: SUCCESS
logan_song@cloudshell:~/Firestore/content-google-cloud-run-deep-dive/image-gallery/3-firestore
$ gcloud config set run/platform managed
Updated property [run/platform].
logan_song@cloudshell:~/Firestore/content-google-cloud-run-deep-dive/image-gallery/3-firestore
$ gcloud config set run/region us-west1
Updated property [run/region].
logan_song@cloudshell:~/Firestore/content-google-cloud-run-deep-dive/image-gallery/3-firestore
$ gcloud run deploy webserver2 --image gcr.io/$DEVSHELL_PROJECT_ID/webserver2
Allow unauthenticated invocations to [webserver2] (y/N)?  y

Deploying container to Cloud Run service [webserver2] in project [dito-contact-center-ai-sandbox] region [us-west1]
OK Deploying new service... Done.
  OK Creating Revision... Creating Service.
  OK Routing traffic...
  OK Setting IAM Policy...
Done.
Service [webserver2] revision [webserver2-00001-tur] has been deployed and is serving 100 percent of traffic.
Service URL: https://webserver2-inpf2htcya-uw.a.run.app
```

Figure 9.7 – Creating and deploying the webserver2 container

From **Google Cloud console | Cloud Run**, we can see the Cloud Run deployments, as shown in *Figure 9.8*:

Figure 9.8 – Cloud Run service is deployed

5. Access webserver2 to test the application:

    From the Cloud Run deployment shown in *Figure 9.7*, we have got the web service URL, which is `https://webserver2-inpf2htcya-uw.a.run.app`, and now we can use it to test the application in three sub-steps:

    I. Access the URL from a new browser, and upload an image, as shown in *Figure 9.9*:

Figure 9.9 – Uploading images to the web service from the Cloud Run deployment

II. Verify that the uploaded images have been put into the GCS bucket we created earlier by the Cloud Run application. The verification is shown in the GCS commands in *Figure 9.10*:

```
$ gsutil ls gs://04092023-temp
gs://04092023-temp/image4.jpg
gs://04092023-temp/image6.jpg
gs://04092023-temp/image7.jpg
```

Figure 9.10 – Images are moved into a GCS bucket

III. Check the backend Firebase database is updated, as shown in *Figure 9.11*:

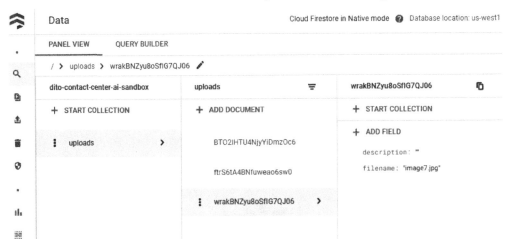

Figure 9.11 – Firestore database updated

In this section, we demonstrated the two Google Cloud Firestore modes and showed how to use them in different use cases. In the next sections, we will briefly discuss Google Cloud Bigtable and Google Cloud Memorystore.

Google Cloud Bigtable

Google Cloud Bigtable is a fully managed, scalable NoSQL database service that can handle massive workloads at high speeds. Bigtable's features include load balancing and auto-scaling, high availability, fault tolerance, support for consistent and strongly consistent reads and writes, and integration with other GCP services. Bigtable fits well with applications that store and process large amounts of data with minimum latency, such as IoT analytics and ad technology.

In general, Bigtable might be best for performance-sensitive use cases that have simple lookups or can tolerate data being potentially inconsistent across tables. Compared to Firestore, it scales better, accommodates larger amounts of data, and costs more. On the other hand, Spanner may perform slightly worse and cost more than Bigtable but will provide strong consistency. More details are available at https://cloud.google.com/bigtable.

Google Cloud Memorystore

Google Cloud Memorystore is a fully managed in-memory data store service that provides users with a fast, scalable, and highly available solution for storing and managing data in memory. Google Cloud Memorystore has scaling and load balancing features, high availability, fault tolerance, support for Redis and Memcached protocols, and integration with other GCP services. Google Cloud Memorystore is particularly well suited to applications that require low-latency access to frequently accessed data, such as e-commerce, gaming, and social media apps. More details are available at `https://cloud.google.com/memorystore`.

After the Google Cloud database service discussions, we will examine Google Cloud's big data services.

Google Cloud's big data services

Google provides a suite of big data analytics tools and services for users to use to collect, process, and analyze large amounts of data in the cloud. Some key services include the following:

- **Pub/Sub**: A cloud messaging service that allows applications to exchange messages reliably, quickly, and asynchronously

- **Dataflow**: This is a fully managed, serverless data processing service that enables users to create data pipelines for real-time and batch processing

- **BigQuery**: This is a fully managed, serverless data warehouse that enables users to store and analyze massive amounts of structured and unstructured data

- **Cloud Dataproc**: This is a managed Hadoop and Spark service that enables users to process large-scale datasets in a scalable and cost-effective manner

- **Looker**: A data visualization tool that allows users to create and share interactive dashboards and reports

Google Cloud's big data services are used for a variety of applications, including business intelligence, machine learning, fraud detection, and more. Let's start with Google Cloud Pub/Sub.

Google Cloud Pub/Sub

GCP's pub/subs are essentially channels where messages can be published by publishers and subscribed to by subscribers. Publishers publish and send messages to a topic, and subscribers can receive those messages by subscribing to that topic. The publishers communicate with subscribers asynchronously, a publisher can have multiple subscribers, and a subscriber can subscribe to multiple publishers. *Figure 9.12* shows a use case where many users upload objects into a GCS bucket. Upon completion of an upload, a message is sent to the topic and received by two subscribers: one triggers a cloud function that processes the uploaded object, another notifies parties via email, and so on:

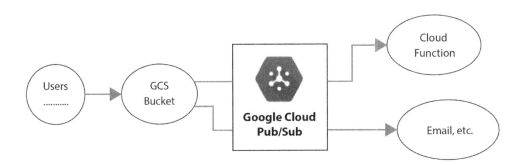

Figure 9.12 – Pub/Sub example

Pub/Sub supports push/pull subscriptions, which allow different ways of receiving messages, and message retention, which allows subscribers to receive messages even if they weren't subscribed at the time the message was published. More details are available at `https://cloud.google.com/pubsub`.

Google Cloud BigQuery

Google Cloud BigQuery is a fully managed, serverless data warehouse service that is designed to enable users to store and analyze massive amounts of structured and unstructured data using SQL queries. BigQuery uses a distributed, columnar storage format for efficient querying and large dataset processing, and thus is a good fit for real-time data analysis and machine learning workloads at the petabyte scale. BigQuery has the following key features:

- It automatically scales to handle petabyte-scale datasets

- It supports standard SQL queries so that users can implement familiar tools

- It integrates with a variety of data sources such as GCS, Cloud Datastore, Cloud SQL, and many third-party visualization tools

- It supports security features including access controls, encryption, and logging

Using Google Cloud Shell, you can use the `bq` command to load data into a BigQuery database and query the tables. *Figure 9.13* shows `bq` commands running in Google Cloud Shell: it makes a `sales` dataset in BigQuery, uploads it to a `sales.sale` table from a CSV file, `sale.csv`, and runs a query against the table.

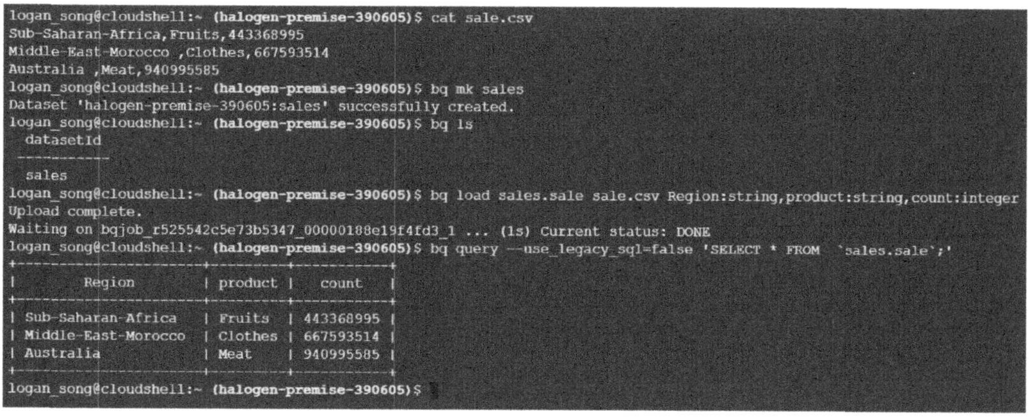

```
logan_song@cloudshell:~ (halogen-premise-390605)$ cat sale.csv
Sub-Saharan-Africa,Fruits,443368995
Middle-East-Morocco ,Clothes,667593514
Australia ,Meat,940995585
logan_song@cloudshell:~ (halogen-premise-390605)$ bq mk sales
Dataset 'halogen-premise-390605:sales' successfully created.
logan_song@cloudshell:~ (halogen-premise-390605)$ bq ls
   datasetId
 -----------
   sales
logan_song@cloudshell:~ (halogen-premise-390605)$ bq load sales.sale sale.csv Region:string,product:string,count:integer
Upload complete.
Waiting on bqjob_r525542c5e73b5347_00000188e19f4fd3_1 ... (1s) Current status: DONE
logan_song@cloudshell:~ (halogen-premise-390605)$ bq query --use_legacy_sql=false 'SELECT * FROM `sales.sale`;'
+--------------------+---------+-----------+
|       Region       | product |   count   |
+--------------------+---------+-----------+
| Sub-Saharan-Africa | Fruits  | 443368995 |
| Middle-East-Morocco| Clothes | 667593514 |
| Australia          | Meat    | 940995585 |
+--------------------+---------+-----------+
logan_song@cloudshell:~ (halogen-premise-390605)$
```

Figure 9.13 – bq command example

BigQuery is very popular and widely used for many applications in business intelligence, machine learning, and real-time analytics, especially in business use cases that require low latency for processing large amounts of data, such as e-commerce, advertising, and finance. More details are available at `https://cloud.google.com/bigquery`.

Google Cloud Dataflow

Google Cloud Dataflow is a fully managed service for stream data processing and batch execution, thus enabling users to create, deploy, and manage data processing pipelines at scale. Dataflow offers a range of connectors to integrate with various data sources and sinks and supports multiple languages, including Python, Java, and Go. Dataflow features auto-scaling, dynamic work rebalancing, and fault tolerance. Dataflow integrates with other GCP services seamlessly, including Pub/Sub, BigQuery, and Cloud Storage.

Now that we have learned about the concepts of Cloud Pub/Sub, Dataflow, and BigQuery, we will use an example to see how these cloud services can integrate to form a data pipeline. In the next example, we will create a pipeline that will process real-time simulated data.

As shown in *Figure 9.14*, the pipeline starts with the simulation of a real-time data generator, which involves executing a Python script that reads from a large Excel spreadsheet, row by row, and generates a message per row, to ingest into Cloud Pub/Sub. The Dataflow job will then get input from Pub/Sub, process the data, and output it to the BigQuery dataset/table, where we can run queries and visualize them using third-party tools:

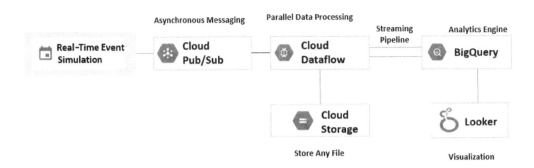

Figure 9.14 – GCP big data pipeline

Let's implement the data pipeline step by step now:

1. Preparing the data generator:

    Go to the Google Cloud console and open a Cloud Shell terminal.

    Upload the `sales.csv` file to Cloud Shell. The file is available in the book's repository: `https://github.com/PacktPublishing/Self-Taught-Cloud-computing-Engineer/chapter9/bigdata/`.

    Copy the data generator from GitHub:

    ```
    git clone https://github.com/PacktPublishing/Self-Taught-Cloud-
    computing-Engineer.git
    ```

    The root directory now has two files: first, `Sales.csv` is a Microsoft CSV file containing all the sales data records.

    Figure 9.15 shows the columns for `Sales.csv`:

	A	B	C	D	E	F	G
1	Region	Country	Item_Type	Order_ID	Units_Sold	Unit_Price	Total_Revenue
2	Sub Saharan Africa	South Africa	Fruits	443368995	1593	9.33	14862.69
3	Middle East and North Africa	Morocco	Clothes	667593514	4611	109.28	503890.08
4	Australia and Oceania	Papua New Guinea	Meat	940995585	360	421.89	151880.4
5	Sub-Saharan Africa	Djibouti	Clothes	880811536	562	109.28	61415.36

Figure 9.15 – Sales.csv data schema

Second, `datagen.py` is the data generator Python script that scans an Excel spreadsheet named `Sales.csv` and generates a data message for each row.

2. Creating a Pub/Sub topic and subscriptions:

    Cloud Pub/Sub is the queue to ingest the real-time data coming from the data generator.

    Go to the **Google Cloud Pub/Sub** console and create a publisher topic called `sales`, noting the topic identifier: `projects/dito-contact-center-ai-sandbox/topics/sales`.

    For the **sales** topic, create a subscription called **demographics**.

    > **Note**
    >
    > There can be many subscriptions, such as shipping, supply, demographics, trends, and so on. Note the subscription name: `projects/dito-contact-center-ai-sandbox/subscriptions/demographics`.

    Figure 9.16 shows the Pub/Sub topic and subscriptions:

Figure 9.16 – Pub/Sub topic and subscriptions

3. Creating an empty table in BigQuery:

    BigQuery is the destination for our data pipeline. Go to the **Google Cloud BigQuery** console and create a BigQuery dataset, `sales`, and a table, `sales_demographics`. Note the table schema needs to match the data source's schema shown in *Figure 9.15*. Record the table ID of **sales.sales_demographics**.

Figure 9.17 shows the empty BigQuery table creation:

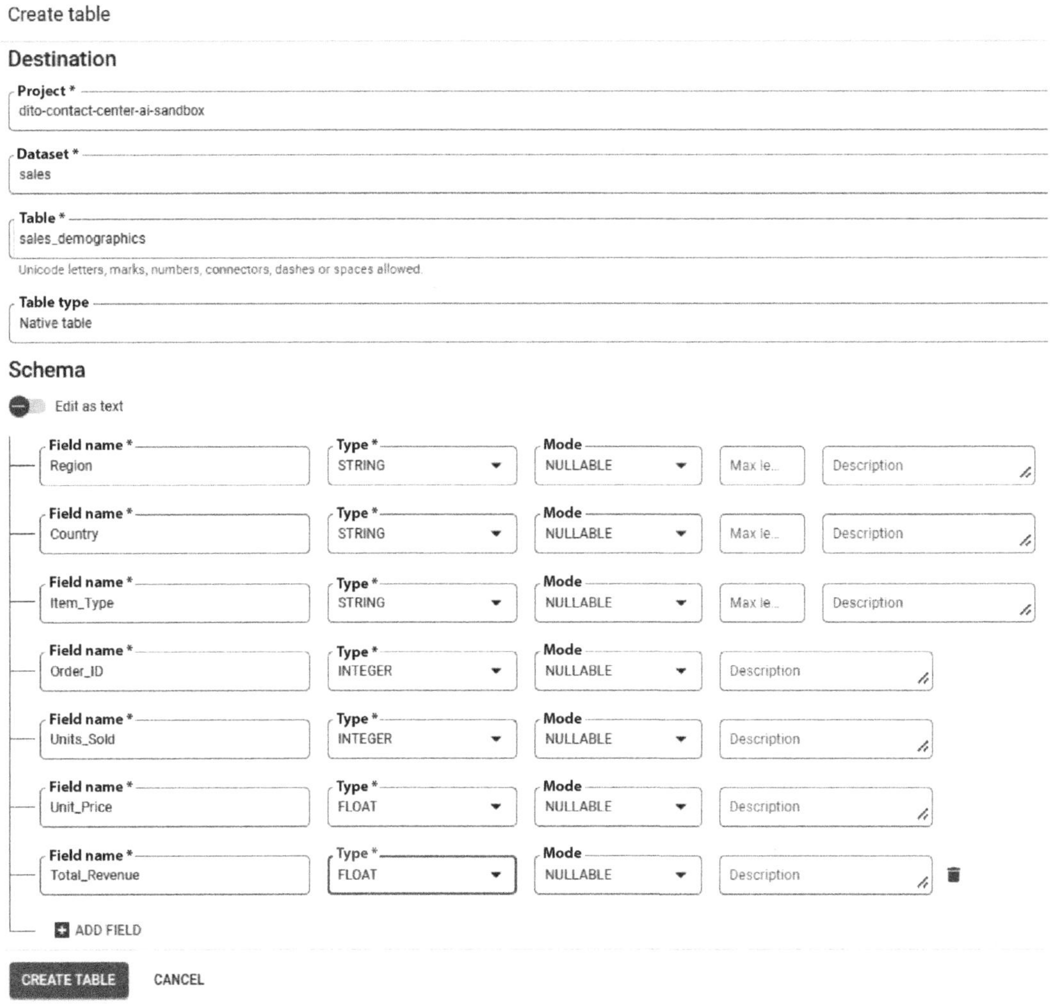

Create table

Destination

Project *
dito-contact-center-ai-sandbox

Dataset *
sales

Table *
sales_demographics

Unicode letters, marks, numbers, connectors, dashes or spaces allowed.

Table type
Native table

Schema

● Edit as text

Field name *	Type *	Mode	Max le..	Description
Region	STRING ▼	NULLABLE ▼	Max le..	Description
Country	STRING ▼	NULLABLE ▼	Max le..	Description
Item_Type	STRING ▼	NULLABLE ▼	Max le..	Description
Order_ID	INTEGER ▼	NULLABLE ▼		Description
Units_Sold	INTEGER ▼	NULLABLE ▼		Description
Unit_Price	FLOAT ▼	NULLABLE ▼		Description
Total_Revenue	FLOAT ▼	NULLABLE ▼		Description 🗑

➕ ADD FIELD

CREATE TABLE   CANCEL

Figure 9.17 – Create the empty BigQuery table

4. Creating a Dataflow job:

The Dataflow job will make ends meet: the Pub/Sub subscription and the BigQuery empty table. It takes Pub/Sub data as input and outputs it into the BigQuery table.

Go to the **Google Cloud Dataflow** console and create a Dataflow job, sub2bq. Choose the **Pub/ Sub subscription to BigQuery** template, and fill it with the Pub/Sub subscription we created earlier for the input, the BigQuery empty table for the output, and the previously created GCS bucket, 04092023-temp/tmp, for the temporary location for the Dataflow job. Click **RUN JOB**, as shown in *Figure 9.18*:

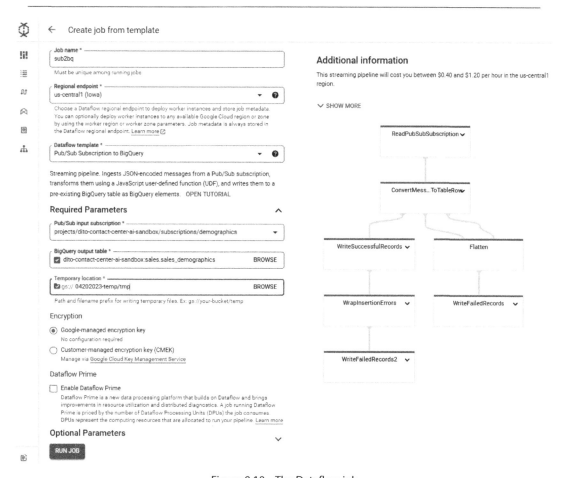

Figure 9.18 – The Dataflow job

So far, we have built the data pipeline, `data generator -> pub/sub -> dataflow -> BigQuery`, and now it's time to light it up!

5. Lighting up the data pipeline:

    We need to light up the data generator using three sub-steps within Cloud Shell:

    I. Install the Pub/Sub library:

    ```
    sudo pip3 install google-cloud-pubsub
    ```

    II. Run the `datagen.py` script:

    ```
    python datagen.py
    ```

III. Verify from the Dataflow console that the data traffic flows through the pipeline, as shown in *Figure 9.19*:

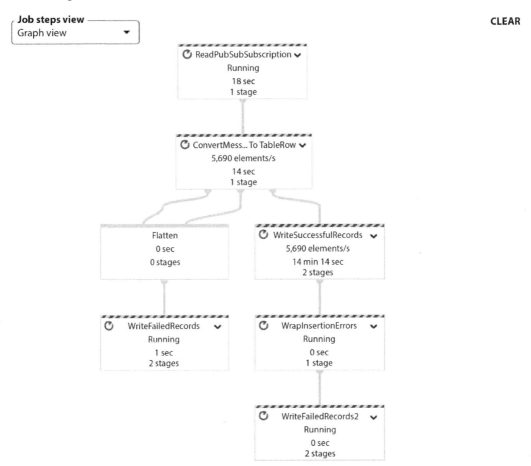

Figure 9.19 – Dataflow job shows the traffic

6. Querying the BigQuery table:

Go to the Google Cloud BigQuery console and preview the **sales_demographics** table. You will see that it was filled by the Dataflow job, as shown in *Figure 9.20*:

Row	Region	Country	Item_Type	Order_ID	Units_Sold	Unit_Price	Total_Revenue
1	Europe	Serbia	Meat	762112843	4981	421.89	2101434.09
2	Europe	Georgia	Beverages	585567700	1350	47.45	64057.5
3	Australia and Oceania	Solomon Islands	Baby Food	979315984	217	255.28	55395.76
4	Central America and the Caribb...	Dominica	Meat	941500270	9707	421.89	4095286.23
5	Sub-Saharan Africa	Mozambique	Baby Food	397630250	6482	255.28	1654724.96
6	Central America and the Caribb...	Jamaica	Beverages	330011117	6478	47.45	307381.1
7	Central America and the Caribb...	Saint Lucia	Meat	666885411	5068	421.89	2138138.52
8	Sub-Saharan Africa	Mozambique	Meat	518784987	8861	421.89	3738367.29
9	Europe	Macedonia	Vegetables	185797536	475	154.06	73178.5
10	Sub-Saharan Africa	Chad	Clothes	885809886	9685	109.28	1058376.8
11	Sub-Saharan Africa	Uganda	Baby Food	121046006	9058	255.28	2312326.24
12	Asia	Japan	Snacks	956860959	5276	152.58	805012.08
13	Australia and Oceania	New Zealand	Clothes	821347606	3864	109.28	422257.92
14	Europe	Albania	Cosmetics	347431313	1501	437.2	656237.2
15	Sub-Saharan Africa	South Africa	Office Supplies	175072562	6717	651.21	4374177.57

Figure 9.20 – BigQuery table preview

Run a sample SQL query; the result is partially shown in *Figure 9.21*:

```
SELECT Country,SUM(Total_Revenue)
FROM sales.sales_demographics
GROUP BY Country
```

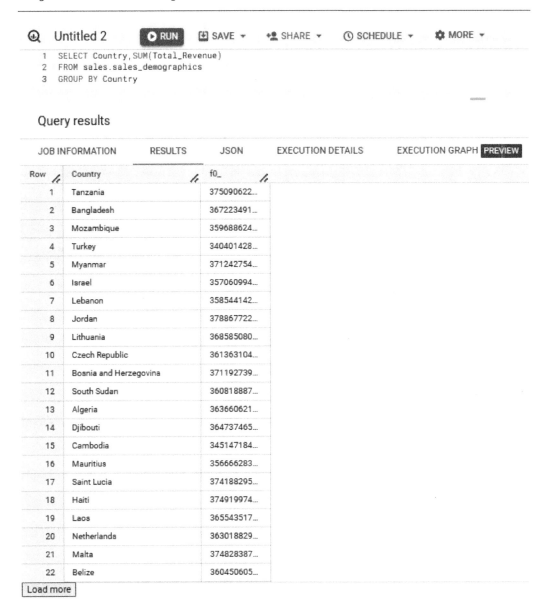

Figure 9.21 – BigQuery query result

The data pipeline is built, and it processed data successfully. Now let's clean the lab.

7. Cleaning up the lab:

Clean up the lab by deleting the Pub/Sub topic and subscriptions, stopping/canceling the Dataflow job, and deleting the BigQuery dataset and table.

Through the previous example, we have built a data pipeline, including Pub/Sub ingesting the real-time data stream and the Dataflow job reading from the subscription and writing to the empty BigQuery table, which can be queried as needed. In the next sections, we will briefly discuss the other GCP big data services, including Dataproc and Looker.

Google Cloud Dataproc

Google Cloud Dataproc is a fully managed, cloud-native big data processing service that enables users to easily process large-scale datasets using open source technologies such as Hadoop, Spark, and Hive. Dataproc offers the following benefits:

- It scales up or down automatically based on demand, allowing users to process large-scale datasets in a cost-effective manner

- It integrates with a variety of Google Cloud Platform services, including Cloud Storage, BigQuery, and Cloud SQL, as well as third-party tools such as Apache Zeppelin and Jupyter

- It supports a variety of open source tools and frameworks including Hadoop, Spark, Hive, and Pig, allowing users to choose the best tool for their use case

- It provides security features such as encryption and access control

Dataproc is used in many use cases, such as real-time analytics, fraud detection, and recommendation systems. It fits applications that process large-scale datasets with popular open source Hadoop tools and frameworks. More details about Dataproc are available at `https://cloud.google.com/dataproc`.

Google Cloud Looker

Google Cloud Looker is a cloud-based business intelligence and data analytics platform that enables users to create and share data visualizations, dashboards, and reports with others, and to analyze large-scale datasets in real time. Looker has the following key features:

- It enables non-technical users to create and share reports and dashboards

- It allows users to collaborate on reports and dashboards in real time, enabling teams to work together more efficiently

- It integrates with a variety of data sources and third-party tools, making it easy to analyze and visualize data from a variety of sources

Looker helps visualize data and supports many business use cases, such as sales and marketing analytics, financial reporting, and product analytics. More details are available at `https://cloud.google.com/looker`.

Summary

In this chapter, we learned about Google Cloud's database and big data services. We have explored Google Cloud SQL, Cloud Datastore, Pub/Sub, Dataflow, and BigQuery with two sample business use cases and hands-on labs. By the end of this chapter, you will have acquired skills in creating and managing databases, ingesting and processing large-scale datasets, and performing data analysis using Google Cloud's big data services.

In the next chapter, we will examine Google Cloud's machine learning services.

Practice questions

Questions 1 to *4* are based on the data pipeline shown in *Figure 9.22*. The pipeline has the default configurations and the following resources:

- Pub topic = t1, and subscription = s1
- Dataflow job = df1, with a GCS bucket called b1
- BigQuery dataset = ds1, and table = ds1-table

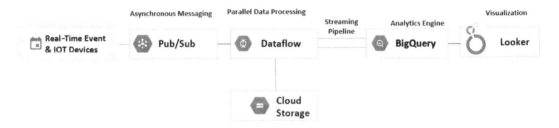

Figure 9.22 – GCP data pipeline

1. Which of the following is not part of df1's metrics?

    A. Latency

    B. CPU

    C. Memory

    D. Storage

2. What machine types will be used by df1's workers?

    A. n1-standard

    B. f1-micro

    C. e2-medium

    D. g1-small

3. When defining BigQuery table names, what's your recommendation?

    A. Use delimited identifiers

    B. Use different versions of SQL

    C. It doesn't matter since you can change the table name on the fly

    D. Use something related to the pipeline

4. We need to update df1 without losing any existing data. What's your recommendation?

    A. Update df1 with the drain flag

    B. Update df1 and provide the transform mapping JSON object

    C. Create a new Dataflow, df2, with s1 as input and cancel df1

    D. Create a new Dataflow, df2, with a new subscription, s2, and cancel the old pipeline

Questions 5 to 8 are based on the GCP database diagram in Figure 9.23:

All the configurations are default

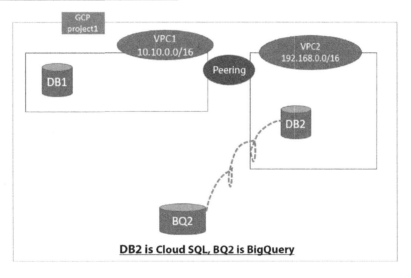

Figure 9.23 – GCP database diagram

5. Applications have performance issues in reading from **DB2**. What is your recommendation?

    A. Create a read replica

    B. Create a memory store

    C. Upgrade to Spanner

    D. Upgrade to Bigtable

6. Applications have performance issues in writing to table XYZ in **DB2**. What is your recommendation?

     A. Create a read replica

     B. Create a memory store

     C. Upgrade to Spanner

     D. Upgrade to Bigtable

7. **BQ2** needs to read data from **DB2**. What is your recommendation?

     A. A read replica

     B. Memorystore

     C. Federated queries

     D. Integrated queries

8. An application needs to read/write DB2 very frequently. What is your recommendation?

     A. A materialized view

     B. A session view

     C. A logical view

     D. A physical view

Answers to the practice questions

1. D
2. A
3. A
4. A
5. A
6. B
7. C
8. A

Further reading

For further insights into what you've learned in this chapter, refer to the following links:

- `https://cloud.google.com/products/databases`
- `https://cloud.google.com/sql`
- `https://cloud.google.com/spanner`
- `https://cloud.google.com/firestore`
- `https://cloud.google.com/memorystore`
- `https://cloud.google.com/learn/what-is-big-data`
- `https://cloud.google.com/pubsub/docs/overview`
- `https://cloud.google.com/pubsub/`
- `https://cloud.google.com/dataflow`
- `https://cloud.google.com/bigquery`
- `https://cloud.google.com/dataproc`
- `https://www.looker.com/`

10

Google Cloud AI Services

Google Cloud provides a set of AI tools and services for developers to build, train, and deploy ML models at scale. Google Cloud AI services provide the ability to build custom **machine learning** (**ML**) models using Vertex AI, which is a fully managed machine learning platform that allows developers and data scientists to build, train, and deploy machine learning models from end to end. Google Cloud AI also offers services based on pre-trained models and APIs for common ML tasks, such as image and speech recognition, **natural language processing** (**NLP**), and other predictive analytics. Google Cloud AI services integrate seamlessly with other GCP services and tools for data preprocessing, training, monitoring, and evaluation. In this chapter, we will cover the following topics:

- **Google Vertex AI**: This is a suite of services for users to develop ML models, including data collection, labeling, training, deploying **automated machine learning** (**AutoML**), and other AI capabilities.

- **Google Cloud ML API**: This is a suite of pre-trained ML models that developers can use to add advanced AI functionality to applications without ML model training. These modules can be integrated into applications to perform various AI tasks.

- **Google Cloud Generative AI**: An AI service newly added to the Vertex AI suite. Since this is an evolving area and some services are still in preview at the time of writing this book, we will briefly discuss them in a separate section.

During our discussions, we will use some examples, and the sample code is available in the GitHub repository for this book: `https://github.com/PacktPublishing/Self-Taught-Cloud-computing-Engineer`. Let us jump into the powerful Google Cloud Vertex AI platform.

Google Cloud Vertex AI

Vertex AI is an integrated set of products, features, and a management interface that simplifies the management of Google Cloud ML services. Vertex AI lets users build, train, and deploy ML models. As shown in *Figure 10.1*, Vertex AI unifies a set of disparate features and has a user interface that makes it easy to develop and integrate ML-related applications:

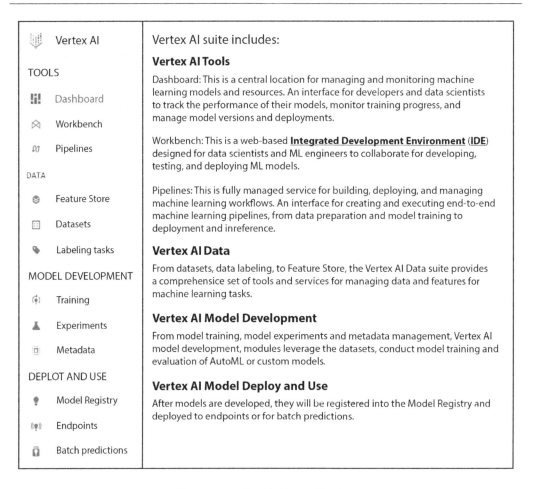

Vertex AI	Vertex AI suite includes:

Vertex AI Tools

Dashboard: This is a central location for managing and monitoring machine learning models and resources. An interface for developers and data scientists to track the performance of their models, monitor training progress, and manage model versions and deployments.

Workbench: This is a web-based **Integrated Development Environment** (**IDE**) designed for data scientists and ML engineers to collaborate for developing, testing, and deploying ML models.

Pipelines: This is fully managed service for building, deploying, and managing machine learning workflows. An interface for creating and executing end-to-end machine learning pipelines, from data preparation and model training to deployment and inreference.

Vertex AI Data

From datasets, data labeling, to Feature Store, the Vertex AI Data suite provides a comprehensice set of tools and services for managing data and features for machine learning tasks.

Vertex AI Model Development

From model training, model experiments and metadata management, Vertex AI model development, modules leverage the datasets, conduct model training and evaluation of AutoML or custom models.

Vertex AI Model Deploy and Use

After models are developed, they will be registered into the Model Registry and deployed to endpoints or for batch predictions.

Figure 10.1 – Google Vertex AI suite

In this section, we will briefly discuss the following Vertex AI concepts first and then spotlight Vertex AI AutoML with a lab to train a simple ML model:

- Vertex AI datasets
- Vertex AI dataset labeling
- Vertex AI Feature Store
- Vertex AI Workbench and notebooks
- Vertex AI custom models
- Vertex Explainable AI
- Vertex AI prediction

- Vertex AI model monitoring

- Vertex AI Pipelines

- Vertex AI TensorBoard

- Vertex AI Metadata

- Vertex AI AutoML

Let us start looking at Vertex AI by looking at datasets.

Vertex AI datasets

Data plays a significant role in any ML process, and the quality of datasets is essential for ML model performance, the so-called *garbage in, garbage out*. With Google Vertex AI, we can create and manage datasets directly from the Vertex AI platform. **Vertex AI datasets** provide users with the ability to upload data of varying types (structured and unstructured) to develop models.

Data uploaded via Vertex AI datasets is automatically stored in Vertex-created, Vertex-managed GCS buckets, and the permissions of the buckets can be managed through GCP IAM configurations within either Cloud Storage or Vertex AI.

Dataset labeling

Vertex AI dataset labeling lets users work with human forces to generate labels for a collection of data used to train ML models. Users that have access to this service can provide instructions directly to human labelers, provided by Google or selected by the user, to review and label the uploaded datasets.

Vertex AI Feature Store

Vertex AI Feature Store is a fully managed service that provides a centralized repository for organizing, storing, and serving ML features. With Vertex AI Feature Store, you can create and manage a feature store, which is a top-level container for the model features and their values. With a central feature store, users in an organization can share and reuse ML features to speed up ML application development and deployment. Vertex AI Feature Store is a central feature store that can be shared with teams for training or to serve tasks in different projects or use cases. Consistency can be maintained across your organization to reduce duplicate efforts, particularly for high-value features. It provides feature search and filter functions for team members to check and reuse features in the store.

Workbench and notebooks

Vertex AI Workbench is a development environment to query and explore data and develop and train ML models. Vertex AI Workbench provides two options: managed notebooks and user-managed notebooks:

- Google managed notebooks provide a convenient and powerful managed environment for data scientists and developers to work on their projects in a collaborative and scalable manner, leveraging the capabilities of Google Cloud Platform. Google takes care of the underlying infrastructure, including provisioning and managing virtual machines, so you can focus on your work without worrying about server management. It offers a JupyterLab interface, which is a web-based **integrated development environment** (**IDE**), where you can work on ML-related tasks without leaving the JupyterLab interface.

- User-managed notebooks allow users to create and manage JupyterLab notebooks within the Vertex AI environment. They are customizable deep learning VM instances that have preinstalled DL packages, providing a flexible and collaborative environment for developers and data scientists to develop and run machine learning experiments and workflows.

With Vertex Workbench and notebooks, you can access and explore your data within a Jupyter notebook. Vertex AI custom models allow us to have complete authority over data processing, model training, and prediction.

Vertex AI custom models

Building a custom ML model provides the ability to deliver highly accurate and robust models. There are two ways you can train a custom model:

- Use a Google Cloud prebuilt container and install a Python package that contains your code for training a custom model.

- Use your own model that has your code for training a custom model.

With a Vertex AI custom model, you can build customized ML models that fit your own business use cases.

Vertex Explainable AI

Vertex Explainable AI provides insights into how much each feature in the data/model contributed to the predicted result to help you with feature selection and researching how to improve your model and training data.

Vertex AI prediction

Vertex AI prediction manages computing resources in the cloud to run your models – it allocates nodes to handle online or batch predictions. When you deploy an ML model, either to endpoints or batch transformations, you can customize the node VM types for the prediction service and optionally configure GPUs for these nodes.

Vertex AI Model Monitoring

Vertex AI Model Monitoring helps you track the performance and behavior of your deployed machine learning models. It allows you to ensure that your models are performing as expected and identify any issues or anomalies in their predictions. It can monitor your model's input data and detect data drift – changes in the statistical properties of the input data over time. It can monitor the predictions made by your deployed model and detect prediction drifting, which occurs when the model's behavior changes over time. It provides metrics and insights into your model's performance. You can monitor key metrics such as latency, error rates, throughput, and resource utilization.

Vertex AI offers interactive dashboards that provide a visual representation of the monitored metrics and insights. It integrates with Google Cloud Monitoring, which allows you to centralize and manage your monitoring data alongside other Google Cloud services. You can leverage Cloud Monitoring's advanced capabilities, such as creating custom dashboards, setting up alerting policies, and analyzing your monitoring data in a unified manner.

Vertex AI Pipelines

Vertex AI Pipelines automates, monitors, and governs your ML systems in a serverless manner. It provides a way to orchestrate and automate the end-to-end machine learning workflow, encompassing tasks such as data preparation, model training, evaluation, and deployment. Vertex AI Pipelines enables you to create scalable and repeatable workflows that streamline the development and deployment of machine learning models.

Vertex AI TensorBoard and Metadata

Vertex AI TensorBoard lets you track, visualize, and compare ML experiments and share them with your team. Vertex AI TensorBoard provides visualizations including the following:

- Metrics such as loss and accuracy over time
- Model computational graphs
- Histograms of weights, biases, or other tensors as they change over time
- Image, text, and audio samples
- Profiling TensorFlow programs

By integrating with TensorBoard, Vertex AI enables you to monitor and analyze the training progress, model performance, and other relevant metrics of your TensorFlow models directly within the Vertex AI environment.

Google Cloud Vertex AI Metadata is a service that allows you to capture, store, and manage metadata associated with your machine learning projects and artifacts within the Vertex AI environment. Metadata provides valuable context and information about the various components and processes involved in your machine learning workflows.

Vertex AI AutoML

Google **AutoML** reduces or eliminates the need for skilled data scientists to build ML models. It enables users with limited ML expertise to train and build their own high-quality models fitting their business needs. Google AutoML allows you to train models on image, tabular, text, and video datasets without writing code.

In the following example, we will use Vertex AI AutoML to train an image classification model. The dataset has 22 images (images 1-22), which are available in the GitHub repository for this book: `https://github.com/PacktPublishing/Self-Taught-Cloud-computing-Engineer`.

We will use Vertex AI Data to prepare the dataset, train an AutoML model using Vertex AI model training, deploy the model to an endpoint using Vertex AI, and test the model with a new image. Let's start with the dataset images:

1. To collect datasets and label them, go to **Google Cloud console | Vertex AI console | Datasets**.

    Import the 22 images and label them – if an image has contents belonging to any of five categories (adult, spoof, medical, violence, or racy), then it is labeled **unsafe**; otherwise, it is labeled **safe**:

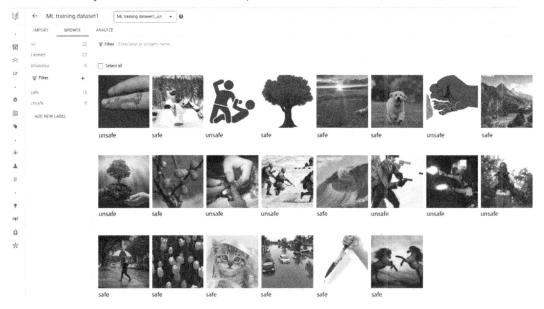

Figure 10.2 – Upload and label the dataset

2.   To train the model with AutoML, take these steps:

    I.   Creating an ML model:

        i.   Go to **Vertex AI console | Training | Create** to generate a new model:

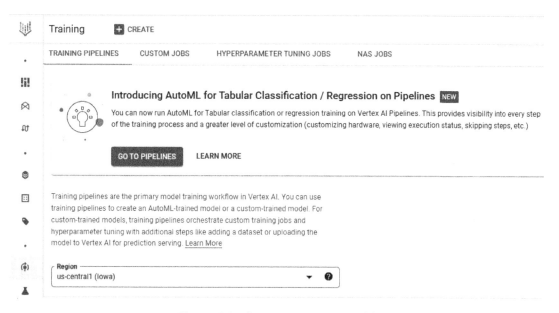

Figure 10.3 – Create a training ML model

ii. Select **AutoML** as the training method and keep the defaults for the rest, as shown in *Figure 10.4*:

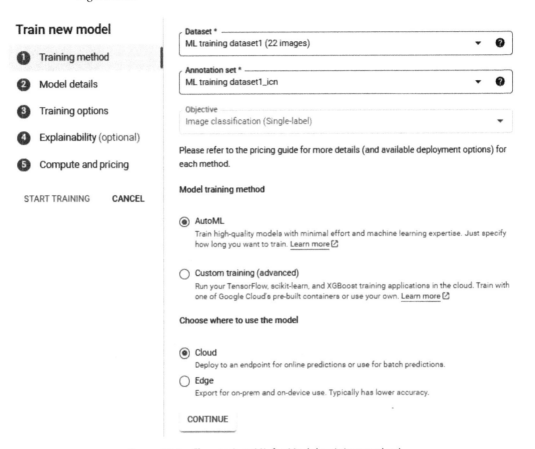

Figure 10.4 – Choose AutoML for Model training method

iii. Fill in more model details. For **Budget**, you can put the maximum node hours to limit the model training time. In our case, we use 8 hours as the limit. Click **START TRAINING**, as shown in *Figure 10.5*:

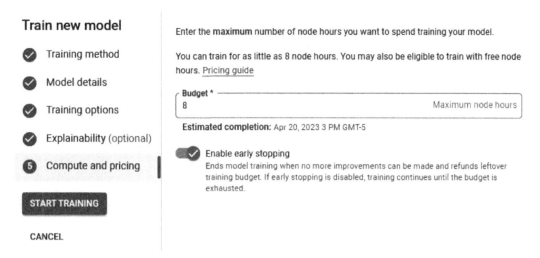

Train new model

✓ Training method

✓ Model details

✓ Training options

✓ Explainability (optional)

⑤ Compute and pricing

START TRAINING

CANCEL

Enter the **maximum** number of node hours you want to spend training your model.

You can train for as little as 8 node hours. You may also be eligible to train with free node hours. Pricing guide

┌ Budget * ──┐
│ 8   Maximum node hours │
└──┘

Estimated completion: Apr 20, 2023 3 PM GMT-5

✓ Enable early stopping
Ends model training when no more improvements can be made and refunds leftover training budget. If early stopping is disabled, training continues until the budget is exhausted.

Figure 10.5 – Start model training

II.   Training the ML model:

It will take some time to do the AutoML training. Once the training is complete, it will send an email to the user indicating the ML training has been completed.

3.   Deploying the model:

After the model is trained, we need to deploy it. In our case, we will deploy it to an endpoint. Go to **Vertex AI console** | **Online prediction** | **Create Endpoint**. Then define the endpoint as shown in *Figure 10.6(a)*:

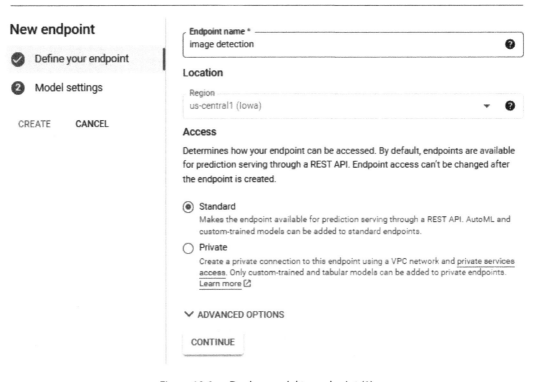

Figure 10.6a – Deploy model to endpoint (1)

Continue to **Model settings** and fill in the details as shown in *Figure 10.6(b).* We will use one node for the deployment:

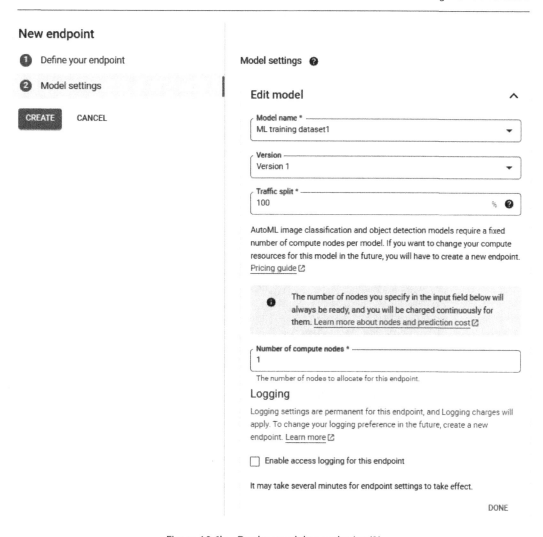

Figure 10.6b – Deploy model to endpoint (2)

It will take some time to deploy the model to an endpoint. After it's done, you will get an email notification and you can then use the endpoint to predict a new image.

4. Predicting content safety for a new image:

    After the model is deployed, we will test it with a new image. Go to **Vertex AI console | Training** and click on the model we have created and deployed. The new page will show four tabs: **EVALUATE**, **DEPLOY & TEST**, **BATCH PREDICT**, and **VERSION DETAILS**. Enter the **DEPLOY & TEST** tab, and we'll upload a new image to test the model and detect whether the image is safe. *Figure 10.7* shows the result of testing a sample image that is 100% safe:

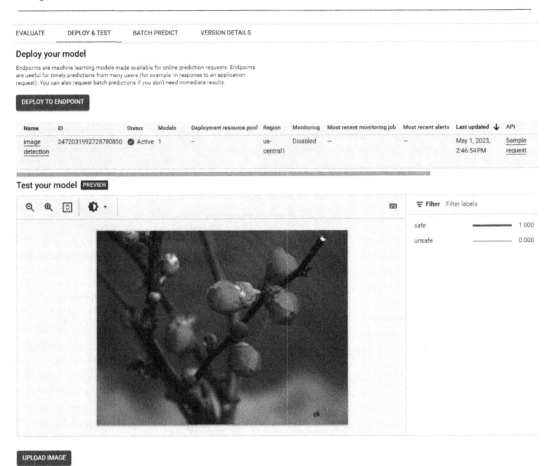

Figure 10.7 – Use the ML model to detect new image content

In the preceding lab, we have shown a Vertex AI AutoML model training process, where we developed a simple model that can classify images, using a small dataset of 22 images. As you can see, Vertex AI provides a comprehensive suite for developers and data scientists to develop ML models easily.

In this section, we introduced the Vertex AI suite, which provides an end-to-end Google Cloud AI suite, from data preparation to feature engineering to model development and deployment. Using Vertex AI, ML model training is the most time and money consuming part and it relates to choosing the notebook/instance types, using CPU/GPU/TPUs, and other factors. For more information about Vertex AI price calculations, please refer to `https://cloud.google.com/vertex-ai/pricing` and `https://cloud.google.com/products/calculator`.

As we discussed earlier, after your ML models are trained and deployed in Vertex AI, they must keep up with changing data from the environment to perform optimally and consistently. **ML operations** (**MLOps**) is a set of practices that improves the stability and reliability of your ML systems (more information about MLOps is available at `https://services.google.com/fh/files/misc/practitioners_guide_to_mlops_whitepaper.pdf`) Google's Vertex AI modules provide services that help you implement MLOps with your ML workflow:

- Vertex AI Monitoring monitors models for data skew drifting and alerts when the incoming prediction data skews too far from baselines

- Vertex AI Feature Store provides a centralized repository for organizing, storing, and serving ML features

- Vertex AI Model Registry provides an overview of your models so you can better organize, track, and train new versions

- Vertex AI Experiments lets you track, analyze, and measure different model architectures to identify the best model for your use case

- Vertex AI TensorBoard helps you track, visualize, and compare ML experiments to measure model performance

- Vertex ML Metadata lets you record and query metadata to analyze, debug, and audit the performance of your ML system

- Vertex AI Pipelines helps you automate, monitor, and govern your ML workflows

In the next section, we will introduce the Google Cloud ML APIs that leverage Google's pre-trained models, and we will also conduct the same image detection/categorizing use case, but with Cloud ML APIs.

Google Cloud ML APIs

The Google Cloud ML APIs are a set of ML API services that provides pre-trained models and tools for developers and data scientists to build custom ML models and ML applications. *Figure 10.8* shows a diagram of the Cloud ML APIs that we will cover next:

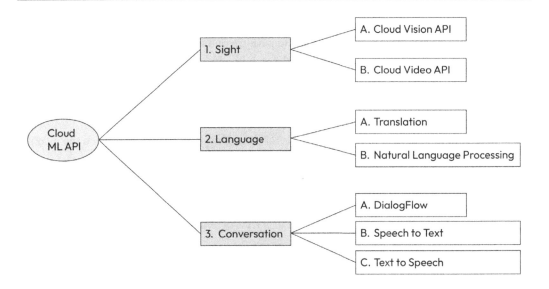

Figure 10.8 – Google Cloud ML APIs

Sight API

Google Cloud Sight API includes Cloud Vision API and Cloud Video API. The former analyzes static images and the latter learns from videos.

Cloud Vision API

Google Cloud Vision API is a cloud-based image analysis tool that helps developers to build applications that can understand the content of images, leveraging pre-trained computer vision models. Here are some key features of Cloud Vision API:

- **Label detection**: It helps to identify objects and the context within an image

- **Optical Character Recognition (OCR)**: It detects and extracts text from images

- **Face detection**: It detects faces and facial features within images

- **Landmark detection**: It identifies popular landmarks within images

- **Image attributes**: It detects attributes of an image, such as contents, colors, and so on

While Cloud Vision API is tailored to image analysis, Cloud Video Intelligence API is specifically designed for video analysis. Both APIs leverage machine learning models to provide powerful capabilities for understanding visual content. The choice between the two depends on whether you need to analyze individual images or analyze video content. Let's look at Cloud Video API.

Cloud Video API

Google Cloud Video API is a machine learning-powered video analysis service that enables developers to integrate video intelligence and analysis capabilities into their applications. Google Cloud Video API provides the following:

- **Label detection**: It analyzes videos and labels them with categories and keywords
- **Shot detection**: It detects changes in the camera angle or scene within a video
- **Object tracking**: It tracks the movements of objects in a video
- **Face detection**: It detects face positions and facial expressions
- **Explicit content detection**: It detects content that may be inappropriate or objectionable

The development of sight and language has played crucial roles in shaping human evolution, cognition, culture, and progress. These faculties have empowered humans to perceive and interpret the world, communicate with one another, and create rich and diverse societies. The fundamentals of AI are to teach machines/computers to learn sight intelligence and language intelligence.

Language API

Language APIs allow developers to incorporate **NLP** and translation capabilities into their applications. GCP Language API offers various features for text analysis, understanding, and language translation.

NLP API

Google Cloud Natural Language API allows users to perform text analysis tasks such as these:

- **Sentiment analysis**: It analyzes the sentiment of a given text and provides a score ranging from -1.0 (negative) to 1.0 (positive), as well as a magnitude that indicates the overall emotional intensity of the text
- **Entity recognition**: It identifies and classifies entities within a given text, such as people, places, organizations, and products
- **Syntax analysis**: It parses the grammatical structure of a sentence, providing information on parts of speech, dependency relationships, and more
- **Content classification**: It classifies text into predefined categories, such as news, politics, or sport

Using text in one language to interpret a text in another language is language translation. GCP provides Cloud Translation API.

Translation API

Google Cloud Translation API enables developers to easily integrate language translation capabilities into their applications. The API supports translation between over 100 languages and provides the following:

- Auto-detection of source language from a given text
- High-quality translations that are contextually accurate and natural-sounding
- Customizable translations for developers to train and deploy custom translation models

Other than text, conversation is an important format in human communications. Google offers Cloud Conversational API for developers to integrate conversations into intelligence applications.

Conversational API

Google Cloud provides several services and APIs that can be used to develop conversational applications. Google Cloud Conversational API includes Dialogflow, Text-to-Speech, and Speech-to-Text. Let's check each of them.

Dialogflow

Google Cloud Dialogflow is a language understanding platform that allows developers to build conversational interfaces for various applications such as chatbots, voice assistants, and other interactive experiences. Dialogflow understands user inputs in natural language and can generate responses in real time. The platform provides tools to understand the meaning behind user inputs and generate appropriate responses. It provides pre-built agents for common use cases such as customer support, e-commerce, and booking systems, which can be customized and extended to meet specific requirements. It provides a drag-and-drop interface for building conversational experiences, as well as analytics and insights into user behavior, including metrics such as user engagement, session duration, and message counts.

Text-to-Speech

Google Cloud Text-to-Speech allows developers to convert written text into spoken audio. Powered by pre-trained ML models, it supports a variety of input audio formats, including MP3, WAV, and Ogg Opus, and generates lifelike voices that sound natural and expressive. The API supports over 30 languages and provides fine-grained control over audio settings, such as speaking rate, pitch, and volume.

Speech-to-Text

Google Cloud Speech-to-Text allows developers to transcribe spoken audio into text. Powered by pretrained Google ML models, the API can transcribe real-time streaming audio or pre-recorded audio files in a variety of formats and transcribe speech with high accuracy. It supports over 120 languages and dialects and can transcribe real-time streaming audio. It can automatically identify and separate different speakers in a conversation and automatically insert punctuation and formatting.

In summary, Google Cloud ML APIs enable developers to integrate the pre-trained ML model services into their applications. The Cloud ML APIs also integrate with other Google Cloud services, such as Google Cloud Storage, Google Kubernetes Engine, Google BigQuery, and so on, to provide a complete end-to-end solution for machine learning projects.

Having explored the Google Cloud ML APIs, we need to practice some hands-on skills. In the next section, we will implement a new solution to the business use case we discussed earlier: detecting input image content and labeling it as *safe* or *unsafe*. Last time, our solution leveraged Vertex AI datasets to import the images and label them, then used Vertex AI AutoML to train an ML model, and used Vertex Endpoint to deploy the model to an endpoint for image detection. This time, we have a different solution – we will use Google Cloud API and leverage the Google pre-trained Cloud Vision models to solve the issue.

We will first create a GCS bucket. Upon uploading an image to the bucket, a cloud function will be triggered. The function will call Cloud Vision API functions to detect whether the image has unsafe contents or not, then move the image to different GCS folders labeled as **unsafe** or **safe** respectively. *Figure 10.9* shows the solution workflow diagram:

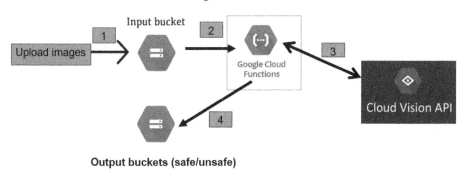

Figure 10.9 – Detect image contents using Cloud Vision API

We will implement the solution in four steps:

1. Create GCS buckets using Cloud Shell:

    ```
    gsutil mb gs://04092023-upload
    gsutil mb gs://04092023-safe
    gsutil mb gs://04092023-unsafe
    ```

    Check the buckets created:

    ```
    gsutil ls
    ```

2. Create three files in Cloud Shell:

- `requirements.txt`

- `target.json`

- `main.py`

  - The `requirements.txt` file defines the library requirements. In our case, it reads as follows:

    ```
    google-cloud-storage
    google-cloud-vision
    ```

  - The `target.json` file includes the target bucket variable in JSON format:

    ```
    {"SAFE_BUCKET": "z04092023-safe",
    "UNSAFE_BUCKET": "z04092023-unsafe"}
    ```

  - The `main.py` file defines a cloud function called `image_checking`.

  Google Cloud Functions is a serverless computing platform that allows developers to write and deploy small functions that automatically scale based on demand. Cloud functions can be triggered by various events, including HTTP requests, Cloud Pub/Sub messages, Cloud Storage changes, and more.

  In our case, the `image_checking` cloud function basically takes the image in the upload bucket folder, calls the Google Cloud API `SafeSearch Detection` function to check whether the image has explicit content (adult, spoof, medical, violence, or racy), and moves the image to the `unsafe` folder if it does; otherwise, it moves the image to the `safe` folder. Details about the Cloud Vision API `SafeSearch Detection` function are available at `https://cloud.google.com/vision/docs/detecting-safe-search`.

3. Deploying the `image_checking` cloud function in Cloud Shell:

  Use the following command in Cloud Shell to deploy `image_checking`:

  ```
  gcloud functions deploy image_checking  --trigger-
  resource  z04092023-upload --trigger-event google.storage.
  object.finalize --runtime python37
  ```

4. Testing with new images:

  Now, when you upload the images into the `z04092023-upload` bucket, the `image_checking` cloud function will perform content detection and move the image to the appropriate folders based on the Cloud Vision detection result.

This concludes our Cloud ML API example. Compared to the solution we had for the same use case in the Vertex AI section, where we trained and deployed our own model using Vertex AI AutoML, this time, we used Google Cloud ML API, which is very powerful since it's based on pre-trained ML models. As a matter of fact, Google ML API is one of the most popular libraries for developers to form business AI applications.

Google Cloud ML API has different price models for sight (vision/video), language (NLP and so on), and other services. Please refer to Google Cloud Pricing Calculator at `https://cloud.google.com/products/calculator` for more details.

Google Cloud generative AI services

Google Cloud generative AI services use **large language models** (**LLMs**) to recognize, predict, and generate human languages. They can be used in many business applications to drive new business opportunities. *Figure 10.10* lists some generative AI use cases in Google Workspace applications.

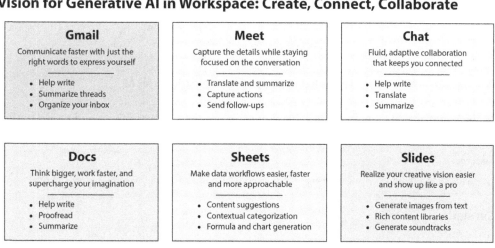

Figure 10.10 – Generative AI use cases in Google Workspace

Since the needs of enterprise customers are different from individual consumers and enthusiasts, Google Cloud generative AI focuses on enterprise business cases and environments. At this time, it offers **Generative AI Studio**, which includes three tabs: **Overview**, **Language**, and **Speech**, as shown in *Figure 10.11*.

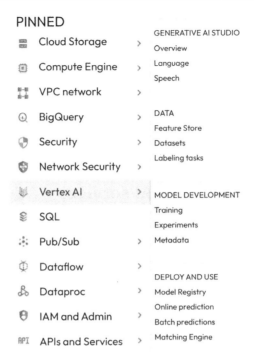

PINNED

🖫	Cloud Storage	>	
▣	Compute Engine	>	
▦	VPC network	>	
⊕	BigQuery	>	
🛡	Security	>	
⬟	Network Security	>	
⚕	Vertex AI	>	
⬚	SQL		
⦂	Pub/Sub	>	
⬡	Dataflow	>	
⅋	Dataproc	>	
❽	IAM and Admin	>	
API	APIs and Services	>	

GENERATIVE AI STUDIO
Overview
Language
Speech

DATA
Feature Store
Datasets
Labeling tasks

MODEL DEVELOPMENT
Training
Experiments
Metadata

DEPLOY AND USE
Model Registry
Online prediction
Batch predictions
Matching Engine

Figure 10.11 – Generative AI Studio in Vertex AI

In the **Language** tab, it provides starting points for prompts, conversations, and model tuning, as shown in *Figure 10.12*:

Language

GET STARTED   MY PROMPTS   TUNING PREVIEW

Get started

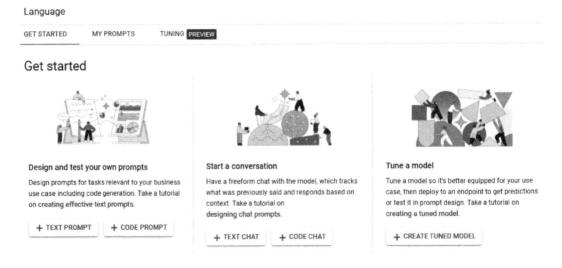

Design and test your own prompts

Design prompts for tasks relevant to your business use case including code generation. Take a tutorial on creating effective text prompts.

    + TEXT PROMPT   + CODE PROMPT

Start a conversation

Have a freeform chat with the model, which tracks what was previously said and responds based on context. Take a tutorial on designing chat prompts.

    + TEXT CHAT   + CODE CHAT

Tune a model

Tune a model so it's better equipped for your use case, then deploy to an endpoint to get predictions or test it in prompt design. Take a tutorial on creating a tuned model.

    + CREATE TUNED MODEL

Figure 10.12 – Generative AI Studio Language tab

It provides many prompts, some of them are shown in *Figure 10.13*:

Figure 10.13 – Generative AI language prompts

Google Cloud generative AI services are part of the Google Cloud AI portfolio to support Generative centric enterprise AI development for business users, developers, and AI practitioners. *Figure 10.14* shows the Google Cloud AI portfolio:

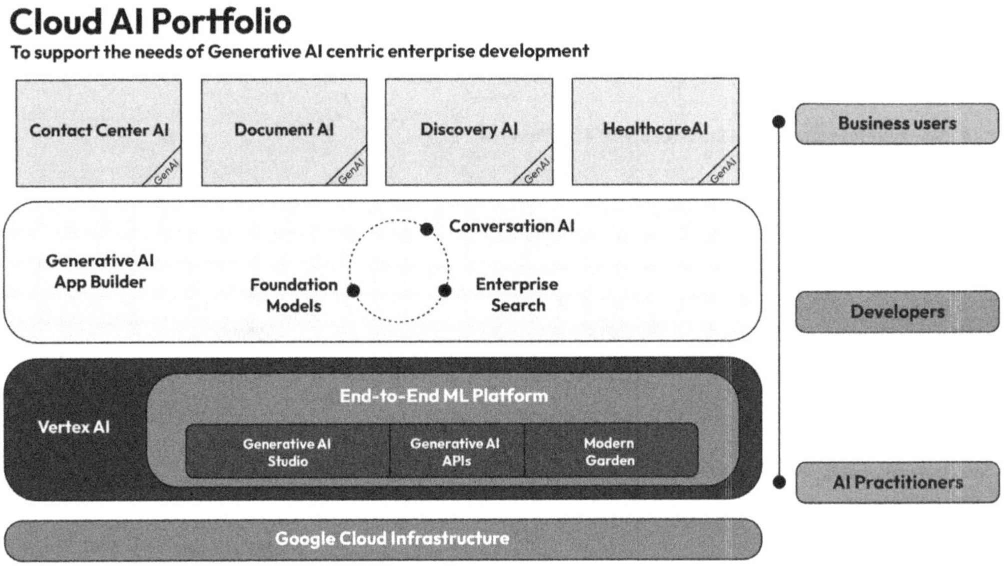

Cloud AI Portfolio
To support the needs of Generative AI centric enterprise development

Figure 10.14 – Generative AI is part of the Google Cloud AI portfolio

More services are being added to it. It would be a great idea to keep track of the generative AI services as they are developed and applied to business use cases.

Summary

In this chapter, we discussed the two main topics in Google Cloud ML: Google Cloud Vertex AI, which provides an end-to-end suite for developing and deploying ML models, and Google ML API, which provides programming interfaces by leveraging pre-trained ML models. We have also covered Google generative AI, which is an emerging AI service added to Vertex AI recently.

In this chapter, you have acquired ML model training and ML application development skills using the Google Vertex AI suite and Google ML API. In the next chapter, we will discuss Google Cloud security.

Practice questions

Questions 1-4 are based on *Figure 10.15*, which is a Cloud Vision system to detect unsafe content in input images.

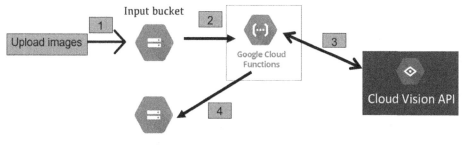

Figure 10.15 – Cloud Vision detection system

We have created three files:

- `target.json`
- `main.py`
- `requirements.txt`

And the following is a snippet of the `main.py` file:

```
def image_checking(data, context):
    uri = "gs://" + data['bucket'] + "/" + data['name']
    image = vision.Image()
    image.source.image_uri = uri
    response = vision_client.safe_search_detection(image=image)
    result = response.safe_search_annotation
```

1. What is the `requirements.txt` file?

   A. It includes the required modules to import

   B. It can be renamed to requirements

   C. It is only for illustration purposes

   D. It is needed for GCP Cloud Vision

2. What is the `target.json` file?

   A. It includes the buckets to put classified images

   B. It includes the dataset for training the model

   C. It is only for illustration purposes

   D. It is needed for GCP Cloud Vision

3. What is `result` in the code snippet?

 A. It is the result of the image safety detection processing

 B. It is the result of image safety dataset labeling

 C. It is the result of the image model training

 D. It is the result of the Vision model validation

4. What is `data` in the code snippet?

 A. It is the input from the cloud function deployment

 B. It is the input for the model dataset

 C. It is the data structure of the image

 D. It is the data for model analytics

Questions 5-8 are based on the following use case:

An engineer is working in a customer support/ticket center for a financial firm and is designing an ML system that will preprocess users' tickets before they are routed to a support agent, as shown in *Figure 10.16*:

The system aims to perform the following tasks:

- Predict ticket priority

- Predict ticket resolution time

- Perform sentiment analysis to help agents make strategic decisions when they process support requests

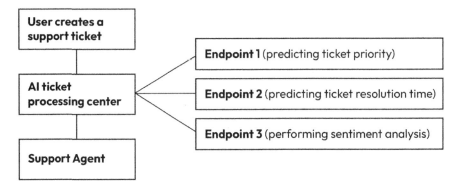

Figure 10.16 – Customer support ML preprocessing system

5. What do you choose for Endpoint 1?

    A. GCP Vertex AI Workbench

    B. GCP Cloud Dialogflow

    C. GCP Cloud Vision

    D. GCP Cloud NLP

6. What do you choose for Endpoint 2?

    A. GCP Vertex AI Workbench

    B. GCP Cloud Dialogflow

    C. GCP Cloud Vision

    D. GCP Cloud NLP

7. What's your recommendation to deal with high call volumes?

    A. Use Vertex AI Workbench distributed training

    B. Use a Dataproc cluster for training

    C. Create a MIG with autoscaling

    D. Use Kubeflow Pipelines to train on a GKE cluster

8. What do you choose for Endpoint 3?

    A. GCP Vertex AI Workbench

    B. GCP Cloud dialogflow

    C. GCP Cloud Vision

    D. GCP Cloud NLP

Answers to the practice questions

1. A

2. A

3. A

4. A

5. A

6. A

7. A

8. D

Further reading

For further insights into what you've learned in this chapter, refer to the following links:

- `https://cloud.google.com/products/ai`
- `https://cloud.google.com/vertex-ai-workbench`
- `https://cloud.google.com/automl`
- `https://cloud.google.com/vertex-ai`
- `https://cloud.google.com/vision`
- `https://cloud.google.com/video-intelligence`
- `https://cloud.google.com/natural-language`
- `https://cloud.google.com/translate`

11
Google Cloud Security Services

As we discussed in *Part 1* of this book, cloud security is all about securing the cloud – addressing the challenges and using risk detection, remediation, and prevention in the cloud. Starting with the shared responsibility model, in which the **cloud service providers** (**CSPs**) are responsible for securing the underlying infrastructure and the customers are responsible for securing their data and applications, Google takes cloud security as a top priority and has built multiple layers of protection in following industry best practices. In this chapter, we will cover the following topics:

- **Google Cloud IAM**: Google has enabled granular control over access and permissions to GCP resources and services

- **Google Cloud endpoint security**: Google provides secure protection for GCP endpoints and services, such as **virtual machines** (**VMs**), **Google Cloud Storage** (**GCS**), and **virtual private cloud** (**VPC**) networks

- **Google Cloud data security**: We will discuss data classification, data encryption, and data loss prevention

- **Google Cloud monitoring and logging**: Google offers various tools for monitoring and logging security events, such as Google Cloud's operations suite

- **Google Cloud Security Command Center** (**SCC**): This is a comprehensive security tool that integrates many GCP security services, and we will have a deep dive into its components and configurations

We will start our Google Cloud security journey with Google Cloud IAM.

Google Cloud IAM

Google Cloud IAM defines cloud identities, resources, and their relationships. It specifies who (users, groups, or service accounts) has what kind of access (roles) to what cloud resources in the GCP resource hierarchy. Key features of Google Cloud IAM include the following:

- **GCP resource hierarchy**: Google Cloud IAM leverages a resource hierarchy (organization, folder, project, and resource) to inherit permissions from higher levels. This allows you to manage access control more efficiently by applying policies at the appropriate level in the hierarchy.

- **Fine-grained access control with roles and permissions**: Google Cloud IAM uses roles, which are a collection of permissions, to grant access to GCP resources. Google provides predefined roles (viewer, editor, and owner) as well as the ability to create custom roles tailored to your organization's needs.

- **Identity federation**: Google Cloud IAM supports identity federation, allowing you to integrate with external identity providers, such as Google Workspace, Cloud Identity, or third-party solutions. This enables you to manage access control in a centralized manner across different systems.

- **Service accounts**: Service accounts are special types of accounts used by Google Cloud applications or VMs to interact with GCP services. GCP IAM enables you to manage and control access to applications through service accounts, ensuring that they have the necessary permissions to function correctly.

We have discussed many cloud IAM concepts in this book, and here we will focus on some key concepts in the GCP IAM domain: users, groups, service accounts, and roles.

Google Cloud users and groups

Google Cloud user accounts here refer to human and not programmatic users, and are usually provisioned and synchronized using the existing company user identity services such as **Microsoft Active Directory** (**AD**), Google **Workspace**, and Okta **identity providers** (**IdPs**), which serve as the *single source of truth* for user/group data. Synchronizing from a single source of truth ensures that users and groups are centrally managed in a consistent manner through their lifecycle. And during their lifecycles, all user/group authentications should be done enforcing MFA, including GCP and other CSP console access, along with any other SSO implementations. Usernames and passwords are simply ineffective for protecting user access these days. Further details on AD and GCP federation can be found at `https://cloud.google.com/architecture/identity/federating-gcp-with-active-directory-introduction`.

Google Cloud groups should be the primary entity to which IAM roles are assigned. It is highly recommended that IAM roles are *not* assigned directly to users but to groups. Once project owners have properly associated groups with their required roles in a GCP project, granting and revoking a user's access to projects should be managed via group membership. Google Cloud groups will be pushed into Google Cloud Identity from the central Cloud Identity management source, such as an AD instance.

Google Cloud service accounts

A Google Cloud service account is a specialized account that can be used by applications to access GCP services. Service accounts are like *programmatic access users* in other public cloud platforms, such as service roles in AWS. Applications can use service account credentials to authorize themselves to cloud APIs and perform actions within the permissions granted to the service account. Specifically, applications running on **Google Compute Engine** (**GCE**) instances use service accounts to interact with other Google services and their underlying APIs.

Google Cloud IAM roles

GCP supports three types of IAM roles: Primitive (basic), Predefined, and Custom:

- **Primitive (basic) roles**: These include the **Owner**, **Editor**, and **Viewer** roles that existed in GCP prior to IAM. Primitive roles such as Owner and Editor should be used sparingly as they confer significant privileges and will likely run afoul of the least privilege requirements.

- **Predefined roles**: These provide very granular access for specific services following role-based permission needs. These are managed by Google and provide what Google believes are the least privileged permissions needed to perform a role for said service.

- **Custom roles**: These roles provide granular access according to the user-specified permissions. They should be used sparingly as the user is responsible for maintaining the permissions.

For GCE VMs, both roles and access scopes can be used to control the access that the VM has to other Google Cloud resources, by following the best practices:

- Creating a new service account rather than using the GCE VM's default service account. Service accounts can be found in the GCP console using the **Service Accounts** page.

- Granting IAM permissions to the service account for only the resources it needs.

- Granting the VM instance service account scope to allow full access to all Google Cloud service APIs so that the instance's IAM permissions are determined by the IAM roles of the service account.

We have highlighted some of the IAM key concepts. More details can be found at `https://cloud.google.com/iam`. In the next section, we will discuss Google Cloud endpoint security.

Google Cloud endpoint security

Google Cloud offers a variety of security features and best practices to help protect Google Cloud endpoints including GCE VMs, GCS, and VPC networks.

GCE VM security

VMs run on GCE, which has security measures designed to secure the underlying infrastructure, protect VM data, and minimize potential vulnerabilities. Key aspects of Google Cloud VM security include the following:

- **Firewall rules**: These allow you to control inbound and outbound network traffic to VM instances. Configuring firewall rules can limit access to specific IP addresses, ports, and protocols, thereby reducing the VM attack surface.

- **Service accounts**: VM instances can use service accounts to authenticate and access other GCP services securely.

- **Secure boot**: This is a technology that helps ensure the integrity of the boot process by verifying that the VM boot firmware and OS have not been tampered with.

- **OS patch management**: This is crucial for security. Google Cloud offers tools such as OS patch management to automate the process of updating and patching VMs.

- **Vulnerability scanning services**: Google Cloud SCC and third-party solutions help identify potential vulnerabilities in your VM instances and suggest remediation actions.

- **Logging and monitoring services**: Cloud Logging and Cloud Monitoring help track VM activities and detect potential security threats in real time.

For GCP VM security, we recommend the following best practices:

- Where possible, prohibit the assignment of public IP addresses. GCE instances that do not have external IP addresses can be configured to use **Identity-Aware Proxy** (**IAP**) or private Google access and leverage existing on-premises remote access services.

- Configure a route egress through a custom firewall solution if needed, and disable VM serial port access.

- Utilize OS Login (`https://cloud.google.com/compute/docs/oslogin`) and leverage MFA/2FA for user access to VMs.

- Within production environments, utilize a bastion host as a jump point for SSH and RDP access. Shut down the host when not in use for added security. Limit source IP access using firewall ingress rules.

- Do not use the GCE default service account. Create service accounts based on instance roles.

- Encrypt disks containing sensitive data with customer-supplied keys if Google-managed keys do not fit the compliance standards.

- When possible, adopt the immutable infrastructure pattern, which leverages automation for provisioning and de-provisioning VM instances.

- Only allow machine image creation from approved base images using **Google Trusted Image Policies**.

By leveraging the security features and following best practices, you can enhance the security of your Google Cloud VM instances and protect your data and applications from potential threats.

GCS security

As we discussed in *Chapter 8*, GCS is a highly scalable and durable object storage service. It is designed with security in mind, offering several features to help protect data and ensure the privacy and compliance of stored information. Key aspects of GCS security include the following:

- Google Cloud IAM allows you to control access to your GCS buckets and objects by assigning roles and permissions to users, groups, or service accounts.

- GCS supports both bucket-level IAM policies and object-level **access control lists** (ACLs) for fine-grained access control. You can configure policies and ACLs to allow or deny access based on the user, group, or domain.

- Private Google access allows your GCS resources to be accessed privately from your VPC network or on-premises network without trespassing the internet.

- GCP **Data Loss Prevention** (**DLP**) can be integrated with GCS to automatically discover, classify, and protect sensitive data stored in your buckets.

- GCS provides data retention policies and object versioning to help preserve data integrity and prevent accidental deletion or overwriting of objects.

- GCS integrates with Google Cloud's audit Logging and Monitoring services to provide visibility into access patterns and help detect potential security threats.

For GCP GCS security, we recommend the following best practices:

- IAM roles should be used to control access at the bucket level. The uniform bucket-level access organization policy can be used to disable ACLs. If control is needed at the object level, ACLs may be used. However, it requires significant management overhead.

- Don't use public buckets unless explicitly required. Compliance tooling should be used to ensure public buckets do not exist and are not created. Leverage signed URLs, (details are available at `https://cloud.google.com/storage/docs/access-control/signed-urls`.)

- Limit the number of publicly accessible GCS buckets. Utilize lifecycle management to automate archival and deletion.

- Apply bucket-level retention rules to data stored within GCS that requires retention policies.

- Leverage customer-managed keys especially for sensitive data (in lieu of Google-managed keys)

By leveraging the GCS security features and following best practices, you can protect your data stored in GCS and maintain a secure storage environment. Now, let us look at the Google Cloud network security.

Google Cloud network security

GCP offers a variety of network security features and best practices to help protect your resources and applications in the cloud. Google provides VPC network security including the following:

- GCP VPCs create isolated and secure virtual networks within GCP. By using VPCs, you can control the network topology, IP address ranges, and routing tables, enabling you to isolate your resources and manage access effectively.

- GCP provides built-in firewalls that enable you to control inbound and outbound network traffic to your resources, such as GCE instances and **Google Kubernetes Engine** (**GKE**) clusters.

- Google Cloud IAM enables granular control over who has access to specific network resources and services.

- VPC service controls create a secure perimeter around your GCP resources, limiting access to only specific VPC networks or authorized users with appropriate context.

- Private Google access allows your GCP resources to be accessed privately from your VPC network or on-premises network without exposing data to the public internet.

- Cloud **Network Address Translation** (**NAT**) is a managed NAT gateway that allows your private instances to access the internet for updates and patches without exposing them to inbound internet traffic.

- VPC network peering connects VPC networks across GCP projects, ensuring low-latency, secure communication between resources without transiting the public internet.

- Shared VPC enables you to centrally manage network resources across multiple GCP projects, allowing for efficient resource sharing and simplified network management.

- Cloud VPN and Cloud Interconnect solutions securely connect your on-premises networks and cloud networks. These options ensure private, encrypted communication between your resources, even across geographical distances.

By leveraging the network security features, you can protect your cloud resources and maintain a secure, well-managed network environment. Among the networking security features, we want to spotlight **GCP Cloud Armor**, which is a cloud network security service integrating with Google's Global HTTP(S) load balancing service. Cloud Armor protects your infrastructure and applications from **Distributed Denial-of-Service (DDoS)** attacks. To mitigate attacks on your GCP resources, Cloud Armor is deployed at the edge of your Google Cloud network, to allow or deny access to your load balancers as close as possible to the source of the incoming traffic. This prevents any unwanted traffic from reaching your network. More details can be found at `https://cloud.google.com/armor/`.

We have discussed Google Cloud endpoint security by examining VM security, GCS security, and network security. The objective of all these Google Cloud security options is to protect our data in the cloud. Let's dive into Google Cloud data security now.

Google Cloud data security

GCP offers a robust set of security features to protect customer data. Many of the data security services are based on basic data security enablement. We will start with data classification.

Data classification and data lineage

Industry data security best practices recommend starting with a classification standard and then assigning a data/resource owner to identify each data resource's classification. We recommend utilizing data classification and maintaining a unified level of permissions on GCP projects and resources, to prevent misconfigurations and unauthorized access to sensitive information.

Data lineage is the practice of tracking the data origin, what happened to it, and where it moves over time. **Data provenance** can be defined as the origins, custody, and ownership of data. It is the documentation of where a piece of data comes from and the processes/methodology by which it was produced. Establishing a data labeling/tagging standard to deal with data lineage and provenance requirements is viewed as a highly recommended practice in data security.

Data encryption

Google encrypts all data channels that it uses to communicate between the cloud services. Customers are responsible for ensuring that communication of their data within the applications is over an encrypted channel.

Google encrypts all data on storage devices to prevent anyone with access to physical devices from being able to inspect the data contained on those devices. Customers can provide their own encryption keys to encrypt **GCE Persistent Disks** and **GCS buckets**. All data stored within Google-managed databases is encrypted at the storage level by default. However, additional encryption is advisable at the application level to prevent users from accessing content and limiting spillage in the event of intrusion.

Google Cloud's virtual network infrastructure enables encryption when data moves among networks/ VPCs and encryption is performed at the network layer within the same VPC or across peered VPCs. For additional information on how Google protects data in transit, please refer to `https://cloud. google.com/docs/security/encryption-in-transit`.

GCP DLP

DLP can be utilized to ensure sensitive data is identified and properly protected. The tool can scan existing datasets and utilize various techniques to obscure sensitive data, including redaction, tokenization, and format-preserving encryption. This ensures that the data is obfuscated before it is stored. With Google Cloud DLP, you can scan objects in GCS, BigQuery, Datastore, and many other data sources, workloads, and applications. Cloud DLP also can be leveraged to transform, mask, or tokenize sensitive data.

When storing PII or other sensitive information, use multiple projects or GCS buckets, and assign permissions based on data sensitivity accordingly. At the project level, the best practice is to create two or more different projects, each with its own data sensitivity. At the GCS bucket level, the best practice is to create two or more different buckets, each with its own data sensitivity. Use DLP to replicate data from sensitive projects/buckets into non-sensitive ones and use IAM to restrict users from accessing sensitive projects/buckets.

Security for the Google Cloud VMs, GCS buckets/objects, VPC networks, and data is all related to cloud resource access activities. In the next section, we will discuss the monitoring and logging of these resource access activities.

Google Cloud Monitoring and Logging

The **Google Cloud operations suite** is a collection of tools and services that help customers monitor, troubleshoot, and improve the performance of their applications and infrastructure on Google Cloud. It is an aggregation suite for Google Cloud Monitoring and Logging. The Google Cloud operations suite offers the following security features:

- **Cloud Monitoring** provides visibility into the performance and availability of cloud applications and infrastructure. It collects and analyzes metrics, logs, and traces to provide insights into the health and performance of applications and services.

- **Cloud Logging** provides real-time log management and analysis for applications and infrastructure. It collects, stores, and analyzes log data from Google Cloud services, third-party applications, and custom applications.

- **Cloud Trace** provides in-depth visibility into application performance by tracing requests across distributed systems. It provides detailed latency information for individual requests, as well as insights into service dependencies.

- **Error Reporting** automatically collects and aggregates errors from Google Cloud services, third-party applications, and custom applications. It provides insights into the root causes of errors and allows customers to prioritize and fix issues quickly.

- **Debugger** allows customers to debug applications running in production without disrupting users. It provides a snapshot of the application state at any point in time, allowing customers to analyze and diagnose issues quickly.

- **Profiler** provides insight into the performance of applications by identifying and analyzing performance bottlenecks. It can help customers optimize application performance and reduce resource usage.

- **Alerting** allows customers to set up alerts based on metrics, logs, and events. Alerts can be sent via email, SMS, or other notification channels.

With all these features, the Google Cloud operations suite provides a comprehensive set of tools to monitor, analyze, troubleshoot, and optimize cloud applications and infrastructure.

In the previous sections, we discussed IAM, endpoint security, network security, data security, and Cloud Monitoring and Logging. Integrating all these security features, Google Cloud **Security Command Center** provides a comprehensive tool for managing Google Cloud security. If there is one service I must recommend for Google Cloud security, it is the Security Command Center. We will closely examine its features and functions thoroughly with some examples in the next section.

Google Cloud Security Command Center (SCC)

Google Cloud **SCC** is a comprehensive security management platform that provides visibility, insights, and tools to help you manage security risks across your GCP resources and applications. Key features of SCC include the following:

- SCC provides a centralized dashboard that gives you an overview of your GCP assets, vulnerabilities, and security findings, enabling you to monitor and respond to potential risks in real time.

- SCC automatically discovers and inventories all the GCP resources, such as GCE instances, **Google App Engine** (**GAE**) applications, and GCS buckets, to understand the scope of your cloud environment and manage resource configurations effectively.

- SCC integrates with various vulnerability scanning and management tools, such as Google Cloud Web Security Scanner and third-party solutions, to identify and remediate vulnerabilities in your web applications and infrastructure.

- SCC collects security findings from various GCP services and third-party security tools, such as Web Security Scanner, DLP, and third-party vulnerability scanners. These findings help you detect potential security issues, such as misconfigurations, policy violations, and threats.

- SCC uses ML algorithms to analyze your GCP resources and activities, detecting and alerting you to potential anomalies and security risks, such as unusual data access patterns or unauthorized API usage.

- SCC enables you to define, enforce, and manage security policies across your GCP resources, ensuring that your environment remains compliant with your organization's security requirements and industry standards.

- SCC provides insights into your security posture by analyzing your GCP assets and security findings, identifying trends, and recommending best practices for improving your overall security.

- SCC integrates with various GCP and third-party security tools, such as Google Cloud Armor, Cloud IAM, and **Security Information and Event Management** (**SIEM**) and **Security Orchestration, Automation, and Response** (**SOAR**) solutions, enabling you to manage and respond to security events effectively.

- SCC allows you to set up notifications for specific security findings or events, enabling you to respond quickly to potential risks. It also integrates with GCP's Cloud Functions to automate remediation actions, such as updating firewall rules or revoking access permissions.

Google Cloud SCC is a basic risk dashboard and analytics system for Google Cloud security and risk management. By leveraging SCC, you can gain visibility into your GCP environment, manage security risks effectively, and maintain a secure, compliant cloud infrastructure. SCC has two tiers: Standard and Premium.

The **SCC Standard tier** is free and provides a good asset inventory capability for the security team. The standard tier has the following features:

- **Security Health Analytics** (**SHA**) provides managed vulnerability assessment scanning that can automatically detect Google Cloud resource vulnerabilities and misconfigurations

- **Web Security Scanner** supports custom scans of deployed applications with public URLs and IPs that aren't behind a firewall

- Integration with many Google Cloud services:

  - Works with DLP to discover, classify, and protect sensitive data

  - Works with Google Cloud Armor to protect against threats and attacks

  - Uses ML to identify security anomalies for your projects, VMs, and other resources

  - Integrates with SIEM and SOAR applications

The **SCC Premium tier** is available via self-service activation in the GCP console. It offers pay-as-you-go pricing at the organization level and individual project levels. More details about SCC pricing are available at `https://cloud.google.com/security-command-center/pricing`. SCC Premium offers the following, in addition to the Standard tier features:

- **Event Threat Detection** (**ETD**) monitors the Cloud Logging stream to detect the following threats: malware, crypto mining, brute force SSH, DoS, IAM anomalous grant, data exfiltration, and so on.

- SHA provides monitoring for many more industry best practices, and compliance monitoring across your Google Cloud assets, including monitoring and reporting for the following standards: *CIS 1.1/1.0, PCI DSS v3.2.1, NIST 800-53,* and *ISO 27001.*

- Web Security Scanner provides managed scans that are automatically configured. These scans identify the following security vulnerabilities: **cross-site scripting** (**XSS**), Flash injection, mixed content, cleartext passwords, and the usage of insecure JavaScript libraries.

- Provides support for granting users IAM roles at the organization, folder, and project levels.

- Continuously and automatically exports new findings to `Pub/Sub`.

Figure 11.1 shows the core features/functions of SCC, and we will now examine these features and configurations closely:

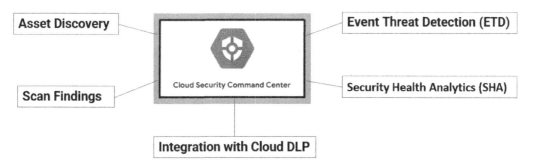

Figure 11.1 – Google Cloud SCC core features/modules

Now, let's examine the SCC modules and their functions, starting with asset discovery.

SCC asset discovery

The SCC asset discovery module discovers and inventory all the resources in your GCP organization. Let's take a look at.

1. Go to **Google Cloud Console** | **Security Command Center** | **ASSETS**, and you will see all the cloud resources for your GCP organization. By default, assets are displayed in the organization and project hierarchy. The asset types currently supported are listed at `https://cloud.google.com/security-command-center/docs/how-to-use-security-command-center`.

2. To view assets grouped by resource type, under the **ASSETS** tab, click **Resource type**. Assets are displayed in categories such as **Application**, **Bucket**, **Project**, and **Service**.

3. To view new and deleted assets, under the **ASSETS** tab, click on **ASSETS CHANGED**. All assets are displayed, including subgroups for new and deleted assets. You can select a time range by clicking the drop-down list at the top of the assets list. *Figure 11.2* shows an asset display from SCC:

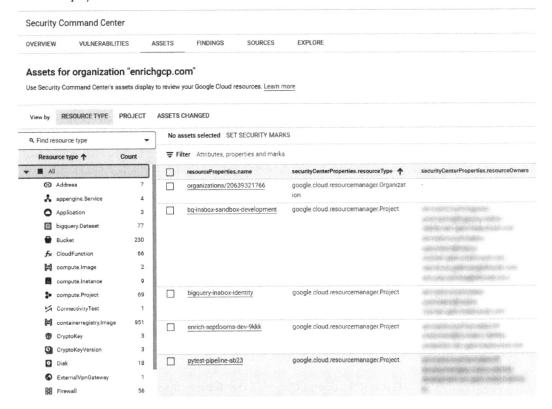

Figure 11.2 – Google Cloud SCC asset discovery

In addition to asset discovery, SCC scans and generate findings for potential risks. We will discuss scan findings in the next section.

SCC scan findings

SCC integrates with native and third-party Google Cloud scanners to surface potential security risks in assets, and findings can be viewed by finding a type or category, source, and changed findings. By default, findings are displayed in specific categories such as XSS and exposure of credit card numbers or phone numbers. If you leave the **Category** field blank while creating a finding, it doesn't have a category in the **FINDINGS** display. To view detailed information about a specific finding, click the finding under **Category**.

A finding source is a provider of findings, such as SHA. You can view findings by source in multiple ways:

- To view findings by source type, under the **FINDINGS** tab, click **source type**
- To view individual findings for a specific source type, under **View by Source type**, select the source type to be reviewed

Figure 11.3 shows an organization with no findings:

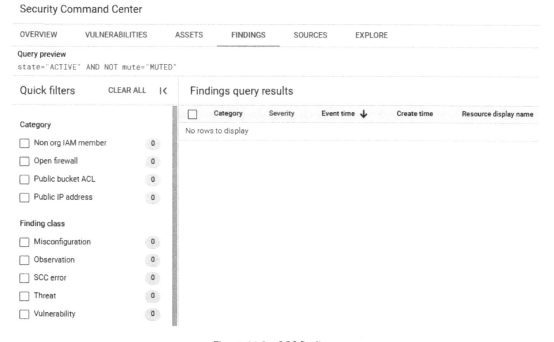

Figure 11.3 – SCC findings

To view new and inactive findings, under the **FINDINGS** tab, click on **FINDINGS CHANGED**. All findings are displayed in the following subgroups:

- **Active changed findings**: Findings that changed to active during the selected time period
- **Active unchanged findings**: Findings that are active and were active during all or part of the selected time period
- **Inactive changed findings**: Findings that changed to inactive during the selected time period
- **Inactive unchanged findings**: Findings that are inactive and were inactive during the selected time period
- **New findings**: Findings that are new during the selected time period

Any findings in a group with a **Changed** tag have changed properties during the selected time range. *Figure 11.4* shows the active findings:

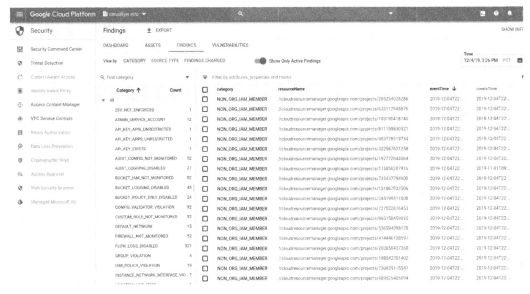

Figure 11.4 – SCC active findings

Now let's discuss how SCC integrates with other GCP services such as DLP.

SCC integration with Cloud DLP

We have discussed DLP in the previous sections, and the following are the steps to enable the integration of DLP into SCC:

1. Enable Cloud DLP by following these steps:

    I.   Navigate to **Security | Data Loss Prevention** and enable the DLP API.

    II.   Create a job and set it to **Publish to Google Cloud Security Command Center**:

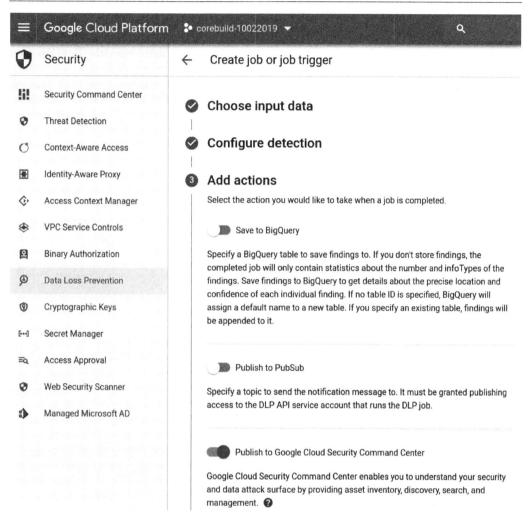

Figure 11.5 – Creating a DLP job that will publish results to SCC

2. Set DLP as a security source for Security Command Center with these steps:

Navigate to **Security Command Center** and select **Settings**. Enable **Cloud DLP Data Discovery** by flipping the switch as shown in *Figure 11.6*:

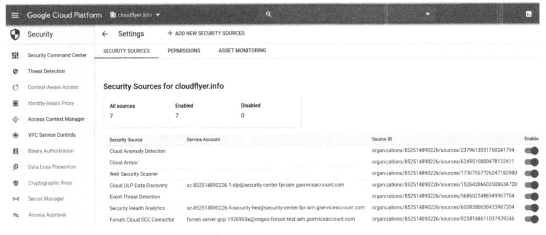

Figure 11.6 – Enabling DLP discovery in SCC

DLP findings are now visible in SCC, as shown in *Figure 11.7*. The finding can be clicked on to view their details:

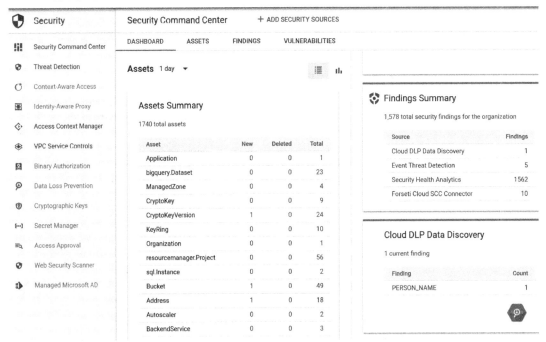

Figure 11.7 – DLP findings in SCC

So far, we have demonstrated SCC's function to discover Google Cloud assets and integrate with DLP and other GCP tools to scan various sources and generate security findings. In the next sections, we will discuss SCC SHA.

SHA

SHA manages vulnerability assessment scanning for Google Cloud. SHA scans for many vulnerability types. It can automatically detect common vulnerabilities and misconfigurations across the following:

- Cloud Monitoring and Cloud Logging
- GCE
- GKE containers and networks
- GCS
- Cloud SQL
- Cloud IAM
- Key Management Service
- Cloud DNS

When SHA is enabled, scans automatically run twice a day, 12 hours apart. More details are available at `https://cloud.google.com/security-command-center/docs/concepts-security-sources`.

1. **Enable SHA**: To view SHA findings in SCC, we need to enable it as a security source. Go to SCC, and the **SECURITY SOURCES** page in the Cloud Console. Under **Enabled**, click to enable **Security Health Analytics**, as shown in *Figure 11.8*. Note this requires the SCC Admin role:

Figure 11.8 – Enabling SHA

After SHA is enabled, you can view the vulnerabilities found in the **VULNERABILITIES** tab in **Cloud Security Command Center**. SHA scans automatically run twice a day, 12 hours apart. The frequency of the scan is currently not customizable.

2. **View the findings**: By using SCC with the available filters, you can focus on the highest severity vulnerabilities, and review vulnerabilities by asset type, security mark, and more. As shown in *Figure 11.9*, the findings can be viewed by the following:

- Project

- Finding type

- Asset type

- Severity

- Security marks

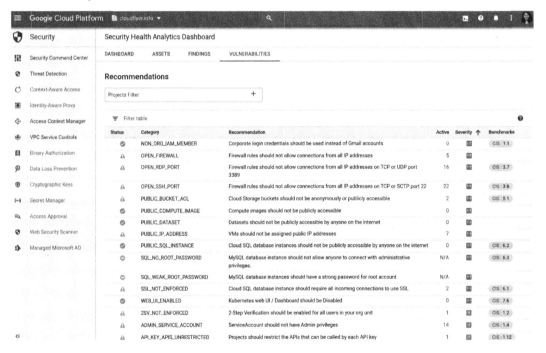

Figure 11.9 – SHA findings

Details on how to filter on findings for SHA can be found at `https://cloud.google.com/security-command-center/docs/how-to-use-security-health-analytics`.

The latest SCC features

Attack Path Simulation is a new SCC feature just announced at the time of writing. With Attack Path Simulation, SCC mimics a real-world attacker's reach and compromises the GCP environment in many ways, generates attack path graphs to provide defenders with insight into how adversaries could exploit security weaknesses or vulnerabilities to access valuable assets, and then provides detailed information on remediations to shore up defenses based on the findings. More details are available on the blog: `https://cloud.google.com/blog/products/identity-security/security-command-center-adds-attack-path-simulation-to-stay-ahead-of-cyber-risks`.

Integrating with **Chronicle SOAR, and Chronicle AI** is another new SCC feature. Chronicle SIEM delivers modern threat detection, investigation, and hunting at unprecedented speed and scale, at a disruptive and predictable price point. Chronicle SOAR enables enterprises to gather data and security alerts from various sources by ingesting orchestration and automation, to detect threats and respond to incidents promptly and effectively. Chronicle AI introduces AI-powered investigations into Chronicle Security Operations. Integrating Chronicle SIEM, Chronicle SOAR, and Chronicle AI in SCC is a great milestone in GCP security.

Summary

In this chapter, we discussed the Google Cloud security concepts, including Google Cloud IAM, endpoint security, data security, monitoring, and logging. We dived into Google Cloud Security Command Center.

This chapter ends the second part of the book: *Google Cloud*. We have covered GCP by examining its foundational services in terms of compute, storage, and the network; the data services of database and big data; the ML services of Vertex AI and ML API; and the security services. In the next chapter, we will start our journey to the Microsoft Azure cloud.

Practice questions

Questions 1 to 10 are based on *Figure 11.10*. All configurations are default.

A cloud engineer team logged in to GCE instances VM-1, VM-2, VM-3, and VM-4, in 4 windows:

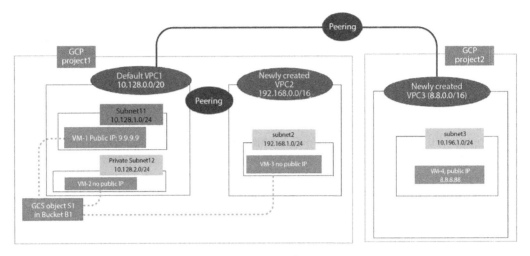

Figure 11.10 – GCP diagram

1. What will they need to do so they can ping www.google.com successfully from VM-1?

    A. Nothing

    B. Open icmp (ping) for the network/VPC1 firewall

    C. Open icmp (ping) for the VPC1/subnet11 firewall

    D. Open IGW routes for VPC1

2. What will they need to do so they can ping VM-1 successfully from the internet?

    A. Nothing

    B. Open icmp (ping) for the network/VPC1 firewall

    C. Open icmp (ping) for the VPC1/subnet11 firewall

    D. Open IGW routes for VPC1

3. What will they need to do so they can ping www.google.com successfully from VM-4?

    A. Nothing

    B. Open icmp (ping) for the network/VPC3 firewall

    C. Open icmp (ping) for the VPC3/subnet3 firewall

    D. Open IGW routes for VPC3

4. What will they need to do so they can ping VM-4 successfully from the internet?

    A. Nothing

    B. Open `icmp` (ping) for the network/VPC3 firewall

    C. Open `ssh` for the network/VPC3 firewall

    D. Open `https` for the network/VPC3 firewall

5. What will they need to do so they can ping `www.google.com` successfully from VM-3?

    A. Nothing

    B. Open `icmp` (ping) for the network/VPC2 firewall

    C. It is impossible

    D. Open `icmp` (ping) for the VPC2/`subnet2` firewall

6. What will they need to do so they can ping VM-3 successfully from the internet?

    A. Nothing

    B. Open `icmp` (ping) for the network/VPC2 firewall

    C. It is impossible

    D. Open `icmp` (ping) for the VPC2/`subnet2` firewall

7. They want to detect any changes for the GCP resources; what is the best way?

    A. Use SCC

    B. Enable VPC flow logs

    C. Enable GCP monitoring

    D. Use a third-party tool

8. They want to scan all the PII in the GCS buckets; what is the best way?

    A. Use DLP

    B. Scan all the buckets

    C. Enable GCS logging

    D. Enable GCP monitoring

Answers to the practice questions

1. A

2. A

3. A

4. B

5. C

6. C

7. A

8. A

Further reading

For further insights into what you've learned in this chapter, refer to the following links:

- `https://cloud.google.com/docs/security/infrastructure/design`
- `https://cloud.google.com/blog/topics/developers-practitioners/data-security-google-cloud`
- `https://cloud.google.com/architecture/framework/security/network-security`
- `https://cloud.google.com/armor`
- `https://cloud.google.com/security`
- `https://cloud.google.com/iam`
- `https://cloud.google.com/security-command-center`
- `https://cloud.google.com/recommender/docs/overview`

Part 3: Mastering Azure Cloud Services

In this part, we will first compare the foundational cloud services – AWS, GCP, and Azure – summarizing the common features of their computer, storage, network, and database services. We will also describe the unique characteristics of the Azure cloud's foundation services. We will then examine the Azure data services by looking at the Azure cloud's database and big data processing services. Further, we will explore the Azure AI services, including the Azure ML workspace and Azure Cognitive Services, which are ML APIs that leverage pre-trained models. We will end this part with a look at the security services in the Azure cloud.

This part comprises the following chapters:

- *Chapter 12, Azure Cloud Foundation Services*
- *Chapter 13, Azure Cloud Data Services*
- *Chapter 14, Azure Cloud AI Services*
- *Chapter 15, Azure Cloud Security Services*

12
Microsoft Azure Cloud Foundation Services

In the first two parts of the book, we dove into AWS and GCP and explored and provisioned the cloud services. We have now reached the third part of the book, which is about the Microsoft Azure cloud. In this part, we will focus on two things:

- Comparing the three clouds as we introduce the Azure cloud

- Expanding to look at more advanced Azure cloud concepts and integrations, based on the cloud discussions we have covered so far

In this chapter, we will explore Azure's foundation services. We will cover the following contents:

- Understanding the Azure resource hierarchy, by comparing cloud resource hierarchies for AWS, GCP, and Azure

- Learning about Azure compute services by comparing VM instances, containers, and serverless services for the three cloud platforms

- Learning about Azure storage services by comparing object, file, block, and archive storage for the three cloud platforms

- Practicing Azure foundation service implementations by integrating VM instances and networking using Azure **Virtual WAN** (**V-WAN**) technologies

Let us start with the Azure cloud resource hierarchy.

Azure cloud resource hierarchy

First, let us review the AWS hierarchy. An **AWS account** is an isolated unit for all the AWS services, such as EC2 instances and S3 buckets. AWS Billing is implemented at the AWS account level to charge for all AWS cloud resource consumption. When a new AWS service resource is created, it is always created within an AWS account. An **AWS organization** represents an organizational entity such as a company, and it includes multiple AWS accounts. In the AWS resource hierarchy, between the organization and the accounts are **Organization Units (OUs)**, which may represent departments, teams, or projects within the company – each OU has one or multiple AWS accounts.

In contrast, a **Google Cloud project** is the isolated unit for Google Cloud resources and can be associated with a billing account that manages the Google Cloud resource consumption costs. Typically, there is a GCP *organization*, which has multiple projects, and between the organization and the projects are the *folders*, which represent the company departments or teams. An organization can have multiple folders, and a folder can have multiple projects, but one project belongs to only one folder and one organization.

Moving to the Microsoft cloud platform, an **Azure subscription** represents a group of Azure resources, and an Azure billing invoice is generated at this scope. An Azure billing account is used to manage costs for one or more Azure subscriptions. Typically, the Azure resource hierarchy has five levels:

- At the top level is the *root* tenant, which manages Azure management groups.
- An *Azure management group* is beneath the overarching *root* tenant. Permissions and policies applied to a management group will flow to all Azure resources below it, including subscriptions and resource groups.
- *Subscriptions* are then assigned to a management group, serving as both a management layer and a billing mechanism for resources within Azure.
- *Resource groups* are the unit from where we provision Azure resources. Usually, we use a resource group for a project or a department/team.
- *Resources* are Azure VMs, storage buckets, networks, and so on.

This is shown in *Figure 12.1*. Creating Azure service resources requires an Azure subscription and at least one resource group, which is used to create, enable, or use the resources. Each resource belongs to one resource group:

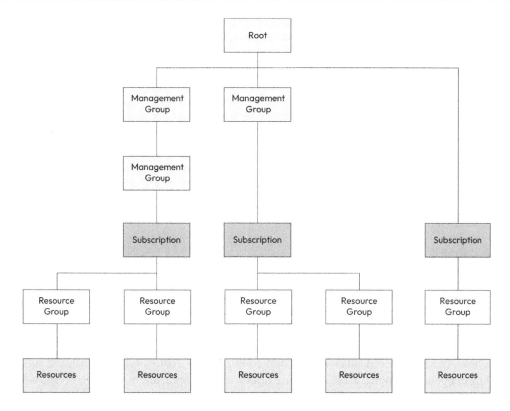

Figure 12.1 – Azure resource hierarchy

Now that we have an idea of the Azure resource hierarchy, we will dive into the foundational Azure services, starting with Azure cloud compute.

Azure cloud compute

Azure cloud compute services include Azure VMs, Azure containers, and Azure serverless.

Azure cloud VMs

Azure cloud VMs are very much like AWS EC2 VMs. To provision a VM instance in the cloud, we need to specify the software (OS and apps) and hardware (CPU, RAM, HD, and so on). While the software categories are very much the same for different cloud platforms, the hardware categories (such as VM types) are named quite differently. *Table 12.1* lists the current VM types for the three cloud platforms: AWS EC2, GCP GCE, and Azure VM:

Use Case	AWS EC2	GCP GCE	Azure VM
General Purpose	A1, M4, M5, M5a, M5n, M5zn, M6g, T2, T3, T3a, T4g, Mac	E2, N2, N2D, N1	B, Dsv3, Dv3, Dasv4, Dav4, DSv2, Dv2, Av2, DC, DCv2, Dv4, Dsv4, Ddv4, Ddsv4
Compute Optimized	C4, C5, C5a, C5n, C6g	C2	F, Fs, Fsv2
Memory Optimized	R4, R5, R5a, R5b, R5n, R6g, X1, X1e, High Memory, z1d	M1, M2	Esv3, Ev3, Easv4, Eav4, Ev4, Esv4, Edv4, Edsv4, Mv2, M, DSv2, Dv2
Storage Optimized	D2, D3, D3en, H1, I3, I3en	N/A	Lsv2
Accelerated Compute and High Performance	F1, G3, G4ad, G4dn, P2, P3, P4, Inf1	A2	NC, NCv2, NCv3, NCasT4_v3, ND, NDv2, NV, NVv3, NVv4, HB, HBv2, HC, H

Table 12.1 – Cloud VM types

Like how AWS utilizes load balancers and auto-scaling groups, Azure uses load balancing and auto-scaling to optimize resource usage, maximize resource throughput, minimize service response time, and improve resource availability. Let's take a close look at them.

Azure provides various *load-balancing services* to distribute/balance your workloads across multiple cloud computing resources: Application Gateway, Front Door, Load Balancer, and Traffic Manager. *Table 12.2* lists these Azure load-balancing features:

Azure Load Balancer	Traffic and Routing Mechanisms	Scope	Traffic
Azure Front Door	URL-based web traffic routing: URL patterns, hostnames, or HTTP headers	Global	HTTP(S)
Traffic Manager	DNS-based network routing to distribute traffic across multiple endpoints	Global	Network
Application Gateway	Layer 7 application load-balancing, including built-in WAF capabilities	Regional	HTTP(S)
Azure Load Balancer	Layer 4 network load-balancing to distribute traffic across VMs or VM sets	Regional	Network

Table 12.2 – Azure load balancing

Like AWS and GCP, Azure provides various *auto-scaling services* to elastically scale cloud resources for high availability and cost optimization. *Table 12.3* lists the auto-scaling features and VM price discount models for AWS, Azure, and GCP:

CSP	VM Scaling Service	VM scaling Metrics	VM Price Discount Model
AWS	**Auto Scaling Groups (ASGs)**	Requires AWS CloudWatch agent	On-Demand, Reserved, and Spot
Azure	**Virtual Machine Scale Sets (VMSS)**	Requires Azure/Linux diagnostics extension	On-Demand, Reserved, and Spot
GCP	**Managed Instance Group (MIG)**	System metrics or cloud monitoring metrics	Sustained Use, Committed Use, and Preemptible

Table 12.3 – Cloud VM scaling and price model

For Azure VM sets, there are two different concepts: availability sets and scale sets. An Azure fault domain is a group of Azure resources that shares a common power supply or network switch, and thus a hardware failure in a fault domain will affect the cloud resources in the same domain. An **Azure VM availability set** consists of two or more fault domains and thus the VMs in an availability set are distributed across these fault domains. When a hardware failure occurs in one fault domain, the VMs in the availability set will still function. An **Azure VM scale set**, on the other hand, is a group of VMs that are in an Azure availability set and will scale up and down as needed. So, the VMs in a scale set are required to have the same configuration, very much like AWS ASGs or GCP MIGs.

Azure cloud container services

We have discussed container concepts, as well as Amazon ECS, which is an AWS fully managed, proprietary container orchestration service for running Docker containers. Amazon also offers **Elastic Kubernetes Service** (**EKS**), which uses the open source Kubernetes framework to manage Kubernetes clusters and orchestrate containers.

Google Kubernetes Engine (**GKE**) provides managed Kubernetes clusters for running containerized applications. GKE offers robust features such as automatic scaling, monitoring, and integration with other GCP services.

Like the other two cloud service providers, Azure provides various container services that enable you to deploy and manage containerized applications in the Microsoft cloud, including the following:

- **Azure Container Instances (ACI)** is the simplest and quickest way to run containers in the Azure cloud without managing the underlying infrastructure.

- **Azure Kubernetes Service (AKS)** is a managed container orchestration service that simplifies the deployment, management, and scaling of containerized applications using Kubernetes. AKS offers advanced features such as auto-scaling, monitoring, and integration with Azure services.

- **Azure Service Fabric** is a distributed systems platform that can host and manage both containers and microservices-based applications. It provides a highly scalable and reliable runtime for building/deploying cloud-native applications.

These Azure container services provide different levels of abstraction and capabilities to suit various business use cases and application scenarios.

Azure serverless computing

We have discussed the evolution history of computers. With serverless computing, developers write and deploy individual functions or small units of code without any concerns about the computing platform executing the code, since the cloud service provider manages all the underlying infrastructure and the code executions in response to events or requests. As we mentioned in *Part 1* of the book, Amazon offers *Lambda* as a serverless computing service that supports a wide range of programming languages and can be integrated with various AWS services. *Google Cloud Functions* is a serverless compute platform that lets you run event-driven functions without managing Google Cloud infrastructure.

Microsoft offers **Azure Functions** as a serverless cloud service. It is highly flexible and can be used for various use cases, such as building serverless APIs, data processing and integration, event-driven workflows, and real-time stream processing. It has the following features:

- Azure Functions can be triggered by various events, such as HTTP requests, timers, messages arriving in a message queue, changes in data within a storage account, or events from other Azure services. Each function is associated with a specific trigger, and when the trigger event occurs, the function is executed.

- Azure Functions supports multiple programming languages, including C#, JavaScript, Python, PowerShell, and TypeScript. You can choose the language that best suits your development needs and preferences.

- Bindings in Azure Functions provide a way to connect your functions to input and output data sources. Bindings allow you to easily integrate with Azure services such as Azure Storage, Azure Cosmos DB, and Azure Service Bus without writing extensive code to connect to these services.

- Functions in Azure Functions are stateless, meaning they don't maintain any state between invocations. Any necessary state information should be stored in external storage such as databases or cache systems.

- Azure Functions automatically scales based on the incoming workload. You pay only for the resources consumed during function execution, as Azure Functions follows a pay-per-use pricing model. This allows you to optimize costs by not paying for idle resources.

Comparing the cloud compute services helps us to find the similarities and differences between the three cloud platforms and understand them better. We will do this when learning about Azure cloud storage services.

Azure cloud storage

We have learned about EBS, EFS, and S3 in the AWS cloud, and PD, Filestore, and GCS in GCP. Azure has similar services. The following is a summary to help us review AWS/GCP storage and learn about Azure storage services.

Object storage

Here is a comparison of object storage for three clouds:

- AWS S3 offers multiple storage classes, **Standard**, **Intelligent-Tiering**, **Glacier**, and **Glacier Deep Archive**, each optimized for different use cases. S3 has object versioning and object life cycle management.

- GCP GCS provides multiple storage classes: **Standard**, **Nearline**, **Coldline**, and **Archive**. GCS offers object versioning and object life cycle management.

- Azure Blob Storage offers similar features to S3 and GCS. It includes Blob Storage, Archive Storage, and Premium Blob Storage tiers. Azure offers blob storage versioning and life cycle management as well.

File storage

The following is a comparison of file storage for three clouds:

- AWS EFS provides scalable and fully managed file storage that can be mounted on multiple EC2 instances concurrently

- GCP Filestore offers managed network file system file storage suitable for shared access across multiple instances

- Azure Files provides fully managed file shares accessible over the server message block or NFS protocols

Block storage

Here is a comparison of block storage for three clouds:

- AWS EBS provides block-level storage volumes that can be attached to EC2 instances. EBS offers various volume types, such as General Purpose SSD, Provisioned IOPS SSD, and Magnetic.

- GCP persistent disk can be attached to GCE VM instances. PD comes in Standard HDD, SSD, and Local SSD types.

- Azure Disk Storage provides block-level storage for Azure VMs, offering disk types such as Standard HDD, Standard SSD, and Premium SSD.

Archive storage

Here is a comparison of the archive storage for three clouds:

- Amazon Glacier is an extremely low-cost storage service designed for long-term archival and backup and provides different retrieval options with varying latency

- GCP GCS Coldline and Archive tiers are suitable for long-term data archival at a low cost

- Azure Archive Storage is a low-cost storage tier for long-term data retention and archival, offering similar features as Glacier and Coldline

Now that we have discussed cloud compute and storage, let's look at the Azure cloud networking service at a high level.

Azure cloud networking

We discussed AWS VPC and GCP VPC previously. They are very similar except that an AWS VPC is regional and a GCP VPC is global (with regional subnets). Azure offers a similar cloud networking service called Azure **Virtual Network** (**vNet**), and it is regional. Like VPC peering in AWS and GCP, Azure vNets can be peered across different regions and different accounts. We know that AWS VPC peering can be initialized from one VPC and accepted by the other, and GCP VPC peering is implemented by creating peering from VPC1 to VPC2, and then from VPC2 to VPC1. In Azure, vNet peering is done similarly, and vNet peering is also non-transitive.

Like AWS provides SGs and NACLs to protect EC2's and VPC/subnets, Azure offers NSGs and Azure Firewall to protect cloud network resources. NSGs provide basic network traffic filtering capabilities at the subnet and network interface level, whereas Azure Firewall offers more advanced traffic control at the network and application levels, and for outbound internet traffic. NSGs are suitable for basic network control within a vNet, while Azure Firewall provides more comprehensive security features and scalability for complex network architectures.

Like AWS provides Direct Connect networking between the public cloud and on-premises, Azure provides ExpressRoute, which enables you to establish dedicated and private network connections between an on-premises network and Azure vNets. It offers more reliable, secure, and high-performance connectivity.

Like AWS provides Route 53 as a public cloud DNS service, Azure provides Azure DNS, which enables you to host and manage your domain names within Azure and provides highly reliable and scalable DNS resolution for your applications and services. By leveraging various routing policies, you can customize the DNS resolution process, optimize performance, implement failover mechanisms, distribute traffic, and ensure efficient routing based on factors such as weight, priority, geographic location, network latency, and subnets.

Like AWS provides CloudFront, Azure provides a global CDN that caches and delivers optimal content delivery by reducing latency.

Like AWS provides TGW, which simplifies connectivity between multiple VPCs and on-premises Direct Connect networks across AWS accounts and regions, and provides centralized AWS network management, Azure offers V-WAN, which provides global connectivity and optimization for Azure vNets, branch offices, and remote users. Via the **hub-and-spoke** architecture, V-WAN simplifies network routing and supports integration with partner **Software-Defined Wide Area Network (SD-WAN)** solutions such as Cisco SD-WAN, Citrix SD-WAN, and VMware SD-WAN. A hub-and-spoke architecture is a network design where multiple branch locations (*spokes*) are connected to a central location (*hub*). With the hub-and-spoke architecture, all network traffic from the spokes is routed through the hub, enabling centralized management, control, and security. More details about Azure V-WAN are available from `https://learn.microsoft.com/en-us/azure/virtual-wan/`, and more details about Azure hub-and-spoke architecture are available from `https://learn.microsoft.com/en-us/azure/architecture/reference-architectures/hybrid-networking/hub-spoke?tabs=cli`.

Now that we have had a brief look at the Azure foundational cloud services, we will conduct a hands-on lab to expand on the basic cloud concepts and integrate them.

Azure Cloud Foundation service implementation

In this section, we will implement an Azure global V-WAN network using the hub-and-spoke architecture. We will build a V-WAN with two hubs, one in `us-east` and the other in `us-west`. Each hub will be connected to two spoke networks: Hub1 connects to spoke networks `vNet1` and `vNet2`; Hub2 connects to spoke networks `vNet3` and `vNet4`. We will create one VM in each spoke. *Figure 12.2* shows a typical V-WAN architecture where all the networks are connected efficiently using a hub-and-spoke topology, including Azure cloud vNets, branch office networks, remote networks, and on-premises networks:

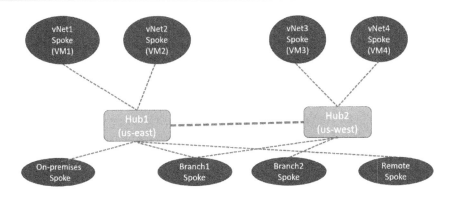

Figure 12.2 – Azure V-WAN infrastructure

In our lab, we will just implement the Azure V-WAN hub-and-spoke network with vNet connections. Let's get started:

1.   Create an Azure V-WAN:

Go to the Azure portal at portal.azure.com, then go to **Virtual WANs**. Create a V-WAN called azure-vwan in the **Central US** region. Choose the **Standard** type. Then, click **Review + create**, as shown in *Figure 12.3*:

Home > Virtual WANs >

Create WAN   ...

Basics   Review + create

The virtual WAN resource represents a virtual overlay of your Azure network and is a collection of multiple resources. Learn more ⌕

Project details

Subscription *	Azure subscription 1	⌄
└── Resource group *	azurerg	⌄
	Create new	

Virtual WAN details

Region *	Central US	⌄
Name *	azure-vwan	✓
Type ⓘ	Standard	⌄

Review + create	Previous	Next : Review + create >

Figure 12.3 – Create Azure V-WAN

2. Create a virtual hub in Azure V-WAN:

    Go to the created resource, `azure-vwan`. From the navigation menu, go to **Connectivity |**
    Hubs | New Hub. In the new window that appears, fill in the **Basics** tab, as shown in *Figure 12.4*.
    Note the region is **East US**.

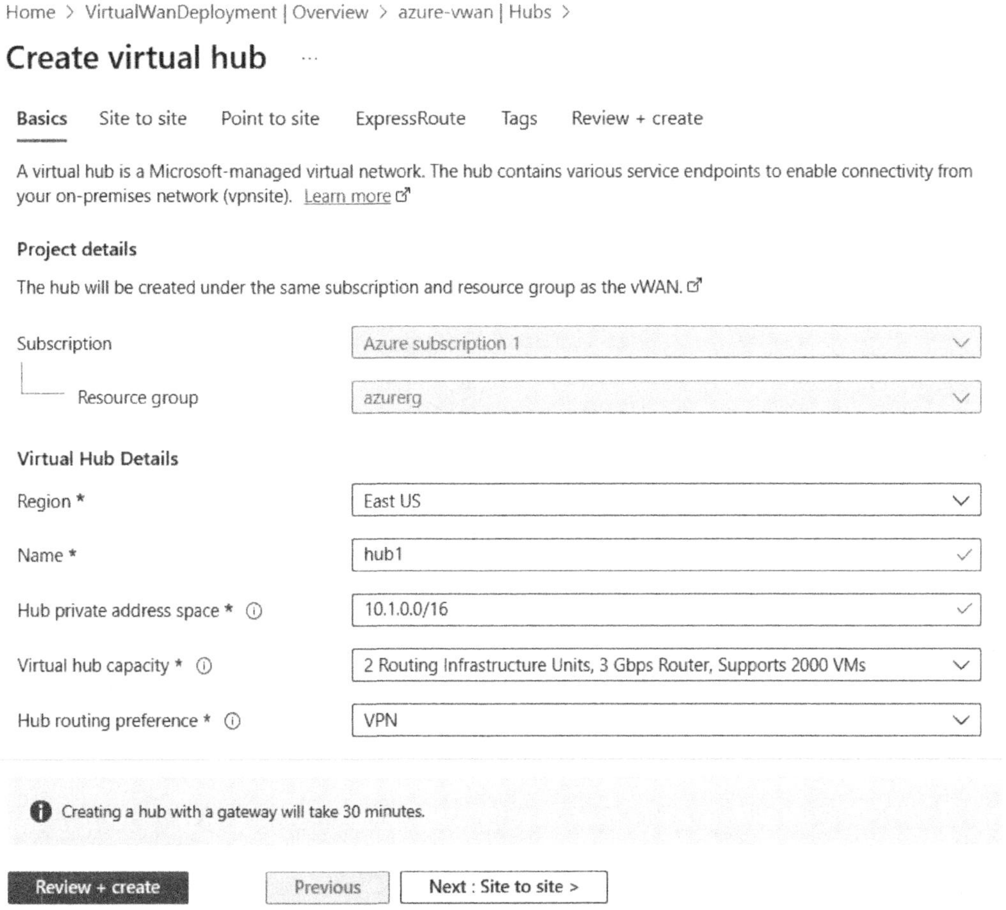

Home > VirtualWanDeployment | Overview > azure-vwan | Hubs >

Create virtual hub ···

| Basics | Site to site | Point to site | ExpressRoute | Tags | Review + create |

A virtual hub is a Microsoft-managed virtual network. The hub contains various service endpoints to enable connectivity from
your on-premises network (vpnsite). Learn more ☐

Project details

The hub will be created under the same subscription and resource group as the vWAN. ☐

| Subscription | Azure subscription 1 | ∨ |
| Resource group | azurerg | ∨ |

Virtual Hub Details

Region *	East US	∨
Name *	hub1	✓
Hub private address space * ⓘ	10.1.0.0/16	✓
Virtual hub capacity * ⓘ	2 Routing Infrastructure Units, 3 Gbps Router, Supports 2000 VMs	∨
Hub routing preference * ⓘ	VPN	∨

ⓘ Creating a hub with a gateway will take 30 minutes.

[Review + create]   [Previous] [Next : Site to site >]

Figure 12.4 – Create virtual hub (1)

Fill in the **Site to site** tab, as shown in *Figure 12.5*. Leave the others as the defaults and click **Review + create**:

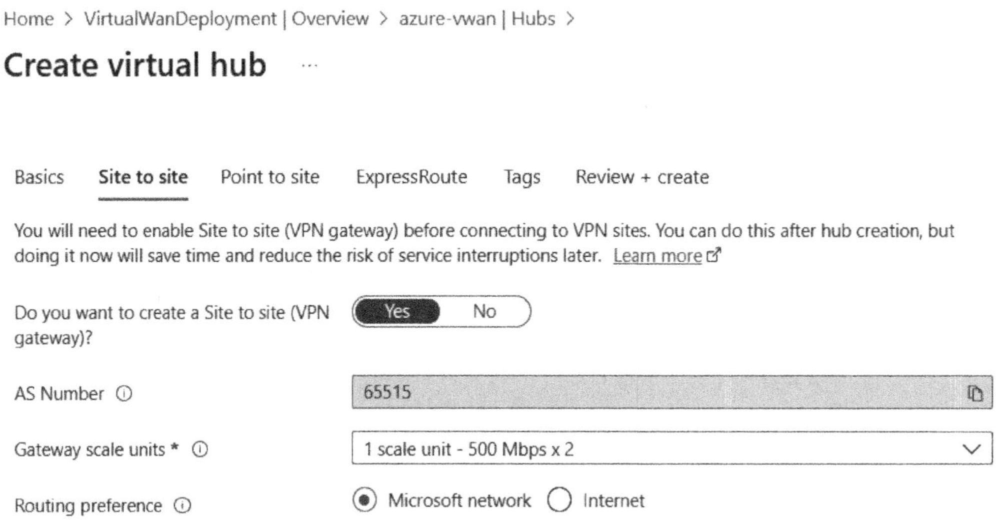

Home > VirtualWanDeployment | Overview > azure-vwan | Hubs >

Create virtual hub   ...

| Basics | **Site to site** | Point to site | ExpressRoute | Tags | Review + create |

You will need to enable Site to site (VPN gateway) before connecting to VPN sites. You can do this after hub creation, but doing it now will save time and reduce the risk of service interruptions later. Learn more ⧉

Do you want to create a Site to site (VPN gateway)?   (**Yes**   No)

AS Number ⓘ   `65515`

Gateway scale units * ⓘ   `1 scale unit - 500 Mbps x 2`

Routing preference ⓘ   ⦿ Microsoft network   ◯ Internet

Figure 12.5 – Create virtual hub (2)

3.   Create the second virtual hub in Azure V-WAN:

I. Use the previous steps to create a second virtual hub (`hub2`) in the **West US** region with the private IP address space of `10.2.0.0/16`.

II. After these two virtual hubs are created, two invisible virtual vNets are created within the V-WAN, along with two invisible vNet gateways. These two hubs are connected by network gateways. *Figure 12.6* shows the V-WAN and hubs:

azure-vwan
Virtual WAN
Search
Delete
Refresh
Overview
Activity log
Access control (IAM)
Tags
Settings
Configuration
Properties
Locks
Connectivity
Hubs
Essentials
Resource group : azurerg
Location : Central US
Subscription : Azure subscription 1
Subscription ID : 535b7401-376a-4d4f-b281-2297b197cf26
Tags (edit) : Click here to add tags
Status : Succeeded
Branch-to-branch : Enabled
Virtual hubs : 2
Topology : View Topology
Hub | Hub status | Address Space | Region | VPN sites | Azure Firewall
hub1 | Succeeded | 10.1.0.0/16 | East US | 0 VPN site(s) | Not deployed
hub2 | Succeeded | 10.2.0.0/16 | West US | - | Not deployed

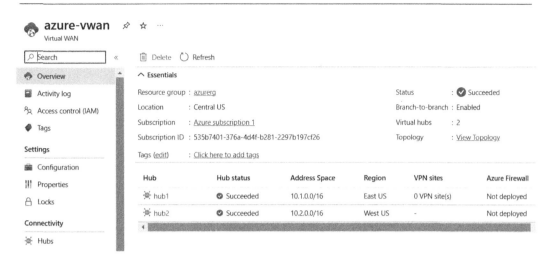

Figure 12.6 – Two hubs are created in azure-vwan

4. Create four Azure vNets – `vNet1`, `vNet2`, `vNet3`, and `vNet4`:

I. Go to the Azure portal, then **Virtual Networks | Create**. Fill in the vNet details as shown in *Figure 12.7* (on the **Basics** tabs).

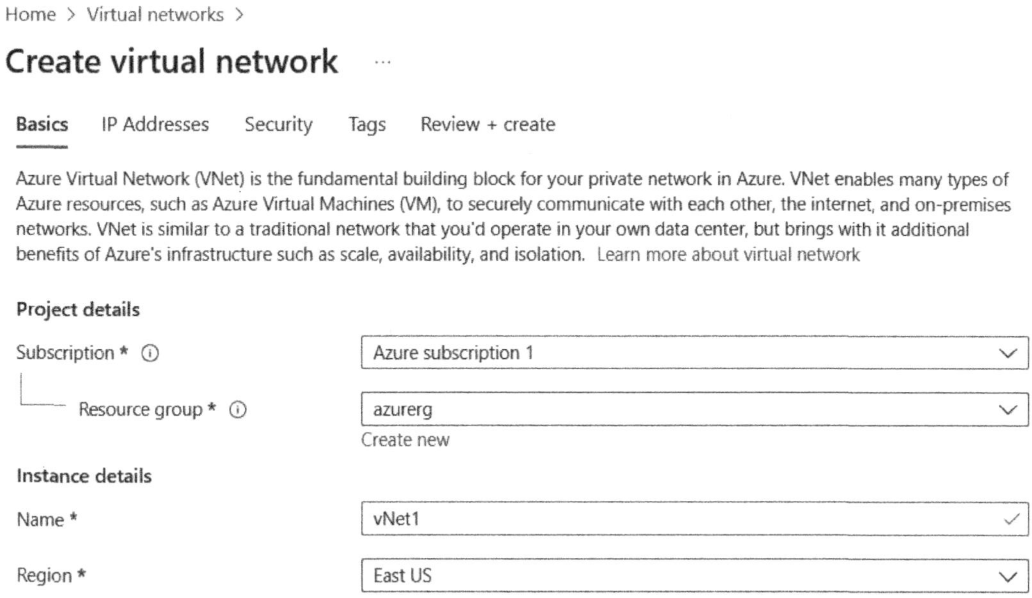

Home > Virtual networks >
Create virtual network
Basics
IP Addresses
Security
Tags
Review + create
Azure Virtual Network (VNet) is the fundamental building block for your private network in Azure. VNet enables many types of Azure resources, such as Azure Virtual Machines (VM), to securely communicate with each other, the internet, and on-premises networks. VNet is similar to a traditional network that you'd operate in your own data center, but brings with it additional benefits of Azure's infrastructure such as scale, availability, and isolation. Learn more about virtual network
Project details
Subscription *
Azure subscription 1
Resource group *
azurerg
Create new
Instance details
Name *
vNet1
Region *
East US

Figure 12.7 – Create virtual network (1)

Fill in the **IP Addresses** tab, as shown in *Figure 12.8*. Click **Review + create** to create vNet1 in the **East US** region:

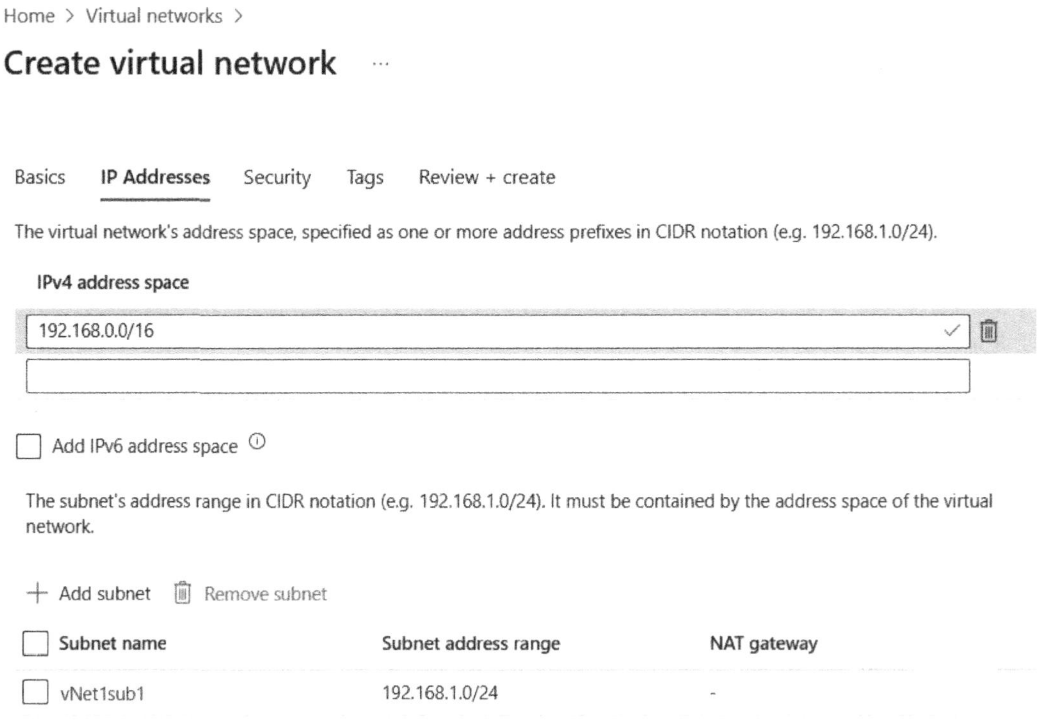

Home > Virtual networks >

Create virtual network   ...

Basics   **IP Addresses**   Security   Tags   Review + create

The virtual network's address space, specified as one or more address prefixes in CIDR notation (e.g. 192.168.1.0/24).

IPv4 address space

| 192.168.0.0/16 | ✓ | 🗑 |

☐ Add IPv6 address space ⓘ

The subnet's address range in CIDR notation (e.g. 192.168.1.0/24). It must be contained by the address space of the virtual network.

\+ Add subnet   🗑 Remove subnet

☐ Subnet name	Subnet address range	NAT gateway
☐ vNet1sub1	192.168.1.0/24	-

Figure 12.8 – Create virtual network (2)

II. Use the same step to create the following:

- vNet2 in East US 2, IP space 10.10.0.0/16, and subnet 10.10.10.0/24
- vNet3 in West US, IP space 172.16.0.0/16, and subnet 72.16.16.0/24
- vNet4 in West US 2, IP space 10.20.0.0/16, and subnet 10.20.20.0/24

Figure 12.9 shows the four vNets created so far:

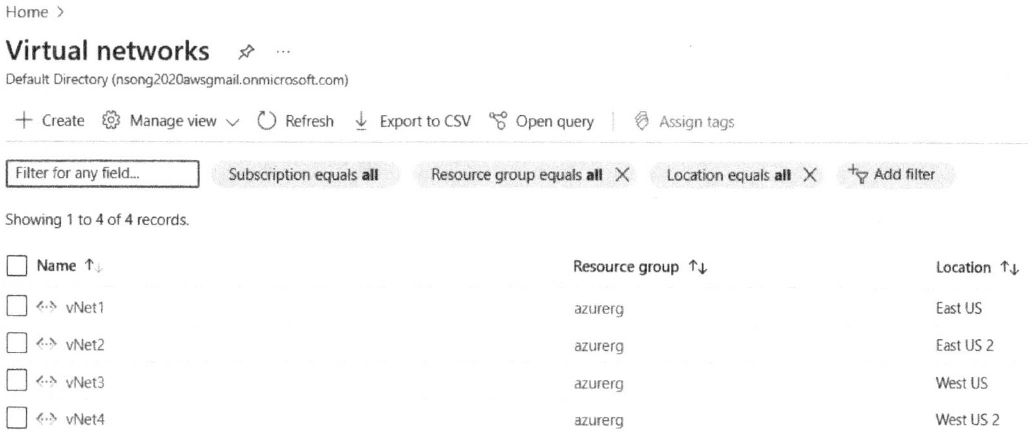

Home >

Virtual networks 📌 ···
Default Directory (nsong2020awsgmail.onmicrosoft.com)

+ Create   ⚙ Manage view ∨   ⟳ Refresh   ↓ Export to CSV   ⟨⟩ Open query | 🏷 Assign tags

Filter for any field...	Subscription equals **all** Resource group equals **all** ✕ Location equals **all** ✕ 🏷 Add filter

Showing 1 to 4 of 4 records.

☐ Name ↑↓	Resource group ↑↓	Location ↑↓
☐ ⟨·⟩ vNet1	azurerg	East US
☐ ⟨·⟩ vNet2	azurerg	East US 2
☐ ⟨·⟩ vNet3	azurerg	West US
☐ ⟨·⟩ vNet4	azurerg	West US 2

Figure 12.9 – The vNets created

5.   Connect the vNets to the hubs in `azure-vwan`:

I. Go to the Azure console and then to **Virtual WAN | azure-vwan | Connectivity | Virtual network connections | Add connection**. Fill in the connection details and choose **Default** for the routing configurations, as shown in *Figure 12.10*. Click on **Create**:

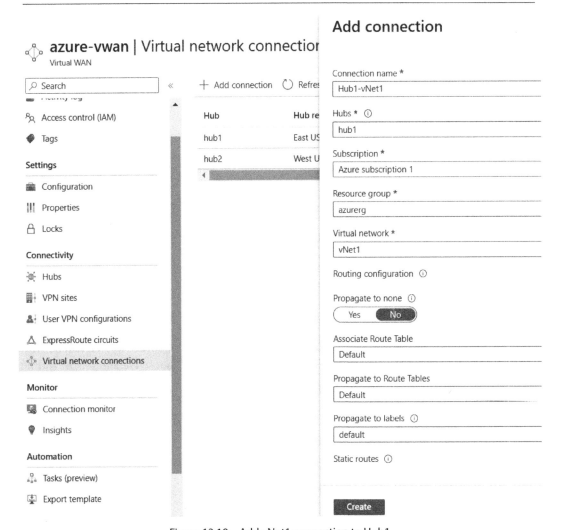

Figure 12.10 – Add vNet1 connection to Hub1

II. Use the same procedure to add vNet2 to Hub1 and vNet3 and vNet4 to Hub2.

Figure 12.11 shows the connections of hubs to vNets:

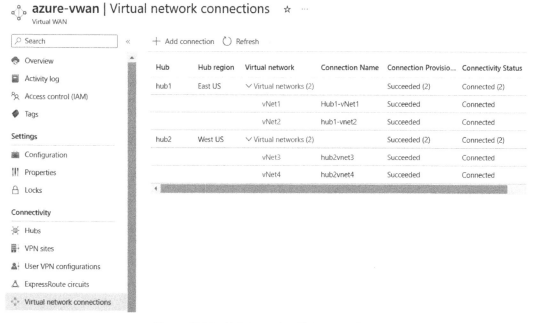

Figure 12.11 – Hub to spoke vNet connections

6.   Create Azure VMs in the four vNets, one in each:

I. Go to the Azure console and then to **Virtual Machines | Create**. Fill in the details and create `Azure virtual machine VM1` in the `vNet1` subnet `vNet1sub1` (the **US East** region). Set up the username/password as needed. Fill in the **Basics** tab as shown in *Figure 12.12.*

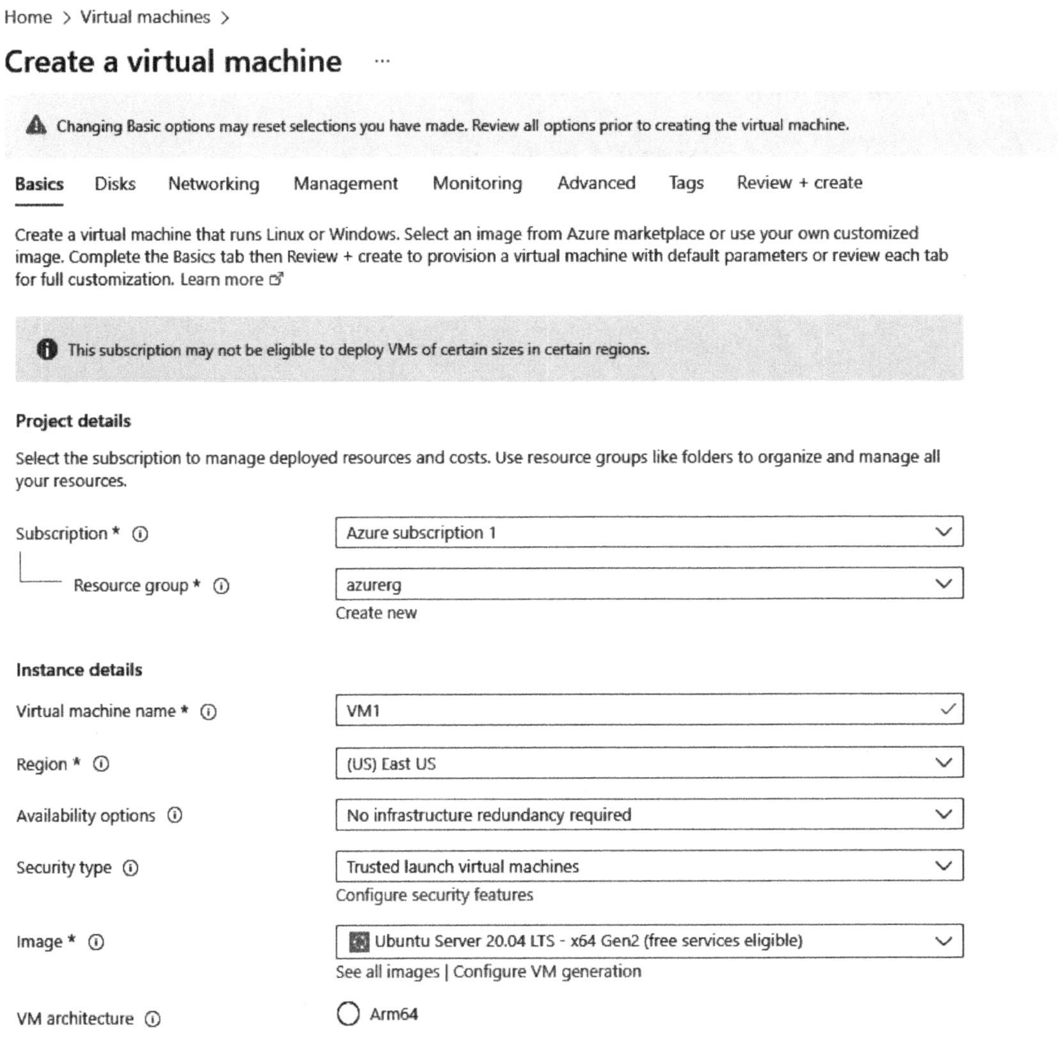

Home > Virtual machines >

Create a virtual machine   ...

⚠ Changing Basic options may reset selections you have made. Review all options prior to creating the virtual machine.

Basics   Disks   Networking   Management   Monitoring   Advanced   Tags   Review + create

Create a virtual machine that runs Linux or Windows. Select an image from Azure marketplace or use your own customized image. Complete the Basics tab then Review + create to provision a virtual machine with default parameters or review each tab for full customization. Learn more ⤤

ⓘ This subscription may not be eligible to deploy VMs of certain sizes in certain regions.

Project details

Select the subscription to manage deployed resources and costs. Use resource groups like folders to organize and manage all your resources.

Subscription * ⓘ

| Azure subscription 1 | ∨ |

⌐— Resource group * ⓘ

| azurerg | ∨ |

Create new

Instance details

Virtual machine name * ⓘ

| VM1 | ✓ |

Region * ⓘ

| (US) East US | ∨ |

Availability options ⓘ

| No infrastructure redundancy required | ∨ |

Security type ⓘ

| Trusted launch virtual machines | ∨ |

Configure security features

Image * ⓘ

| ▣ Ubuntu Server 20.04 LTS - x64 Gen2 (free services eligible) | ∨ |

See all images | Configure VM generation

VM architecture ⓘ

◯ Arm64

Figure 12.12 – Create the VM1 Azure VM instance (1)

Fill in the **Networking** tab as shown in *Figure 12.13*. Leave the defaults for the other tabs. Click **Review + create**:

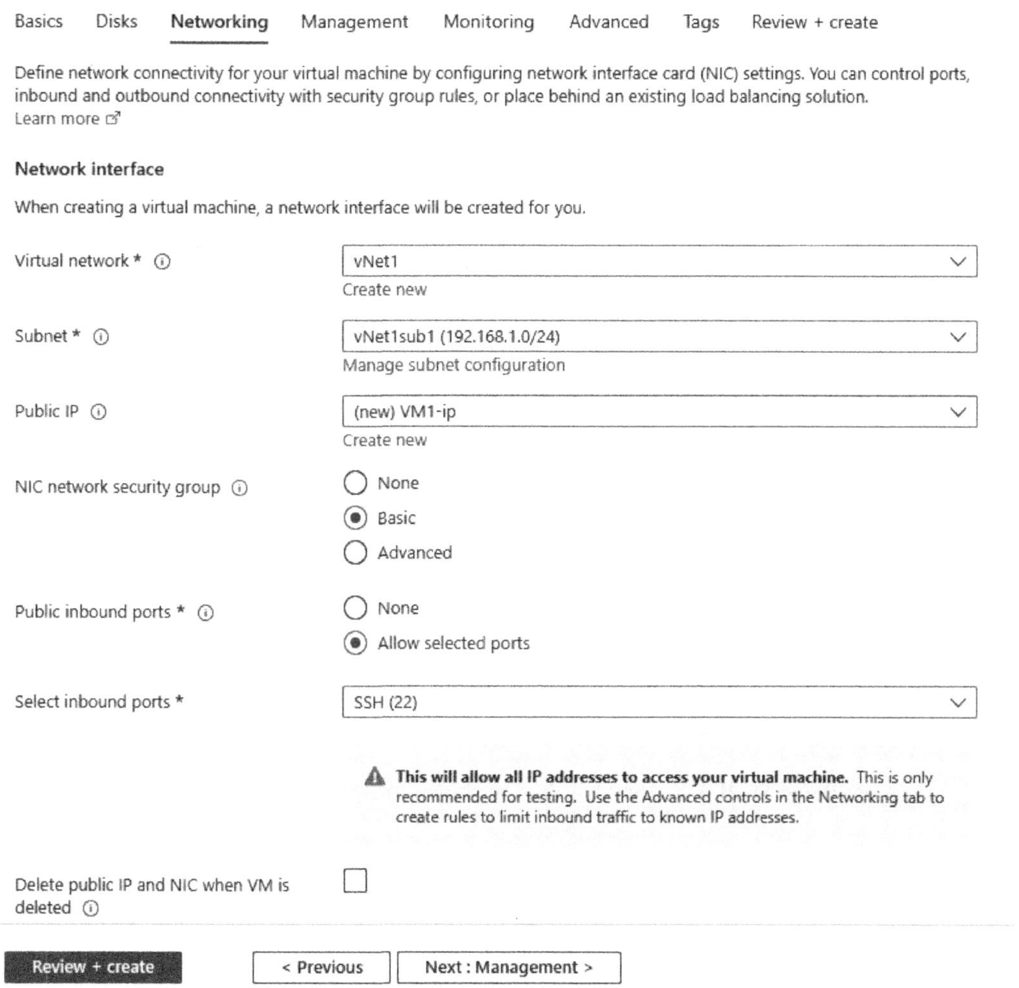

Basics   Disks   **Networking**   Management   Monitoring   Advanced   Tags   Review + create

Define network connectivity for your virtual machine by configuring network interface card (NIC) settings. You can control ports, inbound and outbound connectivity with security group rules, or place behind an existing load balancing solution. Learn more ☐

Network interface

When creating a virtual machine, a network interface will be created for you.

Virtual network * ⓘ	vNet1 ⌄
	Create new
Subnet * ⓘ	vNet1sub1 (192.168.1.0/24) ⌄
	Manage subnet configuration
Public IP ⓘ	(new) VM1-ip ⌄
	Create new
NIC network security group ⓘ	○ None
	⦿ Basic
	○ Advanced
Public inbound ports * ⓘ	○ None
	⦿ Allow selected ports
Select inbound ports *	SSH (22) ⌄

> ⚠ **This will allow all IP addresses to access your virtual machine.** This is only recommended for testing. Use the Advanced controls in the Networking tab to create rules to limit inbound traffic to known IP addresses.

Delete public IP and NIC when VM is deleted ⓘ	☐

Review + create		< Previous	Next : Management >

Figure 12.13 – Create the VM1 Azure VM instance (2)

II. Use the same procedure to create VM2 in vNet2, VM3 in vNet3, and VM4 in vNet4.

Figure 12.14 lists the four VMs:

Figure 12.14 – The four VMs in the spoke vNets

In our case, the internal and external IP addresses for each of the VMs are as follows:

• VM1	192.168.1.4	52.191.51.18
• VM2	10.10.10.4	20.242.12.227
• VM3	172.16.16.4	20.245.115.243
• VM4	10.20.20.4	4.154.83.69

7. Log in to the four VMs from Azure Cloud Shell and verify all the connections:

I. Open **Cloud Shell** from the Azure console. The first time you open it, you need to do some initial setup.

II. First, choose **PowerShell** in the first window, as shown in *Figure 12.15*:

Welcome to Azure Cloud Shell

Select Bash or PowerShell. You can change shells any time via the environment selector in the
Cloud Shell toolbar. The most recently used environment will be the default for your next session.

Bash   PowerShell

Figure 12.15 – Open Azure Cloud Shell

III. Then, set up the region, Storage account, and file share. Note the **Storage account** name needs to be globally unique, as shown in *Figure 12.16*. Click **Create storage**. It will set up and bring you to Cloud Shell:

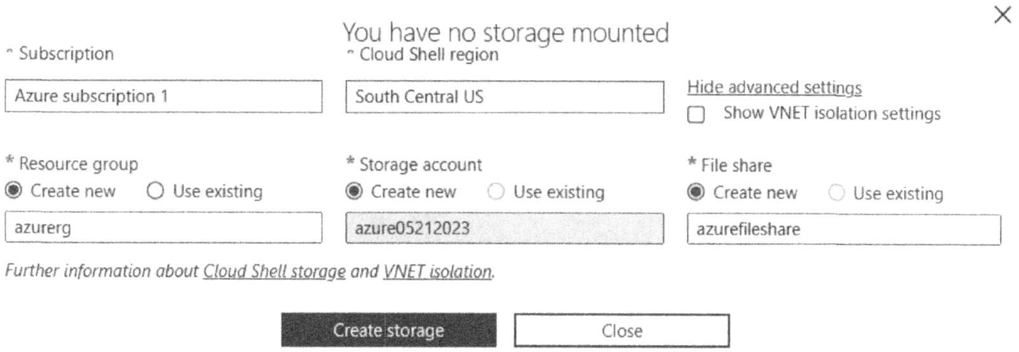

Figure 12.16 – Initial setup of Azure Cloud Shell

IV. In Cloud Shell, log in to VM1: `ssh user222@20.242.12.227`, as shown in *Figure 12.17*:

```
PS /home/n3> ssh user222@20.242.12.227
The authenticity of host '20.242.12.227 (20.242.12.227)' can't be established.
ED25519 key fingerprint is SHA256:GDOV7DPfwIMYtRBbfvJoX6/bulEs14AMEmawL96Ek54.
This key is not known by any other names
Are you sure you want to continue connecting (yes/no/[fingerprint])? yes
Warning: Permanently added '20.242.12.227' (ED25519) to the list of known hosts.
user222@20.242.12.227's password:
Welcome to Ubuntu 20.04.6 LTS (GNU/Linux 5.15.0-1038-azure x86_64)

 * Documentation:  https://help.ubuntu.com
 * Management:     https://landscape.canonical.com
 * Support:        https://ubuntu.com/advantage
```

Figure 12.17 – Log in to VM2 from Cloud Shell

V. Ping the private IP addresses of VM1, VM3, and VM4. As shown in *Figure 12.18*, all the pings are successful. If you log in to each of the other VMs, and ping the rest of the three VMs, they will all be successful:

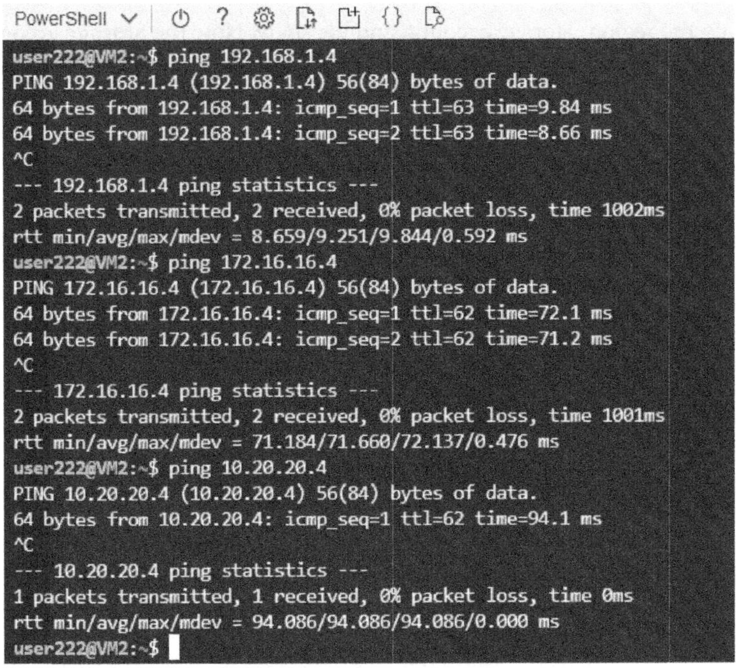

```
PowerShell  ∨    ⏻  ?  ⚙  ⎀  ⎑  {}  ⎚

user222@VM2:~$ ping 192.168.1.4
PING 192.168.1.4 (192.168.1.4) 56(84) bytes of data.
64 bytes from 192.168.1.4: icmp_seq=1 ttl=63 time=9.84 ms
64 bytes from 192.168.1.4: icmp_seq=2 ttl=63 time=8.66 ms
^C
--- 192.168.1.4 ping statistics ---
2 packets transmitted, 2 received, 0% packet loss, time 1002ms
rtt min/avg/max/mdev = 8.659/9.251/9.844/0.592 ms
user222@VM2:~$ ping 172.16.16.4
PING 172.16.16.4 (172.16.16.4) 56(84) bytes of data.
64 bytes from 172.16.16.4: icmp_seq=1 ttl=62 time=72.1 ms
64 bytes from 172.16.16.4: icmp_seq=2 ttl=62 time=71.2 ms
^C
--- 172.16.16.4 ping statistics ---
2 packets transmitted, 2 received, 0% packet loss, time 1001ms
rtt min/avg/max/mdev = 71.184/71.660/72.137/0.476 ms
user222@VM2:~$ ping 10.20.20.4
PING 10.20.20.4 (10.20.20.4) 56(84) bytes of data.
64 bytes from 10.20.20.4: icmp_seq=1 ttl=62 time=94.1 ms
^C
--- 10.20.20.4 ping statistics ---
1 packets transmitted, 1 received, 0% packet loss, time 0ms
rtt min/avg/max/mdev = 94.086/94.086/94.086/0.000 ms
user222@VM2:~$
```

Figure 12.18 – Ping the other three VMs from VM2

Azure V-WAN allows us to connect and manage multiple Azure VNets and on-premises networks in a unified and optimized manner. It simplifies the deployment and management of connectivity across your network infrastructure. In the preceding lab, we utilized a V-WAN as the global transit network, which acts as a group of hubs for network traffic from various connected locations and serves as a central point for network traffic connection and management.

Summary

In this chapter, we learned about the organization of the Azure cloud and its compute, storage, and networking services by comparing them with the AWS and GCP services. We dove deep into the Azure V-WAN infrastructure and concepts, and created a V-WAN with two hubs, connecting to four global vNets. We built an Azure V-WAN and managed all the cloud resources in a centralized manner.

In the next chapter, we will examine the Azure data analytics services, including databases and big data, using the same method of learning by comparison, but going deep and beyond the basics.

Practice questions

The following scenario should be referenced when answering questions 1-10:

An Azure team is implementing a network architecture, as shown in *Figure 12.19*.

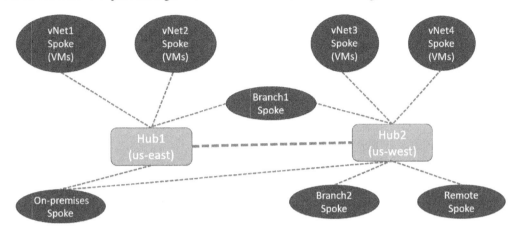

Figure 12.19 – Azure infrastructure architecture

- The subscription is `subs1`.
- The resource group is `azurerg`.
- The Storage account is `store`.
- 200 VMs are in the spoke vNets. The VMs are numbered, and each VM has a public IP and a locally installed application, `App-X`, where `X` is the VM number.
- `vNet1` has two subnets, `sub1` and `sub2`. Azure Firewall is deployed in `sub2`.
- Azure Front Door is deployed.
- **Azure Active Directory** (**AAD**) is used for the infrastructure.
- ExpressRoute is used between on-premises and the Azure cloud.

1. `store` stores blob objects that need to be accessible to Azure Databricks, leveraging AAD. What should be enabled for `store`?

    A. File shares

    B. Hierarchical namespace

    C. Network file shares

    D. Blob access policies

2. They need to ensure that `store` is accessible from `sub1` over Azure's backbone network. What do they need to do?

    A. Modify the firewalls and subnet for `store`

    B. Create an access policy for `store`

    C. Implement a virtual network service endpoint

    D. Remove the firewall

3. How can they move some big blob files from on-premises to `store`?

    A. Use the Azure Import/Export service.

    B. Generate a shared access signature and copy the files via File Explorer.

    C. Use Azure Storage Explorer.

    D. Generate an access key, map a drive, and then copy the files via File Explorer.

4. How can they display the traffic between the 200 VMs?

    A. Leverage the Azure Monitor activity log

    B. Leverage Azure Monitor Metrics

    C. Query from Azure Monitor Logs

    D. Leverage Azure Monitor Workbooks

5. They need to identify underutilized VMs. What Azure tool do you recommend?

    A. Metrics

    B. HDInsight

    C. Monitor

    D. Advisor

6. They are designing a solution to distribute traffic to different VM pools based on rules. What's your recommendation?

    A. Application Gateway

    B. Load Balancer

    C. Traffic Manager

    D. VM-level firewall rules

7. They need to monitor the metrics and logs of the 200 Linux VMs. What is your suggestion?

    A. HDInsight

    B. Analysis Services

    C. Linux diagnostic extension

    D. The Azure Performance Diagnostics extension

8. They need to ensure that app X on VM X only accepts traffic routed from Azure Front Door. What's your recommendation?

    A. Azure Private Link

    B. Azure service endpoints

    C. NSGs with service tags

    D. NSGs with application security groups

9. They need to set up a quick and inexpensive backup for the ExpressRoute connection. What's your recommendation?

    A. Add ExpressRoute bandwidth

    B. Add on-premises internet bandwidth

    C. Add a second ExpressRoute connection

    D. Add a VPN connection

10. They are building a site-to-site VPN connection between on-premises and the Azure cloud and want to make sure the VPN has large bandwidth and high resiliency. What's your recommendation?

    A. They use the VpnGw1 SKU

    B. They use the VpnGw2 SKU

    C. They use the VpnGw1-AZ SKU

    D. They use the VpnGw2-AZ SKU

Answers to the practice questions

1. B

2. C

3. A

4. D

5. D

6. A

7. C

8. C

9. D

10. D

Further reading

For further insights into what you've learned in this chapter, refer to the following links:

- https://azure.microsoft.com/en-us/products/virtual-machines
- https://azure.microsoft.com/en-us/products/category/storage/
- https://azure.microsoft.com/en-us/products/category/networking
- https://learn.microsoft.com/en-us/azure/virtual-wan/
- https://learn.microsoft.com/en-us/azure/architecture/reference-architectures/hybrid-networking/hub-spoke?tabs=cli
- https://learn.microsoft.com/en-us/azure/frontdoor/front-door-overview
- https://learn.microsoft.com/en-us/azure/traffic-manager/traffic-manager-overview
- https://learn.microsoft.com/en-us/azure/application-gateway/overview
- https://learn.microsoft.com/en-us/azure/load-balancer/load-balancer-overview
- https://learn.microsoft.com/en-us/azure/azure-monitor/autoscale/autoscale-overview

13
Azure Cloud Database and Big Data Services

In the first part of the book, we discussed the AWS database and big data services. In the second part of the book, we covered the Google database and big data services. Coming to the third part of the book, after discussing Microsoft Azure's foundational cloud services in the last chapter, we will now focus on the Azure database and big data services, which are like AWS and Google data services but with their own features.

Like Amazon and Google, Microsoft provides many solid data storage and analytics services in its Azure cloud platform. In this chapter, we will cover the following topics:

- **Azure Cloud Data Storage** explores some basic concepts about Azure storage accounts and Azure Data Lake Storage

- **Azure Database Services** examines Azure database services such as Azure SQL Database, Azure NoSQL database solutions including Azure Table Storage and Cosmos DB, Azure data warehouses and Azure Synapse Analytics

- **Azure big data services** include **Azure Data Factory** (**ADF**), Azure Databricks, and Azure HDInsight

Let us start our Azure cloud data journey with cloud data storage services.

Azure cloud data storage

During the launch of Azure Cloud Shell in the previous chapter, you may have noticed that we created an *Azure storage account* before the Azure Cloud Shell launch. An Azure storage account provides unique storage space for your Azure cloud data, accessible from anywhere in the world over HTTP or HTTPS. When an Azure storage account is created, the following Azure storage data objects are created: blobs, files, queues, and tables, in an *all-in-one* fashion:

- **Azure blobs** are blob storage, which is an object storage like AWS S3 or Google GCS

- **Azure files** permit you to manage file-sharing in the cloud – shareable to Azure VMs and on-prem VMs

- **Azure queue storage** is a cloud service similar to **AWS Simple Queue Service (SQS)**, for storing large numbers of messages

- **Azure table storage** stores structured NoSQL cloud data, with a key/attribute store and a schema-less design

An Azure storage account provides all these storage and data services together. *Figure 13.1* shows a sample storage account, `aye4992019`, which will be used in our labs in this chapter, including **Blob service**, **File service**, **Queue service**, and **Table service**:

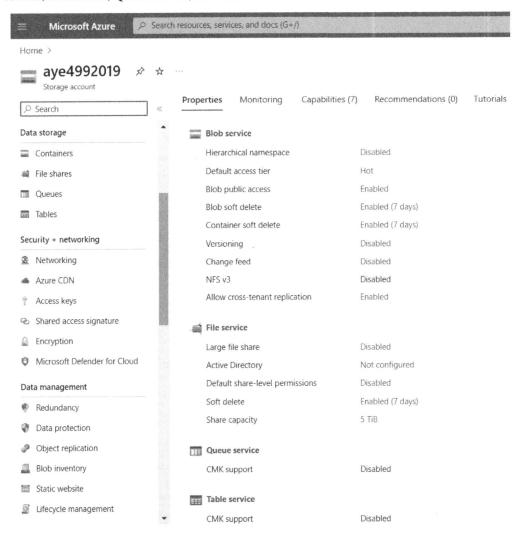

Figure 13.1 – Microsoft Azure storage account

Closely related to Azure blob storage is the **Azure data lake**, which is a storage repository that holds a large amount of data in its native raw format and is optimized for scaling to terabytes and petabytes of data. From *Figure 13.1*, we can see that by default, **Hierarchical namespace** is disabled under **Blob service**, resulting in massive amounts of unstructured data being stored in a single hierarchy – the so-called **flat namespace hierarchy**. Built on Azure Blob storage, Azure Data Lake Storage enables hierarchical namespaces to organize blob data into directories and store metadata about each directory and the files within it. With the structure of hierarchical namespaces, Azure Data Lake Storage is optimized for big data workloads and provides low-cost, scalable, tiered access. It is designed for high security, high availability, high durability, and better data storage/retrieval performance. *Figure 13.2* shows the process of upgrading the preceding storage account, `aye4992019`, to an Azure Gen2 data lake by enabling the hierarchical namespace, in three steps.

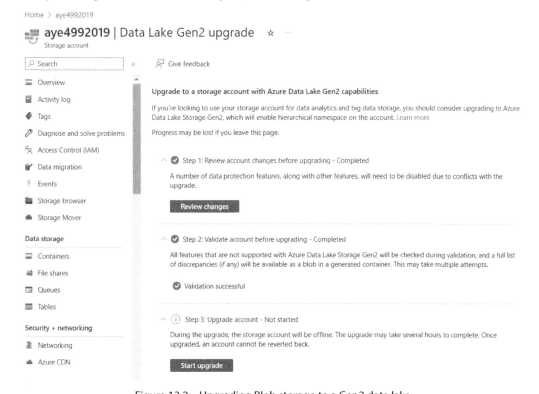

Figure 13.2 – Upgrading Blob storage to a Gen2 data lake

Azure Data Lakes allow developers, data scientists, and analysts to store data of any size, format, and speed, and do all types of processing and analytics, across many platforms and languages. More details about Azure data lakes are available at `https://azure.microsoft.com/en-us/solutions/data-lake/`.

Azure cloud databases

While an Azure data lake stores raw data, an Azure database usually stores formatted data. Azure offers cloud database services categorized into relational databases and NoSQL databases.

Azure cloud relational databases

Like AWS and GCP, Azure offers three options for cloud relational database deployment and usage:

- **Azure SQL virtual machines**: SQL Server built on Azure virtual machines. This is an **Infrastructure-as-a-Service** (**IaaS**) cloud service and thus you will have control of the database edition, version, and size. You will also be fully responsible for managing the virtual machine, including patching and other configuration management. More information is available at `https://azure.microsoft.com/en-us/products/virtual-machines/sql-server`.

- **Azure SQL managed instances**: This is the best for migrating on-premises SQL databases to the cloud. It serves the purpose of migrating many apps from on-premises to a fully managed **Platform-as-a-Service** (**PaaS**) cloud environment, with the minimum migration effort. More details are at `https://learn.microsoft.com/en-us/azure/azure-sql/managed-instance/`.

- **Azure SQL databases**: This is a PaaS cloud service and thus Microsoft will handle all the OS/database management systems, and you will only configure database options.

Figure 13.3 summarizes these three Azure SQL deployment options and use cases:

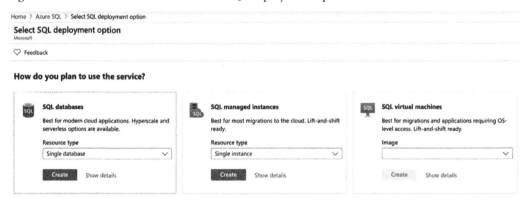

Figure 13.3 – Azure SQL deployment options

With Azure SQL databases, there are three options we can choose from: **Single database**, **Elastic pool**, and **Database server**. *Figure 13.4* shows these SQL database deployment options:

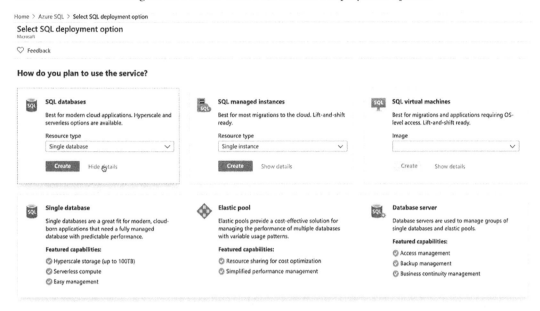

Figure 13.4 – SQL database options

While the single database resource type creates a SQL database with its own set of resources and has its own service tier, an elastic pool allows unused resources to be shared across multiple databases and thus saves the overall cost. A database server is used to manage these single databases or elastic pools. More details about Azure SQL databases can be found at `https://learn.microsoft.com/en-us/azure/azure-sql/database`.

Azure cloud NoSQL databases

Microsoft offers NoSQL cloud database services including *Azure Table storage* and *Azure Cosmos DB*.

Azure Table Storage is a NoSQL database service that is designed to store structured data in a non-relational format, making it suitable for scenarios where fast and flexible data storage is required. Some of the key features of Azure Table Storage include the following:

- Offers a cost-effective solution for storing large amounts of structured data, especially when compared to other database services such as Azure Cosmos DB.

- Data is organized into tables that are collections of entities, which are like rows in a traditional relational database, containing properties with values.

- Each table can be divided into multiple partitions, and each partition can be spread across multiple servers.

- Each entity within a table has a unique primary key, which consists of a partition key and a row key. The partition key is used to distribute data across partitions, and the row key uniquely identifies an entity within a partition.

- Provides a RESTful API for **Create, Read, Update, and Delete** (**CRUD**) operations and querying data.

While Azure Table Storage offers a simple solution for NoSQL databases, Azure Cosmos DB provides a globally distributed, multi-model database service. Cosmos DB is designed to handle large-scale and high-performance applications that require low-latency access to data across the world. It offers multiple data models, including document, key-value, graph, column-family, and tabular. Some of the key features of Azure Cosmos DB include the following:

- Strong service-level agreements for availability, latency, and throughput. It automatically scales based on demand.

- Automatically manages data distribution and partitioning across regions for efficient data access and distribution

- Allows data replication across multiple Azure regions, enabling low-latency access to data for users located in different geographic locations

- Supports multiple data models, including Document DB, Cassandra, MongoDB, Tables, etc.

- Support real-time analytics by integrating Cosmos DB with Azure Synapse Analytics or other analytics services

- Provides built-in security features such as encryption at rest and in transit, RBAC, and virtual network service endpoints

Figure 13.5 compares the features of the two Azure NoSQL databases: **Table Storage** and **Cosmos DB**:

	Table Storage	Cosmos DB Table API
Latency	Fast but no upper bounds.	<15 ms for reads/writes globally
Throughput	Variable, Limited to 20,000 operations per account and 2,000 per table.	Dedicated per table. Accounts have no upper limit on throughout and support >10 million operation/s per table.
Global Distribution	Single region with one optional readable secondary read region. Can't initiate failover.	Turnkey global distribution from one to 30 + regions. Automatic and manual failover.
Indexing	Only primary index on **PartitionKey** and **RowKey**. No secondary indexes.	Automatic and complete indexing on all properties.
Query	Uses index for primary key, and scans otherwise.	Uses automatic indexing.
Consistency	Strong within primary region,eventual within secondary region.	Five consistency levels for various needs.
Pricing	Storage-optimized.	Throughput-optimized.

Figure 13.5 – Azure NoSQL database option comparison

More details about Azure Table Storage can be found at `https://learn.microsoft.com/en-us/azure/storage/tables/`, and more details about Azure NoSQL Cosmos DB are available at `https://azure.microsoft.com/en-us/products/cosmos-db/`.

Azure's cloud data warehouse

Microsoft Azure Synapse Analytics, formerly known as SQL Data Warehouse, is a unified, end-to-end Azure data analytics tool for both traditional database analytics and modern big data analytics. Whatever the data sources and the data types are, you can use Azure Synapse to sort them individually or analyze them together, with one unified interface. Azure Synapse consists of four components:

- **Synapse SQL** – This allows you to deploy a SQL pool or SQL on demand
- **Apache Spark** – This allows you to query big data using the SQL language
- **Synapse Pipelines** – This allows you to accomplish hybrid data integration
- **Synapse Studio** – This unifies the data processing power of Synapse

Azure Synapse has the following modules:

- **Synapse Studio** – Provides a unified user interface
- **Power BI** – Creates rich and dynamic reports and dashboards
- **Query Editor** – Lets you edit queries and run them directly within the portal
- **Data modeling capabilities** – Create semantic models for users to query against

Next, we will show you how to deploy an Azure Synapse workspace, create a SQL pool dedicated to the workspace, and run SQL queries against the pool by leveraging external files and tables:

1. **Deploy an Azure Synapse workspace**:

   Go to the Azure portal at `https://portal.azure.com/`. Currently, we have a resource group and a storage account created in the **Azure for Students** subscription, as shown in *Figure 13.6*:

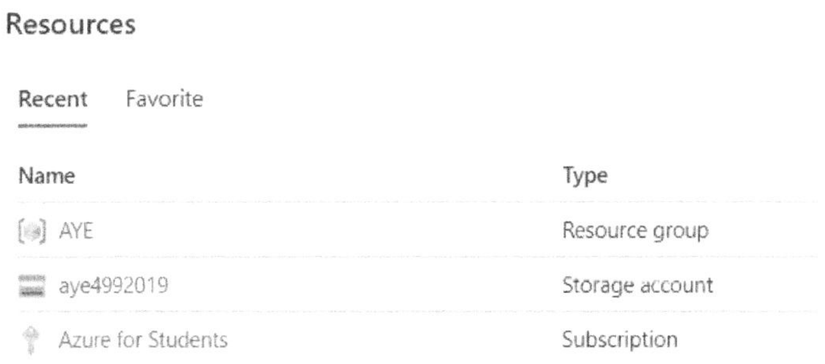

   ## Resources

   Recent   Favorite

Name	Type
[⚙] AYE	Resource group
▦ aye4992019	Storage account
⚲ Azure for Students	Subscription

   Figure 13.6 – Existing Azure resources

   Go to **Azure Synapse Analytics | Create Synapse workspace** and add the details for the workspace. First, fill out the **Basics** tab by using the existing resource group and Data Lake Storage Gen2 account name; adding a unique workspace name and file system name; and choosing a region (**East US** here), as shown in *Figure 13.7*:

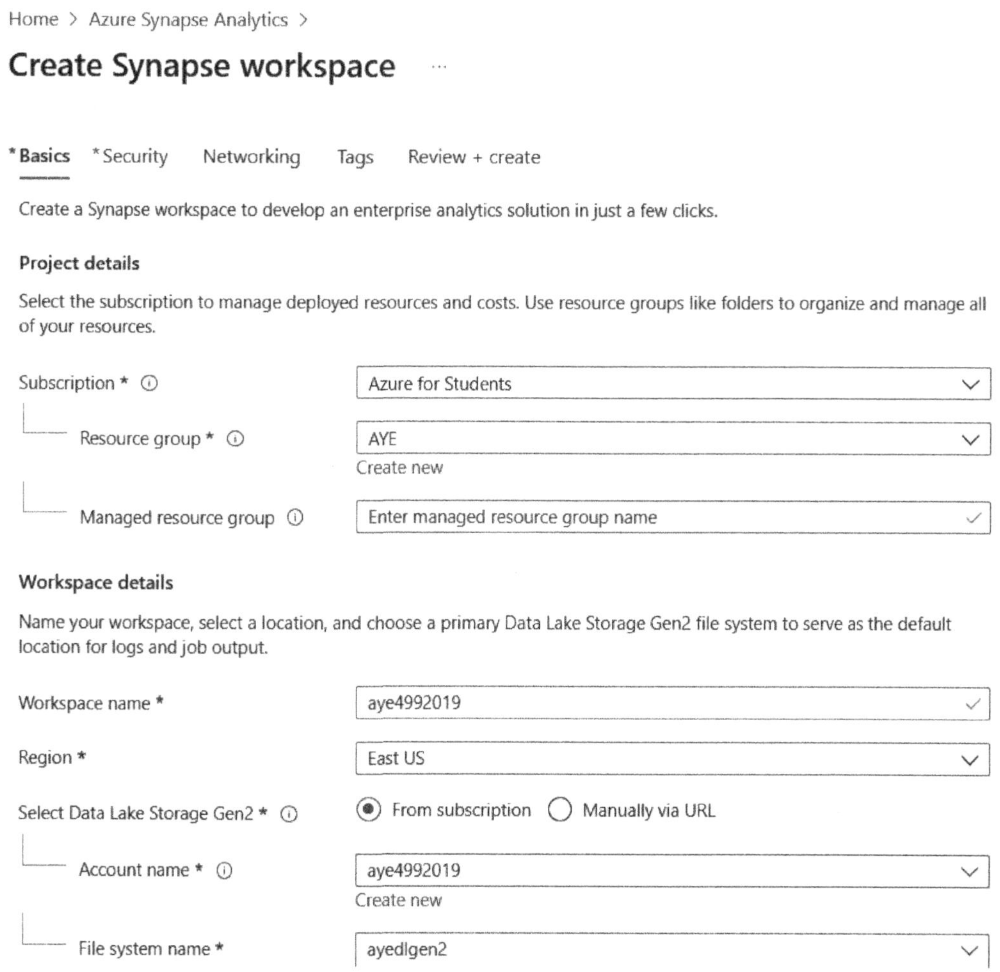

Home > Azure Synapse Analytics >

Create Synapse workspace   ...

*Basics   *Security   Networking   Tags   Review + create

Create a Synapse workspace to develop an enterprise analytics solution in just a few clicks.

Project details

Select the subscription to manage deployed resources and costs. Use resource groups like folders to organize and manage all of your resources.

Subscription * ⓘ	Azure for Students ⌄
Resource group * ⓘ	AYE ⌄
	Create new
Managed resource group ⓘ	Enter managed resource group name ✓

Workspace details

Name your workspace, select a location, and choose a primary Data Lake Storage Gen2 file system to serve as the default location for logs and job output.

Workspace name *	aye4992019 ✓
Region *	East US ⌄
Select Data Lake Storage Gen2 * ⓘ	⦿ From subscription ◯ Manually via URL
Account name * ⓘ	aye4992019 ⌄
	Create new
File system name *	ayedlgen2 ⌄

Figure 13.7 – Create Synapse workspace (the Basics tab)

Then, fill out the **Security** tab by providing a password for the default admin account, **sqladminuser**, and keeping the defaults for the other fields. Click **Review + create** to deploy the Synapse workspace:

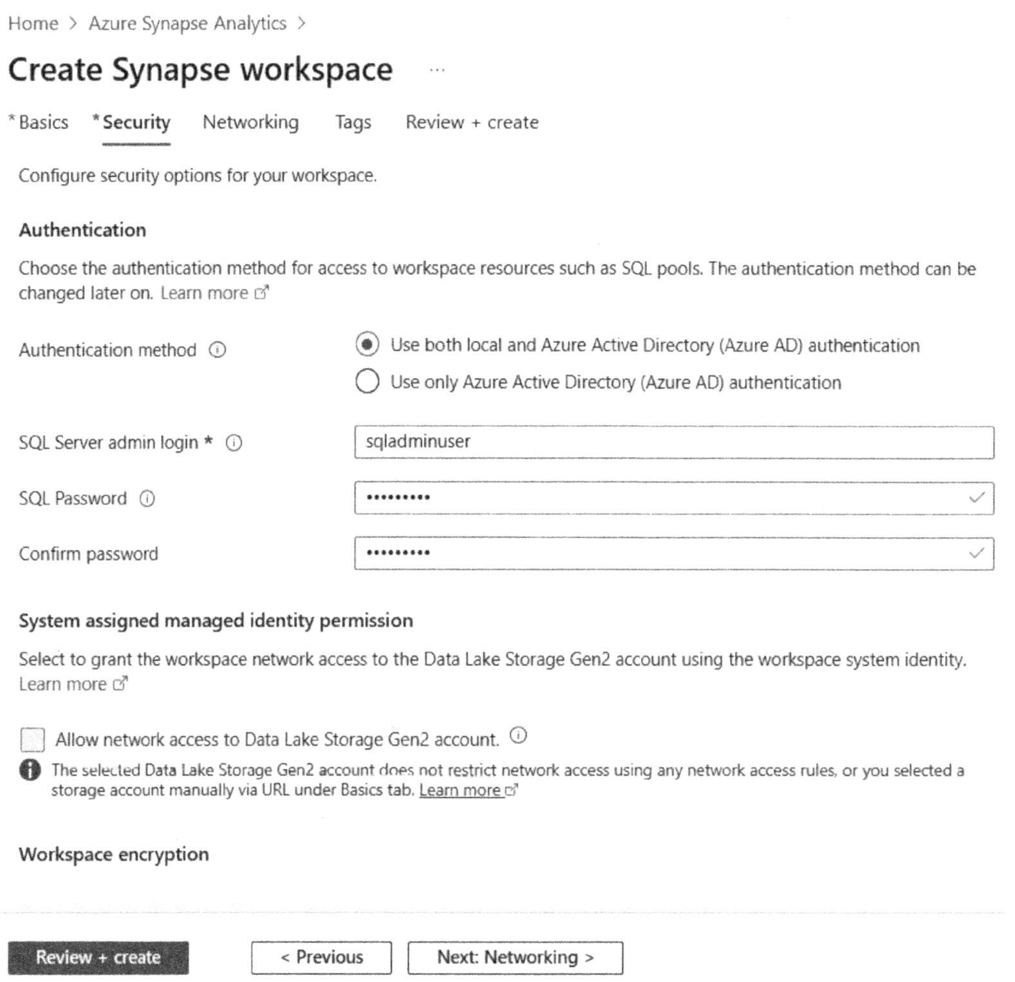

Home > Azure Synapse Analytics >

Create Synapse workspace   ...

* Basics   * **Security**   Networking   Tags   Review + create

Configure security options for your workspace.

Authentication

Choose the authentication method for access to workspace resources such as SQL pools. The authentication method can be changed later on. Learn more ☐

Authentication method ⓘ

- ⦿ Use both local and Azure Active Directory (Azure AD) authentication
- ◯ Use only Azure Active Directory (Azure AD) authentication

SQL Server admin login * ⓘ

```
sqladminuser
```

SQL Password ⓘ

```
·········                                              ✓
```

Confirm password

```
·········                                              ✓
```

System assigned managed identity permission

Select to grant the workspace network access to the Data Lake Storage Gen2 account using the workspace system identity. Learn more ☐

☐ Allow network access to Data Lake Storage Gen2 account. ⓘ

ⓘ The selected Data Lake Storage Gen2 account does not restrict network access using any network access rules, or you selected a storage account manually via URL under Basics tab. Learn more ☐

Workspace encryption

[Review + create]   [< Previous]   [Next: Networking >]

Figure 13.8 – Create Synapse workspace (Security tab)

After the Synapse workspace is deployed, we will go to *step 2*.

2. **Create an Azure Synapse workspace database pool:**

Click on the Azure Synapse workspace we just created, as shown in *Figure 13.9*:

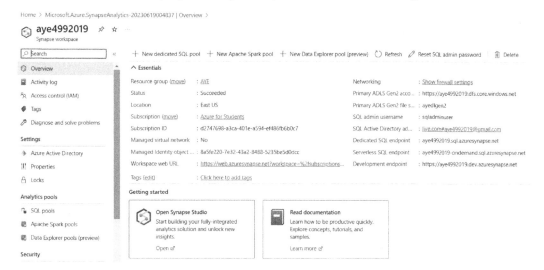

Figure 13.9 – Synapse workspace overview

Click + **New dedicated SQL pool** at the top to deploy a new SQL pool; here, we named it aye4992019.

3. **Open Synapse Studio to query the sample data**:

    After the SQL pool has been created, click **Open** in **Open Synapse Studio** from the Synapse workspace. In the new window, click **Knowledge center | Use samples immediately | Create external table with SQL**, and select the pool we created earlier – **aye4992019** – as shown in *Figure 13.10*:

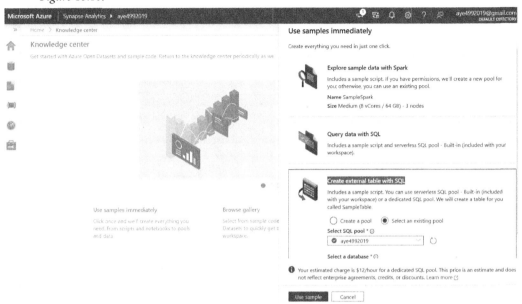

Figure 13.10 – Using a Synapse workspace and SQL pool

Click **Use sample** and it will show a sample SQL script, which will create an external file and an external table using public datasets online. Then, query the external table, as shown in *Figure 13.11*:

```
    Synapse live      Validate all      Publish all

   Create external tabl...   ✕

   ▷ Run   Undo      Publish      Query plan   |   Connect to   ⊘ aye4992019      Use database   aye4992019

 2   IF NOT EXISTS (SELECT * FROM sys.external_file_formats WHERE name = 'SynapseParquetFormat')
 3       CREATE EXTERNAL FILE FORMAT [SynapseParquetFormat]
 4       WITH ( FORMAT_TYPE = PARQUET)
 5   GO
 6
 7   IF NOT EXISTS (SELECT * FROM sys.external_data_sources WHERE name = 'nyctlc_azureopendatastorage_blob_core_windows_net')
 8       CREATE EXTERNAL DATA SOURCE [nyctlc_azureopendatastorage_blob_core_windows_net]
 9       WITH (
10           LOCATION = 'wasbs://nyctlc@azureopendatastorage.blob.core.windows.net',
11           TYPE     = HADOOP
12       )
13   GO
14
15   CREATE EXTERNAL TABLE nyc_tlc_yellow_trip_ext (
16       [vendorID] varchar(8000),
17       [tpepPickupDateTime] datetime2(7),
18       [tpepDropoffDateTime] datetime2(7),
19       [passengerCount] int,
20       [tripDistance] float,
21       [puLocationId] varchar(8000),
22       [doLocationId] varchar(8000),
23       [startLon] float,
24       [startLat] float,
25       [endLon] float,
26       [endLat] float,
27       [rateCodeId] int,
28       [storeAndFwdFlag] varchar(8000),
29       [paymentType] varchar(8000),
30       [fareAmount] float,
31       [extra] float,
32       [mtaTax] float,
33       [improvementSurcharge] varchar(8000),
34       [tipAmount] float,
35       [tollsAmount] float,
36       [totalAmount] float
37       )
38       WITH (
39       LOCATION = 'yellow/puYear=2014/puMonth=3/',
40       -- LOCATION = 'yellow'
41       DATA_SOURCE = [nyctlc_azureopendatastorage_blob_core_windows_net],
42       FILE_FORMAT = [SynapseParquetFormat],
43       REJECT_TYPE = VALUE,
44       REJECT_VALUE = 0
45       )
46   GO
```

Figure 13.11 – Synapse workspace sample script

Click **Run**. The results will be shown in a couple of minutes, as partially shown in *Figure 13.12*:

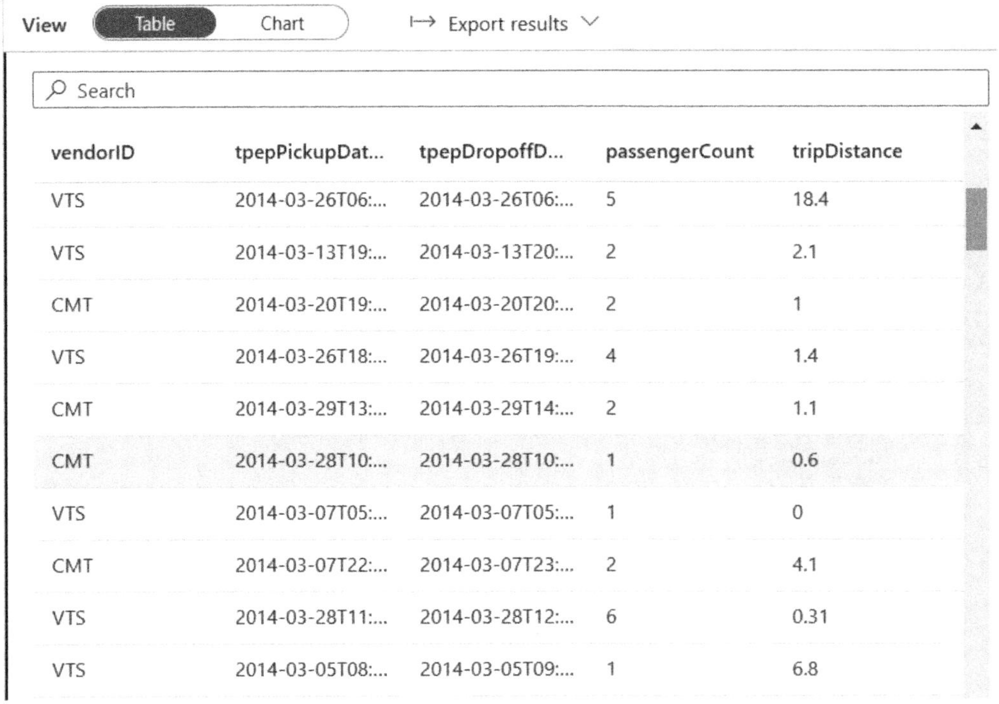

View	Table	Chart	⟼ Export results ∨		

vendorID	tpepPickupDat...	tpepDropoffD...	passengerCount	tripDistance
VTS	2014-03-26T06:...	2014-03-26T06:...	5	18.4
VTS	2014-03-13T19:...	2014-03-13T20:...	2	2.1
CMT	2014-03-20T19:...	2014-03-20T20:...	2	1
VTS	2014-03-26T18:...	2014-03-26T19:...	4	1.4
CMT	2014-03-29T13:...	2014-03-29T14:...	2	1.1
CMT	2014-03-28T10:...	2014-03-28T10:...	1	0.6
VTS	2014-03-07T05:...	2014-03-07T05:...	1	0
CMT	2014-03-07T22:...	2014-03-07T23:...	2	4.1
VTS	2014-03-28T11:...	2014-03-28T12:...	6	0.31
VTS	2014-03-05T08:...	2014-03-05T09:...	1	6.8

Figure 13.12 – Synapse workspace querying results

You can view the results as a table or chat and export them. After checking the querying results, we need to clean up the SQL pool and the Synapse workspace. *Figure 13.13* summarizes Synapse Analytics with its management features and main modules for working with cloud data:

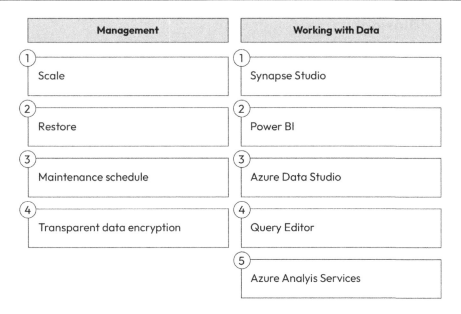

Management	Working with Data
1 Scale	1 Synapse Studio
2 Restore	2 Power BI
3 Maintenance schedule	3 Azure Data Studio
4 Transparent data encryption	4 Query Editor
	5 Azure Analyis Services

Figure 13.13 – Managing and working with Azure Synapse Analytics

In this section, we explored the Azure cloud data warehouse, Azure Synapse Analytics. More details about Azure Synapse Analytics are available at `https://azure.microsoft.com/en-us/products/synapse-analytics/`.

Azure cloud big data services

Like Amazon and Google, Microsoft provides a full stack of big data cloud services, including the big data ETL service, ADF; the big data processing service tool, Azure HDInsight; and the big data analytic service, Azure Data Bricks.

Azure ADF

ADF is a cloud-based data integration service for creating data-driven workflows that automatically move and transform data. ADF is a pipeline – a logical grouping of activities to perform a data-driven task, such as the following:

- **Data moving** – This takes an ingestion source, pulls it into the Azure cloud, and puts it into a data lake

- **Data transformation** – This connects the data lake to Databricks, runs a stored procedure, and transforms data to produce a new dataset for further analytics

Essentially, ADF is a data ETL service integrating hybrid data at an enterprise level. More details about ADF are available at `https://azure.microsoft.com/en-us/products/data-factory`.

Azure HDInsight

We discussed Amazon EMR in a lot of detail in *Part 1* of the book. Like AWS EMR, Microsoft HDInsight is a Hadoop-based big data processing system, and it brings Hadoop and Spark into the same cloud platform for enterprise big data processing. With HDInsight, you can create clusters for Spark, Kafka, HBase, and Hadoop on the Azure cloud, and run big data frameworks in large volumes and at a high velocity. The key features of HDInsight include the following:

- **Global availability** – It is available in many Azure regions to meet global enterprises' data processing needs in foreign areas.

- **Extendability and compatibility** – It can be extended by many productive tools and services, including but not limited to Hue, Presto, and so on. HDInsight is compatible and integrates seamlessly with Azure big data applications.

- **Scalable and low-cost** – It scales out based on workloads, and the cluster can be created on demand, so you pay only for what you use for cost optimization.

There are many business use cases for Azure HDInsight, including IOT data processing, ETL, data streaming, and interactive querying. More details can be found at `https://azure.microsoft.com/en-us/products/hdinsight`.

Azure Databricks

Azure Databricks is a fully managed cloud-native service that enables an open data lake house on top of the Azure data lake. Azure Databricks offers a powerful and collaborative environment for cloud data analytics and machine learning tasks. With Azure Databricks, a whole suite of data analytic tools, both SQL-based database tools and Jupyter-Notebook-based AI tools, can be integrated for common data governance across cloud data lakes. In the next section, we will implement Azure Databricks and see how these tools are integrated together:

1. Creating an Azure Databricks workspace:

   Go to **Azure Databricks | Create Databricks workspace** and add the details for the workspace. After it is created, launch the workspace, as shown in *Figure 13.14*:

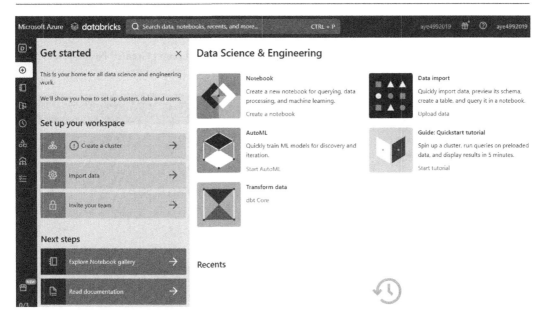

Figure 13.14 – Get started with Azure Databricks

2. Creating a Databricks cluster:

    Click **Create a cluster** from the previous step and fill out the details about the cluster, as shown in *Figure 13.15*:

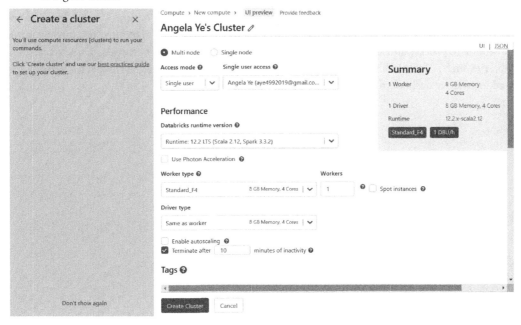

Figure 13.15 – Creating a Databrick cluster

3. Creating a Databricks notebook:

Go to **Databricks** | **Workspace** | **Users** | **aye4992019@gmail.com** | **Create** | **Notebook** to create a notebook, as shown in *Figure 13.16*:

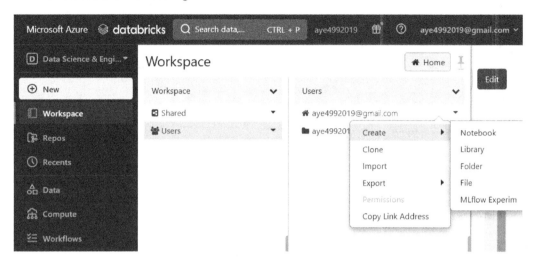

Figure 13.16 – Creating a Databricks notebook

Once a notebook is created, it opens a new avenue for data processing. As shown in *Figure 13.17*, it supports Python, SQL, Scala, R, etc., and we can run many data processing tasks with the Databricks notebook: write and execute code, visualize data, and collaborate with others. Databricks notebooks leverage the power of Apache Spark and can access Spark libraries, APIs, and functions directly in your notebook to process and analyze large datasets. With Databrick notebooks, you can use visualization libraries such as Matplotlib and Seaborn or Databricks-specific visualizations to create charts, graphs, and interactive dashboards.

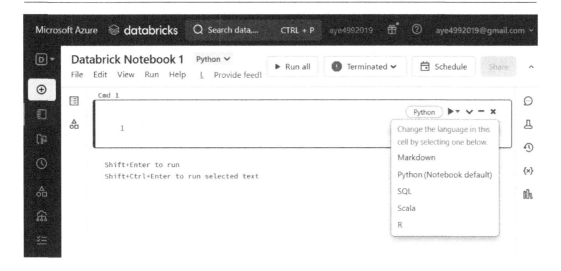

Figure 13.17 – Running scripts in a Databrick notebook

Databricks notebooks are part of the Databricks workspace and provide a powerful and interactive environment for data exploration, analysis, and collaboration, enabling you to leverage Apache Spark's capabilities, integrate with other Azure services, visualize data, and build data processing pipelines. More details are available at `https://azure.microsoft.com/en-us/products/databricks/`.

Summary

In this chapter, we learned about the Azure cloud database and big data services. We explored Azure Data Lake Storage, Azure cloud databases and Azure Synapse Analytics, Azure data ETL tools such as ADF, data processing tools such as HDInsight, and Azure data analytics tools such as Databricks. By the end of this chapter, you will have acquired knowledge on data ingestion, storing, processing, and visualization in the Azure cloud.

In the next chapter, we will examine the machine learning services in Azure's cloud.

Practice questions

Questions 1-3 are based on the following.

The data team for company ABC is building an Azure cloud data analytics platform, with the following objectives:

- The team has two data scientists who are familiar with R, Scala, and Python, and two data engineers who are good at Python. Each team member needs a cluster.

- The team needs to run notebooks that use Python, Scala, and SQL for their job workloads.

- The team needs to optimize their work performance.

1. What platform fits a data scientist?

    A. A High Concurrency Databricks cluster

    B. A standard Databricks cluster

    C. An AFD pipeline

    D. The Azure Synapse platform

2. What platform fits a data engineer?

    A. A High Concurrency Databricks cluster

    B. A standard Databricks cluster

    C. An AFD pipeline

    D. The Azure Synapse platform

3. What platform fits the job workload?

    A. A High Concurrency Databricks cluster

    B. A standard Databricks cluster

    C. An AFD pipeline

    D. An all-purpose cluster

Questions 4-6 are based on the following.

A data team needs to import some Parquet files stored in their Azure Data Lake Storage Gen2 account to an enterprise data warehouse in Azure Synapse Analytics.

4. They need to link the data source to Synapse. What's your recommendation?

    A. Create a remote service binding pointing to the Azure data lake

    B. Upload the files to Synapse

    C. Directly read the source files from Synapse

    D. Create a remote data service from the source table storage

5. They need to get the dataset local to Synapse. What's your recommendation?

    A. Create an external file and external table using the remote data source

    B. Create an external file using the remote data source

    C. Create an external table using the remote data source

    D. Upload the source data files to Synapse

6. They need to load the data to Synapse. What is your recommendation?

  A. Use the **CREATE TABLE AS SELECT** statement from the external table

  B. Use the **CREATE TABLE AS SELECT** statement from the external file

  C. Upload the external file to Synapse

  D. Upload the external table to Synapse

Questions 7-8 are based on the following.

A data team uses Azure Stream Analytics to process Twitter data:

- Input to Azure Event Hubs from Twitter

- Output to an Azure Blob storage account

- Output the tweet counts from the last 10 minutes every minute

7. What is your recommendation about the data ingestion window?

  A. Sliding

  B. Session

  C. Tumbling

  D. Hopping

8. What is your recommendation about the windowing function?

  A. A 10-minute sliding window

  B. A 10-minute session window

  C. A 10-minute tumbling window

  D. A 10-minute hopping window that has a 1-minute hop

Answers to the practice questions

1. B

2. A

3. B

4. A

5. A

6. A

7. C

8. C

Further reading

For further insights into what you've learned in this chapter, refer to the following links:

- `https://azure.microsoft.com/en-us/solutions/data-lake/`
- `https://learn.microsoft.com/en-us/azure/azure-sql/managed-instance/`
- `https://azure.microsoft.com/en-us/products/virtual-machines/sql-server`
- `https://learn.microsoft.com/en-us/azure/azure-sql/database`
- `https://azure.microsoft.com/en-us/products/synapse-analytics/`
- `https://azure.microsoft.com/en-us/products/data-factory`
- `https://azure.microsoft.com/en-us/products/hdinsight`
- `https://azure.microsoft.com/en-us/products/databricks/`

Azure Cloud AI Services

Like Amazon and Google, Microsoft provides many AI tools and services for data scientists and engineers to develop ML models in the Azure cloud. Microsoft cloud AI services include Azure Machine Learning workspaces, which is a fully managed platform for data scientists to build, train, and deploy machine learning models, and Azure Cognitive Services, which helps developers build cognitive intelligence into applications, based on pre-trained AI models and APIs for common ML tasks. Azure cloud AI services integrate seamlessly with other Microsoft cloud services and tools. In this chapter, we will cover the following topics:

- **Azure Machine Learning workspace**, which is an end-to-end platform for data scientists to develop ML models, including data collection, model training and deploying, and other AI capabilities.

- **Azure Cognitive Services**, which enables developers to easily add cognitive features into their applications. The Azure Cognitive Services offerings are available through REST APIs and client library SDKs, with many popular application development languages supported.

- **Azure OpenAI Service**, which enables developers to leverage large-scale, generative AI models and enable new reasoning and comprehension capabilities for building cutting-edge applications.

We will use examples during our discussions to help you understand more deeply. Let us start by jumping into the powerful Azure ML workspace.

Azure ML workspaces

An Azure ML workspace allows you to build, deploy, and manage ML models at scale. It provides a centralized workspace for data scientists, machine learning engineers, and developers to collaborate on machine learning projects, with the following features:

- An Azure ML workspace is an end-to-end suite for organizing and managing ML assets such as datasets, models, notebooks, experiments, and pipelines/resources. It provides a centralized location for team collaboration, version control, and resource management.

- It integrates with Jupyter notebooks and provides an interactive environment for developing and running code, visualizing data, and documenting the ML process.

- It supports dataset versioning and management so you can register and track different versions of datasets for ML model training and evaluation. Datasets can be stored within the workspace or referenced from external data sources.

- It allows you to organize and track different iterations of model training runs. You can define and log various metrics, hyperparameters, and outputs during each experiment run to measure different models and configurations.

- It provides capabilities for model management and deployment. Models can be registered and deployed as web services, containers, or in real-time inference pipelines, making them accessible to both users and applications.

- It includes the capability to automate the process of model selection and hyperparameter tuning.

Azure ML workspaces offer a centralized workspace for data scientists, ML engineers, and developers to collaborate on machine learning projects. The following are some of the tasks you can perform with an Azure ML workspace:

- Create ML model training jobs and group them into experiments for performance measurements.

- Author pipelines to train and retrain your models.

- Register data assets for model training and pipeline creation; register models for deployment.

- Create online endpoints with a registered model.

When creating an Azure ML workspace, the following cloud resources are created, as shown in *Figure 14.1*:

- An Azure storage account, which is a default datastore

- Azure Application Insights

- Azure Container Registry

- Azure Key Vault

Azure Storage Account

Default datastore for our workspace and any Jupyter notebooks.

- General-purpose v1 storage account
- Blobs, files, queues, and tables

Azure Application Insights

Stores monitoring information about our models.

- Request rates, response rates, and response times
- Failure rates
- Dependency rates
- Exceptions

Azure Container Registry

Registers our docker containers used during training and in model deployment.

- Geo-replication
- OCI artifact repository
- Automated container building and patching
- Integrated security

Azure Key Vault

Stores secreats used by compute targets and other sensitive information needed by the workspace.

- Use vault for:
  - Securely storing secrets and keys.
  - Monitoring access and use.
  - Simplifying administration.

Figure 14.1 – Azure ML workspace

Now, let's see how to create an Azure ML workspace and build an ML pipeline:

1. **Deploy an Azure ML workspace:**

   Go to **Azure Portal | Azure Machine Learning | Create a Machine Learning Workspace**.

   Fill out the details as shown in *Figure 14.2*. Note that the following resources will be created along with the new ML workspace:

- **Storage account**: Used to store and access datasets and model artifacts in your machine learning workflows

- **Key Vault**: This is a central location to securely store and manage secrets, such as authentication keys, connection strings, and certificates, for the ML workflow pipelines

- **Application Insights**: Here, you can gain valuable insights into the performance, availability, and usage of your machine learning models and applications

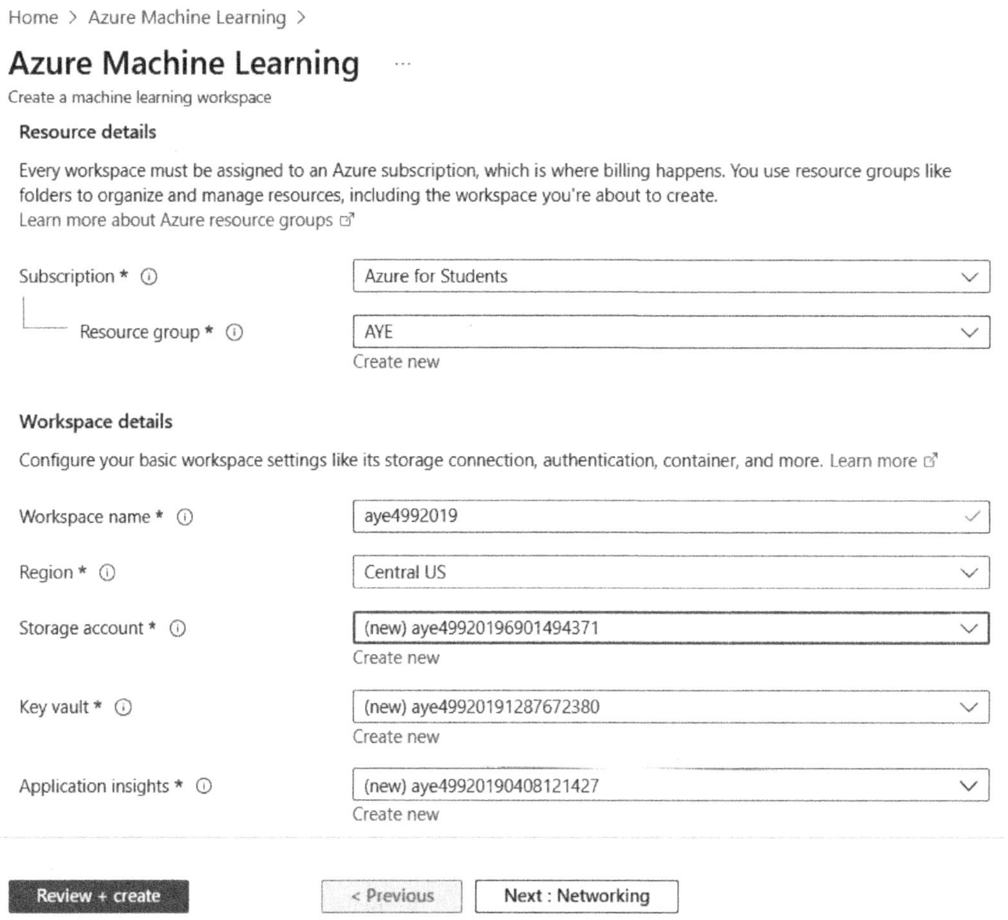

Home > Azure Machine Learning >

Azure Machine Learning ...

Create a machine learning workspace

Resource details

Every workspace must be assigned to an Azure subscription, which is where billing happens. You use resource groups like folders to organize and manage resources, including the workspace you're about to create.
Learn more about Azure resource groups ⬚

Subscription * ⓘ	Azure for Students ⌄
└── Resource group * ⓘ	AYE ⌄
	Create new

Workspace details

Configure your basic workspace settings like its storage connection, authentication, container, and more. Learn more ⬚

Workspace name * ⓘ	aye4992019 ✓
Region * ⓘ	Central US ⌄
Storage account * ⓘ	(new) aye49920196901494371 ⌄
	Create new
Key vault * ⓘ	(new) aye49920191287672380 ⌄
	Create new
Application insights * ⓘ	(new) aye49920190408121427 ⌄
	Create new

Review + create		< Previous	Next : Networking

Figure 14.2 – Create an ML workspace

Click **Review + create**. The aforementioned resources (**Azure Machine Learning workspace**, **Storage account**, **Key vault**, and **Application Insights**) are created, as shown in *Figure 14.3*:

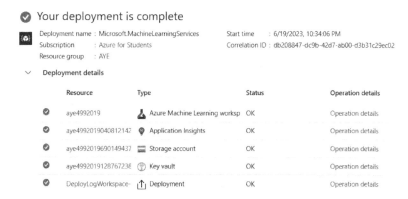

Figure 14.3 – Azure ML workspace is created

Click the **aye4992019** workspace and click **Launch Studio**.

2. **Deploy an Azure ML compute cluster:**

In Azure ML Studio, navigate to **Compute** on the left-hand menu, then click the **Compute clusters** tab at the top. Fill in the details as shown in *Figure 14.4*:

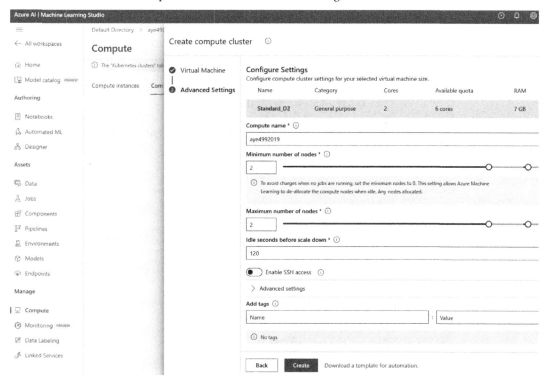

Figure 14.4 – Azure ML compute cluster creation

Click **Create**. Now the ML training compute cluster has been created.

3. **Create an Azure ML dataset:**

After we deploy a model-training compute cluster, we need to have a dataset for the training. For simplicity, we will import from an Azure open dataset.

In Azure ML Studio, navigate to **Data** in the left-hand menu, then click the **Data assets** tab at the top. The **Create data asset** window should appear as shown in *Figure 14.5*. Note that **Type** is set to **Tabular**:

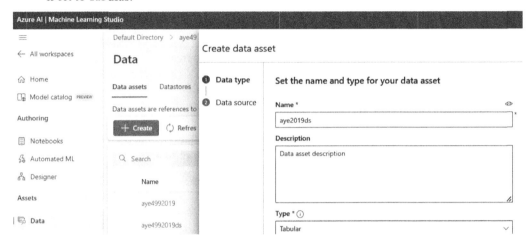

Figure 14.5 – Azure ML data asset basics

Click **Next**. Set the source to **From Azure Open Datasets**. Click **Next** as shown in *Figure 14.6*:

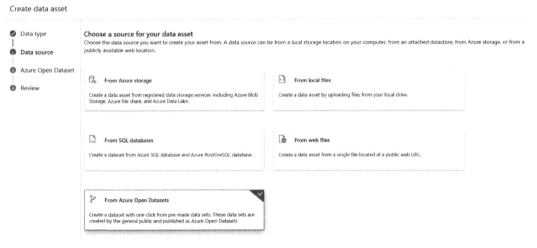

Figure 14.6 – Choosing From Azure Open Datasets

Filter and choose the **Open Dataset Sample: Diabetes**. Click **Create**:

Create data asset

- ✔ Data type
- ✔ Data source
- ✔ Azure Open Dataset
- ❸ Review

Review
Review the settings for your data asset and make any changes as needed.

Data type ✎

Name
aye2019ds

Description
--

Type
tabular

Data source ✎

Type
OpenDataset

Open Dataset ✎

Open Dataset name
Sample: Diabetes

[Back] [Create]

Figure 14.7 – Creating an Azure ML data asset

Now that the dataset is created, we can go to the **Explore** tab to examine the data via the **Preview** or **Profile** options, as shown in *Figure 14.8*:

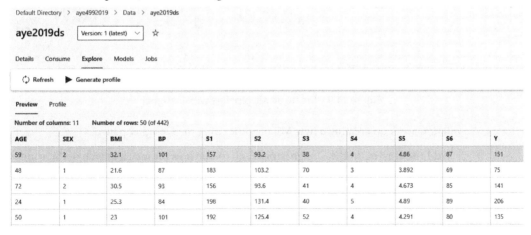

Default Directory > aye4992019 > Data > aye2019ds

aye2019ds   Version: 1 (latest) ⌄   ☆

Details   Consume   **Explore**   Models   Jobs

↻ Refresh   ▶ Generate profile

Preview   Profile

Number of columns: 11   Number of rows: 50 (of 442)

AGE	SEX	BMI	BP	S1	S2	S3	S4	S5	S6	Y
59	2	32.1	101	157	93.2	38	4	4.86	87	151
48	1	21.6	87	183	103.2	70	3	3.892	69	75
72	2	30.5	93	156	93.6	41	4	4.673	85	141
24	1	25.3	84	198	131.4	40	5	4.89	89	206
50	1	23	101	192	125.4	52	4	4.291	80	135

Figure 14.8 – Azure ML data asset exploration

Regarding the Diabetes dataset we are using: this is a public dataset from Bradley Efron, Trevor Hastie, Iain Johnstone, and Robert Tibshirani (2004) published in *"Least Angle Regression," Annals of Statistics (with discussion), pages 407-499.* In this dataset, there are ten baseline variables of age, sex, body mass index, average blood pressure, and six blood serum measurements, which were obtained for each of the 442 diabetes patients, as well as the response of interest, a quantitative measure of disease progression one year after the baseline measurements were collected. These features and the target of the model match the dataset exploration in *Figure 14.8*, where columns *1-10* are features and column *11* is the target.

4. **Create an Azure ML pipeline:**

    Now the training cluster is deployed and the dataset created, it's time to create an ML pipeline! We will use ML Designer with the classic prebuilt components.

    In Azure ML Studio, navigate to **Designer** on the left-hand menu, and click the **Classic prebuilt** tab. Click + to create a new pipeline as shown in *Figure 14.9*:

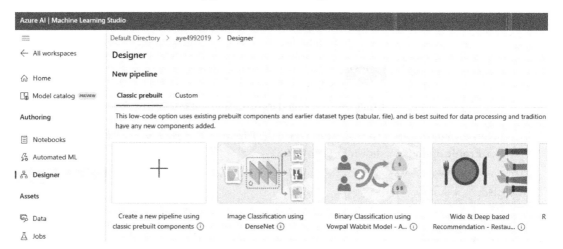

Figure 14.9 – Create an ML pipeline with Designer

We will now work on creating a new ML pipeline using the Designer pane:

I. **Add the cluster**: In the Designer pane, go to **Settings** on the right side of the window and choose the compute cluster we created earlier, **aye4992019**, as shown in *Figure 14.10*:

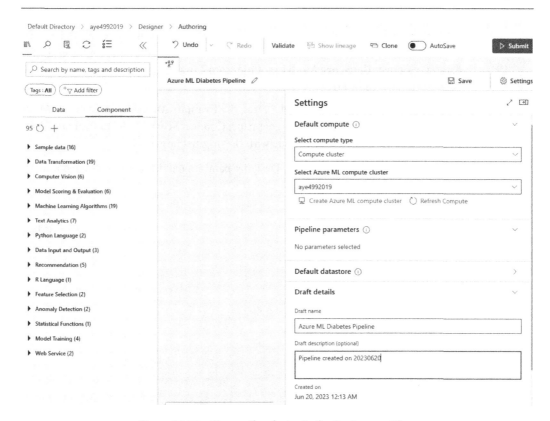

Figure 14.10 – Choose the cluster in the Designer settings

II.   **Add the dataset module**: Go to the **Data** tab on the right side and choose the dataset we created earlier, **aye2019ds**. Drag it to the Designer pane.

III.   **Add the dataset split module**: Go to the **Component** tab on the right side; there will be many modules listed. Drag the **Split Data** module from under **Data transformation** to the Designer pane since we need to split the dataset into a **training dataset** and an **evaluation dataset**. Edit the module for a 70:30 split between the two datasets. Connect the two modules.

IV.   **Add the model training module**: Go to the **Component** tab on the right side and drag the **Train Model** module from under **Model Training** to the Designer pane. Since we need an ML algorithm to train the model, next, drag the **Linear Regression** module from under **Machine Learning Algorithms** to the Designer pane and connect it to **Train Model**. Since we need the training dataset to train a model, connect the training dataset to **Train Model**.

V.   **Add the model scoring module**: Drag the **Score Model** module under **Model Scoring and Evaluation** to the Designer pane. It will predict the target value (Y) for the evaluation dataset. Connect the **Score Model** module from **Line Regression** and the evaluation dataset from the **Split Data** module.

VI. **Add the model evaluation module**: Drag the **Evaluate Model** module under **Model Scoring and Evaluation** to the Designer pane. Connect **Score Model** to **Evaluate Model** to evaluate the predicted target value with the original target value.

Figure 14.11 shows the ML pipeline in the Designer pane after all the aforementioned modules are added:

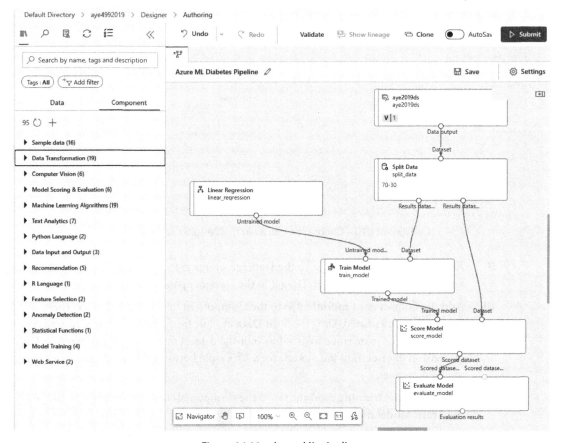

Figure 14.11 – Azure ML pipeline

Click **Submit** and fill in the job details as shown in *Figure 14.12*:

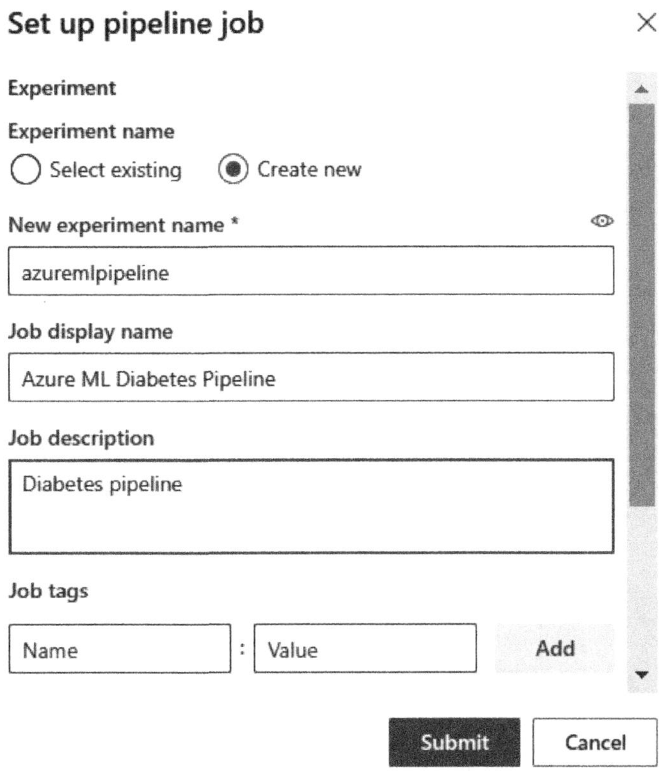

Figure 14.12 – Submit Azure ML pipeline

Click **Submit** again. It will create an ML experiment and execute the pipeline in the experiment. After the job is submitted, you can see the components running in the new ML pipeline, as shown in *Figure 14.13* where the running components are highlighted:

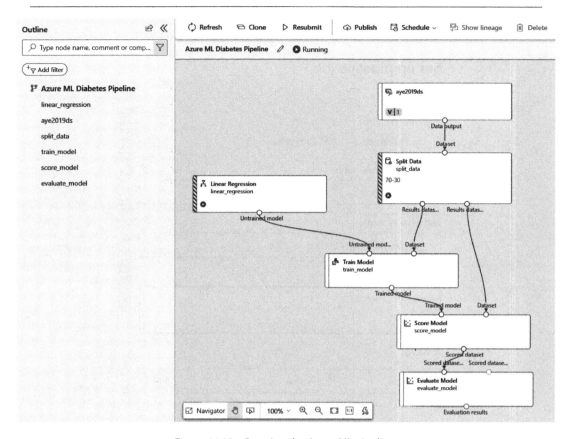

Figure 14.13 – Running the Azure ML pipeline

After a while, the pipeline will be fully executed and all the components will turn green, as shown in *Figure 14.14*:

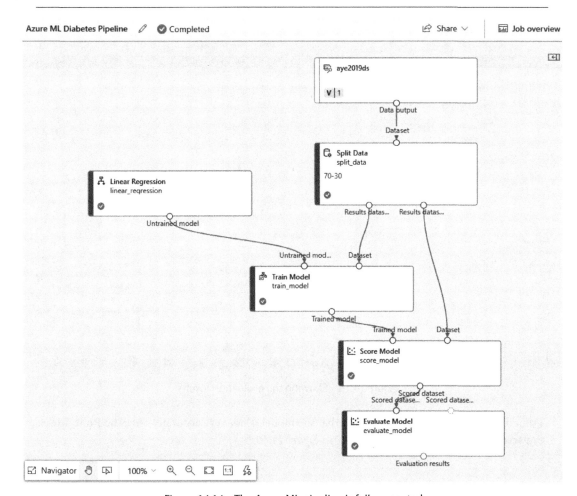

Figure 14.14 – The Azure ML pipeline is fully executed

Right-click the **Evaluation model** module and go to **Preview data | Evaluation results**, as shown in *Figure 14.15*:

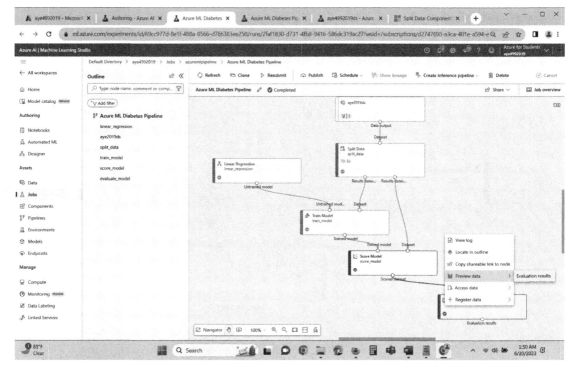

Figure 14.15 – Showing the evaluation results

From the evaluation results, we can see that the model is not very accurate, since the **Root_Mean_Squared_Error** value is high (around 57 in *Figure 14.16*):

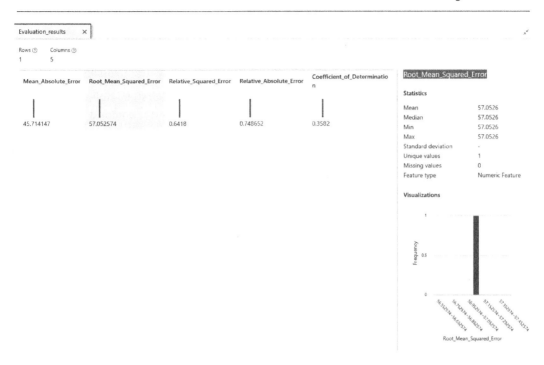

Figure 14.16 – Evaluate the model results

From the model evaluation data, we can see that the ML model needs to be worked on further to improve its accuracy. Nevertheless, we have successfully created and executed an Azure ML pipeline, from dataset creation to model training to model evaluation. This is a great achievement that you should be very proud of. In the next section, we will look at the second aspect of Azure ML: Azure Cognitive Services.

Azure Cognitive Services

Azure Cognitive Services is a collection of cloud-based AI services provided by Microsoft Azure. Like AWS AI services and Google AI APIs, Azure Cognitive Services offers pre-built AI capabilities that can be easily integrated into applications, thus allowing developers to enhance their applications with intelligent features using pre-trained AI algorithms. Some key features of Azure Cognitive Services are the following:

- **Vision**: Azure Cognitive Services includes Computer Vision, which can analyze images and extract information such as objects, texts, and facial expressions. The Face service enables facial detection, recognition, and emotion analysis, and the custom vision option allows you to train custom image classification models.

- **Speech**: The Speech service provides speech recognition, text-to-speech, and speech translation capabilities.

- **Language**: Azure offers several language-related services. Text Analytics performs sentiment analysis, key phrase extraction, and entity recognition. Language Understanding enables natural language understanding and intent recognition. Translator provides text translation in real time.

- **Knowledge**: *Q&A Maker* enables you to create conversational question-and-answer systems from existing content. *Knowledge mining* helps extract information and insights from unstructured documents.

- **Decision**: This service allows you to create personalized recommendations and content rankings based on user preferences. Anomaly Detector helps identify anomalies and outliers in time-series data.

- **Form Recognizer**: This service can extract information from forms and structured documents including invoices, receipts, and contracts.

By leveraging Azure Cognitive Services, developers can add powerful AI capabilities to their applications without extensive AI expertise, and build intelligent and user-friendly applications faster. *Figure 14.17* summarizes the Azure Cognitive Services offerings and their use cases:

Azure Cognitive Services

Infuse your apps, websites, and bots with human-like intelligence

Vision	Speech	Language	Knowledge	Search
Object, scene, and activity detection	Speech transcription (Speech-to-text)	Language detection	Q&A extraction from unstructured text	Ad-free web, news, image, and video search results
Face recognition and identification	Speech Synthesis (Text-to-speech)	Text sentiment analysis	Knowledge base creation from collections of Q&As	Trends for video, news
Celebrity and landmark recognition	Real-time speech translation	Key phrase extraction	Semantic matching for knowledge bases	Image identification, classification and knowledge extraction
Emotion recognition	Speaker identification and verification	Entity recognition	Speaker identification and verification	Identification of similar images and products
Text and handwriting recognition (OCR)	Custom Speech models for transcription and translation	Spell checking	Customizable content personalization learning	Named entity recognition and classification
Video metadata, audio, and keyframe extraction and analysis	Custom voice	Explicit or offensive text content moderation, PII detection		Knowledge acquisition for named entities
Explicit or offensive content moderation		Text translation		Search query autosuggest
Custom image recognition		Customizable text translation		Ad-free custom search engine creation
		Contextual language understanding		

Figure 14.17 – Azure Cognitive Services summary

In the next section, we will explore Azure OpenAI Service.

Azure OpenAI Service

Azure OpenAI Service is newly launched at the time of writing this book. Azure OpenAI Service supports many common AI workloads including ML, computer vision, NLP, conversational AI, anomaly detection, and knowledge mining. It also supports generative AI tasks including the following:

- **Generating natural language**:

  - Text completion: generate and edit text

  - Embeddings: search, classify, and compare text

- **Generating code: generate, edit, and explain code**

- **Generating images: generate and edit images**

We will explore some of these tasks now:

1. Create an **Azure OpenAI** resource:

    Log in to the Azure portal and choose **Azure OpenAI**. Click **Create Azure OpenAI**. Fill in the basics as shown in *Figure 14.18*:

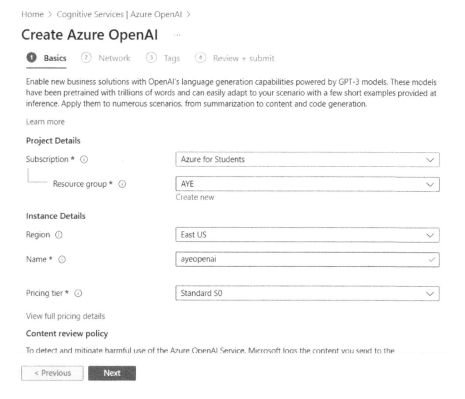

Figure 14.18 – Create Azure OpenAI

2.   Get into Azure OpenAI:

Click the **ayeopenai** resource we have created to enter the Azure OpenAI landing page, where you can explore, develop, and deploy the OpenAI solutions, as shown in *Figure 14.19*:

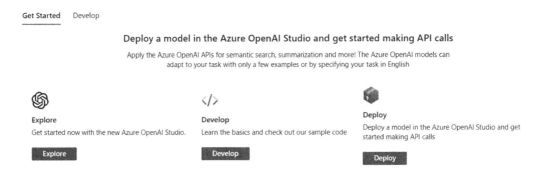

Figure 14.19 – Azure OpenAI landing page

3.   Explore Azure OpenAI Studio:

Click **Explore** and it will bring you to the OpenAI Studio landing page, which looks like something shown in *Figure 14.20* at the time of writing:

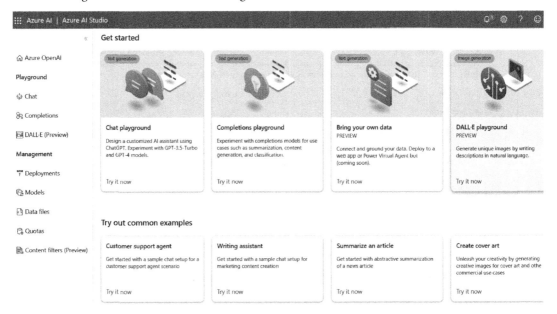

Figure 14.20 – Azure OpenAI Studio landing page

Next, we will demonstrate how to use the **Azure OpenAI Codex** models to generate some code.

Go to **Azure OpenAI Studio | Management | Deployments | Create New Deployment**. Choose **code-davinci-002** from the drop-down menu and create a deployment named `testing`, as shown in *Figure 14.21*:

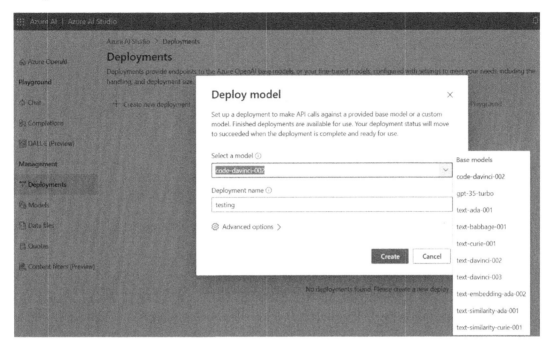

Figure 14.21 – Deploying a model on Azure OpenAI Studio

Go to **Azure OpenAI Studio | Playground | Completions**. The **testing** deployment will be shown, meaning you can now play with it. *Figure 14.22* shows how, after typing `Generate a python loop that lists the prime numbers from 1 to 100` and clicking **Generate**, it will generate a code snippet:

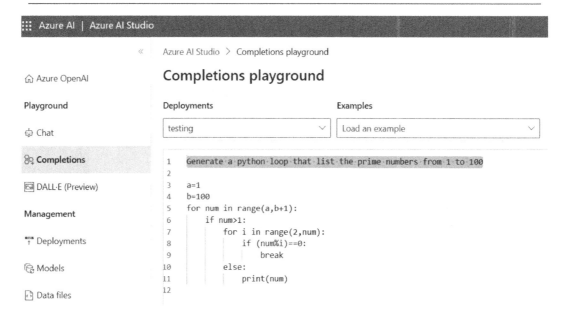

Figure 14.22 – Trying out Azure OpenAI Studio Codex

Next, we will demonstrate how to use **Azure OpenAI DALL.E** to generate some pictures.

Go to **Azure OpenAI Studio | Playground | DALL.E (Preview)**.

Enter the prompt a beach front house facing the ocean with modern structures, click **Generate**, and watch as a picture is generated, as shown in *Figure 14.23*:

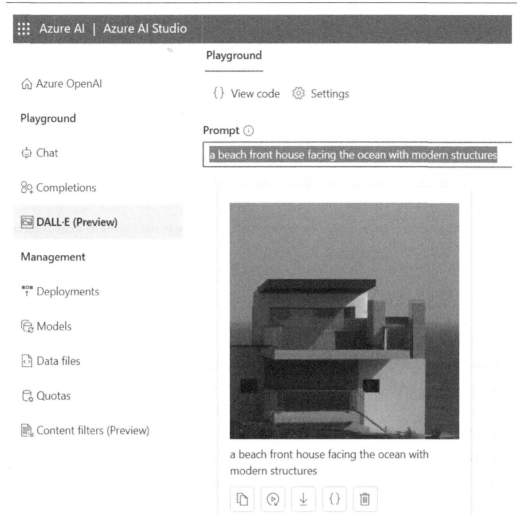

Figure 14.23 – Testing Azure OpenAI Studio DALL.E

We have examined some of the Azure OpenAI Services currently available. Since the OpenAI Service offerings are new and evolve every day, please keep coming back and checking out what's on offer in the Azure portal – you will be sure to have more surprises!

And with that, we can end our discussion of Azure OpenAI.

Summary

In this chapter, we focused on three main topics of machine learning in Azure. We started with the Azure ML workspace, which is an end-to-end ML development suite. Next, we looked at Azure Cognitive Services, which allows us to leverage prebuilt ML models for application development. Lastly, we checked out Azure OpenAI Service, which provides access to GPT-3, Codex, DALL·E, and other pretrained **Large Language Models** (**LLMs**). By the end of this chapter, you have learned the basic concepts of Azure ML and acquired the necessary skills for ML model training and application development using the Azure AI services. In the next chapter, we will discuss Azure cloud security.

Practice questions

1. A cloud engineer team need access to the Azure ML workspace to run a script as a job. What role should they be granted?

    A. Azure ML Data Scientist

    B. Azure ML Compute Operator

    C. Reader

    D. Contributor

2. A cloud engineer team need to run a single script to train a model. What job best fits their requirements?

    A. command

    B. pipeline

    C. sweep

    D. archive

3. And what role should they be assigned?

    A. Azure ML Data Scientist

    B. Azure ML Compute Operator

    C. Reader

    D. Contributor

4. A cloud engineer team need to create/delete Azure ML registries. What role should they be assigned?

    A. Azure ML Data Scientist

    B. Azure ML Compute Operator

    C. Reader

    D. Contributor

Questions 5-8 are based on the following use case:

A cloud engineer is developing applications using Azure Cognitive Services to extract insights from unstructured text. The cloud engineer has created some Azure Cognitive Services resources.

5. The messages between the application and a Cognitive Services resource are transmitted using a REST API. What format should be used for the messages?

    A. XML

    B. JSON

    C. HTML

    D. TEXT

6. How will the applications access the Cognitive Services endpoint?

    A. The application uses a valid subscription key for the Azure resource.

    B. The application user enters a username and password.

    C. Access is granted to anonymous users by default.

    D. Use Azure Key Vault.

7. How does one manage access to the Azure Cognitive Services resources?

    A. Azure Firewall.

    B. Allow traffic from all internal VNets.

    C. Deny traffic from all external networks.

    D. Use Zero-Trust principles.

8. Which Azure Cognitive Services offering should the cloud engineer use?

    A. Azure Text Analytics

    B. Azure Speech to Text

    C. Azure Translator Text

    D. **Azure Language Understanding (LUIS)**

Question 9-10 are based on the following use case:

A lawyer wants to summarize the many cases they have worked on over the past 30 years using Azure OpenAI.

9. What OpenAI Service offering should the lawyer use?

    A. GPT

    B. Codex

    C. DALL·E

    D. Deep Learning

10. What API should the lawyer use?

      A. The Azure Text Analytics API

      B. The Azure NLP API

      C. The Azure OpenAI API

      D. The Azure Cognitive Services API

Answers to the practice questions

1. A

2. A

3. B

4. D

5. B

6. A

7. A

8. A

9. A

10. C

Further reading

For further insights into what you've learned in this chapter, refer to the following links:

- https://learn.microsoft.com/en-us/azure/machine-learning/
- https://azure.microsoft.com/en-in/products/machine-learning
- https://azure.microsoft.com/en-us/products/cognitive-services
- https://learn.microsoft.com/en-us/azure/cognitive-services/
- https://azure.microsoft.com/en-us/products/cognitive-services/openai-service
- https://learn.microsoft.com/en-us/azure/cognitive-services/openai/
- https://learn.microsoft.com/en-us/azure/cognitive-services/openai/concepts/models
- https://azure.microsoft.com/en-us/blog/product/azure-openai-service/

15

Azure Cloud Security Services

In *Chapter 7* of the book, we discussed Amazon cloud security, learned the cloud security concepts, and looked at a case study about auto threat detection and remediation in the AWS cloud. In *Chapter 11* of the book, we explored Google Cloud security measurements and practices, highlighting GCP Security Command Center, which is the most comprehensive security service/tool in Google Cloud. Now, based on our knowledge of cloud security and the Azure cloud, we will go a level up and discuss some advanced cloud security topics related to the Azure cloud. We will first summarize the best practices in Azure cloud security, then discuss the reference architecture of Azure cloud security, and finally, conduct an Azure security case study.

In this chapter, we will cover the following topics:

- **Azure cloud security best practices**, including Azure cloud security center, **Identity Access Management (IAM)**, **Virtual Machine (VM)** protection, network protection, and data security in the Azure cloud

- **Azure cloud security reference architecture**, including Azure cloud security structures and integrations, Azure-native **Security Information and Event Management (SIEM)**, and **Security Orchestration, Automation, and Response (SOAR)** solutions

- An **Azure cloud security case study** of a real-life project that expands existing Azure infrastructure and deploys Palo Alto **Next-Generation Firewall (NGFW)** virtual appliances in the Azure cloud

Now, let's get started!

Azure cloud security best practices

Azure cloud security includes *security of the cloud*, which is the service provider's responsibility, and *security in the cloud*, which is the consumer's responsibility. We will summarize Azure cloud security best practices, including Azure Security Center, IAM, VM security, vNet security, data security, encryption, and privacy.

Azure Security Center

Azure Security Center provides a unified view of Azure cloud resources and offers security recommendations to help you strengthen your security posture. It should be enabled for all Azure subscriptions and resources. We recommend the following Azure Security Center best practices:

- Regularly review and implement Azure Security Center recommendations, which are based on security industry best practices and, thus, can help you address cloud security vulnerabilities and misconfigurations.

- Regularly review Security Center alerts and apply the latest patches and updates to Azure cloud resources. Automate patch management processes with Azure security and DevOps tools.

- Set up an Azure security policy to define and enforce specific security rules and policies for Azure resources.

- Configure **Just-In-Time** (**JIT**) access to restrict access to Azure VMs and other resources within certain network ports and limited time windows, thus reducing the cloud attack surface.

- Enable Azure Defender for all Azure resources to detect and defend against cloud threats effectively.

- Follow the security principle of least privilege in access management and application design. Regularly review and manage cloud accesses, leveraging Azure Active Directory and IAM roles.

- Enable Azure Monitor and Azure Sentinel to collect and analyze logs from Azure cloud resources. Set up alerts and create custom dashboards to gain visibility into potential security incidents.

- Keep up to date with Azure Security Center's documentation, Azure security blogs, and forums to adopt the latest cloud security recommendations.

We recommend leveraging Azure Security Center to centrally manage Azure cloud security services, since it provides a holistic view of cloud assets and integrates with other services smoothly.

Azure IAM

Azure IAM manages the **Authentication, Authorization, and Auditing** (**AAA**) of the Azure cloud. We recommend the following IAM best practices:

- Leverage Azure Active Directory as the central identity management service to enforce authentication and authorization of users, groups, and applications in the cloud.

- Enforce **Multi-Factor Authentication** (**MFA**) for all Azure cloud accounts.

- Ensure that all Azure credentials, including passwords, certificates, and API keys, are rotated regularly to minimize unauthorized access risks due to compromised credentials.

- Follow the principle of least privilege and grant users and services only the permissions necessary to perform their tasks.

- Leverage **Role-Based Access Control** (**RBAC**) to grant granular permissions to cloud identities. Use built-in roles with predefined permissions and create custom roles to tailor specific needs.

- Leverage Azure **Privileged Identity Management** (**PIM**) for time-bound and approval-based privileged access to Azure resources.

- Leverage **conditional access** policies and manage access based on various conditions, such as user location, device type, and risk level. Ensure access is granted only under specific secure conditions.

- Leverage Azure service principles to authenticate applications and services. Protect service principals with appropriate RBAC roles. Manage the credentials securely and review their permissions regularly.

- Enable Azure Monitor and Azure Sentinel to collect, correlate, and analyze cloud logs related to authentication events and user activities. Set up alerts and implement anomaly detections to identify potential security threats.

By following these Azure IAM best practices, you can establish a robust and secure IAM framework in an Azure environment.

Azure cloud VM protection

Protecting Azure cloud VMs is a very important part of cloud security. We recommend the following best practices for Azure VM protection:

- Review and implement the VM recommendations in Security Center.

- Implement JIT access to limit VM access to specific ports and defined periods.

- Implement disk encryption on VM disks for an additional layer of data protection.

- Implement antimalware protection to protect VMs from malware, viruses, and other malicious threats.

- Implement regular backups of VMs to ensure VM recovery from accidental deletion, data corruption, or other disasters.

- Implement RBAC to control access to VMs. Ensure users and applications have only the necessary permissions to perform tasks. Periodically review and audit these permissions.

- Leverage **Network Security Groups** (**NSGs**) to control Azure VM inbound and outbound traffic. Allow only necessary network traffic.

- Leverage Azure Firewall or **Network Virtual Appliances** (**NVAs**) to add an extra layer of protection to VMs.

- Leverage Azure Monitor for VM monitoring and logging. Leverage Azure Sentinel for advanced threat detection, log analytics, and security incident management.

Following these best practices will ensure a strong security foundation for Azure VMs and protect them from various threats and vulnerabilities.

Azure cloud network protection

Protecting Azure **VNets** is essential for Azure cloud infrastructure security. Here are the best practices for Azure network security:

- Divide a VNet into subnets and apply appropriate security controls based on workload requirements. Implement network segmentation to isolate resources, control traffic flow, and minimize the blast radius if there is a security breach.

- Leverage VNet peering to establish connectivity between VNets in a secure and controlled manner, allowing only necessary traffic flows.

- Leverage NSGs to control inbound and outbound traffic at the subnet and network interface level. Regularly review and update NSG rules based on changing requirements.

- Leverage Azure Firewall to centrally manage and enforce security policies across multiple subnets and virtual networks.

- Leverage NVAs to add a layer of security with advanced network filtering, threat intelligence, and security features.

- Leverage a **Virtual Private Network** (**VPN**) or Azure ExpressRoute to establish secure connectivity between on-premises networks and a cloud VNet.

- Implement Azure private endpoints to secure access to Azure services by mapping them to private IP addresses within VNets.

- Implement Azure VNet service endpoints to secure access to Azure services, such as Azure Storage and Azure Databases, from within VNets.

- Enable Azure Network Watcher to monitor and capture network traffic within VNets. Use Azure Monitor and Azure Sentinel to collect/analyze logs and detect potential security incidents, anomalies, or suspicious activities.

- Enable Azure DDoS Protection Standard to protect VNets against **Distributed Denial of Service** (**DDoS**) attacks.

By following these best practices, you can establish a secure and well-protected Azure networking environment.

Azure data protection

Protecting data in Azure is of utmost importance to maintain its confidentiality, integrity, and availability. We recommend the following best practices for Azure data protection:

- Implement data classification based on data sensitivity and regulatory requirements. Identify sensitive data elements, classify them, and apply appropriate security controls accordingly.

- Implement RBAC to control access to Azure resources and data. Assign permissions with the principle of least privilege.

- Regularly back up data to ensure that the critical data is protected and can be restored in any data loss events.

- Establish data retention and deletion policies in compliance with regulatory requirements.

- Enable data encryptions at rest and in transit, whenever and wherever possible. Implement Azure Key Vault for encryption key management.

- Enable Azure Monitor and Azure Sentinel to capture and analyze logs related to data access and activities. Set up alerts and implement anomaly detection to identify potential security incidents or data breaches.

- Use Azure Information Protection and Azure **Data Loss Prevention** (**DLP**) policies to prevent the accidental or unauthorized disclosure of sensitive data.

- Conduct regular security assessments, vulnerability scans, and penetration tests to identify and address any data security weaknesses or vulnerabilities in a cloud environment.

We strongly recommend following the preceding security guidelines for IAM and Security Center to protect Azure cloud VMs, networks, and data. In the next section, we will discuss the related cloud security reference architectures.

Azure cloud security reference architectures

A security reference architecture suggests the optimal delivery of specific technologies to solve certain problems. There are many solution architectures for Azure cloud security, and we will focus on two subjects – Azure hybrid infrastructure, Azure SIEM and SOAR.

Azure hybrid cloud infrastructure

The **Azure hybrid cloud infrastructure** architecture is a framework provided by Microsoft to guide organizations in designing and implementing a hybrid cloud environment. It combines the capabilities of on-premises infrastructure with Azure cloud services, enabling seamless integration, scalability, and flexibility. *Figure 15.1* shows an Azure hybrid cloud infrastructure:

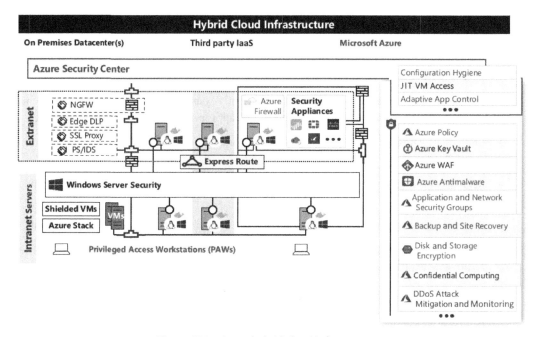

Figure 15.1 – Azure hybrid cloud infrastructure

The key components and concepts are the following:

- **On-premises infrastructure** includes existing data centers, servers, networking equipment, and other resources of an on-premises environment.

- **Azure cloud infrastructure** includes VNets, cloud storage, cloud VMs, cloud databases, cloud load balancers, scale sets, and other cloud resources.

- **ExpressRoute** enables a private and dedicated connection between on-premises infrastructure and the Azure cloud, with high bandwidth, low latency, and better security, ensuring a reliable and consistent hybrid cloud experience.

- **The intranet services** provide security to internal resources such as VMs, windows and Linux stations/services, VMware, and privileged workstations.

- **The extranet resources** provide controlled access to authorized customers, vendors, partners, or others outside the company.

- **Azure Firewall and third-party security appliances** provide an extra layer of security for both on-premises and cloud resources.

- **Azure Active Directory** (**AAD**) is a cloud-based identity and access management service to manage user identities and access controls. It enables single sign-on across a hybrid environment.

- **Azure Security Center** provides centralized monitoring and management for hybrid infrastructure, including VMs, applications, and network resources, to help you gain insights, detect issues, and optimize performance.

These are some core components and services commonly included in an Azure hybrid cloud infrastructure reference architecture. A secure infrastructure will depend on the specific requirements, the existing infrastructure, and the desired outcomes.

Azure SIEM and SOAR

Microsoft provides many cloud services to implement SIEM and SOAR capabilities. *Figure 15.2* shows an Azure SIEM and SOAR reference architecture.

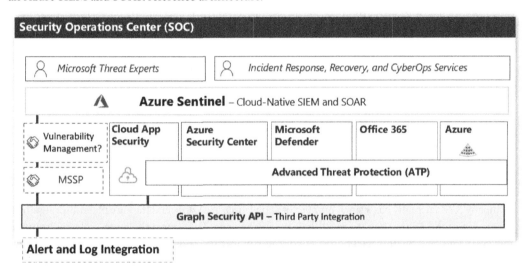

Figure 15.2 – Azure SIEM and SOAR

As shown in *Figure 15.2*, the main components of an Azure SIEM/SOAR solution include the following:

- Data sources from the Azure cloud (AAD, Azure Security Center, Azure Monitor, etc.), on-premises systems, network devices, and third-party applications. These data sources generate security events and logs.

- Azure Security Center provides cloud security posture management and threat protection for data resources. It integrates with Azure Monitor, Azure Sentinel, and other security services for threat detection and incident response.

- Azure Log Analytics is a central component that collects, stores, and analyzes logs and events from diverse sources. It provides a scalable and secure repository to store security data.

- Azure Sentinel is a cloud-native SIEM solution built on Azure Log Analytics. It aggregates and correlates security data from multiple sources, applies advanced analytics and machine learning, and provides real-time threat detection, investigation, and response capabilities.

- Azure Functions is a serverless computing service that allows you to run custom code in response to events.

- Azure Logic Apps is an orchestration service that allows you to automate workflows and integrate various systems and applications.

- Azure Monitor integrates with Azure Sentinel to provide additional monitoring and alerting capabilities. It collects performance and operational data from Azure resources, enabling the detection of suspicious activities and a proactive response.

- Azure Power BI integration can create custom dashboards and reports for security monitoring, incident tracking, and compliance reporting.

When designing the SIEM and SOAR architecture in Azure, you need to consider the specific security needs, compliance requirements, scalability, and operational environment in the organization, and optimize the whole organizational **Security Operation Center** (**SOC**) framework.

After the Azure cloud security best practice and reference architecture discussions, we will now present a real-life Azure infrastructure case.

An Azure cloud security case study

Company XYZ currently has a small number of applications in Azure, and they are planning a significant expansion of the Azure cloud to meet their business needs. To support the large-scale environment, they are building a flexible backbone network to support the connectivity between the Azure cloud and on-prem resources, with a robust security solution to partition internet-facing networks from an intranet environment. In this case study of Company XYZ's cloud deployment project, we will focus on two aspects – cloud infrastructure security and network security.

Organizational infrastructure security

Based on the customer environment, we will architect an organization infrastructure hierarchy of Azure management groups and subscriptions.

Management groups

The Azure **management group** is at the top of the Azure resource management hierarchy. Permissions and policies applied at a management group will flow to all objects below it, including the subscriptions.

Subscriptions

Two subscriptions are designed under the infrastructure management group:

- **Subscription one** is for security functions, including Virtual WAN, Palo Alto supporting components, and associated monitoring components

- **Subscription two** is for common IT functions, such as extending traditional AD domain controllers, DNS zones, and other *back office*-supporting services that are not typically managed by application teams

Policy recommendations

For Company XYZ, we recommend a base policy at the root management group – *network interfaces should not have public IPs*.

This policy will block the creation of public IP addresses attached to network interfaces of the VMs under the root management group. Additional policies include the automatic provisioning of the dependency agent and network watcher agents across VMs in the environment.

Networking infrastructure security

We will design Azure networking with virtual WANs. In *Chapter 12*, we explored the concept of a **virtual WAN** (**VWAN**) and implemented a VWAN infrastructure with the hub-spoke architecture. Here, we will utilize the VWAN features and design two VWANs – the **trusted VWAN** and the **DMZ VWAN**. Each VWAN maintains one hub in each of the US-east and US-south-central regions with the following fictitious IP address ranges:

- Trusted VWAN (111.182.0.0/16): Each VWAN hub acts as a gateway for ExpressRoutes, site-to-site VPNs, and user VPNs, each of which is managed as a separate component of the VWAN hub:

  - East US hub: (111.182.128.0/24 – hub)

  - South Central US hub: (111.182.0.0/24 – hub)

- DMZ VWAN (111.183.0.0/16):

  - East US hub: (111.183.128.0/24 - hub)

  - South Central US hub: (111.183.0.0/24 – hub)

As shown in *Figure 15.3*, we will design the Azure networking for the segregation of trusted and untrusted traffic, with Palo Alto firewalls acting as a boundary between the two traffics – the yrusted VWAN and the DMZ VWAN.

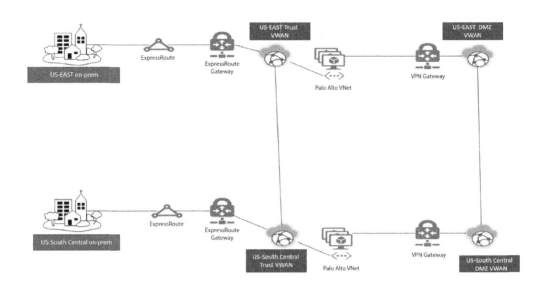

Figure 15.3 – Azure VWAN networking security

Palo Alto networks offer a range of firewall models, including physical appliances, virtual appliances, and cloud-native solutions. Palo Alto firewalls combine traditional firewall functionalities with advanced security features, such as an intrusion prevention system, antivirus, URL filtering, and application awareness, thus enabling granular visibility and control of network traffic at the application, user, and content levels. The deployment of Palo Alto virtual appliances in the Azure network is a key feature in this case study.

Palo Alto networks

We design the Palo Alto networks as:

- US-East: (`111.182.1.0/24`)
- US-South Central: (`111.182.129.0/24`)

The Palo Alto devices/appliances are ultimately VMs deployed to Azure, and they have some limitations – a VM can contain multiple network links, but they must all connect to the same vNet, even though they can connect to different subnets within that vNet. So, we will design a Palo Alto VNet that has four subnets, and the appliance VM has network links that connect to the subnets.

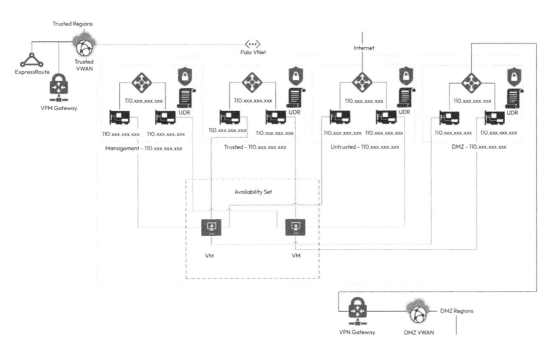

Figure 15.4 – Palo Alto virtual Appliance Architecture

As shown in *Figure 15.4*, the Palo Alto appliance VMs are in an Azure Availability set (to avoid a single point of failure). Each VM connects to four subnets of the Palo Alto VNet, with one subnet for each security zone:

- The management subnet
- The trusted subnet that connects to the trusted VWAN/VNets
- The untrusted subnet that connects to the untrusted internet
- The DMZ subnet that connects to the DMZ VWAN/VNet

By leveraging the Palo Alto virtual appliance firewalls to separate the trusted traffic in the trusted VWAN from the untrusted traffic in the DMZ VWAN, we greatly improve cloud security in the Azure environment.

Summary

In this chapter, we summarized the Azure cloud security best practices to use IAM services and Azure Security Center, manage VMs and vNets, and secure cloud data. We focused on two Azure security reference architectures – the Azure hybrid cloud infrastructure, and the Azure SIEM and

SOAR framework. Finally, we conducted a case study where we designed and implemented a VWAN security architecture, with Palo Alto virtual appliances separating the trusted and untrusted traffic.

This chapter ends the third part of the book, *Azure Cloud*. In this part, we covered the Azure cloud by exploring its foundation services of compute, storage, and network; the data services of databases and big data; the ML services of the Azure ML workspace and cognitive services; and the cloud security services. Since we already discussed the AWS and Google clouds in *Part 1* and *Part 2* of the book, we discussed more advanced cloud services and complicated case studies in this third part, aiming to expand our cloud journey.

In the next chapter, we will start *Part 4* of the book – building a successful career in cloud computing.

Practice questions

1. What is Azure Security Center primarily designed for?

    A. Secure network traffic encryption

    B. Data loss prevention

    C. Threat detection and security posture management

    D. Physical data center security

2. Which service provides secure access management and single sign-on for Azure resources?

    A. AAD

    B. Azure Security Center

    C. Azure Key Vault

    D. Azure Information Protection

3. Which Azure service offers managed encryption keys to protect data at rest?

    A. Azure Key Vault

    B. Azure Security Center

    C. Azure Information Protection

    D. Azure Monitor

4. The Azure DDoS Protection standard provides protection against which type of attacks?

    A. Application-layer attacks

    B. Phishing attacks

    C. Insider threats

    D. Social engineering attacks

5. Which Azure service helps to scan and assess the security vulnerabilities of VMs?

   A. Azure Security Center

   B. AAD

   C. Azure Sentinel

   D. Azure Firewall

6. Which Azure service provides secure access to VMs without exposing public IP addresses?

   A. Azure Key Vault

   B. Azure Virtual Network

   C. Azure Load Balancer

   D. Azure Bastion

7. Azure Monitor helps to monitor and alert for which of the following?

   A. Security events and incidents

   B. Network bandwidth usage

   C. VM performance

   D. Data replication status

8. Azure Firewall provides which of the following capabilities?

   A. **Network Address Translation (NAT)**

   B. VPN connectivity

   C. Load balancing

   D. Application-level filtering and threat intelligence

9. Azure AD Privileged Identity Management helps to manage which type of accounts?

   A. Standard user accounts

   B. Guest accounts

   C. Service accounts with administrative privileges

   D. Service accounts with limited access

10. Azure Sentinel is a cloud-native SIEM solution that integrates with which other Azure service?

   A. Azure Security Center

   B. Azure Key Vault

   C. Azure Active Directory

   D. Azure Virtual Network

Answers to the practice questions

1. C

2. A

3. A

4. A

5. A

6. D

7. A

8. D

9. C

10. A

Further reading

For further insights into what you've learned in this chapter, refer to the following links:

- `https://azure.microsoft.com/en-us/products/category/identity`
- `https://azure.microsoft.com/en-us/products/active-directory`
- `https://learn.microsoft.com/en-us/azure/storage/blobs/data-protection-overview`
- `https://learn.microsoft.com/en-us/azure/security/fundamentals/virtual-machines-overview`
- `https://learn.microsoft.com/en-us/azure/security/fundamentals/network-overview`
- `https://learn.microsoft.com/en-us/training/modules/use-microsoft-cybersecurity-reference-architecture-azure-security-benchmarks/`
- `https://learn.microsoft.com/en-us/azure/virtual-wan/virtual-wan-about`
- `https://learn.microsoft.com/en-us/security/benchmark/azure/baselines/virtual-wan-security-baseline`

Part 4:
Developing a
Successful Cloud Career

In this part, we will focus on achieving cloud certifications and developing a cloud career. We will introduce cloud certification roadmaps and exam-taking strategies. We will study cloud certification exam questions represented by seven certification tracks at various levels. In the last chapter, we will discuss the cloud job market and the soft skills required for a cloud career. I will also share my own cloud journey.

This part comprises the following chapters:

- *Chapter 16, Achieving Cloud Certification*
- *Chapter 17, Building a Successful Cloud Computing Career*

16

Achieving Cloud Certifications

Yes! You have completed all the chapters of the book!

After a full exploration of the three clouds of AWS, GCP, and Azure, it's time for us to integrate our knowledge and skills, which is the goal of *Part 4* of the book – achieving cloud certifications and developing a successful cloud career.

First things first – we will explore cloud certifications in this chapter, as outlined here:

*   Reviewing cloud certification roadmaps for AWS, Azure, and GCP

*   Developing strategies to crack the cloud certification exams

*   Practicing and analyzing sample questions for some certification exams

Achieving cloud certifications is a very important step of your cloud learning journey, and the process of preparing, taking, and passing the certification exams provides a great opportunity for you to review the contents in the book, integrate them, and comprehend the clouds systematically.

Reviewing the certification roadmaps

Let's look at the certification map for each of the three clouds.

AWS cloud certifications

The certification roadmap for AWS consists of three levels:

*   At the foundation level is the **AWS Cloud Practitioner certification** – this is designed for individuals who have a basic understanding of AWS services and want to demonstrate their essential knowledge of the AWS cloud.

*   At the middle level are the **AWS Cloud Associate certifications** – these include **Solutions Architect Associate**, **Developer Associate**, and **SysOps Administrator Associate**. This level of certification is designed for individuals who have a good understanding of AWS services and

want to demonstrate their associate-level knowledge and skills in the AWS cloud in the areas of solution design, application development, and service deployment/management/operations.

- At the top level are the **AWS Cloud Professional certifications** – these include **Solutions Architect Professional** and **DevOps Engineer**. These certifications are designed for individuals who have a comprehensive grasp of AWS services and want to demonstrate their professional knowledge and skills in solution designing and DevOps engineering in the AWS cloud.

Figure 16.1 presents the AWS cloud certification roadmap:

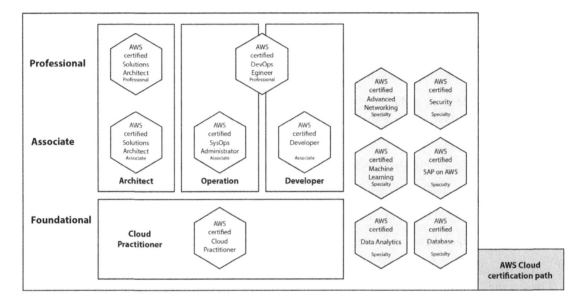

Figure 16.1 – The AWS cloud certification roadmap

As we can see from *Figure 16.1*, there is another level called **AWS Specialty certifications**, which is tailored for individuals with more specialized knowledge and expertise in specific AWS areas. These certifications validate your advanced skills in particular AWS cloud domains (which currently include Advanced Networking, Security, Database, Data Analytics, and Machine Learning) and can help differentiate you in the cloud specialty market.

More details about AWS certifications can be found at `https://aws.amazon.com/certification/`.

Google Cloud certifications

Like AWS, the certification roadmap for GCP consists of three levels:

- At the foundation level is the **Google Digital Leader certification** – this is designed for individuals who have a basic understanding and skills of GCP services.

- At the middle level are the **Google Associate Cloud Engineer certifications** – these are for individuals who have experience working with GCP and want to demonstrate their associate level of knowledge and skills in Google Cloud.

- At the top level are the **Google Cloud Professional certifications** – these include **Cloud Architect**, **Cloud Developer**, and **Cloud DevOps Engineer**. These certifications are designed for individuals who have a comprehensive understanding of Google Cloud services and want to demonstrate their professional knowledge and skills in GCP solution design, application development, and DevOps engineering.

Figure 16.2 shows the GCP certification roadmap. The GCP specialty certifications are designed for individuals with more specialized knowledge and skills in specific GCP areas, including networking, security, database, data analytics, cloud collaboration, and machine learning:

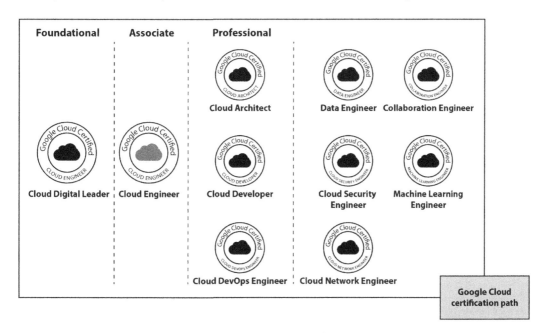

Figure 16.2 – The Google Cloud certification roadmap

More details about GCP certifications can be found at `https://cloud.google.com/learn/certification/`.

Microsoft Azure Cloud certifications

The Azure cloud certification roadmap also consists of three levels:

- At the foundation level is the **Foundations certification** – this is designed for individuals who have a basic knowledge and skills of Azure cloud services. There are three certification exams at this level – **Azure Foundations**, **AI Foundations**, and **Data Foundations**.

- At the middle level are the **Azure Cloud Associate certifications** – these are designed for individuals who have experience working with the Azure cloud and want to demonstrate their foundational knowledge and skills to deploy, monitor, and manage applications in the Azure cloud.

- At the top level are the **Azure Cloud Expert certifications** – these include **Cloud Architect** and **DevOps Engineer**. These certifications are designed for individuals who have an expert level of Azure cloud services and want to demonstrate their professional knowledge and skills in Azure solution design and DevOps engineering.

Microsoft also has Azure cloud **Specialty certifications** in the areas of networking, security, database, data analytics, and machine learning, as shown in *Figure 16.3*:

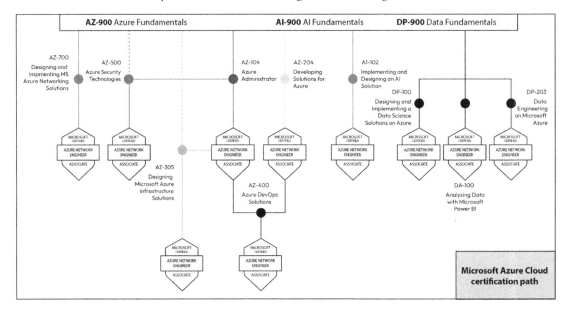

Figure 16.3 – The Microsoft Azure cloud certification roadmap

More details about Microsoft and Azure certifications can be found at `https://learn.microsoft.com/en-us/certifications/`.

Developing cloud certification strategies

The general certification strategy is to *divide and conquer*. For each exam, have a full understanding of the certification exam scope and requirements, and practice as much as you can. To help you prepare for the certification exams, we have collected some practice questions at different levels for the three clouds, along with an analysis of the questions.

We recommend you follow the following steps to prepare for a cloud certification exam:

1. Read the official certification exam guides.

2. Review the chapters in this book that relate to the exam.

3. Complete the hands-on labs in this book that relate to the exam.

4. Study the related practice questions in this chapter.

For each cloud, starting from the foundation level, complete the exams, one by one.

Cloud certification exam practice questions

While we cannot cover all the certification exam questions, we have chosen the following certifications:

- Google Cloud Digital Leader

- Google Cloud Associate Engineer

- Google Cloud Professional Security Engineer

- AWS Cloud Practitioner

- AWS Data Analytics

- Microsoft Azure AI Foundations

- Microsoft Azure AI Engineer

For each of the preceding certifications, we have listed some practice questions, answers, and analytics. For each question in the following sections, please fully understand what it is asking and, out of all the answers provided, why the right answer is right, and the wrong answers are wrong, and make sure you comprehend the analytics of each question.

Google Cloud Digital Leader certification

1. A data science team is designing a Google Cloud service to serve a company's customers worldwide as soon as possible. However, some data is required to be in a specific geographic area. Which of the following is the best option?

   A. A public cloud with services only active in the required geographic area

   B. A private cloud with services only active in the required geographic area

   C. A public cloud with services available in the required geographic area

   D. A private cloud with services available in the required geographic area

   Analysis: The question asks you to choose a worldwide cloud service as soon as possible, so a public cloud with services available in the required areas is the best option. Answer C is the answer.

2. A data science team needs to identify all VMs that have a security vulnerability, among the company's 10,000 VMs in the Google cloud. What's the best way to achieve this?

    A. Use Compliance Reports Manager to download a recent audit report.

    B. Use **Security Command Center** (**SCC**) to identify VMs that do not have up-to-date patches.

    C. Use Terraform to generate and download a SOC 1 audit report.

    D. Use SCC to list all VMs with vulnerable disk images.

    Analysis: This question is about VM security management in Google Cloud. SCC is the best option to identify the vulnerable OS here, so the answer is D.

3. A data science team is designing a GCP cluster, which must have resilience, and its VM nodes must communicate with each other in less than 10 milliseconds. How shall they design the cluster nodes?

    A. In a single zone within a single region

    B. In multiple zones within a single region

    C. In multiple regions, with one zone per region

    D. In multiple regions, with multiple zones per region

    Analysis: This question tests the GCP region/zone concepts. The communication requirement restricts the nodes to be in a single region, and the resilience requirement entails multiple zones, so B is the best answer.

4. A financial company is very concerned about GCP VMs accessing the internet. How can it restrict all the cloud VMs from having an external IP address?

    A. Define an organization policy at the root organization level.

    B. Define an organization policy on all existing folders.

    C. Define an organization policy on all existing projects.

    D. Define a company IT policy that each VM needs to remove its external IP address.

    Analysis: This question is about security policy enforcement in the GCP resource hierarchy. The best answer is A.

5. A healthcare company requires all the VMs in its Google Cloud to access cloud files without trespassing the internet. What do they need to implement?

    A. Private Google Access

    B. A VPN

    C. Partner Interconnect

    D. **Identity-Aware Proxy** (**IAP**)

    Analysis: Private Google Access is the best way to ensure the GCP resources communicate within Google's backbone network. The correct answer is A.

6. A data science team is developing a lightweight code that will activate a data processing pipeline when a web data file is uploaded. The code needs integrations with GCP Pub/Sub and Firebase to orchestrate the pipeline. What GCP service should be used?

    A. GCE

    B. Cloud Functions

    C. GKE

    D. GAE

    Analysis: Among all the answers, Cloud Functions is the best, since it is a serverless service that can be triggered from events such as web uploading and can activate other GCP services/pipelines. The best answer is B.

7. A data science team is developing a cloud application that will ingest data from millions of different sensor devices around the world. The application needs a database to store unstructured data at high speed. What GCP service should they choose?

    A. Firestore

    B. BigQuery

    C. Cloud SQL

    D. Cloud Bigtable

    Analysis: This is a database selection question. Bigtable supports large unstructured data transactions at a high speed. The answer is D.

8. A data science team needs to predict the house sales price covering the 08844 US zip code, based on historical sales data. What service is a good choice?

    A. BigQuery ML

    B. Computer vision

    C. Computer graphics

    D. Classification

    Analysis: This is a regression problem involving structured data. A is the best answer.

9. A data science team needs to detect **Personally Identifiable Information** (**PII**) in the GCS buckets. What service can it choose?

    A. Google KMS

    B. Google Cloud Armor

    C. Cloud **Data Loss Prevention** (**DLP**)

    D. Secret Manager

    Analysis: The correct answer is C – DLP is the best GCP service for PII detection and handling.

10. A data science team has collected many construction pictures and needs to detect objects in new construction pictures. What is the best Google Cloud service to use?

A. BigQuery

B. Picture recognition

C. Vertex AI

D. Cloud Spanner

Analysis: The correct answer is C, since it's ML for image processing.

Google Cloud Associate Engineer certification

1. A data science team launched a GCE Linux VM in the cloud using a newly generated key-pair, and then they ssh-ed to the VM instance from Google's `cloud-shell`. What key(s) are used during this process?

A. A public key on the GCE instance and a private key on the `cloud-shell`

B. A private key stored on the cloud GCE instance

C. A symmetric key on both the `cloud-shell` and the GCE instance

D. A public key stored on the `cloud-shell`

Analysis: This is an SSH key-pair question. When a new VM is launched in the cloud, a public key is generated on the cloud VM. When an SSH session is to be established from a remote VM to the cloud VM instance, the private key from the remote VM is used to match the public key on the cloud VM to authenticate the session. Answer A is the best.

2. A data science team is developing a three-tier GCP web application, which only end users from a specific CIDR range can access. Which product should be used?

A. Shield

B. VPC firewall rules

C. Cloud IAM

D. Cloud CDN

Analysis: GCP VPC firewall rules dictate what network traffic is allowed into GCP. The answer is B.

3. A data science team is working on the database tier for a joint three-tier application project with an engineer from another company, who is building the application tier in their own GCP organization. Communications between the application tiers must not traverse the public internet. Which GCP option is the best choice?

A. VPC peering

B. Cloud VPN

C. Cloud Interconnect

D. A shared VPC

Analysis: GCP VPC peering leverages Google's backbone networking. A is the answer.

4. A data science team is managing GCP workloads, where production VMs must be separated geographically from testing VMs. All the VMs must communicate with internal IPs directly. Which configuration meets these requirements?

   A. A single VPC with two subnets. Create subnets in different regions and with different CIDR ranges.

   B. A single VPC with two subnets. Create subnets in the same region and with the same CIDR range.

   C. Two VPCs, each with a single subnet. Create subnets in different regions with different CIDR ranges.

   D. Two VPCs, each with a single subnet. Create subnets in the same region and with the same CIDR range.

   Analysis: A VPC in GCP is global, meaning its subnets can be in different regions. A is the best answer.

5. A cloud engineer team signed up for a GCP account and logged into the GCP console at `console.cloud.google.com`. They created a VPC, `10.10.0.0/16`, a subnet, `10.10.10.0/24`, and then a virtual machine in the VPC/subnet. They were able to ssh to the virtual machine. From the EC2 instance, what are their permissions?

   A. They cannot access `www.google.com`.

   B. They can access `www.google.com`.

   C. They can access `www.google.com` only after the team configs GCP firewall rules.

   D. They can access `www.google.com` only after the team configs GCP firewall rules.

   Analysis: The key points here are that, by default, the VPC firewall is open to all outbound traffic, and a GCP firewall is also stateful. Therefore, B is the best answer.

6. A data science team is about to run a big query using BigQuery and wants to find out the estimated cost of the query before running it. What should be done?

   A. Switch to flat-rate pricing for this query.

   B. Use Google Cloud Shell to run a dry run query to estimate the number of bytes read, and then estimate the cost using the price calculator.

   C. Use Google Cloud Shell to run a dry run query to estimate the number of bytes read, and then estimate the cost using the price calculator.

   D. Run a select count (`*`) to get an idea of how many records the query will look through, and then convert to dollars using the price calculator.

   Analysis: A dry run query in BigQuery is the right way to estimate. The best answer is B.

7. A data science team wants to protect the default VPC networks from all inbound and outbound internet traffic. What action should be taken?

    A. Create a Deny All inbound internet firewall rule.

    B. Create a Deny All outbound internet firewall rule.

    C. Create a new subnet in the VPC network with private Google access enabled.

    D. Create instances without external IP addresses only.

    Analysis: The best answer is B, since by default all inbound traffic is blocked, but outbound traffic is open.

JencoBank case study

Questions 8–10 are based on the following case study, which is sourced from a Google Cloud architect case:

```
https://cloud.google.com/learn/certification/guides/cloud-architect/
casestudy-jencomart
```

Company overview

JencoBank is a global bank with over 10,000 branches in 16 countries. One of the company's core values is excellent customer service. In addition, they recently introduced an environmental policy to reduce their carbon output by 50% over the next 5 years.

Company background

JencoBank started as a local bank in 1931 and has grown into one of the world's leading brands, known for great value and customer service. Over time, the company transitioned from only physical branches to a branch-and-online hybrid model, with 25% of sales online. Currently, JencoBank has little presence in Asia but considers that market key for future growth.

Solution concept

JencoBank wants to migrate several critical applications to the cloud but has not completed a technical review to determine their suitability for it and the engineering required for migration. It currently hosts all its applications on an infrastructure that is at its end of life and is no longer supported.

The existing technical environment

JencoBank hosts all of its applications in four data centers – three in North America and one in Europe; most applications are dual-homed. There are production, development, and testing networks in each data center.

JencoBank understands the dependencies and resource usage metrics of its on-premises architecture.

Application – Customer loyalty portal

A **Linux, Apache, MySQL, and PH (LAMP)** application is served from the two JencoBank-owned U.S. data centers.

Database

- An Oracle database stores user profiles and has the following properties:

  - 20 TB

  - Complex table structure

  - Well-maintained, clean data

  - Strong backup strategy

- PostgreSQL database stores user credentials:

  - Single-homed in the US West

  - No redundancy

  - Backed up every 12 hours

  - A 100% uptime **Service-Level Agreement (SLA)**

  - Authenticates all users

Compute

- There are 30 machines on the US West Coast, and each machine has the following:

  - Twin, dual-core CPUs with 32 GB of RAM

  - Twin 250 GB HDD (RAID 1)

- There are 20 machines on the US East Coast, and each machine has the following:

  - A single, dual-core CPU with 24 GB of RAM

  - Twin 250 GB HDD (RAID 1)

Storage

- Access to shared a 100 TB SAN in each location
- Tape backup every week

Business requirements

- Optimization for capacity during peak periods and value during off-peak periods
- Guaranteed service availability and support
- A reduced on-premises footprint and associated financial and environmental impact
- A move to an outsourcing model to avoid large upfront costs associated with infrastructure purchases
- Expanding services into Asia

Technical requirements

- Assessing key applications for cloud suitability
- Modifying applications for the cloud
- Moving applications to a new infrastructure
- Leveraging managed services wherever feasible
- Sunsetting 20% of capacity in existing data centers
- Decreasing latency in Asia

CEO statement

JencoBank will continue to develop personal relationships with our customers as more people access the web. The future of our retail business is in the global market and the connection between online and in-branch experiences. As a large, global company, we also have a responsibility to the environment through *green* initiatives and policies.

CTO statement

The challenges of operating data centers prevent a focus on key technologies critical to our long-term success. Migrating our data services to public cloud infrastructure will allow us to focus on big data and machine learning to improve our service to customers.

CFO statement

Since its founding, JencoBank has invested heavily in our data services infrastructure. However, because of changing market trends, we need to outsource our infrastructure to ensure our long-term success. This model will allow us to respond to increasing customer demand during peak periods and reduce costs during off-peak periods.

1. Which one of these is the best target option to migrate the Postgres SQL database to Google Cloud?

    A. Cloud SQL for PostgreSQL

    B. GCP Filestore

C. GCP RDS for PostgreSQL

D. GCP firestore

Analysis: A is the best answer based on the case.

2.   What option is the best target to migrate the shared 10 TB filesystem to GCP?

A. EFS

B. Filestore

C. Firestore

D. Firebase

Analysis: GCP Filestore is a filesystem that can be shared by multiple VMs in the cloud. B is the best answer.

3.   What GCP VM types will be the best migration option for the on-premises VMs?

A. `E2-highmem-4`

B. `M4-xlarge`

C. `Standard_E4_V4`

D. `C2-4xlarge`

Analysis: The best answer is A. The instance type matches the current on-premises machine profiles:

- A twin, dual-core, with 32 GB of RAM

- A twin with a 250 GB HDD (RAID 1)

Google Cloud Professional Security Engineer certification

1.   A data science team has created a subnet in a GCP VPC and launched three Compute Engine instances in the subnet. All the VMs have no external IPs, but they must access a GCS bucket in the same account. What does the team need to do?

A. Configure a tunnel between the subnet and the GCS bucket.

B. Set up VPC sharing.

C. Enable private Google access for the subnet.

D. Enable a VPC endpoint.

Analysis: Enabling private Google access will bring the GCS public endpoint to the VPC. The answer is C.

2.   A data science team needs to have read access to all GCP project resources in a GCP organization for inventory purposes. What roles are needed?

A. Org viewer and project owner

B. Org viewer and project viewer

C. Org admin and folder browser

D. Project owner and network admin

Analysis: The least-privilege security principle dictates that the answer is B.

3. A data science team is implementing a complex GCP organization structure using nested folders and projects. What is the limitation of this architecture?

A. The folders can be nested up to 10 levels deep.

B. A GCP organization can have a maximum of 10 direct folders.

C. A GCP folder can have a maximum of 10 direct folders.

D. A GCP folder can have a maximum of 10 direct projects.

Analysis: This is a GCP organization structure question. A is the right answer.

4. Which one of these is the best practice when conducting application containerization?

A. Ensure that the application does not run as a process ID of 1.

B. Remove unnecessary libraries in the application.

C. Use public container images for the application.

D. Use private container images for the application.

Analysis: B is the best answer.

5. A data science team needs to configure VMs in a GCP to access the workloads that are only accessible from the company's private network. What is the team's best option?

A. A cloud VPN

B. A shared VPC

C. VPC peering

D. Private Google Access

Analysis: This requires a security connection between GCP and on-prem. A is the best answer.

6. A data science team needs to prevent man-in-the-middle attacks, in which hackers hijack the company domain and redirect users to a malicious site. Which one of these should be used?

A. VPC Flow Logs

B. Cloud Armor

C. DNS Security Extensions

D. Cloud IAP

Analysis: This is a cloud DNS security issue. The best answer is C.

7. A data science team needs to audit *"who did what, where, and when"* within a GCP project. Which one needs to be checked?

    A. System Event logs

    B. Data Access logs

    C. VPC Flow Logs

    D. syslog log

    Analysis: Data Access logs provide the information. The answer is B.

8. A data science team needs to make sure that the backend GCP database can only be accessed by a frontend application and no other instances on the network. How should it implement it?

    A. An ingress firewall, allowing access only from the application to the database

    B. Different subnets for the frontend application and the database

    C. Two VPC networks using Cloud VPN gateways to ensure network isolation

    D. Two VPC networks using VPC peering to ensure network isolation

    Analysis: GCP firewall rules can effectively control GCP resource access. The answer is A.

9. A big financial company needs to check its large-scale GCP resources for **National Institute of Standards and Technology** (**NSIT**) compliance and patch them as needed. Which of the following is the best option?

    A. GCP System Manager

    B. Security Command Center Premium

    C. Developing in-house security scripts

    D. Using machine learning tools

    Analysis: The correct answer is B since SCC Premium details NIST compliances for GCP resources.

10. An enterprise needs to grant access for a contract team to work on a GCP application via the internet with two-factor authentication. Which GCP product should be implemented?

    A. Cloud IAP

    B. Cloud Armor

    C. Cloud Endpoints

    D. Cloud VPN

    Analysis: IAP best fits here, so A is the right answer.

AWS Cloud Practitioner certification

1. A company has multiple departments and wants them to share the reserved instances in the AWS cloud. Which service should they use?

    A. AWS Systems Manager

    B. AWS Cost Explorer

    C. AWS Trusted Advisor

    D. AWS Organizations

    Analysis: AWS Organizations optimizes costs across AWS accounts by sharing reserved instances. D is the answer.

2. An AWS customer uses Lambda. Which of the following is their responsibility?

    A. Security inside of Lambda code

    B. The selection of CPU resources executing Lambda code

    C. The patching of an operating system executing Lambda code

    D. The security of underlying infrastructure executing Lambda code

    Analysis: With the shared responsibility model of AWS, B, C, and D fall to AWS while A is the customer's responsibility.

3. A data science team wants to review their monthly costs of EC2 and S3 usage. Which AWS service should they use?

    A. Amazon CloudWatch

    B. AWS Trusted Advisor

    C. AWS Cost Explorer

    D. Amazon Config

    Analysis: Cost Explorer can be used to review the AWS service costs. C is the correct answer.

4. Which design principle fits the need to isolate failures between dependent components in the AWS cloud?

    A. A design for scalability

    B. A design for automation

    C. Loosely coupled components

    D. A design to avoid single points of failure

    Analysis: The principle of *loosely coupled components* is used to isolate cloud component failures. The answer is C.

5. Which AWS service fits the design principle of *loosely coupled components*?

    A. SQS

    B. SNS

    C. EMR

    D. Glue

    Analysis: SQS is a cloud message queuing service that fits the *loosely coupled components* principle. The answer is A.

6. Which AWS service can be used to find the EC2s with low utilization?

    A. Amazon Inspector

    B. Amazon Trusted Advisor

    C. Amazon CloudWatch

    D. AWS Config

    Analysis: Trusted Advisor reports EC2 utilizations, so B is the right answer.

7. Which service can be used to detect malicious activities against AWS accounts?

    A. Amazon GuardDuty

    B. Amazon Trusted Advisor

    C. Amazon CloudWatch

    D. AWS Config

    Analysis: Amazon GuardDuty is a threat detection service that continuously monitors your AWS accounts and workloads for malicious activity. The answer is A.

8. A data science team wants to implement the AWS **Infrastructure-as-Code (IaC)** principle. Which service should they choose?

    A. AWS Config

    B. AWS Systems Manager

    C. AWS CloudFormation

    D. AWS CodeCommit

    Analysis: CloudFormation is a tool to implement IaC. The answer is C.

9. Which AWS service can be used to check cloud resource accesses and gain security recommendations?

    A. AWS Systems Manager

    B. AWS IAM Access Analyzer

C. AWS Trusted Advisor

D. Amazon Config

Analysis: The correct answer is B.

10. Which AWS service can be used to check the inbound and outbound traffic in an Amazon VPC?

   A. VPC Flow Logs

   B. Amazon Inspector

   C. VPC CloudWatch

   D. AWS Trusted Advisor

   Analysis: The correct answer is A.

AWS Data Analytics certification

1. Why do we need to bin numerical features with ranges in data engineering?

   Answer: The value of binning or grouping numerical features with ranges in data engineering is that, for some business use cases, it makes the most sense because the ranges, not the individual data values, affect the target. For example, a diabetes/age dataset would be best fit for a model with age-rangers as features.

2. A data science team has been performing data analytics on logs using Amazon EMR. Due to a recent increase in the number of concurrent jobs running, the overall performance of existing jobs is decreasing. They have determined that it takes longer for the EMR task nodes to process the S3 objects. Which action would *most* likely increase job performance?

   A. Using a hash function to add a random string to the object prefixes when storing the log data in Amazon S3

   B. Using an S3 life cycle policy to change the storage class for the log data

   C. Redeploying the EMR clusters to a different Availability Zone

   D. Increasing the EMR nodes for better performance

   Analysis: This question is about S3 storage performance. Since S3 has a flat structure, adding a random prefix will spread the objects into different storage zones and, thus, gain better performance. The answer is A.

3. A data science team needs to query a subset of a big compressed .csv file (200 MB of about 100,000 property listings) that is archived in S3 Glacier. What is the most cost-effective way?

   A. Load the data into Amazon S3 and query it with Amazon S3 Select.

   B. Query the data from Amazon S3 Glacier directly with Amazon Glacier Select.

   C. Load the data to Amazon S3 and query it with Amazon Athena.

   D. Load the data to Amazon S3 and query it with Amazon Redshift Spectrum.

   Analysis: A is the most cost-effective way to query a portion of .csv data.

4. The data science team needs to identify which department has the best sales performance from the sales data stored in Amazon S3 in the Parquet format. Which solution is the easiest?

A. Use Amazon QuickSight with Athena as the data source and heat maps as the visual type.

B. Use Amazon QuickSight with S3 as the data source and heat maps as the visual type.

C. Use Amazon QuickSight with Athena as the data source and pivot tables as the visual type.

D. Use Amazon QuickSight with S3 as the data source and pivot tables as the visual type.

Analysis: The best answer is A. Amazon QuickSight can be used with Amazon Athena as the data source to visualize data stored in Amazon S3 in the Parquet format, and heat maps can be used as the visual type to quickly identify which sub-organization is the strongest performer in each country. Pivot tables are great to analyze large amounts of data, but they are not the best way to visualize data here.

5. A data science team needs to process a big dataset before ML modeling, which involves mapping, dropping null fields, resolving choices, and splitting data fields. Which of the following is the best solution?

A. Ingest data into S3 and use Apache Spark to curate the data in an EMR cluster. Store the curated data back in S3 for ML modeling.

B. Ingest data into S3 and use AWS Glue to perform data curation. Store the data back in S3 for ML processing.

C. Take a full backup of the data store and ship the backup files using AWS Snowball. Upload the Snowball data into Amazon S3 for ML processing.

D. Ingest the data into Amazon S3 for ML processing.

Analysis: The correct answer is B. AWS Glue is the ideal ETL tool for the data curation process.

6. A data science team needs to process data files within 30 seconds of being uploaded to S3. Which of the following should be used?

A. Use Amazon Kinesis Data Firehose with delivery to S3, invoke a Lambda function to process, and analyze the data.

B. Use Amazon Kinesis Data Firehose with delivery to S3, initiating an event for AWS Lambda to process the data.

C. Use Amazon Managed Streaming for Apache Kafka. Configure Amazon Kinesis Data Analytics for SQL Applications as the consumer application to process data.

D. Use Amazon Kinesis Data Streams. Configure an Amazon Kinesis Data Analytics for Apache Flink application as the consumer application to process and analyze the data.

Analysis: Firehose has a minimum buffer time of 60 seconds, so this eliminates answers A and B. Kinesis Data Analytics for SQL cannot set Managed Streaming for Apache Kafka as a source, whereas Kinesis Data Analytics for Flink can. The correct answer is D.

7. A company has large .csv files stored in an Amazon S3 bucket and partitioned by date. The data is loaded to an Amazon Redshift cluster for frequent analysis, up to 600 GB per day, and then sent to the sales data dashboard. Recently, the process has had performance issues. Which solution will improve the data loading performance?

    A. Compress the .csv files and use an INSERT statement to ingest data into Amazon Redshift.

    B. Use Amazon Kinesis Data Firehose to ingest data into Amazon Redshift.

    C. Split the large .csv files, and then use a COPY command to load data into Amazon Redshift.

    D. Load the .csv files in an unsorted key order and vacuum the table in Amazon Redshift.

    Analysis: Splitting large .csv files and using a COPY command can parallelize the load process and reduce the data load time. Compressing the .csv files might help reduce the storage cost, but it might not improve the data load time. The correct answer is C.

8. A data science team is looking for a high-performing, long-term storage service to store approximately 32 TB of uncompressed data. Each day, the data transactions include a low volume of single-row inserts, a high volume of aggregation queries, and multiple complex joins, and the queries usually involve a small subset of the columns in a table. Which storage service is the best choice?

    A. Amazon Aurora MySQL

    B. Amazon Redshift

    C. Amazon S3

    D. Amazon Elasticsearch

    Analysis: Amazon Redshift meets the requirements. The correct answer is B.

9. The security team requires the Redshift cluster to log all database authentication attempts, connections, and disconnections. The logs must also record the query that runs against the database and the user who ran the query. Which steps will create the required logs?

    A. Enabling Redshift enhanced VPC routing and VPC Flow Logs

    B. Logging cluster access using AWS CloudTrail

    C. Enabling audit logging for the cluster

    D. Enabling Redshift enhanced VPC routing and using Cloudwatch to monitor traffic

    Analysis: When enabled, the Amazon Redshift audit log will capture the connection log, user log, and user activity log. The correct answer is C.

10. Every day, a data science team combines many files from its sources into one file and uploads it to S3. It then uses a batch program to load the file into an Amazon Redshift cluster with the COPY command. Which of the following will accelerate the process?

A. Uploading the individual files to Amazon S3 instead of combining them

B. Splitting the combined file equally into multiple files, with the number of the files equal to a multiple of the number of slices in the Redshift cluster, and then compressing and using the COPY command to load data to the cluster

C. Splitting the combined file equally into multiple files, with the number of the files equal to a multiple of the number of computer nodes in the Redshift cluster, and then compressing and using the COPY command to load data to the cluster

D. Converting the files into the Parquet format and running the COPY command to upload them to the cluster

Analysis: When you load all the data from a single large file, Amazon Redshift is forced to perform a serialized load, which takes a long time. Splitting your data files into ones of equal sizes, and making sure the number of split files is a multiple of the number of slices in your cluster, will ensure that the COPY command loads data in parallel from multiple files, thus dividing the workload among the cluster nodes. The correct answer is B.

Microsoft Azure AI Foundations certification

1. A credit card transaction dataset contains features of user ID, transaction type, transaction location, and transaction amount. What type of ML model can be applied to the data? Choose three:

A. Supervised learning to determine which transactions are most likely to be fraudulent

B. Unsupervised learning to determine which transactions are most likely to be fraudulent

C. Clustering to divide the transactions into N categories based on feature similarity

D. Supervised learning to predict the location of a transaction

E. Reinforcement learning to predict the location of a transaction

F. Unsupervised learning to predict the location of a transaction

Analysis: This is a very good question for you to understand model features and targets, supervised learning, and unsupervised learning. Since we have labels for location and other columns, we can set location as the model target and the other columns as features to conduct supervised learning, which is answer D. With unsupervised learning, we can group/cluster the data, which is answer C. From this grouping, we can reckon the fraudulent transactions, which is answer B. Therefore, the correct answers are B, C, and D.

2. Using an existing dataset of tumor images, we want to adopt a supervised anomaly detection model to classify future images. What supports this method?

    A. There are very few occurrences of malignant tumors relative to benign tumors.

    B. There are roughly equal occurrences of both tumors in the dataset.

    C. You expect future malignant tumors to have different features from the malignant tumors in the dataset.

    D. You expect future malignant tumors to have similar features to the malignant tumors in the dataset.

    Analysis: This question is about how we can use ML to find existing data patterns and predict new data. D is the answer.

3. For ML model training/evaluation, how should you split the dataset?

    A. Use features for training and labels for evaluation.

    B. Randomly split the data into rows for training and evaluation.

    C. Use labels for training and features for evaluation.

    D. Randomly split the data into columns for training and columns for evaluation.

    .**Analysis**: A dataset is randomly split into rows for training/evaluation. The answer is B.

4. A data science team wants to make sure that their Azure ML model meets the Microsoft transparency principle of responsible AI. What needs to be done?

    A. Set the validation type to **auto**.

    B. Enable the Explain model.

    C. Set the primary metric to **accuracy**.

    D. Set the maximum concurrent iterations to 2.

    Analysis: Microsoft's responsible AI framework has a core set of principles – fairness, reliability and safety, privacy and security, inclusiveness, transparency, and accountability. The Explain model meets the transparency principle. The answer is B.

5. A data science team is training an ML model to predict the fare of a taxi journey from a taxi-trip dataset. Which column from the dataset should be used as a feature of the model?

    A. The trip ID of individual taxi journeys

    B. The driver of the taxi journeys in the dataset

    C. The trip distance of individual taxi journeys

    D. The fare of individual taxi journeys

    Analysis: The fare of a taxi journey depends on the trip distance, which needs to be a feature of the model. C is the answer.

6. A data science team is using ML to predict the traffic on Highway 95 for the next year. Which type of model should they build?

    A. Classification

    B. Regression

    C. Clustering

    D. Reinforcement

    Analysis: It's a continuous value prediction, so the answer is B.

7. A data science team uses a large, anonymized dataset of CT-scan images that are categorized as benign and malignant to build an ML model. What type of ML are they conducting?

    A. Reinforcement

    B. Regression

    C. Classification

    D. Clustering

    Analysis: The model is built to classify an image as benign or malignant. The answer is C.

8. Which of the following helps to define an ML problem?

    A. A domain expert in the problem area

    B. A traditional coded solution

    C. Sufficient hardware to run ML training

    D. A neural network

    Analysis: We need domain experts in ML problem framing. The answer is A.

9. A data science team is processing a dataset that includes credit card transactions, of which 1% are identified as fraudulent. How can the team improve the performance of their classifier?

    A. Use MS Excel records.

    B. Normalize numeric features.

    C. Oversample the fraudulent transaction.

    D. Use one-hot encoding.

    Analysis: The correct answer is C, since the dataset is unbalanced, and we need to use oversampling skills.

10. Which of the following is *not* a common technique for feature scaling?

    A. Min-max scaling

    B. Standardization

C. Normalization

D. Mean imputation

Analysis: The correct answer is D.

Microsoft Azure AI Engineer certification

1. A data science team needs to extract some information from receipts, including the vendor and the transaction amount, with minimum development effort. Which Azure service should be used?

    A. Custom Vision

    B. Language processing

    C. Form Recognizer

    D. Computer Vision

    Analysis: Form Recognizer is the right service for this use case. The answer is C.

2. A data science team needs to analyze extracted information with Microsoft Power BI, leveraging an Azure Cognitive Search instance that indexes purchase orders by using Form Recognizer. What should they add to the indexer?

    A. A projection group

    B. A table projection

    C. A file projection

    D. An object projection

    Analysis: The table projection feature in Azure Cognitive Search allows you to flatten complex data structures into a format that can be easily indexed and queried. The answer is B.

3. A data science team has collected blog posts that include a `category` field. Now, they need to index the posts using an Azure Cognitive Search solution that does the following:

- Includes the `category` field in the search results

- Ensures that users can search for words in the `category` field

- Ensures that users can perform drill-down filtering based on category

- Which index attributes should you configure for the `category` field?

    A. `searchable`, `sortable`, and `retrievable`

    B. `searchable`, `facetable`, and `retrievable`

    C. `retrievable`, `filterable`, and `sortable`

    D. `retrievable`, `facetable`, and `key`

Analysis: `Searchable` allows users to search for words in the category field. It can be included in full-text searches. `Facetable` allows users to perform drill-down filtering based on category. Faceting is used for self-directed drill-down filtering on query results in a search app, where your application offers controls for scoping search. Azure Cognitive Search provides the data structures and filters to support the experience. `Retrievable` allows the category field to be included in the search results. This means that the field can be included in the search results returned by the search service. The answer is B.

4.   An Azure IoT app receives sensor data from sensors and detects an anomaly across multiple correlated sensors. It identifies the root cause and sends incident alerts if the process stops. Which service should be used?

A. Azure Metrics Advisor

B. Azure Form Recognizer

C. Azure Machine Learning

D. Azure Anomaly Detector

Analysis: Azure Metrics Advisor uses AI to perform data monitoring and anomaly detection in time-series data. The correct answer is A.

5.   A data science team has set up a language service resource named `lsr` and a virtual network named `vnet1`. How can they make sure only resources in `vnet1` can access `lsr`?

A. Set up NSG for `vnet1`.

B. Set up Azure Firewall for `vnet1`.

C. Set up a service endpoint in `vnet1`.

D. Set up a language service container in `vnet1`.

Analysis: A service endpoint is the way to go here. The answer is C.

6.   An Azure monitoring system is used to analyze gas pipe sensor data, such as temperature, pressure, and flow speed, and generate alerts when atypical values are detected. What service should be used?

A. Azure Monitor with Application Insights

B. Azure Monitor with metric alerts

C. Multivariate Anomaly Detection

D. Univariate Anomaly Detection

Analysis: The Multivariate Anomaly Detection APIs enable developers by integrating advanced AI to detect anomalies from groups of metrics, without the need for machine learning knowledge or labeled data. The answer is C.

7. A data science team uses an Azure Cognitive Services model to identify anomalies of a time-series data stream in a location with limited connectivity. What service should be used?

    A. Azure Kubernetes Service

    B. Azure Container Instances

    C. A Kubernetes cluster in Azure

    D. Docker Engine in Azure

    Analysis: The answer is B. Azure Container Instances is a serverless container runtime that allows you to run containers without managing the underlying infrastructure. It suits scenarios with limited connectivity, since it eliminates the underlying infrastructure, such as a Kubernetes cluster or Azure Stack Hub. Also, you can deploy and run individual containers directly, without any additional overhead.

8. A data science team deploys a Docker server named `s1`, which will host an instance of an Azure cognitive service, to the on-premises network. Which parameter should they include in the `docker run` command?

    A. `Fluentd`

    B. `Billing`

    C. `Http Proxy`

    D. `output`

    Analysis: The `Billing` option must be specified to run the container. The answer is B.

9. A data science team is developing a new sales app that will process video and text from a public-facing website. Which responsible AI principle provides guidance to make sure that the app provides equitable results, independent of the user's location or background?

    A. Transparency

    B. Fairness

    C. Reliability and safety

    D. Privacy and security

    Analysis: The correct answer is B.

10. In Azure Cognitive Search, what is the effect of using server-side encryption with a *CMK* stored in Azure?

    A. Query times will increase.

    B. An `X.509` certificate is required.

    C. The index size will decrease.

    D. Query times will decrease.

Analysis: Customer-managed keys require Azure Key Vault. Enabling CMK encryption will increase query time. The correct answer is A.

Summary

In this chapter, we reviewed the cloud certification roadmaps, briefly discussed the certification exam-taking strategies, and provided practice questions and analysis for seven certification exams in GCP, AWS, and Azure. Practice, practice, practice – that is the best way of preparing for any certification exams.

In the next chapter, we will discuss cloud career development.

Further reading

For further reading on cloud certifications, use the following links:

- `https://aws.amazon.com/certification/`
- `https://learn.microsoft.com/en-us/certifications/`
- `https://cloud.google.com/learn/certification`
- `https://www.coursera.org/articles/cloud-certifications-for-your-it-career`

17

Building a Successful Cloud Computing Career

Starting or transferring to a professional cloud career requires cloud knowledge, cloud hands-on skill development, and passing cloud certifications, all of which we discussed in the previous chapters – the so-called *hardware* for a cloud career. In this final chapter of the book, we will discuss the *software* that is needed to develop a successful profession in cloud computing. We will focus on three topics:

- The cloud job market
- The soft skills in a cloud career
- My cloud story

Without question, cloud computing is booming, and we need both hard skills and soft skills to stand on top of the cloud.

The cloud job market

The cloud computing job market continues to grow rapidly as organizations increasingly adopt cloud technologies. Here are some key observations of the cloud computing job market at the time of writing:

- The cloud computing job market offers a wide range of roles, catering to different skill sets and expertise, including cloud engineers, cloud administrators, DevOps engineers, security specialists, data engineers, ML engineers, and solution architects.

- Cloud computing technology has become an integral part of modern business and technology operations, leading to an increased need for skilled cloud professionals who can design, deploy, manage, and secure cloud infrastructure and applications, across various industries and sectors.

- Many companies and organizations are in the process of migrating their existing infrastructure and applications to the cloud or implementing cloud-native solutions. Professionals with expertise in cloud migration strategies, architecture design, and cloud-native development are highly sought after.

- Cloud computing roles often offer remote work opportunities, since cloud technologies enable remote management and access to resources. This flexibility in work arrangements allows professionals to work remotely or in hybrid environments, expanding job opportunities geographically.

- Cloud computing offers excellent career growth opportunities. As you gain experience and expertise, you can progress into more senior or specialized roles.

- Cloud certifications, offered by AWS, Azure, Google Cloud, and so on, are highly valued in the job market. Certifications validate skills and knowledge of specific cloud platforms and can give candidates an advantage when seeking cloud-related roles.

- Cloud computing professionals are in high demand and, thus, their salaries tend to be competitive. The high demand for cloud expertise often leads to competitive compensation packages and additional benefits.

The cloud computing job market offers big opportunities for skilled professionals. Staying up to date with the latest cloud technologies, gaining hands-on cloud experience, and obtaining relevant cloud certifications will significantly enhance your chances of success in this growing field.

Soft cloud skills

While hard/technical skills are essential in a cloud computing career, soft skills are equally important for success. From my observations, the following are some key soft skills that can benefit professionals in a cloud career:

- **Communication skills**: Effective communication is crucial in cloud computing roles. You need to convey complex technical concepts to both technical and non-technical stakeholders. Clear and concise communication skills help in documenting requirements, collaborating with team members, and presenting ideas or solutions to clients.

- **Collaboration and teamwork skills**: Cloud computing often involves collaborative working with cross-functional teams, including developers, system administrators, network engineers, and business stakeholders. Being able to work well in a team, share knowledge, and collaborate on projects is essential.

- **Problem-solving skills**: Cloud computing professionals frequently encounter complex technical challenges. Having strong problem-solving skills helps to identify and analyze issues, evaluate possible solutions, and implement effective resolutions. Problem-solving skills also involve critical thinking, creativity, and the ability to think outside the box.

- **Adaptability and flexibility**: Cloud technology is ever-evolving, with new services and updates introduced regularly. Professionals in the cloud industry need to be adaptable and embrace changes. Being open to new technologies, frameworks, and methodologies and quickly adapting to shifts in the industry is important for cloud career growth.

- **Continuous learning and curiosity**: The cloud industry is dynamic, with constant advancements and new technologies. Demonstrating a passion for learning, being curious, and staying up to date with the latest industry trends is essential. Continuous learning helps you expand your cloud skill set, adapt to new technologies, and remain competitive in the field.

- **Time management and organizational skills**: Cloud computing professionals often work on multiple projects simultaneously and need to prioritize tasks effectively. Good time management and organizational skills enable you to meet deadlines, stay focused, and manage your workload efficiently. Being organized helps you track progress, maintain documentation, and stay on top of project requirements.

- **Customer service and client-facing skills**: Cloud computing roles often involve direct interaction with clients or end users. Strong customer service skills, including empathy, active listening, understanding, and addressing client needs, contribute to positive client relationships. Being able to provide technical guidance and support in a user-friendly manner is very valuable in cloud careers.

- **Leadership and management**: As you progress in your cloud computing career, leadership and management skills become increasingly important. Leadership skills involve guiding and mentoring team members, taking initiative, and driving projects to successful completion. Management skills help you coordinate teams, set goals, make decisions, and oversee project execution.

- **Ethical and professional conduct**: Upholding ethical standards and professional conduct is vital in the cloud computing industry. This includes respecting data privacy, maintaining client confidentiality, adhering to industry regulations, and displaying integrity in your work. Being trustworthy and accountable contributes to building strong professional relationships.

Soft skills complement technical expertise and can make you stand out in the cloud computing job market. Developing and nurturing these soft skills alongside your technical capabilities can lead to steady growth and successful outcomes in your cloud computing career.

In the next section, I will share my story of transferring to the cloud and standing steady on the cloud.

My cloud story

I came to the United States with $400 borrowed from my advisor at Tsinghua University. When I entered US customs at the San Francisco port, on August 17, 1992, I was asked by the US customs officer, *"How will you survive here with 400 dollars?"*

Four years later, with a PhD in industrial engineering and a master of science in computer science, I started working at Chase Manhattan Bank as a Unix administrator. Working as a Unix administrator, a Cisco internet expert, and then an advisory **Storage Area Network** (**SAN**) architect, it took me eight years at Wall Street financial firms and 12 years in IT firms (EMC/VMware) to build a solid foundation in all aspects of IT infrastructure (server, network, storage, database, high availability, and disaster recovery). At that time, I had worked in the **traditional** IT industry for over 20 years and was very comfortable with my professional life.

My life changed in 2014. I was made aware of the *cloud computing concepts* of **Amazon Web Services** (**AWS**) and was inspired by *Steve Jobs' 2005 speech* at Stanford University. With a mindset of *"stay hungry, stay foolish,"* I started self-learning the basic AWS cloud services and was certified as an AWS solution architect at the associate level in 2015. In August of 2016, I joined AWS as a **Technical Account Manager** (**TAM**), which was my *first lifetime breakthrough* – I started my cloud journey!

During my first month at Amazon, I was shocked by two things – one was the dollar cost of the invoices Amazon charged to their enterprise customers, such as Intel and Citrix, for their cloud usage (I had never seen such big cloud resource consumption), and the other was how my coworker built a cloud data center, which consists of large-scale networks, server farms, and database pools, within a couple of hours. Coming from a traditional IT data center environment, I was intimately acquainted with how long it took to build a physical data center – not to mention the time allocated for hardware purchasing, installation, testing, and rolling to production!

Life in AWS was full of challenges but fruitful. In two years, I completed all the AWS cloud certifications and learned so much from the job! At the beginning of 2018, my manager called me into his office and assigned me a big task – I was to complete two white papers and conduct presentations at the district level. My first reaction was, *"It's not fair – no one in my group has done any of this! Why do I have to do it?"* But after some thinking, I took on the challenge! In the following three months, I spent so much time working on AWS security projects, writing the two white papers, and presenting at various AWS meetings. And guess what? Several months later, when I was interviewed for a principal cloud architect position in 2019, the last round was with the company's "C-level" leadership team, and the final question was, *"Logan, can you send us some technical papers you have written?"* I replied without any hesitation, *"Of course!"* Imagine how embarrassing it would have been if I had not completed those two white papers – the only paper I had would have been my PhD publication from 20 years ago! At the same time, because I was so adept at cloud security presentations, the University of Texas in Dallas offered me a full-time position shortly after my on-campus presentations. This was my *second lifetime breakthrough* – I stepped up in my cloud journey!

My days after AWS were amazing. Based on my strong AWS background, I absorbed the details of Microsoft Azure and Google Cloud like a sponge, developed a plethora of hands-on skills in multiple cloud platforms, and completed every Azure and GCP certification in two years. In 2021, together with the company VP of engineering, I led a team and completed an important Google Cloud project, which was so successful that we secured 10 more projects thereafter, and I was promoted to **chief architect and director of cloud computing**. In the meantime, I have taught cloud computing and machine learning courses at the University of Texas in Dallas. The students love my courses so much that, at the beginning of the semester, there's always a long waiting list for my classes, and at the end of the semester, the students give me a standing ovation. And this was my *third lifetime breakthrough* – standing high on the cloud and gaining a new perspective on cloud computing!

There are many things that I have learned in my career, and the most important ones are as follows:

- **Thanksgiving**: As the American author Zig Ziglar said, "*Gratitude is the healthiest of all human emotions. The more you express gratitude for what you have, the more likely you will have even more to express gratitude for.*"

- **Forever learning**: As Albert Einstein said, "*The more I learn, the more I realize how much I don't know.*"

Always being grateful, always learning, taking ownership, taking initiative, and helping others whenever possible – these are the soft skills that I have developed on my cloud journey, and they made me the person I am today.

Summary

In this chapter, we discussed the job market and soft skills in cloud computing career development, and I also shared my cloud story, hoping to provide some inspiration for your cloud journey.

This chapter concludes the fourth part of the book, and we have now reached the end of the book. Nevertheless, our cloud journey continues, and I look forward to seeing you in the clouds.

Index

H

Hadoop 126
hash key 89
Health Insurance Portability and
    Accountability Act (HIPAA) 199
high availability (HA) 18
Hive 128
Hue 128

I

Identify Aware Proxy (IAP) 288
Identity Access Management (IAM) 188, 381
    reference link 287
identity providers (IdPs) 286
Infrastructure-as-a-Service (IaaS) 338
Infrastructure as Code (IaC) 6
in-memory cache database 82
in-memory cache databases examples
    Memcached 83
    Redis 82
internet 47
    EC2 instances, accessing from 55-58
Internet Control Message
    Protocol (ICMP) 11
Internet Gateway (IGW) 55
Internet Protocol (IP) address 46
Internet Service Provider (ISP) 9

J

JencoBank case study 406
    AWS Cloud Practitioner
        certification 412, 413
    AWS Data Analytics certification 414-417
    CEO statement 408
    CFO statement 408, 409

company background 406
company overview 406
CTO statement 408
customer loyalty portal application 407, 408
existing technical environment 406
Google Cloud Professional Security
    Engineer certification 409-411
Microsoft Azure AI Engineer
    certification 420-422
Microsoft Azure AI Foundations
    certification 417-419
solution concept 406
JupyterLab interface 262
Jupyter notebook
    launching 153
    working in 155
Just-In-Time (JIT) 382

K

Keras 163
Key Management Service
    (KMS) 35, 178, 191
key pairs 188

L

Lambda 314
Language APIs 273
large language models (LLMs) 277
Letter of Authorization and Connecting
    Facility Assignment (LOA-CFA) 72

M

machine learning (ML) 3, 145, 146
management group 388
MapReduce 126

www.packtpub.com

Subscribe to our online digital library for full access to over 7,000 books and videos, as well as industry leading tools to help you plan your personal development and advance your career. For more information, please visit our website.

Why subscribe?

- Spend less time learning and more time coding with practical eBooks and Videos from over 4,000 industry professionals

- Improve your learning with Skill Plans built especially for you

- Get a free eBook or video every month

- Fully searchable for easy access to vital information

- Copy and paste, print, and bookmark content

Did you know that Packt offers eBook versions of every book published, with PDF and ePub files available? You can upgrade to the eBook version at www.packtpub.com and as a print book customer, you are entitled to a discount on the eBook copy. Get in touch with us at customercare@packtpub.com for more details.

At www.packtpub.com, you can also read a collection of free technical articles, sign up for a range of free newsletters, and receive exclusive discounts and offers on Packt books and eBooks.

Other Books You May Enjoy

If you enjoyed this book, you may be interested in these other books by Packt:

Python Essentials for AWS Cloud Developers

Serkan Sakinmaz

ISBN: 978-1-80461-006-0

- Understand the fundamentals of AWS services for Python programming
- Find out how to configure AWS services to build Python applications
- Run and deploy Python applications using Lambda, EC2, and Elastic Beanstalk
- Provision EC2 servers on AWS and run Python applications
- Debug and monitor Python applications using PyCharm and CloudWatch
- Understand database operations on AWS by learning about DynamoDB and RDS
- Explore the API gateway service on AWS using Python to grasp API programming

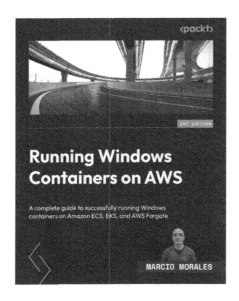

Running Windows Containers on AWS

Marcio Morales

ISBN: 978-1-80461-413-6

- Get acquainted with Windows container basics

- Run and manage Windows containers on Amazon ECS, EKS, and AWS Fargate

- Effectively monitor and centralize logs from Windows containers

- Properly maintain Windows hosts and keep container images up to date

- Manage ephemeral Windows hosts to reduce operational overhead

- Work with the container image cache to speed up the container's boot time

Packt is searching for authors like you

If you're interested in becoming an author for Packt, please visit `authors.packtpub.com` and apply today. We have worked with thousands of developers and tech professionals, just like you, to help them share their insight with the global tech community. You can make a general application, apply for a specific hot topic that we are recruiting an author for, or submit your own idea.

Share your thoughts

Now you've finished *The Self-Taught Cloud Engineer*, we'd love to hear your thoughts! Scan the QR code below to go straight to the Amazon review page for this book and share your feedback or leave a review on the site that you purchased it from.

`https://packt.link/r/180512370X`

Your review is important to us and the tech community and will help us make sure we're delivering excellent quality content.

Download a free PDF copy of this book

Thanks for purchasing this book!

Do you like to read on the go but are unable to carry your print books everywhere?

Is your eBook purchase not compatible with the device of your choice?

Don't worry, now with every Packt book you get a DRM-free PDF version of that book at no cost.

Read anywhere, any place, on any device. Search, copy, and paste code from your favorite technical books directly into your application.

The perks don't stop there, you can get exclusive access to discounts, newsletters, and great free content in your inbox daily

Follow these simple steps to get the benefits:

1. Scan the QR code or visit the link below

https://packt.link/free-ebook/978-1-80512-370-5

2. Submit your proof of purchase
3. That's it! We'll send your free PDF and other benefits to your email directly

Made in the USA
Las Vegas, NV
20 July 2024

92658172R10260